The Genius

The Genius

Elijah of Vilna and the
Making of Modern Judaism

ELIYAHU STERN

Yale UNIVERSITY PRESS
New Haven & London

Published with the assistance of the Frederick W. Hilles Publication
Fund of Yale University and with assistance from the Annie Burr
Lewis Fund and from the foundation established in memory of James
Wesley Cooper of the Class of 1865, Yale College.

Yale University Press books may be purchased in quantity for
educational, business, or promotional use. For information, please
e-mail sales.press@yale.edu (U.S. office) or
sales@yaleup.co.uk (U.K. office).

Set in Bauer Bodoni type by IDS Infotech, Ltd.
Printed in the United States of America.

Library of Congress Cataloging-in-Publication Data

Stern, Eliyahu, 1976–
    The Genius : Elijah of Vilna and the making of modern Judaism / Eliyahu Stern.
      p. cm.
    Includes bibliographical references and index.
    ISBN 978-0-300-17930-9 (alk. paper)

    1. Elijah ben Solomon, 1720–1797. 2. Rabbis—Lithuania—Vilnius—
Biography. 3. Judaism—History. 4. Vilnius (Lithuania)—Biography. I. Title.
    BM755.E6S77 2013
    296.8'32092—dc23
    [B]

                                                                    2012015866

A catalogue record for this book is available from the British Library.

This paper meets the requirements of ANSI/NISO Z39.48–1992
(Permanence of Paper).

10 9 8 7 6 5 4 3 2 1

For Sholom and Batya Stern, my Abba and Imma

Contents

Acknowledgments

THIS WORK IS THE PRODUCT OF GREAT FRIENDSHIPS, HEATED CONVERSATIONS, sage counsel, and unending generosity. Hearing my grandfather Eliezer Rabinowitz of Vilna-Baltimore studying in song in the wee hours of the morning inspired me to write on the Gaon—although it was not until some point between the *beit midrash* and Alan Brill's seminars that I came to know what my grandfather was learning. It was Elisheva Carlebach who reminded me not to be frightened of my own voice, giving me the intellectual confidence to pursue this project. The book's historical core emerged under her guidance, was further developed by Martin Jay's depth and breadth, and was refined and polished by John Efron. Choosing to study with Daniel Boyarin—an *eynikel* (descendant) of the Gaon—was one of the best decisions I ever made. Daniel's genius and spirit can be found on every page of this book.

After finishing my studies at Berkeley I had the good fortune of having Shaul Stampfer and David Myers advise me to be patient with my manuscript and expand the scope of the project. I am forever grateful to Shaul for at the last stages of production generously giving his time to fine-tune and sharpen the manuscript. The editorial staff of *Jewish Quarterly Review*, led by David and Eliot Horowitz, was instrumental in bringing forth the ideas addressed in the chapters on Mendelssohn and the modern yeshiva.

Writing this book was made considerably more enjoyable by the High Tables and by the intellectual freedoms served to me during my years at Brasenose College and the Oriental Institute at the University of Oxford.

Jordan Finkin, David Rechter, Aaron Rosen, Francesca Bregoli, Martin Goodman, Edward Fram, Elchanan Reiner, Theodore Dunkelgrüen, Islam Dayeh, Joanna Weinberg, Piet Van Boxel, Abigail Green, and Jenny Barbour remain good friends.

My colleagues at Yale—Ivan Marcus, Paula Hyman, z"l, Steven Fraade, Christine Hayes, Benjamin Harshav, Hindy Najman, Paul Franks, Phylis Granoff, Dale Martin, Stephen Davis, Andrew Quintman, Kathryn Lofton, and Skip Stout—have given me a home and inspired me to ask the larger questions that hover over this work: What are the essential features of the modern Jewish experience, and what is the place of religion in modern Western life and thought?

I have indeed been blessed to have the most remarkable friends, who read countless drafts, listened to endless rants, and nonetheless still pick up the phone when I call. Daniel Septimus and Meir Katz continue to be study partners, my *havruta*. The three years Meir and I spent studying and laughing together at yeshiva prepared us for the six months we spent poring over the *Biur* together. Since our days arguing about the world in Jerusalem, Daniel has remained a moral and spiritual compass in my life, reminding me of what really matters.

Barry Wimpfheimer saved me on the treacherous streets of Washington Heights. His mentorship and confidence have been pillars holding me up throughout my studies. My dear friend Dov Weiss has been there at any hour of the day to read an obscure commentary of the Gaon, offer sober advice, or lend a hand to a friend. Since my first week of graduate school, Noah Strote has been my most trusted intellectual companion and sounding board. Only if Noah thought a chapter was up to snuff would I allow myself to move on to the next.

The style and substance of the manuscript were greatly improved by David Billet's clarity, Amos Bitzan's precision, and Gabriel Posner's craftsmanship.

I would like to thank Yale University Press and especially Jennifer Banks, who from our first correspondence has supported this manuscript and made the publication process a pleasure. Julie Carlson's and Susan Laity's economy of language and eleventh-hour suggestions greatly lightened the burden of my readers. The book was published with the assistance of the Frederick W. Hilles Publication Fund of Yale University.

Through their teaching, friendship, or advice the following individuals have played a significant role in the publication of this book. My loving and caring sister, Danya Stechler, Aryeh Stechler, Leora Behor, Rebecca Brygel, David Horowitz, George Newmark, Ruth Bevan, Rebecca Shalomoff, Lionel Beehner, Julie McCarthy, Yehuda Sarna, Saul Austerlitz, David Biale, Menachem Butler, Sandra Valabregue-Perry, Michah Perry, Amanda Katz, Eli Scheiman, Shaya Ish-Shalom, Yaakov Elman, Saba Mahmood, Ben Skydell, Yehuda Mirsky, Shaun Halper, Sara Doris Labaton, Karen Collis, Zvi Septimus, David Henkin, Hoffer Kaback, Steven Bayme, Steven Katz, Noah Feldman, Gershon Hundert, Jim Ponet, Irving Greenberg, and my brother Jacob Morris. I was lucky to have met at a young age a lion in Judah, David Hartman, who fired my imagination and showed me the power of ideas.

Finally, Batya and Sholom Stern's integrity, honesty, and love of learning continue to be my touchstones. It's easy to read a finished book; it's much harder to read first drafts. I am forever indebted to the time and energy they put into a terribly rough manuscript, when few imagined a book.

It is an honor to acknowledge the institutions and their leadership that supported me over the last decade: the YIVO Institute; David Ariel, president of the Oxford Center for Hebrew and Jewish Studies; Principal Roger Cashmore and the Fellowship of Brasenose College, Oxford; Donniel Hartman, president of the Shalom Hartman Institute; Rabbi Arthur Schneier and the members of Manhattan's Park East Synagogue; Jack Rosen, Chairman of the Council for World Jewry; and Richard Haass, president of the Council on Foreign Relations.

A Note on the Transliteration

THE TRANSLITERATION SYSTEM IN THIS BOOK WAS DESIGNED TO MEET TWO objectives: to give readers a sense of Jewish life in eighteenth-century Polish-Lithuanian lands and to allow them easy access to the sources cited. I use Polish names for towns (Międzyrzecz) and Hebrew or Polish names for individuals, according to common usage (Józef Hilary Głowacki instead of Josef Hilary Glowacki, Elijah ben Solomon instead of Eliasz Zelmanowicz). However, when there is an accepted English spelling, I have used that version (Hayyim of Volozhin instead of Hayyim of Wołożyn, Vilna rather than Vilnius or Wilno, Safed for Tzfat).

My transliterations of Hebrew follow the conventions of the Jewish Publication Society. The letter *kaf* is transliterated as *kh* when soft and *k* when hard, *chet* as *ch*, *heh* as *h*, *kuf* as *k*, *zayin* as *z*, and *tzadi* as *tz*. Exceptions, by reason of common convention, are Hasid, Hatam Sofer, and Hayyim. Diacritical marks are not used. Apostrophes are used to clarify syllabic distinctions, for example, *Ne'emanah, Be'er, hashpa'ato, Ma'aseh, ta'anit*.

I transliterate the six consonants /b g d k p t/ as single letters (*b, g, d, k, p, t*) when they appear with a dagesh at the beginnings of words, after other consonants, and after a sheva. In all other cases, they are transliterated as double letters (*bb, gg, dd, kk, pp, tt*). If the bet has a dagesh, as in *batei midrash*, it is rendered *b*; without the dagesh, as in *u-vatei*, it is rendered *v*.

The Yiddish transliterations are based on the system devised by the YIVO Institute for Jewish Research, and book titles follow the spellings used in the YIVO library catalogue.

In my citation style, Hebrew prefixes are set off with a hyphen—for example, *ha-Kehilah ha-Ivrit be-Vilna*. I follow English capitalization rules for transliterated titles. Prefixes (*ha-*, *ba-*, *she-*) are not capitalized, except when the title begins with a prefix (for example, *Ha-Minhag*). Because many of the texts are difficult to locate, I cite works as they are most commonly referenced—thus, *Aderet Eliyahu* (Dubrovna: 1804) and *Biur ha-Gra al Shulchan Arukh Yoreh Deah* (Grodno: 1806) rather than the more abstract *Chamisha Chumshei Torah* (Dubrowna: 1804) and *Ashlei Ravrivei* (Hrodna: 1806). English names are used for cities in all bibliographic information (Jerusalem, not Yerushalayim, Mogilev, not Mohylów).

Introduction

TOWERING OVER EIGHTY-EIGHT SAGES OF ISRAEL, ELIJAH BEN SOLOMON (1720–1797), prayer shawl draped over his shoulders, grips a tome in his left hand while writing one of his seventy works with the other. A white halo encircles his face, highlighting his sacrosanct position among Jewry's most celebrated masters. Beneath him rest Jewry's luminaries, among them the stately medieval philosopher Maimonides, regally dressed in a turban, and the learned commentator Isaac Alfasi, cradling his head in his hand while poring over a pile of books. Such is just one of the dozens of pictures featuring Elijah that hung in Jewish homes and study houses across eastern Europe in the late nineteenth century.[1]

For two centuries, Elijah has been known simply by the name "Genius," or "Gaon." His biographers claim that "one like him appears every thousand years."[2] Born into a respected rabbinic family, Elijah from early adolescence distinguished himself by his mastery of rabbinic literature, mathematics, and scientific knowledge. In the manner of other pious scholars of the time, he wandered anonymously about various towns and villages, finally settling in the Lithuanian city of Vilna (today Vilnius). Fiercely reclusive, he held no public position and spoke out only on the most pressing political matters. Still he would become known as the patron sage and spiritual leader of the Vilna Jewish community, which by the late eighteenth century had emerged as the epicenter of eastern European Jewish life.

Elijah's contributions as author, leader, and genius—along with the sociocultural makeup of eighteenth-century Vilna, of which Elijah was so vital a part—laid the groundwork for the central institutions and ideologies of modern eastern European Jewry. By the time of his death at the age of seventy-seven in 1797, he had written commentaries on a wider range of Jewish literature than any writer in history. He had so mastered the Jewish canon that there is hardly a major rabbinic or kabbalistic text untouched by his erudite commentary. His originality, command of sources, and clarity of thought not only place him among Jewry's luminaries, but establish him as the equal of other religious and intellectual giants such as Aquinas and Averroes. On the social plane, his works contributed to the unmooring of European Jewry from the rabbinic legal codes and political communal structures that had governed sixteenth- to eighteenth-century eastern European Jewish life. His commentaries and worldview encouraged the establishment of privately funded religious institutions such as the "yeshiva" (study house), whose doors were at least in theory open to all comers. Under his influence, public religious institutions and local communal identities yielded to a new "privatized" religious culture in which identity became determined less by place of residence than by ideological commitments.

During the eighteenth century, Jews came to form a majority among Vilna residents—a demographic development replicated throughout eastern Europe over the course of the nineteenth century. As the Vilna Jewish community grew in size and stature, it assumed greater political and economic power both within Jewish life and in regional politics. Jews may have been powerless in the geopolitical affairs of the highly decentralized Polish Sejm (parliament) and the king's court, but they played critical economic roles where they resided as virtual majorities.

Elijah exemplified the newly emboldened posture of a leader of a majority culture. He was engaged in developing his own constituency's literary heritage, language, and political tradition—all while being neither threatened by, nor overly interested in, the ideas and institutions of other religious or ethnic groups.

Elijah's confidence and genius inspired not only those nineteenth-century Jews who were privileged enough to attend yeshivot (and later, universities), but also the masses, who embraced the ideal of intellectual achievement as a means of upward social mobility. While during his lifetime Elijah's reputation was limited to a select group of scholars and lay people living around Vilna and its environs, after his death the masses of European Jewry immortalized Elijah. They hung his portrait on their walls, read middlebrow hagiographies extolling his brilliance, and reminded their children "Vil-nor Goen" (playing on the Yiddish vocalization of the Gaon's name); "if you will it, you too can become a Gaon [genius]" like Elijah.

Elijah's immense popularity, his retreat from the public sphere, and his expressions of political agency as the leader of a majority culture distinguish him from his predecessors, and express in embryonic form the unique experiences of modern eastern European Jewry. Yet Elijah's legacy is today primarily guarded by those often identified as staunch traditionalists, who cast him as the right pillar of medieval rabbinic culture.[3] These seemingly opposing views point to a deep misunderstanding in scholarly and confessional literature not only about the Gaon and his legacy, but also about the relationship between tradition and modernity.

Who then was Elijah of Vilna, and which contemporary movement, if any, is his rightful heir? These questions thrust us toward the essence of modernity, and more particularly, modern Jewish history.

Tradition and Modernity

In the common narrative, modern Jews exchanged their belief in messianic redemption for citizenship in the nation-state, leaving the ghetto walls of the *kehilah* (the pre-modern Jewish governing structure) for the freedom of the coffee houses, and abandoning rabbinic study halls for universities. This approach is closely identified with the Hebrew University historian Jacob Katz, who documented the ruptures and crises of the emancipation of European Jewry and the demise of "Jewish traditional society" as Jews emerged from social and cultural segregation. In his telling, the rise of Jewish "rationalism" seen during the eighteenth-century Haskalah (Enlightenment) eroded and eventually destroyed the "traditional society" of the high Middle Ages.[4]

Katz's immensely influential studies provided subsequent generations of historians with a framework to understand how "traditional" Jews entered modernity.[5] In their textbook *The Jew in the Modern World*, for example, Paul Mendes-Flohr and Jehudah Reinharz argue that Jewish modernity derives its primary energy and legitimization from sources other than the sacred authority of the Jewish tradition. "With this in mind," they explain, "the documents we have selected make little reference, for instance, to Hasidism. . . . To be sure, the custodians of Jewish tradition—and the Hasidim were among the most forceful—did respond to modernity and were quick to note its 'dangers,' often with impressive understanding of its radical nature."[6] They continue this line of thought with the following caveat: "Although historians generally agree that Hasidism had no direct impact on the shaping of Jewish modernity, it has been argued [by the likes of Gershom Scholem and Jacob Katz] that Hasidism . . . indirectly—dialectically—prepared the way to the secularization of eastern European Jewish life."[7]

Mendes-Flohr and Reinharz relate to "traditional" Jews in the modern period in three ways. They either dismiss such Jews as irrelevant; view them as reactionaries against their modernizing counterparts; or (in a minority of cases) transform them into clandestine enlighteners or harbingers of modernity whose contribution to Jewish history consists of infrequent and "subtle" allusions in their voluminous writings to modern signposts such as science, Israel, and the nation-state.

The first position, that of dismissing "traditional" Jews, was illustrated at a 2007 conference of the Association for Jewish Studies in Toronto. In a session entitled "Where Does the Modern Period of Jewish History Begin?" Michael Meyer, a distinguished historian of German Jewry, suggested that most rabbinic Jews living in the modern period "are not modern at all," and are best understood as "medieval." Meyer follows a long line of scholars who assert that the terms "tradition" and "modernity" have been "at odds since the eighteenth century."[8] In this view, the powerful and protean force of modernity erodes (or in some instances fails to erode) an almost static, unchanging world of tradition.

The putative opposition of traditional and modern has been a staple of historical studies, pitting various groups, ideologies, and institutions against one another. More recently, however, this dichotomy has been challenged by those suggesting that while the terms might be opposed, when tradition becomes an ideology ("traditionalism") the two become intertwined, reacting to each other's positions. "Ironically," David Gross writes, "though traditionalism is based on a rejection of modernity, it can come into being only within modernity."[9]

Jacob Katz's student Michael K. Silber expressed this point, citing the case of Moses Sofer (1762–1839), a leading Hungarian rabbinic figure who vehemently and famously opposed many of the developments and innovations of his age. Sofer's battles showed how "tradition" is not something that exists only before or on the periphery of modernity; instead it functions as an ideology that contests modernity's claims. Following Katz, Silber suggested that Sofer's and his disciples' militant Orthodoxy was as much a product of "modernity" as was the ideology of the enlighteners he attacked. In a groundbreaking essay called "The Emergence of Ultra-Orthodoxy: The Invention of Tradition," Silber showed that "belying the conventional wisdom of both its adherents and its opponents, [ultra-Orthodoxy] is in fact not an unchanged and unchanging remnant of pre-modern, traditional Jewish society, but as much a child of modernity and change as any of its 'modern' rivals."[10]

Katz himself identified a select number of traditional Jews as forerunners of the Jewish Enlightenment. His work on Hasidism and the Haskalah illuminated the subtle and dialectical processes by which traditional Jews began to adopt modern modes of thought and behavior in the late eighteenth and early nineteenth centuries. Since the 1960s this more nuanced approach has enjoyed a warm reception in Modern Orthodox academic institutions such as Bar-Ilan University in Israel and Yeshiva University in New York. These institutions' journals (like *Bekol Derakhekha Daehu* and *Torah u-Madda*) regularly feature articles about rabbinic figures and organizations that reflect a more harmonious relationship between modern and traditional spheres. Such studies have been conducted in large part by Modern Orthodox scholars seeking precedents for their own hybrid identities. *Torah u-Madda*'s founding editor states in the introduction to its second volume (1990) that the journal's purpose is to explore "the interaction between Torah and secular culture throughout Jewish history."[11] Such an approach may adequately account for a rare breed of highly acculturated western European rabbinic figures whose struggles to resolve the tension between these two spheres made their modern tendencies overt.[12]

One might, however, be forgiven for calling this approach a needle-in-the-haystack rendering of "tradition," for it involves combing through reams of literature to locate instances where a rabbinic figure addressed "modern" issues. The dry hay of tradition—including whole Talmudic tractates, volumes of exegesis, and massive collections of legal rulings—that constitutes the bulk of the material and of the authors' concerns is feverishly winnowed in the hope of chancing across the five times an author mentions the Hebrew word for "science," the twenty times someone refers to the actual Land of Israel, or the two responsa written about the permissibility of shaving one's beard, wearing fashionable clothing, or owning books written by gentiles.[13]

Historians such as Shmuel Feiner and David Sorkin have improved on this approach. They focus on the more subtle and disguised elements of modernity that appear in the writings of those whom many scholars have otherwise depicted as traditional figures, and zero in on the points of tradition that appear in the writings of those whom many others have identified as modern thinkers. Their careful research has raised the possibility that several different "modernities" emerged in the eighteenth century.[14] Specifically, in addition to the more commonly cited anti-religious Enlightenment that challenged the canons of tradition, Sorkin identifies a *religious* Enlightenment exemplified by the "early Haskalah."[15]

The categories of what constitute modernity, however, still rely heavily on the experiences of Jews in western Europe. In most studies on eastern European Jewish intellectual history, a large portion of the subject's intellectual accomplishments and social significance is all too often ignored in the hope of excavating a statement or position that conforms to a certain process of secularization.

Katz's and Silber's approaches toward traditional Jews in the modern period can be traced genealogically to studies conducted by Katz's teacher Karl Mannheim (1893–1947) and, in turn, to his predecessor Max Weber (1864–1920). Weber examined numerous competing elements of Judaism, such as its charismatic and rationalist elements. He believed, however, that Judaism's "genuine ethic" was "traditionalism as shown from the Talmud."[16] These German scholars laid the groundwork for Katz's and Silber's studies—by largely ignoring traditional figures and their worldviews, by casting them in opposition to secular trends, or by nominating a select group as harbingers of modernity.

Typically, Weber and his students contrasted the static nature of traditional societies with modernity's dynamism.[17] According to Weber, "a system of imperative co-ordination will be called 'traditional' if legitimacy is claimed for it and believed in on the basis of the sanctity of the order and the attendant powers of control as they have been handed down from the past, [as they] 'have always existed.'"[18] Weber's contemporaries used the placeholder "traditional" to describe those societies that have seemingly "not changed greatly over many years, and [where such] changes have occurred [they] are primarily adaptations to changes of external circumstances of the societies."[19] This description of tradition has led many to simply ignore those groups deemed traditional or express surprise when they locate "change" in a tradition, a traditional society, or a traditional structure of authority.[20]

In other cases, Weber identified certain sixteenth- through eighteenth-century Protestant pietistic figures—including John Calvin (1509–1564), Philip Jakob Spener (1635–1735), Nikolaus von Zinzendorf (1700–1760), and John Wesley (1703–1791)—as harbingers for trends and movements ranging from capitalism to secularism.[21] Weber's analysis of these thinkers' contributions to secularism, however, came at the expense of understanding how they also gave rise to various extreme and often highly "traditional" worldviews that flourished in modernity.[22]

Weber's student Karl Mannheim likewise placed tradition in opposition to modernity—and to conservative thought in particular. Whereas conservatism is "meaningful," "conscious," and "reflective," Mannheim defines "traditionalism" as "a general psychological attitude which expresses itself in different individuals as a tendency to cling to the past and a fear of innovation."[23] Conservatism appears as something rational and deliberate; traditionalism is reactive and irrationally defends the status quo against deliberate challenges.

Much in the same way that scholars of Chinese and Indian civilizations, which are often labeled as traditional, have come to take issue with Weber and Mannheim for not adequately explaining these civilizations,[24] so too have I come to believe that Katz's and Silber's notion of tradition and traditionalism fails to explain the experience of the overwhelming majority of eighteenth- and nineteenth-century eastern European Jews, who did not spend their days either combating the western European secular pursuit of science, philosophy, and mathematics or holding on to the same political and social structures of their sixteenth- and seventeenth-century ancestors. Katz and Silber might have been right about Sofer (although even he spent only a small fraction of his intellectual resources battling reformers). But figures such as the Gaon of Vilna or Hayyim of Volozhin (the Gaon's student and Sofer's contemporary), who did not express hostility toward modernity, elude their grasp.

Yet although Elijah of Vilna evinced an appreciation for certain aspects of what might be identified as western European modernity (such as embracing various elements of secular knowledge and offering a new approach toward Jewish education), these aspects remained tangential to his concerns.[25] The true nature of his life and his impact on modern Jewry are far more profound and have generally been overlooked. The piecemeal nature and paucity of research produced on Elijah's life and writings are the result of applying the experiences of western European Jews—religious reform, acculturation, and emancipation—to evaluate eastern European Jews, who lived under radically different circumstances.

This book provides a new narrative of the modern Jewish experience and challenges the description of eastern European Jewry as "traditional" in the Weberian sense of the term. It suggests that the differentiation between public and private spheres, the weakening of religious governing structures, and the democratization of knowledge in Jewish society—all processes that emerged in tandem with principles such as civil rights, equality, functional differentiation, and skepticism—produced a host of unforeseen ideologies and movements, including Hasidism, Mitnagdism, the Haskalah, Zionism, and Jewish anti-statism. Many writers divide these movements into modern, anti-modern, and pre-modern tendencies. Such divisions generate imprecise terminology, concealing more than they illuminate. Most important, they fail to grasp that modernity was not just a *movement* based on a certain set of liberal philosophical principles that only certain elite sectors of society experienced. Rather, it was a *condition* that restructured all aspects of European life and thought, in diverse and often contradictory ways. Exclusivist ideologies such as Hasidism, institutions such as the yeshiva, and self-assertive Jewish political expressions all emerged from the same democratization of knowledge and privatization of religion that gave rise to the Haskalah. Those contemporary religious movements that diverge from—and at times threaten—secular and liberal conceptions of Judaism express the unforeseen side effects of a seminal tension in modernity. This tension gave rise simultaneously to exclusivist, as well as various liberal, intellectual and political movements, which were created alongside and not originally in opposition to one another.[26]

Elijah and Eighteenth-Century Eastern European Jewry

This book follows Elijah through the course of events that mark eighteenth-century eastern European Jewish history. It opens with an overview of his life and the seventeenth- and early eighteenth-century influences on his worldview. It then distinguishes his work from both the mid-eighteenth-century German Haskalah and the Hasidic movement and explains his connection to the establishment of the early nineteenth-century yeshiva. Finally, the book addresses the way Elijah's students crafted and popularized his legacy as "the Genius of Vilna" to nineteenth-century eastern European Jewry. This approach corrects both biographies[27] and other studies that document the way he was appropriated by later generations[28] and offers a non-hagiographic rendering of Elijah's life, while keeping an eye on the larger question: What about Elijah and his ideas made them so critical to the emergence of modern Jewry? To answer these questions and steer clear of pitfalls posed by the myriad editors involved in the publication of Elijah's writings, I will primarily rely on Elijah's commentaries listed in David Luria's bibliography and only on those ideas that reappear throughout Elijah's writings, irrespective of editor or commentary.

Chapter 1 presents an account of Elijah's life that draws on the most historically verifiable material offered by Vilna archives, Elijah's own work, and his immediate students' reflections. The reflections that describe the way Elijah was experienced in his lifetime are distinguished both from Elijah's own words and from later hagiographic statements.[29] Such insights by Elijah's immediate students shed light on his relationship to the town in which he resided and the way he was experienced. By the end of his life Elijah was nearly deified among his supporters in Vilna. But his name remained obscure among the masses of eastern European Jewry until the first decades of the nineteenth century, in part because he was reticent to publish in his lifetime or occupy an official rabbinic position. Chapter 1 thus provides a historical framework to understand his writings and the role he played in the emergence of Vilna as a central locale for European Jewry.

Chapter 2, the most philosophically technical section of the book, explores the Gaon's worldview in relation to eighteenth-century intellectual culture. It examines the Gaon's work in its broad intellectual context, tempered by modest causal claims regarding those whose work influenced him. The Gaon does not cite any eighteenth-century work. This omission suggests something beyond an attempt to follow Maimonides's advice to veil philosophic sources in consideration of the masses' ignorance.[30] It might be argued that the Gaon's citation style evinces what Harold Bloom has identified as an "anxiety of influence," the fear that one's work will be derivative.[31] A true genius, Bloom argues, is one who works through this anxiety to a point where he or she creates something original and unprecedented. The Gaon's terse writing style, coupled with the ways he emends texts and dismissal of rabbinic works published in the eighteenth century,[32] suggests a concerted effort to remove evidence of influence (or simply indifference). Elijah read widely, but what he read, and to what degree it influenced him, can be gleaned only by carefully comparing his writing to that of scholars living before and during his lifetime.

Elijah was a product of an idealist philosophic tradition that resurfaced in eighteenth-century European intellectual circles. He borrowed from rabbinic thinkers like Moses Hayyim Luzzatto (1707–1746) and Raphael Levi of Hannover (1685–1779), both of whom applied the idealist worldview of Gottfried Wilhelm Leibniz (1646–1714) to Jewish thought. Leibniz and his contemporaries, like Elijah, embraced early kabbalistic ideas, reinterpreted Aristotelian categories to fit mathematical schema, and emphasized the role played by motion in the genesis of the world. For both the Gaon and Leibniz, the mathematics of motion replaces God as the principle for evaluating the reason behind being. The Gaon's removal of God from the concrete workings of nature (he instead places God *behind* nature) grants human beings the opportunity to assert themselves in history and to take an active role in the redemption of the world.

Chapter 3 examines the Gaon's relationship with his mid-eighteenth-century contemporaries in Berlin, especially the philosopher Moses Mendelssohn (1729–1786, another follower of Leibniz). A comparison of how each man interacted with the rabbinic tradition sheds light on the sharp social and political contrasts between Vilna and Berlin during the mid- to late eighteenth century, and more generally, on the dramatic differences between the Jewish communities of modern eastern and western Europe. In Vilna there were as many Jews as there were Catholics, while Jews lived in Berlin as a minority among the mostly Protestant population. Acting as the leader of a community that lived as a virtual majority encouraged Elijah to develop ideas that in other contexts would have been deemed threatening. Unlike Mendelssohn, who resided in Protestant Berlin, the Gaon, living in Jewish Vilna, was unfazed by its local Catholics and by whatever criticisms they may have had of the rabbinic tradition. The lack of a perceived intellectual threat provided Elijah an intellectual freedom not afforded Mendelssohn, who defended Judaism and the rabbinic tradition against both a hostile radical Enlightenment and Protestant biblical scholarship.

Despite the differences and similarities between these two intellectual giants, neither ever directly addressed the other. Whatever criticisms the Gaon may have had of the mid-eighteenth-century Maskilic movement with which Mendelssohn was associated, they never appear in his writings. Rather, the Gaon is best known for his forceful public condemnation of the Hasidic movement at the end of the eighteenth century.

Chapter 4 details the battle between the Gaon (and his followers) and the Hasidim. The Gaon feared that Hasidic ideas and practices had links to the seventeenth-century false messiah Sabbatai Tzvi. While many may see Hasidism as having triumphed in its battle with Elijah, twentieth-century Jewry's privileging of the yeshiva over the Hasidic court (even in many Hasidic communities) highlights the Gaon's enduring influence.[33]

The Gaon's inspirational role in establishing the modern yeshiva is the subject of Chapter 5. His glosses to Joseph Karo's definitive code of Jewish law, *Shulchan Arukh*, encouraged nineteenth-century Jews to move away from the code-based learning culture supported by the *kehilah* (the elaborate lay-led self-governing structure used by eastern European Jews in the sixteenth and seventeenth centuries). The Gaon encouraged his students to focus their studies on the Talmud, a text known most for being open-ended and not legally binding. Ultimately, the Talmud replaced legal code as the central text studied in the nineteenth-century modern yeshiva founded in Volozhin. This paradigm shift—from code to commentary, from *kehilah* to yeshiva—restructured the hierarchy of authority in rabbinic Judaism and should be considered one of the many expressions of religious privatization that followed the *kehilah*'s downfall and the rise of the modern state.

Indeed the nineteenth-century yeshiva was unique in Jewish history. Previously only a chosen few were permitted entry into Jewish study halls, and even fewer were afforded the opportunity to attend secular universities. These study halls were locally run, usually comprising no more than six to ten students.[34] A prominent community such as Vilna, for example, granted its chief rabbi, Baruch ben Moses Meir Kahana Rapoport, twenty students in 1708.[35]

The book's final chapter, Chapter 6, assesses Elijah's immortalization and the defining aspect of his life and legacy—his sobriquet Gaon, or "Genius"—in part by tracing the intellectual genealogy that popularized his "genius" in the first half of the nineteenth century. In recent years scholarship dealing with Elijah has revolved around his and his students' relationship to the Land of Israel. Most notably, Arie Morgenstern and Israel Bartal have engaged in a robust debate over the place of Elijah's students in the history of Zionism. Though an important issue (one that I hope to fully address in the future), it narrows Elijah's life and legacy to concentrate on a specific idea and group of students. Since this work focuses on the master's life and thought writ large, it explores how his genius was employed and refashioned by those associated with various modern ideological movements. Elijah's genius was understood as a product of individual will: he was revered for actualizing his inner potential and cultivating a taste for knowledge. It was a human feat, devoid of any external influences or divine intermediaries. Theoretically, any member of society could replicate it with adequate intelligence and dedication. In this sense, the lore and mystique surrounding the Gaon's genius and his intellectual charisma—more than any text he wrote, position he expressed, practice he adopted, or institution he envisioned—permanently enshrined him in the modern Jewish imagination.

1

Elijah and Vilna in Historical Perspective

ELIJAH BEN SOLOMON'S LIFE AND HIS RELATIONSHIP TO THE CITY WHOSE name he would share remain somewhat obscure—especially when compared to what is known about other outstanding figures of his age. Trails of correspondence and memoirs have provided ample material for scholars to document the experience of the "Jewish Socrates" Moses Mendelssohn in eighteenth-century Berlin, for instance, but few have been able to ascertain even the most basic details of Elijah and eighteenth-century Jewish Vilna.[1] That the life of one of the most influential figures in Jewish history remains opaque is the result of both personality and profession. Since Elijah held no official rabbinic position and had little contact with the non-Jewish residents of his city, he is only tangentially mentioned in Jewish communal documents and government archives. Unlike Mendelssohn's, then, only a few hundred of Elijah's words can be found scattered in letters of approbation or condemnation published during his lifetime—even though after his death in 1797, the task of organizing his voluminous literary estate required scores of individuals to complete.

What is clear from the archival and published data, however, is the symbiotic relationship that made both Elijah "the Genius of Vilna" and

Vilna the "mother of eastern European Jewry." By the nineteenth century, Vilna and Gaon had become synonymous. Over the course of Elijah's life, Vilna was transformed from a poor town with no more than a thousand Jews subjected to local anti-Semitism and economic discrimination into an economic and intellectual center where Jews lived as a majority vis-à-vis the local Catholic and Polish population. Moreover, Elijah's genius almost singlehandedly turned what otherwise might have been simply a demographically and economically vibrant town into the center of the Jewish intellectual aristocracy. "Just as Vilna was the jewel of Ashkenaz," it was said, "so was the Gaon the jewel of Vilna."[2] Conversely, Vilna's Jewish population boom turned what otherwise might have been a brilliant social hermit into a patron sage of modern Jewry.

Vilna in Ashes and Elijah's Youth

When Elijah was born to Solomon Zalman and Traina of Słutzk[3] on the first day of Passover, 1720, Jewish Vilna was in shambles, a shadow of the large community it had been before the Muscovite invasion in the mid-seventeenth century.[4] Vilna was just then emerging from the throes of the Great Northern War (1700–1721), when Russian and Swedish troops had invaded its territory. Fires (1706), plagues (1710), and famines (1706, 1724) decimated Vilna's Jewish population, leaving it debt-ridden and with little more than a thousand members. In size and prestige, it was dwarfed by Kraków and Brody, then the major centers of European Jewish life.

Elijah was the first of five boys born into a family whose piety, economic self-sufficiency, and intellectual pedigree were well known to Vilna residents. He was a descendant of two of the town's most celebrated rabbinic figures, Moses Rivkes (d. 1672)[5] and Moses Kraemer (d. 1688).[6] Both were pious scholars who gave of themselves freely to the townspeople, and both financially supported themselves—Moses Rivkes from his father-in-law's fortune, and Moses Kraemer from his own shop.

By all accounts Elijah was a child prodigy. As legend has it, by age nine he had mastered the Bible, Mishnah, and Gemara,[7] and he was capable of reading an astounding 140 folios of the Talmud in half an hour.[8] At age ten, he is said to have mastered kabbalistic literature, including the *Zohar, Sefer ha-Pardes*, and the writings of Isaac Luria. By age twelve he reputedly had taught himself the "seven sciences": logic, rhetoric, grammar, arithmetic, music, geometry, and astronomy. He expressed an interest in pursuing medical studies, but was discouraged by his father, who pushed his son to return to the Talmud.[9] Even when compared to hagiographic accounts of other Jewish figures, Elijah's contemporaries' reflections on the nature of his genius are remarkable. One of Elijah's students was later celebrated for knowing all of Talmudic literature by age twenty-four—fifteen years longer than Elijah purportedly took to master it.[10] Hyperbole and hagiography aside, his genius was described as incomparable in the annals of Jewish history.

Elijah's intellectual accomplishments were not the result of any particular school or institution. He did not attend the Vilna *cheder* (primary school),[11] established in 1690 by the Vilna community (in conjunction with the Council of the Four Lands). The *cheder* taught children from the "aleph-bet until mishnayot" and offered to instill "linguistic and writing skills."[12] Most of these types of schools in eastern Europe remained poorly administered and staffed by teachers whose pedagogic qualifications amounted to little more than their lack of qualification to do anything else.[13] The curriculum was unsystematic and students of various ages and with different levels of knowledge were often squeezed into the same classroom. Elijah was known to have dismissed the *cheder* system outright: "no word of truth was ever uttered in such a place," he remarked.[14]

Unlike Ezekiel Landau of Prague, one of his best-known contemporaries who studied in the Brody *kloiz* (a permanent study house for elite scholars supported by the community), Elijah did not attend any advanced study house. Nor does it seem that he benefited from a great teacher, as Moses Sofer did in Frankfurt with the mystic Nathan Adler (1741–1800). Instead Elijah studied alongside his peer Aryeh Leib Tshanavith, perhaps supplemented by very infrequent sessions with rabbinic luminaries.[15] Later some would cite Elijah's dismissal of the *cheder* system as support for revising the educational institutions of eastern European Jewry.[16]

In the 1730s Elijah moved from a decimated Vilna to the town of Kėdainiai (Keidan), sixty-eight miles northwest,[17] where he punctiliously fulfilled the Talmudic dictum: "[at age] eighteen to the wedding canopy" (Avot 5:24). Shortly after his marriage to Hannah in 1738,[18] Elijah followed in the path of other itinerant scholars, leaving his wife and journeying across the continent[19] with his friend and eventual student Hayyim of Sereje.[20] Though it may seem odd that he set off traveling so soon after his marriage, throughout his life Elijah left his family for considerable periods of time for spiritual reflection.[21] Self-imposed exile had strong roots in the rabbinic tradition and was commonly practiced by eighteenth-century spiritualists. Along with Elijah, other pietists such as Aryeh Leib ben Asher Gunzberg (1695–1785) and Nachman of Bratslav (1772–1810) left home to wander about in unknown lands. By detaching from family, friends, and material comforts, they aimed to cultivate a sense of humility and religious dedication—or to atone for sins.[22]

While Elijah focused on his spiritual well-being, Vilna's Jews fought for their very survival. The long-standing and complex relationship between the Polish-Lithuania Commonwealth and Vilna's local governmental institutions created a perilous environment for the city's Jews. In the 1730s the residents of Vilna nearly expelled the city's Jewish residents in response to the decision by King Friedrich Augustus III (1696–1763) to grant Jews trading rights in 1738. Local merchants and craftsmen balked because the ruling threatened their monopoly on the local economy. In 1740 they convinced the local magistrate court not only to overturn the king's law but also to demand that the Jews be expelled from the city.

The contradictory messages issuing from local officials, the king, and magistrate courts were a function of a weak Polish government and Vilna's position as the capital of the historic Grand Duchy of Lithuania. Founded in the fourteenth century by the pagan leader Gediminas (1275–1341), the Grand Duchy of Lithuania spanned the length of the Baltic Sea to the Black Sea and covered the territory between Lublin and the Moscow Duchy. Though the Polish-Lithuanian Commonwealth subsumed the Grand Duchy in the sixteenth century, the historic bloc still maintained its own government, treasury, and army. Further complicating its internal political affairs was its position as the seat of the Lithuanian-Polish Catholic bishop, the powerful Radziwiłł family, and other members of the Polish landowning *szlachta* (nobility) who were *voivodes* (governors) and *castellanes* (senators) in the Polish national legislative arm, the Sejm. These authorities and chieftains vied for power and control of Vilna, leading to a highly decentralized relationship with the king and the Sejm.[23] This decentralization created a situation in which "what was authorized on one street was made illegal on another."[24]

The vulnerable Jews tried to leverage this decentralization to their advantage, appealing to each of the parties for support. In the 1740s it was the Lithuanian "general" (the chief beadle and recorder of testimony for the court) and *voivode* Michał Serwacy Wiśniowiecki (1680–1744) who defended them, arguing that the expulsion of the Jews from Vilna would ultimately harm the town's economy. Wiśniowiecki brokered a deal with local officials and townspeople to allow Jews to remain in Vilna on the condition that their residential and trading rights be severely curtailed to a three-block radius bounded by Żydowska (Jews Street), Juatkowa (Slaughters Street), and St. Michael (also called Glass Street). Some exceptions continued to be permitted for Jews who lived in housing complexes on Vokietchių Street (German Street), which bordered the synagogue complex, owned by various noblemen. The three blocks were connected like a maze—or, in the words of one nineteenth-century observer, like "an old wrinkly face."[25] Jews were not even secure about their place on this shriveled plot of land, however. Various Christian denominations owned and hoped to expand monasteries and other religious institutions on precisely the same three-block radius, thereby effectively pushing Jews out of their only area of residence.[26]

While the fate of Vilna's Jews was being negotiated, Elijah wandered the continent. The few verifiable facts about Elijah's odyssey in the 1740s have given rise to numerous fantastical hagiographic stories, many of which are almost certainly not true. Elijah supposedly dazzled local rabbis with his vast knowledge,[27] awed hosts with his pietistic and ascetic practices,[28] outmatched German professors in debate,[29] and combed Amsterdam libraries for variant manuscripts of the Talmud.[30] Elijah's biographer Shmuel Luria claims that Elijah "wandered about various lands in order to locate precious hidden texts and manuscripts and bring them back to his home."[31] Irrespective of the veracity of these stories' details, they do at least provide us with important kernels of information about Elijah's vast library, which extended beyond normative religious texts. More to the point, these stories also hint that he was not a cloistered mystic unacquainted with those living beyond the walls of his study house in Vilna. His travels certainly brought him to Königsberg and likely to Berlin and Amsterdam, putting him in contact with a wide range of individuals, communities, ideas, and texts across Europe.

When Elijah returned to Vilna in 1748, the city's Jews still faced harsh economic, religious, and social discrimination. Around this time, the Jewish community's growth was stunted by the threat of expulsion and more fires (most notably those in 1748 and 1749). The fires ravaged the Jewish quarter, including the old study house where Elijah's great-grandfather had studied, part of the main synagogue, Jewish stores, and twelve churches and monasteries. The community remained afloat only by drawing from loans it received from local Christian groups such as the Basillians (a monastic order established in the seventeenth century in memory of Basil the Great and affiliated with the Greek Catholic Church), from European creditors (such as the Jewish community of Amsterdam), and from prominent Jewish families such as the Friedländers.[32]

Leading Polish officials, including the Catholic bishop Franciszek Antoni Kobielski (1679–1755), blamed these fires on Jews and incited anti-Semitic attacks.[33] At the same time, the priest Stephen Turczynowicz (d. 1773) launched a Mariavite mission to promote the conversion of Jewish women.[34] Apparently some financially strapped and unattached Jews were enticed by Turczynowicz's promises of prosperity and upward social mobility. Some historians claim that from 1743 to 1753, as many as 153 Vilna Jews converted to Christianity.[35] Moreover, Turczynowicz was said to have abducted and forcibly converted young Jewish children, ignoring King Jan III Sobieski's 1690 edict that prohibited the practice.[36]

The shrinking of Vilna's Jewish community and the economic hardships it faced forced *kehilah* leaders to sell or relinquish most of the community's real estate to Christian monasteries and churches.[37] Turczynowicz himself purchased from the Jewish leader Michel Gordon his home, which was eventually named after the Mariavite mission.[38] In 1690, Jews owned twenty-one of the thirty-two homes in the Jewish quarter; by the mid-eighteenth century they retained only a handful. One of the few residences they still owned was the "Fatel house," named after the seventeenth-century Vilna patron Michael ben Fatel,[39] whose heirs had donated it to the *kehilah* in 1682. The community used it to house religious functionaries, among them Elijah and his growing family, which by 1750 included three daughters. The Fatel house (or perhaps more appropriately, housing complex) sheltered some 51 families totaling 178 people. According to Klausner, there were no windows, nor even "a crack in the walls to allow for air circulation."[40] Elijah's very frugal accommodations underscore how impoverished the Vilna Jews were during the first half of the eighteenth century.

Elijah's Return and Vilna's Rebirth

From the mid-1740s until the mid-1760s, the Jews of Vilna struggled to support themselves. While the community's merchants toiled in the marketplace, trying to break the monopoly of the local townspeople,

Elijah locked himself in his room, feverishly writing notes and commentaries to classical rabbinic and kabbalistic works, and cultivating a mystique of genius that would eventually come to embody Vilna's return to glory. Elijah limited his contact with loved ones to the point that he resisted lifting his head from his books even upon hearing that his children were sick.[41] He was known to donate the family's food to the poor and paid little attention to his family's well-being.[42] Hannah described her husband as "not caring about worldly matters, his household, the health of his children, or his livelihood."[43] Still, he demanded strict obedience from her, reminding her that "a good wife follows the will of her spouse."[44]

Hannah cared for the family and provided Elijah with the time and space needed to write his commentaries.[45] Not since the medieval sage Rabbi Shlomo Yitzchaki (Rashi) had anyone written on as many classical rabbinic texts as Elijah, and not since the famed Safed mystic Isaac Luria (1534–1572) had a scholar penned as many works on kabbalah—among them magisterial commentaries to the early kabbalistic works *Sifra di-Tzniuta* and *Sefer Yetzirah*. Indeed, according to one historian, "The kabbalistic writings of . . . Elijah alone exceed in volume those of all his Hasidic contemporaries put together."[46] Elijah's energies were primarily focused on writing what some claim amounted to thirty full-length commentaries on the *Zohar*.[47]

Elijah's kabbalistic commentaries, like his writing on rabbinic literature, tended to focus on works he believed were of ancient origin.[48] Elijah interpreted these sacred kabbalistic texts according to the same principles he used when emending and interpreting Talmudic literature. Just as he freely emended two-thousand-year-old Talmudic texts, uninhibited by medieval commentators, Elijah altered kabbalistic works and boldly challenged Luria's hitherto unassailed interpretations.[49]

The majority of Elijah's kabbalistic works can be divided into two groups, according to their editors. The first and most authoritative group (including the earlier-mentioned works) was published posthumously by his family and those students whom he taught personally. The second group, published in the late nineteenth century by Shmuel Luria, includes Elijah's commentaries to *Heikhalot, Ra'ayah Mehemnah,* and *Tikkunei ha-Zohar.*

Elijah saw himself as a direct student of the earliest Talmudic and kabbalistic sages, if not their peer. According to his son Avraham, Elijah said

"with full certainty that he had no compunction about reciting his interpretations of the *Zohar* in front of Rabbi Shimon Bar Yochai [its purported
author] himself."[50] Avraham claims that his father wrote commentaries to
the Bible; the Mishnah; the Babylonian Talmud; the Palestinian Talmud; the
Tosefta; the Midrashic works *Sifra, Sifrei, Mekhilta, Seder Olam Rabbah,
Pirkei de-Rabbi Eliezer, Zohar*; the mystical and kabbalstic works *Tikkunei
ha-Zohar, Sefer Yetzirah*, and *Sifra di-Tzniuta*; as well as two commentaries
to Karo's *Shulchan Arukh*. He also wrote works on the *masorah* (the transmission of the Hebrew Bible), grammar, logic, algebra, and geometry. His
students marveled that if one were to live a thousand years one would not be
able to produce as prolifically as Elijah.[51] Not all of these works found their
way to publishing houses, and those that did were sometimes edited heavily,
but by the late nineteenth century most of Elijah's commentaries on biblical,
kabbalistic, and rabbinic literature could be found in Jewish libraries.

Yet more than the sheer size of his oeuvre, it is the unsurpassed quality
of Elijah's work that stands out. It is distinguished by its precise and
economical language; by Elijah's full command of sources and a mastery
of the entire canon of rabbinic and kabbalistic literature; and, finally, by
its originality. Though Elijah's writings are primarily commentaries on
preexisting literary texts, they nonetheless express unrivaled inventive-
ness, almost never containing the positions of any of his contemporaries
or immediate predecessors. Never once does he mention any teacher,
nor does he ever cite his own father Solomon or his brothers Abraham
(1712–1797) and Yissaschar (d. 1807), all of whom also spent their lives
immersed in study.[52] Elijah goes so far as to say that in some instances it
would have been better had his own great-grandfather Moses Rivkes
"kept his mouth shut."[53] Though these features of his commentaries will
be explored further in later chapters, one can surmise that Elijah's
commentaries reflect the stature of a scholar who is not a dwarf standing
on the shoulders of giants but a giant who dwarfs his predecessors.

It comes as no surprise that Elijah never published any of his own works.
He had little interest in recognition and little taste for the controversy likely
to be brought about by attaching his name to a document. Moreover, that it
would take some of the sharpest rabbinic minds over a century to edit his
commentaries suggests that there was simply not enough time for Elijah to
be both a genius with an unending devotion to study and a published
author. "He did not want to waste his time," was how one student explained
his reluctance to publish and circulate his works.[54] This reticence limited his

renown, especially during the 1750s and 1760s, to those with whom he came in direct contact or who learned of his reputation through word of mouth. Consequently only a few scholars in central Europe knew of Elijah's piety and brilliance.[55] His name remained known primarily within the confines of Vilna, where by 1755 he was referred to as the Hasid, an honorific bestowed on his grandfather, Vilna's seventh chief rabbi, Moses Kraemer.

Though revered by Vilna residents, there is no evidence from communal records available from the 1750s through the 1770s to suggest, as some have, that Elijah was financially dependent on his community. The truth of the matter is that during these years he was funded by the largesse of family members such as Eliyahu Pesseles (d. 1771),[56] who administered a fund established by his grandfather and by Elijah's ancestor, the remarkable scholar Moses Rivkes. Before his death, Rivkes created the fund that would bear fruit for the Vilna community well into the latter part of the eighteenth century. Pesseles's patronage and Hannah's dedication to her husband's studies were indispensable to Elijah's intellectual development. It is doubtful that during this period the financially strapped Vilna Jewish community, still trying to rebuild itself, could have provided Elijah with a stable salary or stipend.

Pesseles's generosity supported Elijah's growing family, which by 1758 included four children living under his roof: Khiena of Pińsk (1748–1806), Pesia Bassia Disna (b. 1750), another daughter whose name is unknown (b. 1752), and the newborn Shlomo Zalman (1758–1780). In 1756, Pesseles allocated the very respectable sum of three hundred gold coins from Rivkes's fund for a dowry for Elijah's eldest daughter (1741–1756), whose name is unknown.[57] Elijah would not see her under the wedding canopy, however; she passed away during her engagement.

Elijah was deeply affected by the death of family members. After going to his parents' graves, he refused to visit them again, telling his brother that it was simply too depressing for him to bear.[58] A fear of death would haunt him throughout his life. Nightmares of the dead caused him to shudder in his sleep.[59]

The year that Elijah's father died (1758), Pesseles donated the necessary funds to establish Elijah's study house in the heart of Vilna's Jewish quarter, next to the rebuilt main synagogue.[60] Moneys previously dedicated to the father were freed up for the son,[61] who by 1758 was living in increasingly cramped conditions in the Fatel house.[62] The establishment of Elijah's study in the town center highlights the rebuilding of Vilna's

Jewish quarter and the town's recognition of Elijah's importance to the city's intellectual life.

The founding of Elijah's study house in 1758 roughly coincides with the date of 1760 that Elijah's son Avraham gave for his father's emergence from solitude and his turn toward teaching. Vilna's Jewish population now totaled roughly 3,500. Contributing to this growth spurt were refugees who had fled to Vilna after being expelled from Kovno (Kaunus) in 1753 and 1761.[63] More importantly, as Zdzisław Budzyński and Gershon Hundert have shown, the Jewish population of the Polish-Lithuanian Commonwealth doubled between 1720 and 1760 largely due to low infant-mortality rates. While during this period "the Christian population in the [Polish-Lithuanian Commonwealth] grew 2.2 times, the Jewish population increased 3.7 times."[64]

Demographic growth generated greater economic needs for the Jewish community, and more lucrative opportunities for its merchants.[65] A number of Vilna's Jews became wealthy trading in grain, lumber, and medicine across eastern Europe.[66] The English traveler William Coxe remarked on the ubiquity of Jews during his sojourn through the region in the second half of the eighteenth century: "If you want an interpreter, they bring you a Jew; if you come to an inn, the landlord is a Jew; if you want post horses, a Jew procures them and a Jew drives them; if you wish to purchase, a Jew is your agent."[67]

The increasing presence of Jews beyond their designated quarter reflected a new social confidence as well as the tolerance of new local Catholic officials who subscribed to Enlightenment values. Vilna's leading Catholic figure in the second half of the eighteenth century, the enlightened bishop Ignacy Massalski (1729–1794), actually rebuffed Jewish would-be converts. Breaking with the conversion tactics supported by his predecessor, the virulently anti-Semitic Kobielski, Massalski instead scolded "individuals who were taking by force heretics' children and baptizing them against their will." These actions, Massalski claimed, "generated more enmity and bad will towards religion than they helped the Church."[68] Vilna Jewry's newfound economic and demographic strength certainly contributed to the bishop's decision to shut down Turczynowicz's Mariavite mission in 1774.[69] Massalski, who developed a warm personal and business relationship with Chief Rabbi Shmuel ben Avigdor, was not without his detractors. Like the chief rabbi, the bishop would years later be accused of accepting bribes. In addition, some members of the Lithuanian Catholic diocese, enraged by Massalski's warm relations with the Jews, appealed to the pope, claiming that the bishop had been lax in his conversion efforts. While Massalski could point to a tradition of tolerance dating back to the sixteenth century when, in the context of brutal religious conflicts, Lithuanian nobles passed laws guaranteeing religious freedom to all residents, his stance cannot be divorced from the emerging demographic and economic reality.[70]

There are no records of Elijah interacting with Massalski or any other Catholic official. But Elijah was aware of Vilna's reputation throughout Europe as a cosmopolitan city, the home to various Christian denominations, Muslims, and even the remnants of a small Karaite community.[71] Vilna boasted one of the only universities in the Polish-Lithuanian Commonwealth, Vilnius University.[72] Firsthand reports from the period describe Vilna's Jewish doctors breaking bread with their Christian counterparts, a practice that surprised at least one western European observer.[73] Elijah's student and grandson-in-law Avraham Danzig relates Elijah's concerns about the overlap between the various communities; he records "the Gaon's outlawing Vilna Jews from using palm fronds on the festivals of the Pentecost as the non-Jews do on their holiday."[74] Palm fronds were one of the most sacred symbols for Vilna Catholics, who claimed that their forefathers had consecrated palm trees when the city became Christian in the fifteenth century. From Shrove Tuesday through Easter, Vilna residents crafted them into Christian trinkets, dolls, and crosses. The use of the very same palm fronds by Jews for their own festival, Shavuot, just a few weeks later, disturbed Elijah, who saw the Shavuot custom (as opposed to the custom of using palm fronds on the fall holiday of Sukkot) as having Catholic connotations.

By 1764, then, Vilna's Jews were spilling over the three-block radius to which they had been confined. And just as Vilna was reemerging as an economic and spiritual center of eastern European Jewry, Elijah ben Solomon was beginning to be recognized as its intellectual leader.

Elijah as Spiritual Leader

As Vilna's Jewish population grew, the major debates and polemics shifted; rather than addressing external threats posed by Catholic bishops and anti-Semitic economic legislation, they began to address points of division within the Jewish community itself. For nearly thirty years the town's financial resources and emotional energy were sapped by the battles surrounding the *kehilah*'s attempt to remove Shmuel ben Avigdor (d. 1791) from his position as chief rabbi of Vilna. In 1762, the Vilna community, ignoring the rulings of rabbinic courts, charged Shmuel with bribery and with meddling in the affairs of the *kehilah*.[75] Over time, the chief rabbi enlisted the support of Jewish leaders from other locales such as Königsberg (where he traded in lumber), while Vilna's *kehilah* was backed by members of the Pińsk *kehilah*. Each side aligned itself with its own complement of noblemen, governmental officials, and Catholic clergy. Bishop Massalski defended the chief rabbi, while the Polish nobleman Karol Radziwiłł backed the Vilna *kehilah*. The fights between the two sides so poisoned the town's political atmosphere that never again would Vilna officially appoint another chief rabbi. The protracted internecine battle reflects the luxury and challenges of managing a large community. That none of the outside authorities such as Massalski or Radziwiłł had enough clout to mediate the fight indicates the extent to which the Jewish community had become its own independent political universe.

Though it is unclear if Elijah took a side in the dispute, the fight itself made him even more important to the community's self-image.[76] Without a chief rabbi, the *kehilah* leaders needed a figure to whom they could look, if not for political support, then at least for spiritual authority. Thus in the 1760s Elijah's stature in Vilna was catapulted to new heights.

It came as no surprise, then, when in 1767 the *kehilah* granted Eliyahu Pesseles permission to renovate and expand Elijah's study hall. The renovations were carried out around the same time as the Vilna community hired the Baroque architect Johann Christoph Glaubitz (1700–1767) to redesign the interior of the synagogue that had been ravaged by fires earlier in the century.[77] The renovations perhaps made room for Elijah's growing family, which now included two more sons, Avraham (1750 or 1765?–1808) and Yehudah Leib (1764–1816), as well as a new daughter, Tauba (1768–1812), additions that brought the total number of children to eight. (It remains unclear whether Elijah's family moved in with him or remained in the Fatel house.) As a mark of the community's increasing respect for Elijah, it threatened to excommunicate a candlemaker, Yosef, who lived atop Elijah's study house and was disturbing his important downstairs neighbor with the putrid smell of burned goose fat from his candles.[78]

The comfortable life Elijah was now enjoying in Vilna could not, however, quiet his spiritual yearnings. Sometime between the mid-1760s and early 1770s, he embarked on what would turn out to be a failed attempt to reach Palestine.[79] Arie Morgenstern claims that Elijah got as far as Amsterdam, where he had hoped to board a ship to Turkey and sail from there to the shores of Jaffa.[80] If Elijah was trying to reach Palestine, this was not the most direct route; going south through Italy would have been less circuitous. Except for a letter that Elijah penned to his wife,[81] and a document that Morgenstern unearthed in an Amsterdam archive stating that the Amsterdam Jewish community had donated a small sum of money to one "Rabbi Elijah ben Solomon of Vilna for his trip to the Land of Israel," we possess no other archival sources about his journey—further evidence that prior to the mid-1770s very few outside of Vilna found it important enough to note his presence in their city. Elijah's attempt, however, eventually inspired many of his students to reestablish Jewish life in Palestine in the nineteenth century.

In 1772 Elijah made himself and Vilna known throughout eastern European Jewry. That year he signed a ban against the revolutionary pietistic movement known as the Hasidim. Elijah and the Vilna community were not alone in condemning the new group. Spurring them to join the battle were numerous rabbinic figures, such as the elders of Shklov and the embattled chief rabbi Shmuel ben Avigdor. Other venerable eastern European cities, such as Brody with its roughly nine thousand Jewish inhabitants and elite *kloiz* (study house), also spoke out against the Hasidim. But the condemnations issued by the Gaon and "the Vilna Jewish community" were immediately noticed and cited in rabbinic and communal correspondence of the period. The opposition of Elijah and Jewish communal leaders in Vilna made the city the bulwark against the new group. The battle waged in Vilna stirred heated passions, bringing the issue of Hasidism to the forefront of eastern European Jewish politics. As Chapter 4 will show, the warring pamphlets and condemnations published by both Hasidim and Mitnagdim demonstrate that Elijah was viewed not as simply another leading rabbinic figure, nor was Vilna regarded as just another large town.

Elijah's hard stance against the new movement must have worried many of his co-religionists. That Elijah—a dedicated scholar who never dirtied his hands in communal affairs—bothered to involve himself in this dispute signaled that something seriously disturbing was afoot. His concerns were directed at the threat that Hasidism posed to the centrality of Torah study in the Jewish tradition. While some have suggested that the Vilna opposition to Hasidism consolidated the various pietistic groups into a spiritual movement, it could just as easily be said that the battle against Hasidism established Vilna and Elijah as the epicenters of eastern European Jewish intellectual life. Combating the "pseudo-pietism" of the Hasidim, in other words, made Elijah into the torchbearer of Jewry's intellectual tradition.

As will be discussed in depth later, sometime between 1772 and 1776 the Lithuanian Hasidic leaders Menachem of Vitebsk (1730–1788) and Shneur Zalman of Liadi (1745–1812) attempted to visit Elijah in Vilna, in the hopes of assuaging his fears about the new sect. Elijah literally slammed the door on them. "For if a person says something that you believe to be incorrect," he remarked in other contexts, "what shall you do? If you continue speaking to them in a pleasant manner, you will have deceived them, because in your heart you know the person is in the wrong. And if you are honest and tell them that they said something wrong, they will ignore you anyway and end up hating you."[82]

Elijah's refusal to meet with Hasidic emissaries in the early 1770s contrasts with the warm welcome that he and Vilna bestowed on the enlightened Barukh of Shklov upon his return from Berlin. Barukh had befriended members of Moses Mendelssohn's circle such as the early Haskalah figure Naftali Herz Wessely (1725–1805).[83] In 1778 Elijah greeted Barukh in Vilna and endorsed his translation into Hebrew of the Greek mathematics book *Euclid*. Barukh thought Elijah to be as well versed in the sciences and mathematics as in rabbinic literature. Elijah reinforced this impression by writing his own concise mathematical work, posthumously titled *Ayil Meshulash*.

Late eighteenth-century Vilna Jewry developed strong ties with western European Maskilim. Yosef ben Eliyahu Pesseles, for example, enjoyed warm relations with David Friedländer (1750–1834), who was not only a student of Mendelssohn, but also a Berlin leader and reformer of Judaism.[84] Elijah was at least vaguely known in Berlin both by Wessely[85] and by the son of Berlin's chief rabbi, who in 1779 referred to Elijah as "ha-Gaon ha-Hasid."[86]

Vilna Jewry's intellectual ties to western European Maskilim were reinforced by its increasing commerce with cities such as Königsberg. In 1783, restrictions against Jewish business were lifted and Jews were allowed to trade throughout the city, a change that brought new commercial opportunities to Vilna residents. From 1765 to 1784, the number of Vilna's Jewish laborers increased by nearly 25 percent, from 359 to 452.[87] Along with the increased circulation of goods, new ideas, books, and scholars trickled into Vilna.[88]

Vilna as an Intellectual Epicenter

Toward the end of the eighteenth century, Elijah's reputation as an obscure recluse was transformed, and he became known as a force to be reckoned with in the major political and intellectual debates of the day. By 1780 elite students had begun frequenting the Gaon's study house, many of them from nearby Shklov, a bastion of anti-Hasidism and where Elijah's respected and learned brother Abraham had moved in 1779.[89] To accommodate his students, Elijah acquired, with funds raised from private donors, space in the "Slutzki" home, which had the distinction of being one of the first housing complexes owned by Vilna Jews and located outside the courtyard of the synagogue.[90] Making use of their newfound prosperity, Vilna Jews in the second half of the eighteenth century bought back numerous properties from monasteries and Christian denominations, cementing their foothold in the city's real-estate market.

Vilna's improved living conditions, coupled with the Gaon's wide-ranging intellectual interests, made the city a magnet for scholars and students alike. The Gaon's method was enticing to various groups. To students like the Maskil Menashe of Illya (1767–1831), he interpreted the Bible according to its plain sense, "systematically distinguishing between rabbinic interpretation and *sensus literalis*."[91] To others such as Shraga Feivush of Dubrowna, "he followed the early sages of the Mishnah and Talmud, locating all aspects of the law within Scripture."[92] For mystically minded students like Hayyim of Volozhin, he could reveal the kabbalistic significance of texts. The Gaon's dexterity in juggling different interpretations led one student to reflect that "even when he heard the Gaon on consecutive days, it was as though he was a different person."[93]

Many earlier scholars had spoken theoretically about the multifaceted nature of the Torah, repeating the common refrain that the Torah had "seventy faces." But the Gaon rigorously applied such an outlook to every text he analyzed. This in turn attracted a diverse cadre of students. Even more alluring was Elijah's incomparable grasp of what at that time was seen as all of Jewish literature. So profound was his knowledge of the Jewish canon that some of his students made his commentaries and emendations the final word on rabbinic literature, ignoring and sometimes zealously removing from printed editions all other commentaries and variant traditions that had come before him.[94]

Elijah's unique status was due not merely to his polemical talents (as in the case of Jacob Emden of Altona), nor his communal leadership (as with Ezekiel Landau of Prague), nor his piety (like Nathan Adler of Frankfurt). Rather, for his students he represented the very apex of the rabbinic tradition; he offered them a radically new understanding of Judaism that tossed aside customs followed for hundreds of years, treated kabbalah as a science containing not only the deepest metaphysical secrets but also a code for understanding the mechanics of nature, and replaced (though never eliminated) *mitzvot* (deeds) with the study of the Talmud as the locus of religious authority. In effect, Elijah gutted the medieval corpus of Jewish literature that had stood as a barrier between him and the classical rabbinic and kabbalistic texts. He turned the medieval rabbinic tradition into a secondary literature that could be argued with or ignored. He put himself in the closest possible contact with the source of knowledge, all the while upholding the binding nature of the law.

Elijah's brilliance was directly experienced only by a select few: his most prominent and earliest disciples included his brothers,[95] his children,[96] and elite scholars,[97] some of whom also served as his beadles.[98] Elijah also studied with a number of more distant family members.[99] In his final years, a host of dedicated scholars from Shklov spent time with him before emigrating to the Holy Land, where they spread his teachings.[100] Of these scholars, his most dedicated and gifted pupil was Menachem Mendel of Shklov, who would later found the first *yishuv* (settlement) in Palestine. His most illustrious and influential student, however, was Hayyim of Volozhin (1749–1821), founder of the Volozhin yeshiva.[101]

Students visited the Gaon only after spending years with other teachers.[102] For example, Hayyim of Volozhin had already studied with Aryeh Leib ben Asher Gunzburg (1695–1785) before arriving at Elijah's study hall. Moshe of Pińsk (d. 1836) and Sa'adya ben Natan Nata (d. 1813), both grown men thoroughly versed in rabbinic and kabbalistic literature, left their wives and children to sit at the Gaon's feet.

The Gaon's teaching method largely entailed speaking while his students took notes. In his meetings with Menachem Mendel of Shklov, he essentially dictated his ideas to his student, who occasionally asked the master for a clarification. The Gaon answered plainly by shaking his head.[103] Others claimed that Elijah's style of teaching involved simply "reading out loud and people around him listening."[104]

The Gaon's students were astounded by his economy of language and intellectual confidence.[105] Every idea expressed, they claimed, contained nothing superfluous or unsubstantiated, no half-baked thoughts. His students relate stories about those who questioned the Gaon only to have him stubbornly repeat himself verbatim until the questioners realized the flaw in their logic.[106] At other times, he would interrupt students "in the middle of their question," as if he could divine their query before it could be fully articulated, and then summon sources from the depths of rabbinic and kabbalistic literature in reply.[107]

In contrast to the cult of personality that developed around Hasidic rebbes, a cult of genius developed around the Gaon. His disciples relate stories about the master sleeping only two hours a day, or turning deathly ill if he failed to understand some passage or other.[108] His donnish and preoccupied manner, it was said, led him to accidentally bump into people while he was studying.[109] A wide range of students who worked directly with Elijah captured these impressions. Some, like Sa'adya ben Natan Nata, spent years with Elijah, studying with him, caring for his needs, acting as his emissary to local communities, and issuing updates to others about his master's stance against the Hasidim. Menachem Mendel of Shklov, by contrast, a student who aside from Elijah's children was the figure most intimately involved in editing the Gaon's manuscripts, spent only a year and a half with Elijah himself (though during that time he reportedly never left the Gaon's side).[110] Hayyim of Volozhin frequently visited the Gaon over a twenty-year period but stayed in the city only sporadically.[111]

Elijah limited his relationship with his students to strictly intellectual matters. Unlike his Hasidic contemporaries, almost none of his students mention him addressing their personal lives or dispensing marital or professional advice.[112] His austere scholarly lifestyle prevented him from developing close friendships. Nonetheless, softer sides of Elijah are detected in the concern he sometimes showed toward his students' emotional well-being,[113] and the joy he took in the companionship of

Jacob ben Wolff Kranz (1740–1804), known as the Dubner Maggid (preacher);[114] Raphael the Av-beit Din of Hamburg (1722–1803);[115] and the Słonim-based rabbi Yehudah Edel (1759–1827).[116]

Hannah, Elijah's wife of over forty years, died in 1782 at the age of fifty-nine.[117] Shortly thereafter, Elijah took the hand of Gittel, the widow of Rabbi Meir of Chełm.[118] Yet Elijah probably had even less time to attend to her than he had when he was married to Hannah. By 1780, his reputation—and Vilna's—had reverberated beyond Lithuania due to his charisma, the town's economic dynamism, and the community's steadfast opposition against the Hasidim.

Vilna Politics

Vilna's economic and demographic expansion gave it the means to provide more assistance to Elijah and his growing family. By 1784, communal records indicate that Elijah was exempt from paying taxes and was receiving a very respectable 28 Polish złoty a week. The Gaon earned far more than the community doctor (12 złoty a week) but slightly less than the scribe and judge David ben Shimon (32 złoty a week).[119] The tax exemption reflects Elijah's value in the eyes of communal leaders. Few eastern European Jewish communities could afford to waive such fees for someone who did not serve in any official capacity. Leading rabbinic figures like Akiva Eiger of Posen (1761–1837) took rabbinic positions only because they failed to secure funds from patrons or communities to support full-time study. The monies paid to Elijah may have come from the *kehilah* itself or from the interest from Moses Rivkes's general charity fund.[120] Elijah received an additional 18 złoty a week from his relatives and from the Vilna patron and businessman Yitzchak ben Yosef Mechotievitz.[121]

With all the tension surrounding the battle against the Hasidim, the *kehilah*'s attempt to remove Chief Rabbi Shmuel ben Avigdor, and other contentious issues, it is not surprising that communal officials relying on the Gaon's spiritual capital compensated him accordingly. But the community did not actually have sufficient funds in its coffers. It was still paying back heavy interest on loans that it had taken out at the beginning of the century. Thus the Gaon's weekly salary and tax exemption became controversial, drawing the ire of some who charged the community with wasting its money on intellectual decadence.[122] Some of these townspeople were enraged that a portion of the taxes they paid for every circumcision, dowry, home sale, and purchase of meat or milk was paying for Elijah's studies.[123] While the *kehilah*'s coffers were considerably fuller than at the start of the century—a result of increasing tax revenues from the town's growing Jewish population—these concerned citizens wondered what the cash-strapped, debt-ridden *kehilah* was doing spending its tax revenues on Elijah, someone who seemed to offer no instrumental value to the city's residents. Some residents even demanded that Elijah return to the community what the *kehilah* paid him. According to Peter Wiernik, echoes of these grumblings could still be heard in nineteenth-century Vilna, where some claimed that their grand-parents had said "the Gaon's children went around with diamonds."[124] Vilna's communal leaders, however, who regarded the Gaon as the pride of the city, rebuffed any such complaints. Instead the *kehilah* threatened to sanction those who dared to speak against their Gaon.[125]

Elijah spent the final years of his life mired in the rough and tumble of Vilna's politics. The pious recluse living in a burned-down Lithuanian town had become a prominent leader of a Jewish capital. Elijah's stature as Vilna's spiritual leader existed in symbiosis with Vilna Jewry's self-perception as a political force in local and regional affairs—as a remark-able kidnapping case would soon show. On December 2, 1787, a seventeen-year-old named Hirsch ben Abba Wolf walked into the Vilna Dominican monastery and asked to convert to Christianity. It seems that his conversion was brought on more by teenage ennui or rebellion than anything coercive or sinister. Even so, Hirsch was the son of Abba ben Wolf, a wealthy member of the Vilna *kehilah*, sworn opponent of the chief rabbi, and staunch supporter of the Gaon. Abba himself had been accused by his enemies of having converted in his youth. Much to the consternation of his rivals, the *kehilah* had just approved Abba to replace Shmuel ben Avigdor as chief rabbi.[126] His son's conversion lent support to those who deemed Abba unfit for the appointment, such as the Vilna strongman Isaac ben Leib.

Earlier in the century, youth conversions in Vilna had often been the result of kidnappings of young Jewish children by Catholic officials there. Later too, in the nineteenth-century Italian case of Edgardo Mortara, a six-year-old Jewish boy was kidnapped by the Catholic Church.[127] Weak minority Jewish communities like those were often helpless in reclaiming kidnapped children. But the large late eighteenth-century Vilna community had no such inhibitions. Instead, the Vilna Jewish leader Abba, his sons, and Elijah confidently hatched a plan to abduct Hirsch and bring him back into the Jewish fold. Their plan involved bribing another recent convert from Judaism to Christianity, a boy from Grodno roughly the same age as Hirsch named Kwiatkowski. Hirsch's family paid Kwiatkowski to travel to Vilna, where Abba's children took him to visit the Gaon. Three times Kwiatkowski was given an audience with the master, who impressed on him the importance of bringing Hirsch back to his family. The Gaon persuaded the boy not to relate any of the proceedings to local authorities and promised him a portion in the world to come if he succeeded in rescuing Hirsch.[128] With the Gaon's blessing and a substantial sum of money handed to him by Hirsch's brother, Kwiatkowski entered the monastery and befriended the impressionable and newly christened Hirsch, who had subsequently taken the name Wincenty Nueman. On January 23, 1788, Kwiatkowski finally coaxed Nueman (Hirsch) into taking a walk outside the monastery. A few minutes into their stroll, Hirsch was grabbed by his brothers and other members of the Vilna *kehilah*, shoved into a carriage, redressed in women's clothing, and smuggled to Vilkomir, forty-three miles north of Vilna, and thence to Dvinsk.

Five days after the kidnapping, local officials interrogated Abba ben Wolf, along with Elijah and other Jewish leaders. The Gaon responded to his interrogators as if he were a head of state being forced to stand in front of petty bureaucrats: he shrugged his shoulders and steadfastly declined to answer the questions posed to him. He was jailed for over a month, but never uttered a word to local authorities. On February 29, 1788, he and Abba ben Wolf were released. A few months later the Gaon signed his name on a document produced by Abba ben Wolf denying culpability in the kidnapping of Nueman (Hirsch). Even so, on September 15, 1789, the Vilna tribunal sentenced Abba ben Wolf, his family, leading members of the *kehilah*, and the Gaon each to twelve weeks in jail.

It is unclear how long the sixty-nine-year-old Elijah was imprisoned.[129] While he was not listed among those freed on December 12, 1789, we do know from other testimony that he celebrated the holiday of Sukkot in jail. Those who shared his cell report that he paced the room and held his eyes open, doing everything in his power to remain awake so as not to be guilty of sleeping outside the sukkah during the holiday.[130]

Still unsure about the whereabouts of Nueman (Hirsch), authorities remained confused by the false testimony and inconclusive leads until, in October 1788, Kwiatkowski was turned over to Vilna leaders from authorities in Warsaw, where he had been apprehended while seeking employment. Once in Vilna, he testified extensively about the Gaon, Abba ben Wolf, and the plot to kidnap Hirsch.[131] His testimony, however, was riddled with internal contradictions and deemed dubious by local authorities. A year later, in December 1789, authorities were offered a different version of events from Nueman (Hirsch) himself, who suddenly reappeared in Vilna. In February 1791 the Vilna tribunal began final proceedings on the case, and on March 3 it issued its rulings: Kwiatkowski would be jailed for five weeks, during which he would be lashed a hundred times every Friday. Abba ben Wolf and six others were freed after swearing they took no part in the kidnapping. Abba's wife was jailed for six weeks, and his son was given the same sentence as Kwiatkowski. The Gaon and other Jewish officials were ordered to appear before the community in the main synagogue and publicly deny involvement in the kidnapping.[132]

The kidnapping case, and the local skirmishes involving the Hasidim, forced the Gaon to flee briefly to his son Yehuda Leib's residence in Sereje, sixty-eight miles from Vilna.[133] The possibility that Elijah may have had to escape Vilna due to communal pressure is not discussed by his biographers, but may very well have merit. Even those awed by the Gaon were not enthralled by his close ties to Abba ben Wolf or by the immense communal power both wielded. One Vilna resident complained to Polish authorities in 1788 that the Gaon had "the ability to excommunicate, and without his approval it was impossible to enact any important decision, especially in matters concerning religion."[134]

There was more tumult to come. In 1795, Russian forces gained control over Vilna and the remaining territories of the Polish-Lithuanian Commonwealth. Elijah is said to have led prayers for the safety of the city during this period.

The various scandals, fights, and fiascos must have weakened terribly the aging Elijah. By his seventy-sixth birthday he was in failing health and had to be looked after by his family and his trusted students.[135] In 1796 he instructed his son to write one last condemnation of the Hasidim and charged his loyal beadle Sa'adya with traveling across Europe to spread the message that, contrary to rumor, he remained steadfast in his opposition to the new movement. On Yom Kippur of 1797, Elijah became deathly ill, and a week later, October 9, 1797, on the holiday of Sukkot, he passed away.

Bedlam broke out in Vilna's Jewish community (now ten thousand strong).[136] As the Gaon's followers wept, the Hasidim continued to celebrate the holiday. Against his own rulings, Elijah's body was ushered into the synagogue where eulogies were offered and placed before the ark (a custom frowned on by the Gaon).[137] The townspeople then traveled to the nearby Śnipiszki cemetery to lay the body to rest.[138] After World War II, Russian authorities built a housing project on the Śnipiszki cemetery, and Elijah's remains were disinterred and transferred to Saltonishkiu cemetery, where they are to this day.[139]

The Gaon's Legacy—and Vilna's

Elijah's reputation was closely bound up with that of the city now variously described as a "city of glory," the "capital city" of European Jewry, and a "city of praise."[140] Vilna's Jewish population comprised a majority of the local population, and formed an essential part of the city's vibrant cultural and economic order.[141] If in the seventeenth century Jews looked "at Vilna as a great metropolis of the nations of the world,"[142] by the end of the eighteenth century non-Jews regarded Vilna as a city in which "Jews make their appearance without end."[143]

There would always be cities, like Warsaw in the nineteenth century, that could boast of larger Jewish populations. Already at the end of the eighteenth century Lwów and Brody could be given such honors. Likewise, by the mid-nineteenth century the Greek city of Salonika was 51 percent Jewish and cities such as Grodno shared with Vilna the status of being the governmental seat of a major Russian district. What distinguished Vilna, however, was not merely its numbers but rather the intellectual, spiritual, and political gravitas lent to it by the legacy of the genius who shared the city's name. Lwów, Warsaw, Brody, Grodno, and Salonika were undoubtedly great centers of Jewish culture, but none attracted the caliber of intellectual found in Vilna and none could boast a figure comparable to Elijah.

At the dawn of the nineteenth century the wars over Hasidism, the Haskalah, and eventually Zionism's forerunners would each be influenced by Elijah's legacy. Despite unanimous assent that the Gaon embodied the ethos of Vilna's Jewish community—intellectual dynamism, social confidence, and political agency—great debate and confusion ensued as to the proper uses of his intellectual inheritance. Who exactly was the Gaon? The leader who encouraged a return to Zion? The man who befriended and supported the enlightener Barukh Schick? The mentor of Hayyim of Volozhin, founder of the Volozhin yeshiva? These questions would animate Vilna Jewry for the next hundred and fifty years.

Just thirty days after his burial, a bitter dispute arose among Elijah's sons, his students, and the Vilna community over who controlled the Gaon's estate.[144] More was at stake than the question of property. Ultimately, his children were forced to sell their father's Slutzki home, with the proceeds going to establish a permanent *kloiz* (elite synagogue/ study house). The *kloiz* would become a place of homage to the Gaon, where men were paid by the community to study day and night in the master's memory. Vilna's communal leaders wanted to claim Elijah's mantle, even at the cost of upsetting his family. Although the Gaon's family eventually obtained a foothold in the administration of the new *kloiz*, the rabbinical courts ruled that Vilna's Jewish residents, not his direct heirs, had proprietary rights. The Vilna community now owned, in a metaphorical sense, the Gaon's legacy of study.

More fundamentally, Elijah's spiritual and political positions were being contested. Few outside of Vilna knew anything about him other than his opposition to Hasidism and his reputation for brilliance. So obscure were the details of Elijah's life at the time of his passing that even a great admirer, Akiva Eiger of Posen (1761–1837), wrote to the Gaon's children to request their father's writings and ask how to eulogize him properly.[145] Elijah's sons Avraham and Yehudah Leib prophetically predicted such confusion. On at least one occasion, they asked their father to consider writing an autobiography or perhaps allow them to draw a brief sketch of his practices. "It was [our] will to fulfill the wishes of [our] people and write the little of which [we] knew [about our father]," they wrote. Eventually, they confronted their father. "[We] said, to him, please tell [us] and [we] will write a large volume about your life . . . provide [us] with a broad sketch and it will provoke people's interest and satisfy their wish." The Gaon, they said, "dismissed the idea" out of hand, but Avraham and Yehudah Leib ignored his wish. "[We] have chosen to write about his greatness," they admitted.[146]

Elijah's life would be documented not by means of biography, however, but "in the context of publishing his many works."[147] The Gaon's children inherited Elijah's *nachlass* (literary estate), which totaled thousands of pages.[148] One of Elijah's eulogizers, Tuviah Gutmann, spoke for many when he remarked: "For those of us who were distant from him in his lifetime and were unable to hear Torah from his holy mouth, we will take pleasure in reading his books."[149]

2

Elijah's Worldview

ELIJAH'S WORLDVIEW BEARS THE MARKS OF BOTH JEWISH AND GREEK philosophical sources. His ideas took shape in an age typified by an attempt by Gottfried Wilhelm Leibniz (1646–1713) to locate a universally valid coherent system that could be justified by and contained within a first and Absolute Idea (that is, God).[1] like Leibniz and early Enlightenment idealist philosophers—including Christian Wolff (1679–1754), Johann Martin Chladenius (1710–1759), Georg Friedrich Meier (1718–1777), and Moses Mendelssohn (1729–1786)—Elijah believed that all components of experience emerge from, and can be understood by, our minds.[2]

Elijah was certainly influenced by at least one of Leibniz's students, Raphael Levi of Hannover (1685–1779), a rabbinic scholar whom Leibniz considered to be one of his foremost pupils.[3] Levi's work *Tekhunot ha-Shamayim* (*The Properties of Heaven*), published in Amsterdam in 1756 (but notes and drafts of which had circulated already in the mid- 1720s when Elijah was still in his youth), provided a conduit for post-Copernican theories to enter into rabbinic thinking. Levi offered new understandings of the lunar calendar and emphasized the philosophical implications of the discovery that the earth was in constant motion. Elijah may have been one of the very first rabbinic thinkers to study *Tekhunot ha-Shamayim*. His association with Levi's work was documented as early as 1804 in his sons' introduction to Elijah's commentary on the Bible, *Aderet Eliyahu*.[4] Before the age of thirteen, Elijah was purportedly already "studying books on engineering for half an hour a day, and during that time he would study *Tekhunot ha-Shamayim*."[5]

Levi was not the only follower of Leibniz whose work impressed Elijah. Another was the Italian sage Moses Hayyim Luzzatto (1707–1746), who read and appropriated Leibniz's ideas on theodicy (God's relationship to the concept of evil or badness).[6] Elijah adopted Luzzatto's positions especially with regard to redemption and evil.

Yet despite the influence exerted by Levi and Luzzatto,[7] it is doubtful that Elijah read Leibniz's works, many of which were not even published until the very end of or after Elijah's life. Elijah refused to speak (or perhaps did not even know) Belorussian, Polish, German, Lithuanian, or Ruthenian (as will be discussed later). He also never cites any non-Jewish philosophical work, which makes it difficult to suppose that he perused the *Monadology*. Yet Elijah, Luzzatto, and Leibniz were working with an overlapping set of kabbalistic and philosophical texts, ideas, and questions that pervaded eighteenth-century European intellectual life.[8]

In addressing the problem of theodicy, for example, Elijah, Leibniz, and other eighteenth-century idealist thinkers employed kabbalistic and philosophical arguments interchangeably.[9] The problem that idealists faced can be simply put: if God created all ideas, God must also have created evil. And if every idea—both those deemed good and those deemed bad—comes from God, how does one distinguish between them? This problem was not only theological but also epistemological. If God created all knowledge, how does one mediate among various claims, each maintaining to be true? Elijah tries to answer these questions through the lens of his worldview, which is unique in its strong idealist commitments and radical critical tendencies. Like Leibniz, he sees the world as the expression of an Absolute Idea. Yet he spent his life not only justifying and explaining every aspect of nature, but also removing and critically emending what he believed to be the evil and error that had distorted nature. That is, Elijah addresses the criticisms expressed by idealism's detractors by developing a hermeneutic category of emendation as a response to the problem of evil and error. Idealism's most notable opponent was Voltaire, who quipped in his play *Candide* that "in the best of all possible worlds—everything is for the best," even the Lisbon earthquake of 1755. While Leibniz himself hints at possible responses to Voltaire's charge, it is in Elijah's work that we see the latent critical side of eighteenth-century idealist thought fully developed and practically deployed in solving the problem of theodicy in the idealist tradition. More important than the causal relationship between Leibniz and Elijah is the way that Elijah addresses the fundamental challenges raised against the idealist project.

Eighteenth-Century Idealism

The Platonic-idealist tradition assumes that God is to be understood as the Absolute Idea. For God to become fully complete, God had to become manifest through the infinite ideas that make up this world. Thus that which seems disgusting or evil is as much a part of the Absolute Idea as that which is perceived to be good or beautiful. God created the world full of all possible ideas, even those that seem to be evil.

Some religious exegetes, including Elijah, merged this Platonic idealism with the biblical account of creation; they included "evil" in God's pronouncement in Genesis that "it was good." In his commentary to Genesis, Elijah contends: "God's creations are all 'good' and even their opposites. Even death falls under the rubric of the good. For there is nothing that is found in this world that is outside the rubric of the good."[10] Leibniz had made a similar claim: "Evil is useful for the good . . . all providential events are good for the good."[11] As Luzzatto argued, "it should not be said that good and evil are separate influences."[12] As will become evident later, however, unlike Leibniz and Luzzatto who saw evil as being inherently connected to the good, Elijah contends that while God created evil, which ultimately has a good purpose, evil was created independently. Evil's independent identity makes it easier for it to be identified when employed for purposes other than those intended by God.[13]

It is not that Elijah, Leibniz, and Luzzatto believed that all expressions of evil were good. Rather, they argued that evil has a specific role to play in the best of all possible worlds—the world as it should be in its original state of harmony with *the least possible evil and error*. Just because an event had sufficient reason for occurring did not make it necessary. That which "is" must be distinguished from what "ought" to be.[14] Irrational behavior and unnecessary evil separate the "is" from the "ought." The task of philosophy is not only to explain but also to remove evil and error as much as possible from human existence.[15]

Though he never articulates it in quite this way, Leibniz suggests that humanity is charged with eradicating *humanly* caused evil and thereby with bringing the world in line with pre-established rational principles that can be proven to be true under any and all circumstances. Leibniz hints at such a project when he distinguishes between what he calls eternal truths and factual truths. Eternal truths (also referred to by Leibniz as necessary truths) are distinguishable from mere factual truths—those objects, statements, and beliefs that can only be causally justified—by their capacity to be formulated into a stable mathematical equation. Eternal truths are propositions that express full agreement between subject and predicate. "All squares have four sides" is an eternal truth because its subject and predicate agree under any and all circumstances. Factual truths, by contrast, are true only under certain circumstances; their subject and predicate are not stable. For example, the proposition "apples are red" is factually true, since there is no necessary connection between the subject "apple" and the predicate "red." In the process of locating eternal truths, Leibniz also engages in removing that which is irrational or false. In his view, mathematics can be used as the human equivalent of a divine litmus test for evaluating, removing, or emending the human error or evil that can taint propositions, objects, and beliefs.

Leibniz's students Johann Martin Chladenius and Christian Wolff employed their teacher's mathematical litmus to locate the sufficient reason for every statement, object, or action. This required reformulating all material objects and texts into a set of mental ideas and then distilling those ideas into a pure Leibnizian mathematical language. According to this conceptualization, creation at its core represents a divine calculation of the universe.[16] Moreover, underlying the order of the world is a kind of "divine mathematics." Thus for Leibniz, the logic of math represented the possibility of restoring a rational "original harmony.[17]

The notion that a "divine mathematics" undergirds nature and is the basis of all ideas goes back to Platonic as well as kabbalistic sources.[18] Elijah explains that mathematics can be used not only to understand the world, but also to identify errors that have crept into nature:

Sefar [mathematics], *sippur* [story], and *sefer* [book] represent the genesis of the world. For the creation of the world needs thought, speech and action. Based on this, Scripture teaches us "In the beginning" which symbolizes thought, after which God "said," which symbolizes the story [the speech], and after which it is said "and there was" which symbolizes action, after which "God looked and saw it was good" which symbolizes that God reviewed [His creation] and made sure all was good. So too in the writing of Scripture the scribe must *think* about what he is writing, he then must *say* what it is [he will write], and then he *writes*, and afterwards he looks and *emends* [*magiah*] what he has written.[19]

According to Elijah, the world is understood through the concepts of *sefar, sippur,* and *sefer.* Each concept stems from the same Hebrew root: *sfr.* When the root appears in the form *sefar,* it refers to a type of calculation, counting, or mathematical schema. For Elijah, *sefar* (mathematics) denotes a realm of pure thought.[20] *Sippur* designates the telling of a story and represents the realm of speech. *Sefer,* the most common permutation of the root, translates as book. For Elijah, the writing of a book—the production of a text's letters and signs—corresponds to the category of action. Just as God creates through a process of thinking, speaking, acting, and reviewing or emending, so the mortal author thinks, speaks, writes, and emends.[21]

In so doing, Elijah adopts the ancient "world-book" trope—identifying the book as a means for understanding the world.[22] He adopts, too, a basic idealist assumption: ideas first emerge in the mind, are then articulated in speech, and are finally written down on paper or put into an object (existing as its essence or soul).[23] In his commentary to *Sefer Yetzirah,* Elijah explains that one first looks at the text (*sefer*) to see if its signs are correctly placed. After glancing over the textual terrain, the reader "repeats orally what is written." The act of reading is converted into an act of speaking. For every written sign there is a spoken word (story) that is speech.[24] Therefore, interpretation—the act of rendering something intelligible—requires imagining the text as if it were being *told.*

Vocalized reading features prominently both in stories told about Elijah's education and in his philosophy.[25] According to Elijah, "Understanding entails knowing something through and through. Acquiring such knowledge entails reading out loud."[26] Speech begins a process of harmonizing various independent elements.[27] Expressing a similar sentiment, Georg Friedrich Meier (1718–1777), a philosopher of aesthetics and follower of Leibniz, remarked, "An expression is a sign of knowledge, and such an expression normally consists of a human voice, or can be heard."[28]

But "understanding" the conceptual essence of objects and texts— written or material—requires that the spoken word be put into mathematical terms (*sefar*), thereby unlocking the full logical and rational order of the text, the speaker, or the world. A text or any material object is created by *sefar* (a divine mathematics or a kind of book comprised of mathematical code), *sippur* (spoken word), and *sefer* (writing); but it is grasped or interpreted in reverse order. Thus, any divinely inspired or humanly perfected text contains a logic that is revealed when the text is transformed into a set of signs that correspond to numbers. For example, Elijah explains how the first twelve verses of Proverbs can be mathematically charted out by dividing four "categories" of action (study, taking, giving, and hearing) into three "concepts" (wisdom, ethics, and understanding). He charts twelve categories corresponding to the outcome of each permutation of category and concept. Elijah's commentary tries to demonstrate the *sefar*, the logical mathematical structure of the *sippur* (story) written in the *sefer* (text). Furthermore, Elijah argues that when something does not cohere or cannot be mathematically proven, one must *magiah* (emend) the written text. This final point further distinguishes Elijah's work from his predecessors and highlights the critical side that mathematics plays in his worldview.

Mathematics represents both a litmus test for evaluating the truth value of a text and the most accurate language to describe what the world should look like. Elijah's concept of *sefar*, mathematics, assumes that numbers lack concrete material definition; they exist only in the mind. "[While] all things in the world are differentiated from each other through quantity and purpose, a number is not recognized except through thought. Numbers have purpose in thought but not in space."[29] In Leibnizian terms, numbers are "real" (they do not exist in time or space) but are exact (not divisible).[30] Elijah's commentary to *Sefer Yetzirah* is an attempt to chart out a " '*mathesis universalis*'—an unequivocal, universal, coherent, yet artificial language to capture our 'clear and distinct' ideas and their unique combinations."[31] Elijah's notion of a *mathesis universalis* is based not only on kabbalistic texts but also on classical mathematical works, such as the first six books of Euclid's *Elements*, which was famously translated into Hebrew and published in The Hague in 1780 by Barukh Schick of Shklov (1744–1808), who according to Schick, had been encouraged by Elijah to translate and publish the ancient work. In fact, Elijah's interest and knowledge of mathematics can be seen in his own work on geometry and algebra, *Ayil Meshulash*, which is based on Euclid's work.[32]

Leibniz's and Elijah's views converge around the respective kabbalistic and philosophical idea that knowledge can be represented in mathematical terms, and this convergence provides an area of overlap for Leibniz's and Elijah's views. That is, while Leibniz borrowed heavily from Euclidian mathematics,[33] he was also indebted to kabbalistic ideas regarding his notion of *mathesis universalis*. Leibniz, who was familiar with works such as *Sefer Yetzirah*, admits that "certain forms of kabbalistic mathematics could contribute to our understanding of calculus generalis."[34] According to Leibniz, "when God calculates and employs thought, the world is made."[35]

Allison Coudert accounts for the kabbalistic overtones in Leibniz's philosophy by explaining that Leibniz believed that "all knowledge could be reduced to a number of simple ideas, which could be arranged logically and expressed as suitable signs." For example, she suggests, "Leibniz's claim that man is a rational animal can be understood as "animal + rational = man or mathematically as $2 \times 3 = 6$."[36] Leibniz explicitly contends, like Elijah, that numbers are points that do not exist in space or time and are indivisible. According to him, these points are both similar to and different from what he calls "monads":

["Monads" are similar to] mathematical points, which are their points of view for expressing the universe, but they are not themselves mathematical points because they have something alive about them, and a kind of perception. When a bodily substance is contracted far enough, all its organs together make what to us is only a physical point. So physical points only seem to be indivisible. Mathematical points really are indivisible, but they are not things. It is only metaphysical or substantial points (constituted by forms or souls) that are both exact and yet real, and without them there wouldn't be any thing real at all, because without true unities there would be no multiplicity—without true ones there would be no manys.[37]

Leibniz and Elijah's emphasis on math offered a different way of conceiving the universe. In breaking with the traditional theosophic kabbalistic model, which described creation as the result of a series of divine emanations, Elijah's system was unique in the annals of Jewish history.[38] He and his students reinterpreted a strand of kabbalah developed by Abraham Abulafia (1240–1291?) that privileged the role played by numbers and mathematics in the unfolding of the universe. As Menachem Mendel of Shklov wrote, "The word *cheshbon* [calculus] comes from the word *machshava* [thought] and this [calculus] is the first form that emerges from the essence of thought."[39] Though many viewed Abulafia as a heretic, Elijah's circle borrowed heavily from his ideas regarding the mathematical underpinnings of the world.[40] In his work *Rav Pe'alim*, Elijah's son Avraham approvingly cites the much-maligned Abulafia, and bestows the honorific "z"l" (the Hebrew acronym for "may his memory be blessed") on the controversial medieval thinker.[41]

In short, numbers can both explain the structure of an ideal world and identify that which is irrational. Lacking material definition, they represent in ideal terms what the world ought to look like and express the apex of human understanding. Unlike monads, however, numbers do not contain an active force and as such fail to fully explain the act of creation or the cause for the emergence of evil in nature.

Creation and Form

Leibniz and Elijah also relied heavily on similar strands of Aristotelian and neo-Platonic thought in order to explain the process of creation. Elijah's knowledge of Aristotle is attested to by a letter that he and his brother, Yissaschar Ber, sent in 1776 to Shaul ben Aryeh Leib Lowenstam (1717–1790), the head of the rabbinic court in Amsterdam. They requested that he deliver to them manuscripts of "Moses Cordovero's commentary to the *Zohar* and other wondrous works as well as Aristotle's *Ethics*."[42] Elijah and Leibniz read Aristotle alongside his medieval interpreter Moses Maimonides.[43] Leibniz began reading Maimonides sometime after 1700,[44] roughly when Raphael Levi of Hannover came under his tutelage. It is not unreasonable to conjecture that Levi's interest in Maimonides encouraged Leibniz to take a more careful look at the medieval thinker. In his introductory notes to his Latin commentary to *Guide of the Perplexed*, Leibniz admits that he found Maimonides's work "remarkable" and believed "it deserves careful reading." In particular, Leibniz adopted Maimonides's position that while God must have created the world, nature unfolds according to its own logic. Leibniz concurred with the medieval Jewish philosopher that the "the fabric of science is too coherent, too valuable, and too significant as an expression of the divine wisdom in nature for the theologically motivated concept of continuous creation to be allowed."[45]

In his commentary to Genesis 1:3, as in numerous other texts, Elijah challenges Maimonides and argues for a neo-Platonic notion of creation:

> And God said, "let there be light": In *Pirkei de-Rabbi Eliezer* our Sages asked, "Whence were the heavens created?" [They answered that God took part of the light of His garment, stretched it like a cloth, and the heavens were extending continually, as it is said: "He covered Himself with light as with a garment, He stretched the heavens like a curtain."] And Maimonides tried to answer this question according to his own view and all those [*pashtanim*] who came after him also tried to answer this question. [Maimonides, however, was wrong to assert that one must believe in creation ex nihilo.] For it would seem that light was not created from nothing. While regarding the sky and the earth it is written "and He created," teaching us about their origins; with regard to light, Scripture simply teaches "it was," written in the language of the present, teaching us that something came from something.[46]

Maimonides (*Guide*, 2:26) argues that although *Pirkei de-Rabbi Eliezer* could be construed as suggesting that matter existed eternally, this reading echoes a misguided position that was espoused by Plato in his work *Timaeus*.[47] But following kabbalists like Isaac the Blind (1160–1235), Elijah adopts the simple interpretation of *Pirkei de-Rabbi Eliezer* that in fact matter existed eternally.[48] Unlike Isaac, however, Elijah justifies his position with the Aristotelian philosophical language of creation ex nihilo (*yesh me-ayin*).[49] In his comments to Genesis 1:21 he explains that he does "not read the word '*ayin*' as 'absolute nothing' ('*eyn biuro she-eyno mamash*'). Rather, the term '*yesh me-ayin*' means: 'It created from that which exists above, for the matter above creates the forms below. For everything that lacks a direct causal explanation is called *yesh me-ayin*.'"

For Maimonides, then, the term *yesh me-ayin* means creation from nothing; for Elijah, it means creation from matter. Elijah contrasts *yesh me-ayin* (form from matter) with *yesh me-yesh* (one form generating another form). Whereas *yesh me-yesh* denotes something causally created from a preexisting form—something that has definition—*yesh me-ayin* involves the figuring of primordial matter, that is, of something that lacks definition or form and thus is unintelligible. Elijah believes that God created the world, but he contends that He did so by shaping "something" that is eternal.

Leibniz too challenges a strict notion of creation ex nihilo:

> Creation from nothing (ex nihilo) is not grounded in Sacred Scripture, but rather in a certain tradition and in a certain reasonable sense it is acceptable but as commonly understood, it is not free from error. The truth indeed is that it is certain that Chaos or Atoms, or another material did not exist coeternal with God from which the world was made. But nevertheless it is false that the earth is strictly speaking made from nothing as if from matter. It is an eternal truth: nothing comes from nothing. It is more correctly said, therefore, with the author of the Letter to the Hebrews, chap. II, verse 3, that the visible is made from the invisible.[50]

While it is a matter of debate as to what exactly Leibniz means here, he certainly seems to go further than Plato (and for that matter Elijah) in asserting that form was not created strictly out of matter. Something more than just chaos or matter existed prior to creation, for how could something be created out of nothing? Leibniz and Elijah are well aware that their respective positions are controversial.[51] Echoing Leibniz, Elijah notes that "all of the interpreters of religion [*mifarshei ha-dat*] are of the opinion that the world was created *ex nihilo*."[52] Plato's notion of creation was "rejected by Saadia, tolerated by Yehudah ha-Levi and vigorously rejected by Maimonides."[53] Over time, Maimonides's position became so entrenched in classical Jewish thought that, ironically, one writer went so far to assume (without citation) that Elijah himself subscribed to a strict notion of creation ex nihilo: "The idea of the creation of the World out of nothing (*yesh mi-ayin*) is that boundary that separates Jewish thinkers from pagan (ancient Greek) thinking."[54] Others have correctly noted that "to this day traditional Jewish cosmological speculation tends to defend the *ex nihilo* conception of creation."[55]

The taboo surrounding the denial of creation ex nihilo revolves around the extent of God's sovereignty in the world. Most notably, the Gnostics asserted that powers other than God exist and that primordial matter indicated God's limitations. In fact, the Gnostics claimed, primordial matter symbolized that other powers (usually those responsible for evil-ness or badness in the world) exist outside of God's dominion. Elijah, like other seventeenth- and eighteenth-century thinkers grappling with matters of theodicy, dismisses the Gnostic challenge by arguing that God created evil. Like Leibniz, Elijah thought that evil was part of the pre-established harmony of the world. Evil is not simply an aberration or signals another competing divine force, but was created by God and plays a productive role in the universe.

Elijah's dismissal of the Gnostic understanding of primordial matter also ran up against seventeenth- and eighteenth-century Occasionalists, such as Nicolas de Malebranche (1638–1715), who proffered that, despite appearances, all movement and change in the world is the result of an intervening God. While the Gnostics' understanding of matter limited God's role in this world, Occasionalists' understanding of form limited nature's sovereignty. Occasionalism is often identified as a response to René Descartes, whose strong distinction between matter and mind made it difficult, for some, to see how one object made of matter could cause another object to move.[56] The Occasionalists, with more nuance than space permits, described so-called causes as occasions for God to move something in a particular direction. While it may seem to us that there is a natural order that functions on its own through secondary causes, in fact there is no actual inherent power, freedom, or agency on earth, because every act is the direct result of God's meddling in history in order to allow for the movement of matter.

Elijah responds to the problems posed by Occasionalists by rejecting the neo-Platonic notion of form as an ideal archetype that exists beyond nature. Elijah does not have "ideal" forms. Instead, he argues that form and matter are inseparable and that form only exists after creation in this world. Whereas primary matter only exists in Heaven and remains unde-fined, all bodies in this world possess form and as such are defined and in constant motion.[57]

Creation entails God's imposition of form onto matter. In his commen-tary on the kabbalistic work *Sifra di-Tzniuta* (*Book of Concealment*) Elijah explains: "Primordial matter is nothing but matter and exists without any form. . . . As it says [in Genesis 1:1] regarding the creation of the world: 'and God said' (*va-yomer Elohim*) and then 'He acted' (*bara*). 'God said' refers to divine knowledge (*chokhmah*), but 'acted out his will' refers to human knowledge/understanding (*binah*) and that means God created form." In this world, Elijah concludes, "matter is never separated from form."[58] Elijah thus explicitly connects human knowledge with form: "the acquisition of knowledge and the ability to comprehend suggest the ability for something to possess a specific form."[59] By identifying bodies as forms in which motion inheres, Elijah can account for changes in the world without having to appeal to the momentary actions of a divine potter who is constantly shaping matter.

This shift to a form-based world is the lynchpin of Elijah's worldview; it allows him to see nature as operating on its own terms and human beings to be the agents that transform nature. Human beings are able to create new entities from preexisting forms. In freeing nature from the arbitrary whims of God and putting it in the minds of human beings, Elijah and Leibniz carefully distinguish between two types of "creation." Elijah refers to the type of creation described earlier as "origination" (*etzem*), or what Leibniz calls "creation."[60] Here God endows entities (both inanimate and living) with a life force (a substantial form). Originally these entities existed in the most perfect manner, in line with the creation of the best of all possible worlds. God continues to conserve these entities at all times, ensuring the constancy of the life force that has been imparted within them.[61] But these entities are not stable; they can be transformed (think of melted copper, or the example used by Elijah of a tree made into a table). Elijah argues with Nachmanides, who suggested that "the Genesis story is only about Creation, with each entity retaining the stable identity given to it by God."[62] Rather, he claims, "this process continues at all times." The Genesis story is thus not about creation, but rather explains how "composites are constantly being separated and forming new entities."[63] Creation is a process and not a single historical moment.[64]

At this point Elijah and Leibniz describe a second type of creation. Human beings have the ability to "make" (*la'asot*)—or what Leibniz calls to "produce"—new entities from preexisting God-given entities.[65] Nature functions on its own and humans can manipulate it according to their needs. Thus Elijah and Leibniz cannot (nor do they ever claim to) explain why earthquakes (a result of God's creation) befall humanity or why a seemingly healthy child can die in his or her sleep. Elijah and Leibniz cannot explain the kind of random badness expressed in bold relief by filmmaker Terrence Malick in his pictorial depiction of primordial matter, *The Tree of Life*. Yet most of what we consider to be evil is in their view a result of human "production." While God creates a certain balance between various entities, human beings throw off that balance by producing new entities from the forms given to the world by God. This ability to produce new entities carries with it the potential for evil. Consequently, human beings are the ones who produce "evil" and as such they are also tasked with the responsibility of removing it, rectifying nature, and reestablishing the world's "original harmony."

Interpreting the Book of Nature

So far we have laid out Elijah's theory of the World-Book—from Idea to Creation to Nature. Now we ask what happens when the World-Book becomes corrupted by the "production" of human error (evil). What does Elijah mean when he says that after the book has been written an author "looks and *emends* what he has written"? To decipher what is meant by "emendation" is to understand the ideal World-Book itself and what constitutes a corruption of that ideal. It is here, in Elijah's emendation project, that he overcomes the theodicy problem presented by eighteenth-century idealist thought.

In his approach to texts, Elijah sought to discover the "authentic-ideal book"—one that lived up to his reverence for ancient texts and conformed to mathematical-rational principles that transcend historical circumstance. Early Enlightenment interpreters believed that "discourse and books determine the selection and ordering of signs and expression . . . and serve a normative function of providing a specific medium of application for any given content. The author does not create, but rather *integrates* this content within a discourse or book type."[66] An authentic-ideal book addresses a specific idea and expresses all of that idea's various dimensions.

For Elijah—as for Meier, Chladenius, and Wolff—interpretation entailed identifying the purpose of the book as well as the type of knowledge and discourse that the book conveyed. According to Elijah, "If one wants to study a book, one must know who the author is . . . *in order to understand* the greatness of wisdom in the book."[67] The author is important only as a *means* to understanding the eternal truth encompassed in his book.[68] Thus Elijah asks not "where did the *author* write the book?" but "where was the *book* written?"[69] Likewise, he does not employ the Hebrew word *kavanah* (intent) as much as he uses the word *takhlit* (purpose) to describe what he hopes to uncover.[70] Just as God is known only through the uncorrupted state of nature, an author's purposes are discerned only through the ideal that his book purports to express.

The book's conceptual makeup and mathematical design occupied the interpretive energies of early Enlightenment thinkers, who did not experience a gulf of time separating them from the book they were reading. They do not depict the relationship between reader and writer through the trope of an author interacting with a reader, but rather favor the model of a teacher communicating with a student.[71] Putting the reader in such close proximity to the text's production blurs the historical lines between interpretation and the text itself. The original text is "reconstituted" by the reader, whose comments become part and parcel of the text. Not only is the text re-created; the past version is nullified as well. There is no history of the text, only iterations of what is deemed the ideal or most perfect text.

The eighteenth-century interpreters' emphasis on the ideational qualities of the book itself stands in marked contrast to the dominant trends in nineteenth-century scholarship.[72] For Chladenius and Elijah, the reader may understand a text's *ideational* intent better than the author himself.[73] Because concepts are eternal, the reader and author are on a level playing field in terms of their ability to express a specific idea or a mathematical equation. Leveling the playing field allowed early Enlightenment interpreters full license to fill in missing information, add new material, or delete incorrect statements, phrases, sentences, and sections. The individual reader was empowered, in a quasi-divine manner, to evaluate critically and to rearrange text, nature, and knowledge in line with reason. What was important was the idea, not the person through whom it happened to have been expressed. Interpretation and criticism, for Elijah, did not involve the knowledge of manuscripts or their histories, but rather the exercise of reason to disclose what the text ideally ought to include. Error and evil were subjected not to detached historical analysis but to aggressive acts of removal aimed at preserving and conveying the text's ideal nature.[74]

This idealistic view, as many have noted, is caught in a kind of "vicious" self-referencing circle. The only way a reader can know the idea on which a text is based is from the error-filled text itself. As Heidegger put it, "Any interpretation which is to contribute understanding, must already have understood what is to be interpreted. . . . But if interpretation . . . must draw its nurture from this, how is it to bring any scientific results to maturity without moving in a circle . . . this circle is a *circulus vitiosus*."[75] According to Heidegger this "circle" becomes "vicious" when the interpreter claims philosophical objectivity.[76] In other words, all philosophical endeavors are somewhat circular insofar as they begin inside a particular discourse, but projects undertaken by scholars who fail to admit these constraints are even more problematic.

Elijah, however, never claims that one can fully understand God or the metaphysical foundations of the world; to him, even mathematics is nothing but a language to make sense out of the world only as *we* (*mi-tzideinu*) perceive it. In his view, the truth-value of an idea or a book can be evaluated by the degree to which the idea or the content of a book adheres to the framework in which the idea is expressed or to the intended purpose of—or subject matter addressed in—the book. A book's subject could be said to be "ethical," "historical," or "poetic." For example, Elijah identifies Proverbs' subject as "the attainment of God-consciousness [*chokhmah*] and ethics" (1:2). In his letter, *Alim li-Terufah*, Elijah classifies Proverbs as an "ethical work." In his commentary on Proverbs, he tries to prove how each verse refers to humanity's attempt to attain God-consciousness and to act ethically. For early Enlightenment thinkers, as for Elijah, "to judge a book by its authorial intention mean[t] ascertaining the degree to which its author had succeeded in adhering to the generic requirements of the particular discourse he had chosen."[77]

A book's subject matter is announced in its introduction or opening verses. According to Elijah, the introduction or the title page acts as the seed or origin of the book, where all of the various elements in the book are contained in embryonic form.[78] As Luzzatto claims, "The makeup of a book follows from its introduction. One should not try to understand the subject of a book before understanding the book's overall structure."[79] Elijah's students suggest that the purpose and subject matter of a book can be gleaned from a quick glimpse at its title pages or introduction.

> When one wants to purchase a book . . . one should first find out the book's purpose. And this is revealed at the very beginning of most ancient books. The introduction of books tells one about the nature of the book. . . . And if the author himself does not directly explain the purpose of the book, such information can sometimes be obtained by reading the [preface] written by another person.[80]

Likewise, Elijah's son Avraham remarks, "It is a major principle among scholars (*chokrim*) that the introduction contains the essence of something."[81] Or as Elijah himself claims more generally: "In the beginning the outcome is revealed."[82] Elijah's ideas regarding the role of introductions can be traced back to Aristotle through medieval works ranging from Maimonides's *Guide* to Joseph Albo's *Sefer ha-Ikarim*.[83]

According to Christian Wolff, "The design of the whole book is known either from the title page, or the preface wherein we generally find what gave occasion to write."[84] One is made aware of the things that the author has "omitted" by comparing the content of a book with the title page.[85] Wolff assumes, like Leibniz, that "we can express the identity of concepts by the identity of signs which we immediately perceive."[86] The reader encounters a book through the lens presented in its introduction.

But Leibnizian hermeneutics are not merely based on which image happens to strike one's eye first.[87] As mentioned earlier, Leibniz's quest for eternal truths was the product of a particular epistemological understanding of the relationship between subject and predicate.[88] Leibniz suggests that a proposition is eternally true only if its subject and predicate agree with each other under all circumstances. According to Leibniz, "Always in every true affirmative proposition, necessary or contingent, universal or particular, the notion of the predicate is somehow included in that of the subject, the predicate is present in the subject."[89] For example, the proposition that "all things that are green are green" is eternally true because if a thing x is called green but is not *actually* green, then calling x green in the first place was an error. In addition, the only way x can be called green (if x is not green) is if there is such a thing as a true contradiction—a possibility that Leibniz denies. Thus, x either is green, must be made green, or must be placed under a different conceptual heading that accounts for its non-greenness.

Leibniz's theory of contradiction and subject-predicate relationship explains the vexing question posed earlier regarding the epistemological foundations of Elijah's emendations and more generally his notion of evil. The beginning of a book indicates the book's subject (its "book type"). The predicate (the rest of the book) follows the subject. The monad, seed, or introduction holds within itself the entire future history (the preformation) of the element, tree, or book.[90] For an object, book, or proposition to be mathematically formulated and proven to be universally and eternally true (that is, understood rationally), its predicate (the content of the book) must conform to its subject (that which is stated in the introduction) in all cases and under all circumstances. This theory is stated almost explicitly by Moses Hayyim Luzzatto in his work *Derekh Tevunot*, where he argues that for a book's logic to be fully revealed, the interpreter must be able to discern an agreement between the book's *noseh* (subject) and *nasu* (predicate).[91] Without such agreement, the book would be nothing more than a contradiction and thus would be unintelligible and false. Luzzatto argues that there is an order and structure to every utterance. "When one understands the intent of the speaker, one will realize that the speaker of course was intent on making sure that the subject and predicate of his statements fully agreed with one another. . . . Therefore, when you are interpreting one's words do not pay heed to the manner in which he speaks. Instead, focus on the idea he is intending."[92]

A book's rationality is expressed by the extent to which its predicate fully accords with its subject. If the subject of the book is ethics, the book's contents must reflect ethical concerns. Where the book's content fails to conform to its purported subject, or deals with topics that are not pertinent or are superfluous to the subject matter, the text must be either reinterpreted to make sense with the subject or fully removed from the book and reclassified as part of a different conceptual order.

While such an undertaking might at first glance seem reasonably simple, it is in fact a bold and challenging task to harmonize the "subject" and "predicates" in a text that has been composed over a long period of time from numerous competing voices and stories, then handed down for generations. And it is precisely this undertaking that lies at the heart of Elijah's project of emending classic texts in order to redeem the world.

Emending the Text, Redeeming the World

Elijah's theory of emendation and redemption is foregrounded in his glosses of *Sifra*, *Sifrei*, and *Mekhilta*, a group of rabbinic works that are today commonly referred to as *Midrash Halakha*.[93] Compiled mainly between 300 and 600 C.E., these texts record the biblical sources for the earliest sages' halakhic (legal) statements. (The first of Elijah's glosses was not published until 1844.)[94] For nineteenth-century rabbinic figures confronting a range of contemporary social and intellectual charges against Judaism, including challenges of the Bible's divine authorship and the veracity of the Masoretic tradition, much was at stake in the reading of these rabbinic works.[95] Elijah's commentaries, however, address a different set of issues: the dissonance between the idea (or subject) of the Midrashic text and the way its content (predicate) has been corrupted by history.

To understand Elijah's hermeneutic-theological project, one must first realize that the Gaon did not consider *Sifra, Mekhilta,* and *Sifrei* to be part of *Midrash Halakha.* In fact, the term *Midrash Halakha* was first invoked after Elijah's era, by the nineteenth-century rabbi and philosopher Nachman Krochmal in his work *Moreh Nevukhe ha-Zeman* (*Guide for the Perplexed of the Time*), where Krochmal used it to define a certain type of Talmudic literature.[96] Elijah, in contrast, refers to these texts as *Midrashei ha-Torah,* which he sees as outside the corpus that includes the Babylonian Talmud and the oral law.[97] According to Elijah, *Midrashei ha-Torah* are texts with their own function, meaning, and identity—not simply an extension of the Babylonian Talmud. As Jay Harris put it, these texts gave "voice to the Gaon's conviction regarding the ideal interrelationship of all rabbinic documents, and the thoroughly intertwined nature of the oral and written Torahs."[98]

Midrashic works, then, merge the written law and the oral law.[99] In Leibnizian terms, we might say that Midrash represents the ideal pre-established harmony of the world. In his kabbalistic writings, Elijah identifies the concept of pre-established harmony with the concept of *mishkal* (the "scale" through which the world is created and balanced).[100] But he sees Midrashic works "as representing [the shape] that is taken through the connection between the two corpora of Torah—for they bring the *halakha* of the oral law into Scripture." In his commentary to Genesis 49:19, for instance, Elijah explains how Midrash "brings together the Oral and Written Torah, and upon them [*Midrashei ha-Torah*] it is written: 'also together.'" Yet this harmonization of the oral and written law, he adds, "is difficult labor; so too the creation of *Midrashei ha-Torah* is difficult labor."[101] Reestablishing the original harmony, like Midrash, involves resolving the tension between seemingly contradictory elements. Creating the ideal balance requires undoing the errors that have distorted texts—and the evil that has corrupted nature—by emending, deleting, and sometimes adding various elements to restore the original harmony. These corruptions represent the process by which a text or the world regresses back to a state of *tohu* (confusion), and thereby generates unnecessary and irrational evils in thoughts and deeds alike.[102]

ELIJAH'S WORLDVIEW

The Gaon's textual emendation can be understood as part of his larger project of eradicating evil and error in society. Little wonder, then, that he refers to the editing of Midrashic works as "difficult labor." A typical emendation of Elijah's can be found in one of his glosses to *Sifra* (Parshata 7, Perek 9, Halakha 1–3). There the Midrashic text comments on Leviticus 4:27–28: "If any person from the populace unwittingly incurs guilt by doing any of the things which by the Lord's commandments ought not to be done and he realizes his guilt—or the sin of which he is guilty is brought to his knowledge—he shall bring a female goat without blemish as his offering for the sin of which he is guilty." The rulings in Halakha 2 and 3—which focus on the liability of an individual who follows an incorrect court ruling—are repeated in slightly different language in Halakha 8, and because of their similarity, Elijah took the liberty of deleting Halakha 8.[103] Elijah's emendation is obviously histori-cally inaccurate; the Midrash contains both sections. But his purpose in emending the Midrash has nothing to do with the historicity of the Midrash, or with the conceptual harmonization of this text with other recorded opinions, or even with making the text conform to the Babylonian Talmud. Rather, he refines the text according to what he believes the text ideally ought to look like.[104] The Gaon's emendation accords well with his grandson's claim that he believed "the Gaon was in agreement with scholars (*chakhamei ha-mechkar*) that one should use only as many words as necessary to properly express himself."[105] Elijah in his own commentaries assumes "that students should be taught using the fewest words possible."[106] If there is no "sufficient reason" for a word to be used or written, it should be removed. Many of his predecessors emended texts, but Elijah was the first rabbinic sage to emend texts in order to correct literary or conceptual superfluity (*meyutar*).[107]

On the surface, Elijah's emendation could be seen as rather benign; there is seemingly very little conceptual difference between the original and emended texts. But the blunt sacrilege of his method (which did away with historical accuracy in favor of a principle of sufficient reason) was lost on no one. The nineteenth-century historian and founder of Reform Judaism, Abraham Geiger, saw Elijah's emendations as being so original, so respected, and yet so anti-historical that he expressed relief that the Gaon did not live before the eighteenth century, lest later generations not have access to any historically accurate rabbinic texts.[108] Geiger realized that Elijah's students were so awed by their master's emendations that they were prepared to do away with all previously authoritative versions of rabbinic texts. Geiger was far from the only person to recognize the temporal violence wrought by Elijah's emendations; more than one rabbinic scholar could only countenance Elijah's emendations by attributing to them divine sanction.[109] Yisrael of Shklov, quoting from Hayyim of Volozhin, went so far as to claim that he "heard from his [Elijah's] holy mouth that for every emendation he made in texts that are *nigleh* [legal; literally, open or revealed], he would first reference not less than 15 to 20 *sugyot* [Talmudic topics], and concerning texts that are *nistar* [philosophic or kabbalistic; literally, hidden] he would not emend until he had 150 reasons to emend."[110]

While such comments might be an apologetic exaggeration of Elijah's humility, they also highlight the radical nature of his emendation project. Elijah's emendations of the Midrash challenge even Luzzatto, who under Leibnizian influence recognized humanity's main task as the removal of error in the world, but still asserted that if one could not understand or make sense of a rabbinic text, the problem lay with the reader and not the author or the text itself. In *Derekh Tevunot* Luzzatto writes:

> After you have identified the intent of the section of Talmud before you, according to the rules I have laid out here, then you will be able to return and understand the section's specific sub-structures. It is a good sign if the sub-structures conform with the rest of the text according to the natural rules I have stated above. If you find that the sub-structures do not make sense with the entirety of the text, you should go back and work hard on trying to figure out the appropriate logic that will allow the text to be understood according to its language.[111]

When the "predicate" of a text veers off from the text's stated "subject," a fork emerges in the interpretive road. Luzzatto, along with the vast majority of rabbinic interpreters, places the burden of interpretation on the reader. "If the text is missing something," says Luzzatto, "fill it in your mind."[112] The text as it appears cannot be changed. If there is a problem in the text, it must be the reader's failing—not the author's. Elijah, however, validates the reader's critical capacities. He emends the text to conform to reason. According to his view, Talmudic texts are malleable and susceptible to human error.

Elijah's emendations correspond with his broader philosophic project of restoring the rational pre-established harmony of a world confused by unnecessary human error and evil. To achieve this act of restoration, he addressed those ideas and texts that were unclear, mistaken, and therefore not yet rational or ideal. In his writings on rabbinic literature, then, such as Midrashic texts, Elijah labors to pare away synonymous and repetitive language.

Leibniz vividly explains the philosophical problem that idealists like himself (and Elijah) had with synonymy:

> Wisdom requires variety. To multiply exclusively the same thing, however noble it be, would be superfluity; it would be a kind of poverty. To have a thousand copies of Virgil in your library; to sing only airs from the Opera of Cadmus and Hermione; to break all your porcelain in order to have golden cups; to have all your buttons made of diamonds; to eat only partridges; to drink only the wine of Hungary or of Shiraz—could anyone call this reasonable? [113]

Synonymy nullifies the individuality, difference, and plenitude in nature. Reason dictates that each and every thing has its own independent identity and cause for being. While it is doubtful that Elijah would have wasted his tears on bottles of Shiraz wine or a few extra copies of Virgil, the same cannot be said with regard to rabbinic texts that he saw as being invested with a quasi-divine quality. For Elijah, rabbinic literature is quasi-divine in the sense that it ideally is meant to be perfect—and yet, in practical terms, it was not "created" by God but "produced" (written) by human beings and hence can include errors, superfluities, and synonymous ideas. Unlike Karaites, who rejected rabbinic literature, Elijah saw the errors in Talmudic texts not as grounds to dismiss them outright, but as calls to restore them to their ideal state. While many before him emended texts, none did so in accordance with the principles of synonymy and hermeneutic ideality. As Ya'akov Spiegel notes, Elijah's emendations are unique in both their "their expansive scope and in their very nature. That is, his emendations express something not testified to by any other later sage." [114]

Elijah's treatment of Talmudic literature stands in marked contrast to his relationship to biblical literature. With respect to the Bible, Elijah assumes the absolute perfection and therefore full rationality of each and every word. Any "errors" found in the Bible are there as part of God's "best of all textual worlds." By contrast, "errors" found in the writings of the rabbis are humanly generated. This philosophic distinction is most pronounced in the way Elijah relates to linguistic superfluity. With regard to the Bible, Elijah argues against biblical synonymy; in his view, every word must, by virtue of being in the Bible, have its own meaning and purpose. Rabbinic literature, however, contains wasted words and imprecise language that the interpreter is tasked with correcting. Rabbinic literature is thus a textual site where humanly produced mistakes (evil) exist and must be eradicated.

The discrepancy between Elijah's treatment of biblical works (which are never to be emended) and Talmudic literature (which demand emendation) finds a parallel in Leibniz's ideas concerning divine (perfectly rational) and non-divine (yet-to-be rationally realizable) forms of knowledge, and in Leibniz's distinction between that which was "created" by God and that which was humanly "produced." Jacques Derrida illustrates this distinction with the image of someone tasked with marking points on a sheet of paper in a helter-skelter fashion and then being instructed to find a geometrical line whose concept is uniform and constant, that is, in accordance with a certain formula, and that passes through all those points in the same order in which they were jotted down. Nature has no "fact whose contour does not form part of a geometrical line and which cannot be traced entirely by a certain mathematical motion." This is what it means to encounter something that was divinely "created." Leibniz employed such a mathematical picture to explain a certain imperfect resemblance between mathematics and divine wisdom. He did not, however, pretend to explain "the great mystery upon which depends the whole universe." As concerns non-divine works read by finite minds, Leibniz is much less confident in their mathematical-spatial makeup. These works should be treated "with more prudence and less abandon than formerly."[115] One is not responsible for locating a line that connects all the dots. Rather, under such circumstances one might emend or remove some of the dots that serve no purpose or defy reason.

In Leibniz's early notes on St. Augustine's *De trinitate*, he was in effect adamant that one should not "change any dots." He accepts that "the word of God was true, and that its meaning should not be distorted in order to accommodate it to human reasoning; [even] where the literal meaning contradicted what was evident to reason, a metaphorical interpretation should be preferred, provided it did not do violence to the text."[116] In his posthumously published *New Essays on Human*

Understanding, Leibniz (writing as Theophilus) engages Locke (Philalethes) in a fictional Socratic conversation that revisits the question of Scripture's status vis-à-vis other texts. Leibniz once again asserts the special kind of knowledge contained in Scripture.[117] Arguing with Locke's claim "that we can do without . . . the writings of antiquity," Leibniz asserts that with regard to the ancient writings we need to understand "Holy Scripture above all things." Leibniz addresses the question explicitly: "Suppose on the one hand we have a literal sense of a text from Holy Scripture, and on the other hand, we have a strong appearance of a logical impossibility or at least a recognized physical impossibility; then is it more reasonable to give up the literal sense or to give up the philosophical principle?" In response, Leibniz never entertains the possibility of rejecting the words of Scripture outright. Instead he argues: "There are certainly passages where there is no objection to abandoning the literal sense—for instance, where Scripture gives God hands, or attributes to him anger, repentance and other human affects. . . . This is where rules of interpretation come into play; but . . . it is safer and indeed more reasonable to keep to the letter."[118]

Leibniz does, however, call for identifying and uprooting those errors that have been historically generated and have mistakenly been given a false stamp of divine authority: "Children have propositions insinuated into them by their father and mother, nurses and tutors, and others around them; and once these propositions have taken root they are treated as sacred, like a *Urim* and *Tummim* set up in their minds . . . by God himself."[119]

A similar distinction between divine and human knowledge can be found in Elijah's contrast of divine and human authorship: "Regarding humanly authored texts, many times we should not accept what they say for two reasons: 1) Because what is expressed lacks clarity or is unintelligible; 2) Even if it does make sense, because it is superfluous or it incorrectly connects ideas that never should have been brought together. In contrast to such [writings], Scripture does not contain anything that is confused or unintelligible."[120]

For both Leibniz and Elijah, everything in Scripture and nature, being God-created, has sufficient reason for existing. Every substance, point, and word that has God's imprint must have its own unique sufficient reason and can never be identical with any other substance, point, or word. Even if two words appear synonymous, it could never be the case that both meant the same thing. Even that which seems bad or erroneous must have a purpose, and divine texts are *eternally true*. The interpreter has an imperative to "connect" the various "dots" through whatever means afforded to him and without rearranging the given dots, signs, or words.

But when a text, idea, or object is *humanly authored*, an interpreter is not only granted more leeway to emend and fix the text, but is indeed *obligated* to do so. This is because the text has no political or religious authority per se. Theoretically Talmudic literature might be more important than the Bible for organizing contemporary Jewish life, but in its current state it remains confused and requires perfecting. In contrast to Luzzatto, Elijah contends that Talmudic texts are mere *factual truths* waiting to be either emended into *eternal truths* or dismissed as false. Unlike late medieval/rabbinic texts, such as Karo's code, which Elijah rejected outright, classical rabbinic works were considered by Elijah to be at the very least divinely inspired (but, unlike the Bible, not of divine origin) and thus in need and deserving of emendation.

For Leibniz, a humanly authored sentence or speech that does not express perfectly the ideas it intends to convey, or worse, distorts those ideas, must be tossed aside or rewritten (emended).[121] In 1670, Leibniz pointed to the often-ignored philosophical implications of his theory; he noted that "we may thus regard it as established that whatever cannot be explained . . . is nothing and should be exorcized from philosophy as if by an incantation."[122] What Leibniz only spoke about in theory—ensuring plentitude and removing irrational synonymy—Elijah put into practice. Elijah's emendations of humanly authored texts exorcise from rabbinic history redundant, synonymous, and logically confused statements.

The novelty of Elijah's approach is thrown into high relief if we compare it to the hermeneutics of the rabbinic scholars identified with the fifteenth-century Iyyun School, which was dedicated to justifying all seemingly synonymous language in biblical and rabbinic texts. According to Daniel Boyarin, Isaac ben Jacob Campanton (also Canpanton, 1360–1463), the founder of the Iyyun School, "recognized the exegetical and Talmudic-interpretive implications of Aristotle's linguistic-semantic philosophy."[123] For Campanton, every sacred text worthy of interpretation is devoid of synonymy; the reader is ultimately responsible for determining how the text can be understood in a logical manner:

At the beginning of your in-depth examination you should realize that each one of the speakers involved—both the questioner and respondent—are people of intellectual means. All their statements are well thought out. Their words do not show misunderstanding or a lack of knowledge. [As it is stated,] "Are we dealing with stupid people?" Therefore the burden is on you to understand their words. Therefore you should look into each of their statements and see if it makes sense. Is the reasoning logical and sound, or is the evidence weak and illogical? Does it seem reasonable to you or not? Analyze their statements and try to understand them properly. Make sure that you understand the logic, and that [your understanding] is not built on faulty or flimsy reasoning. Their words were not said carelessly. Rather, they are all "words of the living God." If anything is lacking, it is you. This is what is meant by "In the beginning what was assumed? And in the end what is known?" A person must try to understand what was meant in the beginning and what was meant in the end.[124]

The Iyyun School's interpretive approach assumes that even medieval commentators such as Rabbi Shlomo Yitzchaki (1040–1105), better known as Rashi, composed perfect texts. Their interpretive presupposition was *"kol medaber be-chokhmah"*—"all 'speakers' in a canonized text express themselves in a wise manner." In other words, the interpretive burden is placed on the reader to discern the writer's wisdom.

Elijah, as can be seen from his interpretations of Deuteronomy 1:1 and Proverbs 1:1, employs the same principle and follows the Iyyun School in assuming that every element in a text must have sufficient reason for being present. But he challenges the Iyyun School in the way that he understands *human* error and history. Elijah adopts the Iyyun School's philosophic assumptions when interpreting biblical texts, yet takes a different approach with regard to the interpretation of humanly produced rabbinic texts, where he believes errors do not rest with the interpreter but with the text itself.

Elijah's emendation project addresses the charge that Leibnizian idealism leaves no room for the possibility of progress, redemption, and critique. Indeed, Elijah's emendations demonstrate the critical possibilities of idealism. Elijah embroidered the theological concept of evil around the idea of textual error.[125] According to this view, the transformation of human-produced evil and error into the good and the right is a sacred endeavor; it is the very telos of man's existence.[126] Elijah's emendations are indicative of this raison d'être and highlight humanity's ability to employ critique and reason in religious life.[127] Emendation is the path toward redemption and a restored original harmony.

Elijah's emendation project actualizes what Leibniz only hints at. Yet the Gaon's contributions to idealist thought were not the result of his ties to German philosophical circles (it would have been historically impossible for him to have read many of Leibniz's and his students' most important works). If anything, the opposite is true. As we will see, Elijah's ability to see Jewish texts as the basis for an idealist philosophical system, with its attendant universal claims, emerged in large measure from his unique position as the intellectual leader of a Jewish culture that did not depend on "non-Jewish" intellectual traditions. That is, Elijah never had to confront the challenges posed by Christian theologians and Protestant exegetes who saw the New Testament as the ideal reading of the Hebrew Bible. Those challenges would be taken up by Elijah's contemporary and Leibniz's best-known Jewish follower, the acculturated German Jewish thinker Moses Mendelssohn.

3

Elijah and the Enlightenment

ELIJAH BELIEVED THAT JUDAISM AND JEWISH TEXTS EXPRESSED UNIVERSAL and rational principles. In contrast, Moses Mendelssohn, Leibniz's best-known Jewish follower, attempted to convince Germans that rabbinic Judaism highlights the social and political limitations of idealism.

This is not the way Elijah and Mendelssohn are commonly represented. Generally, historians have described the men as two poles of eighteenth-century Jewish history, with the Gaon (Elijah of Vilna) described as the defender of rabbinic or "traditional" Judaism,[1] and the "Jewish Socrates" (Mendelssohn) characterized as the founder of "modern" Judaism.[2] The historian Heinrich Graetz, for instance, went so far as to liken Mendelssohn's accomplishments, specifically his translation of and partial commentary to the Hebrew Bible, *Biur al ha-Torah* (published 1780–1783), to the reforms of Martin Luther.[3] And "just as Luther had overthrown the papacy," Heinrich Heine wrote, "Mendelssohn overthrew the Talmud, for he rejected tradition and asserted that the Bible is the most important aspect of religion."[4] When Shraga Feivush of Dubrowna published *Aderet Eliyahu*, the commentary to the Pentateuch written by his father-in-law, Elijah, he too played into the stereotypes, arguing that the Gaon was a traditionalist. He explained, "The Gaon Rabbi Elijah's exegetical approach was to [follow] the early Sages of the Mishnah and Talmud, locating all aspects of the law within Scripture."[5]

A closer examination of these two important figures, however, suggests that scholars have misunderstood their protagonists. In fact, it was the Gaon's hermeneutic idealism that called into question the canons of rabbinic authority, while Mendelssohn tirelessly defended the historical legitimacy of the rabbinic tradition to German-speaking audiences.

The confusion has in large measure resulted from scholars' efforts to employ the dyad of "modern" and "traditional" instead of considering fully the distinct social dynamics of Vilna and Berlin. Often considered the eastern and western capitals of modern Jewish Europe, Elijah's Vilna and Mendelssohn's Berlin were vastly different types of Jewish centers that hosted distinct intellectual experiences: Vilna was a large provincial town with a Jewish majority, whereas Berlin was a cosmopolitan city with a tiny Jewish minority.[6] And even though the Gaon never engaged directly in the high-stake debates surrounding biblical exegesis in eighteenth-century Christian academic quarters, Mendelssohn already in 1759 was ardently defending the sages and Judaism in general to German intellectual elites.

Only by ignoring this social context could a historian like Graetz mistakenly conjecture that a "traditionalist" like the Gaon was someone "who, in a more favorable environment might, like Mendelssohn, have effected much for the moral advancement of his co-religionists."[7] Rather, living in the densely populated Jewish locale of Vilna and *not* as a minority in acculturated Berlin was precisely what allowed the Gaon to challenge the rabbinic tradition. Evaluating the Gaon by his proximity to Enlightenment trends in western Europe misses the essential point that his role as a leader of a majority culture had a profound effect both on the formation of his worldview and on the legacy of Jewish intellectual confidence and political agency that he bequeathed to nineteenth- and twentieth-century eastern European Jewry. Indeed, the demographic strength of Vilna Jewry allowed the Gaon to adopt positions that Mendelssohn would have considered detrimental to the cause of Jewish emancipation, and perhaps even would have deemed sacrilegious. Meanwhile, Mendelssohn mobilized his defense of the rabbinic tradition precisely because he was fighting for the political recognition of German Jewry. Mendelssohn's understanding of Judaism was not an apology for an increasingly acculturated German Jewry, but a forceful argument for pluralism and minority rights.

The Long Road between Vilna and Berlin

Vilna and Berlin are 514 miles (828 kilometers) apart. In good weather, a hasty trip on horseback in the eighteenth century would have taken roughly two weeks.[8] Germans referred to Vilna as *die Wilde*, a nod to the city's various ethnic groups and ideological unruliness, as well as to the treacherous forests that surrounded the city.[9] In the late eighteenth century, people typically traveled from Vilna to Königsberg, and from there sailed westward. The majority of Jewish scholars immigrating to Berlin during this period were from the western provinces of the Polish-Lithuanian Commonwealth.[10]

Berlin grew rapidly in the eighteenth century. Jews and numerous other émigrés flocked to the Prussian administrative offices, commercial opportunities, and mercantile businesses sprouting up in the city.[11] Berlin, known for its intellectual ferment, was home to thinkers such as Gotthold Ephraim Lessing (1729–1781), Christoph Nicolai (1733–1811), and Johann Georg Sulzer (1720–1779), all of whom were long-standing friends of Mendelssohn by 1755. Mendelssohn frequented Nicolai's garden and Lessing's home, and was a "pioneer," along with the women of the Berlin salons, in cultivating contacts with the city's elite.[12] His wife, Fromet Gugenheim (1737–1812), attended the theater with Christian friends.[13]

By 1750, the 3,000 to 3,500 Jews living in Berlin were a minority in Old Berlin (population 22,000), and comprised only 3 percent of the 120,000 total population of regional Berlin.[14] Only a handful cultivated social relationships with Christian sectors of society. Those who were afforded such opportunities did so, like Mendelssohn, by mastering German, studying western philosophy, and dressing in contemporary styles. As this trend toward acculturation gathered force, some would leave the Jewish fold entirely. There are records of 345 Jews in Berlin converting to Christianity from 1770 to 1804.[15]

Berlin Jewry's minority status shaped the style of its intellectual output. Mendelssohn's efforts were primarily devoted to communicating with a Protestant majority culture in Berlin and in Prussian lands more broadly.[16] His Jewish writings offered a philosophic response to his Christian interlocutors' harsh criticisms of the rabbinic tradition. As

Lessing's play *Nathan the Wise* illustrates, Mendelssohn was recognized by his Christian peers as the undisputed leader of a minority group and defender of Judaism, due to his reputation as a genius as well as his participation in the debates on the rabbinic tradition. Well before the publication of his own biblical commentary, Mendelssohn reviewed Robert Lowth's groundbreaking work on biblical poetry, *De sacra poesi Hebraeorum, praelectiones academicae Oxonii habitae* (1763).[17] In Prussian lands, Lowth's work was privileged over what was perceived as the more heretical and radical historical criticism expressed by Spinoza's followers in England.[18] Nonetheless, even Lowth, whose theories in some respects were adopted by Mendelssohn, made it a point to inform his readers that he "pays no attention to the fictions of the Masorites [*sic*]."[19] Lowth mocked the ignorance of the rabbis in matters of poetic under-standing and literary scholarship.[20] He was not alone in this estimation of rabbinic interpretation. His student Johann David Michaelis, in the introduction to his *Mosaisches Recht* (1770), demurs that while the "intellectually deficient rabbis" of the Talmud may have something to teach us about Jewish law as it developed in Second Temple culture, their words have little value for illuminating Mosaic law itself.[21] Though some like F. A. Wolf saw value in the Masoretic tradition,[22] most German scholars from Johann Gottfried von Herder (1744–1803) to Mendelssohn's close friend Lessing contested, and in many instances detested, rabbinic methods of interpretation.

Criticism of the rabbinic tradition was often connected to the debates surrounding Jewish emancipation. The great champion of Jewish political rights Christian Wilhelm Dohm (1751–1820) suggested that Jews leaned on the laws of the despised Pharisees because they had been denied full partic-ipation in civil society. Dohm believed that for Jews to become "upright" they would need—with German encouragement—to reclaim their biblical roots. He was convinced that as soon as Jews were accepted into civil society, they would cast aside what he saw as the crutch of rabbinic law.[23]

Mendelssohn anticipated Dohm's critique in 1759, in a passionate defense of the Masoretic tradition and rabbinic exegesis.[24] Prompted by Johann Jacob Rabe's announcement of a new German translation of the Mishnah, he wrote an anonymous essay in the prominent progressive German journal *Literaturbrief: Briefe die Neueste Litteratur betreffend*. Mendelssohn's essay is written from the point of view of a non-Jew skep-tical of Judaism and especially of the rabbinic tradition. When the non-Jew "once upon a time . . . happened upon a rabbi, a well-known sage of his people," he asked the rabbi for his thoughts regarding rabbinic interpretation and Talmudic study. The rabbi admits that he "is well aware of the miserable and dishonest view, even the wisest of your people, have towards our [rabbinic] knowledge." As the rabbi tells it, German academics distort rabbinic literature and exegesis and incite "bloody persecutions" against Jews. Eventually, the rabbi launches into a spirited, albeit apologetic, defense of rabbinic exegesis, pointing out that only a small percent of the Talmud contains "fairy-tale like" elements, and these are meant to be interpreted allegorically. "The rest of the Talmud," he contends, "contains thorough examinations and evaluations of our laws and rituals and the commandments of the Old Testament."[25]

Mendelssohn expanded his fictional rabbi's argument—this time in his own voice—in his commentary to Ecclesiastes, published in 1770 in Berlin. Only one year after Mendelssohn produced his commentary, in 1771, Jacob Rabe published a German translation. Mendelssohn unabashedly and publicly defended the rabbinic tradition in that commentary and elsewhere. In the summer of 1770, he boasted to his friend Elkan Herz that he never wavered in the authority he granted to the sages. "I am far removed from declaring a single utterance of our Sages of blessed memory to be a *Scharteke* [trash]," Mendelssohn asserted. "There is not a single gentile scholar who has leveled this charge against me or misrepresented my words to this effect."[26]

Finally, Mendelssohn would forcefully argue in *Jerusalem* (published in 1783) that rabbinic law was not an impediment to Jewish emancipation, but rather the very standard against which the state's tolerance could be measured. Jews would gain emancipation not as members of a universal biblical religion (as Dohm had argued) but as members of a religion valued for its distinctive features as expressed by the rabbinic tradition. Hence Mendelssohn's plea to governments not to "feign agreement where diversity is evidently the plan and purpose of Providence."[27]

Around the time that Mendelssohn was writing *Jerusalem*, he tacitly agreed to coauthor the *Biur*.[28] One might assume that Mendelssohn wrote the *Biur* with an exclusively Jewish readership in mind and therefore addressed strictly Jewish communal concerns.[29] His views in the *Biur* vis-à-vis rabbinic authority, however, were consistent with those exegetical and philosophical positions that he had expressed before German Protestant audiences.

In his introduction to the *Biur*, Mendelssohn repeated his interpretive credo: "If we see that the *sensus literalis* of the text contradicts and opposes the authoritative interpretation—as it has been given to us by the Sages—to the point that there is no way to justify both readings, then we are obligated to follow the reading of the Sages. . . . For we have been given the tradition of the Rabbis, whose interpretations enlighten."[30]

While Mendelssohn wrote the *Biur* for a primarily Jewish audience, his positions regarding the authenticity of rabbinic exegesis were largely a response to attacks launched against the rabbis by non-Jewish German scholars. No fewer than twenty-one subscribers to the first printing of the *Biur* were non-Jews.[31] Though the *Biur* itself was written in Hebrew script, a German script edition—translated by Mendelssohn and Friedrich Christian Löffler (1752–1816) and intended for a Christian audience—appeared not long after the original publication.[32] More importantly, by 1780 a translation of Mendelssohn's *Alim li-Terufah*, where his fullest defense of rabbinic exegesis appears, was distributed throughout Protestant intellectual circles. Indeed, Mendelssohn personally sent the translation to Protestant clergymen.

By connecting rabbinic exegesis and biblical literature, Mendelssohn hoped to refute those like Dohm who distinguished Mosaic law from rabbinic norms. Separating rabbinic exegesis from the biblical word and world gave ammunition to those seeking to further separate Judaism from Christianity and Jews from German society. Mendelssohn's defense of rabbinic exegesis vindicated the central ideas and practices of a minority group living in a majority culture. The rabbinic tradition, like the Jewish people itself, shared a biblical background with its German surroundings, while retaining distinct features.

Mendelssohn co-wrote the *Biur* with, among others, the scholar and bibliophile Shlomo Dubno (1738–1813). Born in Poland in the town of Dubno, Shlomo studied in his youth under prominent European rabbis such as Shlomo ben Moshe of Chełm (1715–1778).[33] In 1772, after years of cataloguing Hebrew books in Amsterdam, he arrived in Berlin, where he worked with Mendelssohn for nine years on the *Biur*. Then, abruptly, Dubno left Berlin.[34] In a letter he sent to the publisher and Hebrew grammarian Wolf Heidenheim (1757–1832), Dubno explains that he left because some of his teachers across eastern Europe had questioned his association with the new Maskilim.[35] Despite leaving, however, Dubno did not cease to promote his exegetical project. He traveled the continent collecting subscriptions in the hope of republishing his commentary on the Pentateuch without Mendelssohn's controversial translation.

When Dubno moved to Vilna, the city he found was by no means intellectually isolated. Though there was no "beckoning bourgeoisie" in Vilna, its wealthy members, some invested in the lumber trade, traveled regularly to German lands.[36] Economic ties developed in tandem with intellectual affinities. The fourteen Vilna residents who subscribed to the first edition of the *Biur* dwarfed the number of subscribers in other eastern European towns (Kovno and Shklov were next closest, with three each).[37] Many of the same individuals also subscribed to the German Maskilic publication *ha-Me'asef*. Scholars in both locales focused on examining universalistic biblical texts such as Job, Proverbs, and Ecclesiastes.[38] Vilna scholars like Yehezkel Fievel (1755–1833), Shmuel ben Avigdor (d. 1791), Yosef ben Eliyahu Pesseles, Yehudah Hurwitz (1734–1797), and the Gaon's own sons all maintained contact with members of the Berlin Haskalah.

The best-documented exchange of ideas between the Berlin Maskilim and Elijah in Vilna is the case of Barukh Schick of Shklov (1744–1808). After spending a year in Berlin with Mendelssohn and other Maskilim such as Naftali Herz Wessely (1725–1805) and David Friedländer (1750–1834), Schick visited the Gaon.[39]

Vilna's Jewish intellectual vibrancy and demographic strengths appealed to rabbinic intellectuals like Schick and Dubno who had spent time in western Europe.[40] Vilna's Jewish establishment, for instance, encouraged Dubno to reprint his commentary with the introduction that Mendelssohn would not publish.[41] Among the notables who showered Dubno with approbations was Vilna Chief Rabbi Shmuel ben Avigdor, who explained that because "some living in Ashkenaz and Poland did not embrace the method adopted by [Mendelssohn in his] German translation, Rabbi Shlomo will print the Pentateuch with the Aramaic translation of Onkelos."[42] The chief rabbi never condemns Mendelssohn by name, simply noting that "some" had complained. Other supporters of Dubno's exegetical project were Hayyim of Volozhin and his brother Zalman (1756–1788).[43]

Dubno brought to Vilna at least part of his magnificent library,[44] which now also contained the works of not only Mendelssohn and Wessely, but also the bibliophile, grammarian, and philosopher Isaac Satanov (1732–1804). He ingratiated himself to those in the Gaon's inner circle, especially the Gaon's son Avraham, with whom he shared bibliographic interests.[45] Dubno also befriended the town's financial elite, such as Yosef ben Eliyahu Pesseles, in whose house he resided.[46] In correspondence written in 1783 to the Berlin Maskil David Friedländer, Pesseles tried to smooth over the ill feelings and negotiate a financial settlement between Dubno and his Berlin associates in the wake of Dubno's abrupt departure.[47] Some speculate that Pesseles welcomed Dubno with the express purpose of helping him edit an edition of the Torah, Prophets, and Writings that would be supported by the Gaon.[48] This is probably incorrect. Though Elijah and Mendelssohn never mention one another's work, Dubno's close contacts within both of their circles lends credence to the claims made by the historian Graetz (1817–1891) and the Maskil Kalman Shulman (1819–1899) that at one time documentation existed showing that the Gaon read the *Biur*, and that he not only refused to condemn the work but actually had a favorable impression of it.[49]

Like in Berlin, Vilna's Jews lived in close proximity to their Christian neighbors. In addition to its synagogues and Jewish study houses, the city had thirty-two Catholic churches with fifteen monasteries, and five Uniate churches with three monasteries. Catholic functionaries lived throughout the city.[50] As mentioned in Chapter 1, beginning in the early modern period, Vilna was seen as a city situated between eastern and western Europe where various ethnicities and religious groups lived side by side, with occasional hostilities among them. Warsaw may have been a larger economic center, but by the end of the eighteenth century, Vilna was the intellectual hub of eastern European Jewry. It was Vilna, not Warsaw, that since 1579 could claim one of eastern Europe's most respected institutions of higher learning, the University of Vilnius.

Yet for all the intellectual overlap, Vilna and Berlin could not have been more demographically and spiritually different. Whereas the 3,000 Jews in Berlin comprised only a tiny fraction of the total regional population, the roughly 5,500 Jews in and around Vilna (Wojewoda) made up nearly 30 percent of the population, and the 3,500 to 4,000 Jews living within Vilna proper formed an overwhelming majority of the local population.[51] As discussed in Chapter 1, the Jews of Poland and Lithuania in this period were "virtual majority populations," which meant that the eastern European Jews developed very different cultural reference points vis-à-vis their western European counterparts.[52]

Unlike Berlin, where conversion to Christianity was encouraged by Protestant clergymen who offered the keys to the modern German city, Vilna's leading Catholic figure in the second half of the eighteenth century, the physiocrat Bishop Ignacy Massalski (1729–1794), tried to prevent forced conversions and closed the doors of missions to converts.[53] His position, however, was largely a response to the growing economic status of Jews living in Vilna. The unique experience of living as a virtual majority is highlighted in the Gaon's response to questioning by the police regarding his role in the famous kidnapping of the seventeen-year-old Christian convert named Hirsch, son of the wealthy Vilna communal leader Abba ben Wolf. When Elijah was interrogated by local Polish officials, they noted the Gaon's defiant response: "An old Jew, knowledgeable in the Talmud, looked at us in a bewildered fashion, as if he did not understand Polish. Nonetheless, he understood everything being said. Irrespective of the language in which the questions were posed, he refused to answer any of them."[54]

That the Gaon could support the kidnapping (from a monastery, no less) of a child who seems to have converted out of his own will to Christianity, and could then refuse to respond to the police, bespeaks a chutzpah toward local non-Jewish authorities unfathomable to a Jew living in Berlin in that period. Moses Mendelssohn admitted as much: "When living in a foreign land, a Jew must be prepared to forgo what he believes is just. He should speak to ruling authorities with fear and humility in an ethically appropriate way and not in a strident fashion which would provoke anger."[55]

Living as virtual majorities in their respective locales offered eastern European Jews a sense of political and intellectual agency. The luxury— and Achilles' heel—of living under such conditions is that one need not be constantly self-conscious of one's own primary identity. Living among a critical mass of those with whom one shares a common culture and language creates a sacred canopy that withstands outside criticisms as well as inventions and ideas that emanate from alien sources. Vilna's Jews were more aware of the differences among Maskilim, Hasidim, and Mitnagdim, and were less engaged in the happenings of the minorities that lived among them, such as Catholics and Protestants.

The Gaon embodied the confidence of someone who saw himself as a leader of a majority culture. This self-perception is evidenced as well in his intellectual proclivities. That is, the Gaon's and Mendelssohn's respective political positions as leaders of minority and majority communities is reflected in the way they understood the rabbinic tradition as well.

Exegetical Method

Both the Gaon and Mendelssohn saw the Pentateuch as a blueprint for the history of the world.[56] Each composed immensely influential Jewish biblical commentaries that employed innovative interpretive techniques and broke new ground in Jewish scholarly literature.[57] Before the eighteenth century, according to Hans Frei, most exegetical traditions combined the literal and religious meanings of Scripture. "The point to realize," he writes, "is not that they had been conceived to be in harmony with each other but that they had not even been generically distinct issues."[58] Over time, the ties holding together these two interpretive categories unraveled, however, and the literal sense of Scripture gained its own prominence separate from the text's religious, spiritual, homiletic, or mystical significance. Canon law, *halakha*, and dogma that had been "read into" the words of Scripture were now ignored or bracketed by eighteenth-century exegetes trying to locate the text's plain sense. In Jewish circles, the growing gap between the religious and plain-sense meanings was exemplified by Mendelssohn and the Gaon in their theories of the medieval, kabbalistic conception of the fourfold hermeneutic system *PaRDeS*[59]—a Hebrew acronym for the different kinds of meaning derived from a text: *peshat* (literal or plain sense), *remez* (allusive or allegoric), *derash* (rabbinic intertextual), and *sod* (kabbalistic or esoteric).

Jewish biblical interpretation and the fourfold hermeneutic method have a long and much studied history. Though Bachya ben Asher (1255–1340) employed *PaRDeS* as an exegetical system in his biblical commentary *Midrash Rabenu Bachya* (Naples: 1492), Edward Breuer has detailed how, prior to Mendelssohn, few if any Jewish interpreters laid out in any conscious way a defined rigorous hermeneutic strategy that accounted for the rabbinic interpretation of the Bible.[60] Most medieval Jewish commentators related to *PaRDeS* as an abstract kabbalistic concept, whereas Mendelssohn and the Gaon applied this interpretive scheme to their Scriptural reading practices. In his commentary to Ecclesiastes, Mendelssohn explains: "There are four approaches to the explanation of the Holy Torah and they are *peshat*, *derash*, *remez*, and *sod*. All are words of the living God and are simultaneously correct. They are not contrary to the ways of reason and logic, nor are they difficult to understand."[61]

Mendelssohn tries to justify how the four methods of *PaRDeS* are all simultaneously correct—more specifically, how the plain sense of the biblical text squares with rabbinic interpretation (*derash*). These two approaches can generate either complementary or contradictory readings. When a contradictory reading occurs, Mendelssohn is adamant that "one is obligated to follow rabbinic interpretation."[62] According to Mendelssohn, distinguishing between rabbinic interpretation and the text's *sensus literalis* turns on the issue of biblical synonymy. In the introduction to his commentary to Ecclesiastes, he writes:

> Every statement has a meaning agreeable with all the purposes of the speaker and the one listening. [The meaning] that follows the continuity and flow of words, stated without any additions or deletions, is called the primary meaning, and the explication of this meaning is called *peshat*. . . . The manner of *peshat* is to pay attention to the sense and not to the words. [According to this approach] there is no difference between "Remember [the Sabbath day]" and "Observe [the Sabbath day]." . . . For what is intended by them . . . is itself one matter as Rabbi Abraham Ibn Ezra explained in *Yitro*.[63]

Mendelssohn's understanding of *sensus literalis* was based on a theory of authorial intention advanced by the medieval commentator Ibn Ezra (1089–1164).[64] Ibn Ezra argues that the biblical use of synonyms is nothing more than a poetic device. The sages' interpretation of every biblical word, in his view, is to be understood only on the level of a secondary meaning and is not to be confused with the simplest reading of the text (the author's primary meaning). Interpretation involves understanding the writer's levels of intention.[65] According to Mendelssohn, *peshat* is the author's primary intent, while *derash* represents the author's secondary or indirect intent.

Mendelssohn's position on synonymy ran up against contemporary rabbinic interpretive practices. For example, Mendelssohn's co-contributor to the *Biur*, Naftali Herz Wessely, wrote some of the most controversial Enlightenment tracts, stressing the need for the full integration of Jews into German intellectual, social, and political life. Yet with regard to biblical synonyms, the great reformer implicitly challenged

Mendelssohn: "There is no redundancy in different words. In our view the Torah's repetition of words was not meant in order to improve a poem. Because God's Torah is not, God forbid, like books of poems."[66] Wessely's view of biblical synonymy was echoed by numerous eighteenth-century biblical commentators, including the Gaon, whose commentary to Proverbs argues that each biblical work has a sufficient interpretive reason to stand uncontested.[67] The fact that Mendelssohn adopted Lowth's position even though it contravened that of the overwhelming majority of his rabbinic contemporaries suggests that his defense of Talmudic reading practices had little to do with a fear of ruffling the feathers of his rabbinic colleagues.

Before Mendelssohn, however, the Gaon used *PaRDeS* as a self-reflexive method of interpretation rigorously applied to classical texts. In this spirit, the Gaon penned three different commentaries to the book of Esther—one following the rules of *peshat*, a second according to the rules of *remez* and *derash*, and a third according to *sod*.[68] In his work on Proverbs, the Gaon expounds his understanding of *PaRDeS*:

> Torah is broken up into two parts . . . they include *peshat* and *sod*. Within each, there exist two parts—in *sod* there exist the essence of something [the actual *sod*] and *remez*, which represents the entrance into the city of *sod*. In *peshat* there are *peshat* and *derash*. "Outside knowledge" refers to those who still stand on the outside [of the city of *sod*]. He who stands on the outside knows only the *peshat*. . . . "In the street" refers to the *derash* where *halakha* is found and it is this road that leads into . . . the gates of *remez* . . . which leads [into] the city of *sod* which is the inner world of Torah.[69]

Elijah represents hermeneutics as a landscape, with *derash* imagined as a road, *remez* as a gateway, and *sod* as a city. *Peshat*, or the *sensus literalis*, is depicted as that which stands alone on the outskirts, separate from other forms of interpretation. A little later in the same comment, he identifies *peshat* with children and others who have little background in Jewish texts.[70] The *sensus literalis* of the text requires one to read without preconceived notions. It expresses the interpretation of someone freed from all traditions (what the Gaon considers the road of *derash*) or notions of community.[71] In his commentary to the Bible, *Aderet Eliyahu*, the Gaon provides a more precise definition. *Peshat*, he writes there, "is an explanation of the word that takes into account the subject matter that comes after it. . . . According to [the hermeneutic] of *peshat*, no word is superfluous."[72] For the Gaon, *peshat* entails explaining the significance of each word in a plain-sense manner while taking account of a verse's context.[73] That is, he defines *peshat* as that which operates outside of any specific system, provides the plain-sense meaning, and is derived from the full context of a verse.

Both the Gaon and Mendelssohn agree on a contextual notion of *sensus literalis* defined by "the continuity and flow of words, stated without any additions or deletions." While the Gaon employs *PaRDeS* to lay out a theory of gauging one's proximity to the essence of a text, Mendelssohn uses it as a framework for his theory of linguistic synonymy.

The similarities between the Gaon's and Mendelssohn's exegetical approaches are eclipsed, however, by the differences that mark their descriptions of the relationship between the *sensus literalis* of the text and its *derashic*, rabbinic interpretation. For example, both grapple with the verse on torts in Exodus 21 that seemingly prescribes *lex talionis*—"an eye for an eye." Most rabbis of the Talmud insist that the verses in question concern only the monetary payment assessed to the criminal and Mendelssohn agrees, under the general principle that the sages' interpretations are correct in all circumstances:

> We have not forgotten the general principle we adopted in the introduction to this book regarding the distinction between things contradictory and complementary. Exegetically, the plain sense of Scripture may stand in complementary relationship with the tradition of our Sages, but cannot contradict them with regard to strictures and law. . . . Thus in every instance that the apparent meaning of the plain sense of Scripture seems to contradict a tradition of our Sages concerning strictures or laws, the exegete is obligated to completely abandon the approach of *peshat* and to follow the path of true tradition, or to effect some compromise [if this can be achieved].[74]

Instead of taking "an eye for an eye" literally, Mendelssohn harkens back to the interpretation offered by the medieval rabbi Sa'adya ben Joseph (882–942).[75] According to reason, Mendelssohn claims, the text must refer to financial liability because "what happens if someone damages only a third of one's eyesight, how does it figure that we could exact a form of retribution that would not lead to additional or less damage to the individual?"[76]

The Gaon, however, takes a different tack:

> *"When men fight, and one of them pushes a pregnant woman and a miscarriage results, but no other damage ensues, the one responsible shall be fined according to the woman's husband, [who] may exact from him the payment to be based on reckoning."* And this is a rule regarding the meaning of damage through the Torah . . . and it can be applied through the principle of general-specific. In the first verse [21:23] we are dealing with a case of [damages] to life, one kills another person [and we would apply payment based on the law of reckoning] and in the second verse [21:24] we are dealing with a case of [damages] to limbs, one damages someone's eye [and we would apply payment based on the law of reckoning] and in the third verse [21:25] we are dealing with damages done to the body, someone cuts or bruises another person [and we would apply the law of reckoning].[77]

The Gaon deviates entirely from the accepted rabbinic interpretation, arguing instead that according to its plain sense the payment for such damage (*ason*) does not mean a monetary payment. Rather, he contends that these verses assume a general principle of *lex talionis*, and specify the cases in which *lex talionis* is applied.

The Gaon's approach toward the rabbinic tradition is reflected throughout his commentary.[78] He contends that one is free to read the text in such a manner because Jewish law does not necessarily conform to the *sensus literalis* of Scripture. Not only does the Gaon express no need to justify the lack of textual or biblical rationale behind Jewish practices, but he also cleverly quotes the subversive Talmudic dictum (Makkot 22b): "How stupid are the people of Babylonia who stand before a Torah scroll but not before a great sage."[79] The suggestion is that the Bible receives its authority only because of the way it is read and received by the sages (not vice versa). The Gaon does not defend Scripture or the rationale of rabbinic interpretation; nor does he hesitate to distinguish between these two corpora. In his view, rabbinic authority is not derived from the rabbis' connection to the biblical text itself, but rather is based on the fact that the Torah as a whole was given to human beings to interpret as they see fit. Mendelssohn, unlike the Gaon, could ill afford to mock those "Babylonians." He lived among them, and many of them occupied prominent places in German intellectual life.

Levita and Rashbam

During the eighteenth century, the work of two of the most controversial biblical commentators in Jewish history once again rose to prominence: that of the twelfth-century rabbi Shmuel ben Meir (1085–1174?) and that of the sixteenth-century grammarian Eliyahu Levita (Bachur) (1469–1549). Both figures can be found lurking in the background of commentaries by the Gaon and Mendelssohn. At the end of *Tosefet Ma'aseh Rav* (Jerusalem: 1891), a commentary to a book written about the Gaon's customs, we are informed "that in the field of grammar, Gra followed Rabbi Eliyahu Bachur [Levita] and somewhat the approach of Rabbi David Kimchi, except in matters involving cantillations [the accents over biblical words printed in the Masoretic text of the Hebrew Bible that provide the syntactical structure of Scripture], where [the Gaon] followed Rabbi Shlomo Zalman Hanau's work *Sha'arei Zimra*."[80] While *Tosefet Ma'aseh Rav* is far from an objective source, its claims call out for investigation.

The Hebrew grammarian Levita wrote some of the greatest works of Old Yiddish literature, including the chivalric epic *Bove-bukh* (1507). He gained notoriety in Jewish circles—and a modicum of fame in Christian-Hebraic ones—for teaching the Christian monk (and later cardinal) Egidio da Viterbo (1469–1532).[81] Levita's book *Masoret ha-Masoret* (1538)[82] focused on the Masoretic tradition (diacritic markings and marginal notes dealing with the way biblical words are written and pronounced). Levita contested the established position that the Masoretic tradition emanated from the revelation at Sinai, insisting instead that the Hebrew vowel marks were unknown to Jews until post-Talmudic times.[83]

In his bibliographic work *Rav Pe'alim*, the Gaon's son Avraham lends credence to those who saw a connection between his father and Levita: "See the work *Masoret ha-Masoret*, written by Rabbi Eliyahu Bachur. [There] he analyzes in depth as to whether or not the *masorah* came from Sinai or from Ezra the prophet and he concludes in line with the authors of the Tosafot [the medieval school of Talmudic interpretation] that it came after the time of Ravina and Rav Ashi [the redactors of the Talmud]."[84] Avraham in his introduction to *Midrash Aggadat Bereishit* again refers to Levita and the Tosafot, claiming: "the Tosafot agree that the *masoret* contradicts the Talmud."[85] While the authors of *Tosefet Ma'aseh Rav* wanted to distance the Gaon from Levita's controversial ideas on the *masorah*, one senses that in this case perhaps the lady doth protest too much. The Gaon was certainly influenced by Levita's ideas generally.[86] In his commentary to *Shulchan Arukh, Even ha-Ezer*, the Gaon addresses the veracity of the cantillations of the Bible and explicitly endorses Levita (though not by name): "In numerous cases the *masorah* disagrees with the Talmud."[87]

The Gaon was far from the only eighteenth-century exegete touched by the critical ideas of Levita. The 1771 edition of *Masoret ha-Masoret*, translated into German by Johann Salomon Semler (1725–1791), was dedicated to Moses Mendelssohn.[88] Yet Mendelssohn in his own writings rebukes the controversial rabbi, and devotes a large portion of his introduction to the *Biur* to challenging Levita. After paying Levita requisite respect, he fiercely defends the Mosaic origins of the *masorah*. "Also with regard to the orally pronounced and written words recorded in the Bible," Mendelssohn argues, "Moses wrote all of the written words down and then orally read the text to Joshua and passed on to him the secret behind the difference between the two versions."[89] Mendelssohn draws a connection between Levita's position and "Christian scholars," who in his view

> do not possess the tradition of the Rabbis, pay no attention to the *masorah*, and do not accept the vowels and cantillations. These scholars make the Torah like an unguarded wall, where each person according to his own intellectual abilities can rise up and say what he pleases. They add, subtract and change the content of God's Torah. They do not stop with the vowels and cantillations, but also alter letters and words (for what will stop them from following such a path?) according to their own beliefs and ideas.[90]

Levita's treatment of the *masorah* and the vowel points reminds Mendelssohn of certain Protestant forms of biblical interpretation. By distancing his project from Levita's, Mendelssohn highlights the differences between his and the Gaon's exegetical projects and, more generally, between their respective views of rabbinic exegesis.

Another exegetical fault line between the Gaon and Mendelssohn can be detected in the way each treated the recently republished biblical commentary of Rabbi Shmuel ben Meir (1085–1174?), known by the acronym Rashbam. A grandson of Rashi, Rashbam regularly interpreted biblical verses in ways counter to the readings offered by the rabbis. His biblical commentary is hardly ever cited in the medieval period, but it is no wonder that in an age of critical inquiry the critical commentary of the Rashbam would find an audience.[91]

According to some, it was Mendelssohn who rescued the text from historical oblivion. But Mendelssohn himself registered his discomfort with Rashbam:

> I have composed my commentary to Scripture according to the simplest reading of the text and according to Scripture's primary meaning [as opposed to Scripture's *derashic*—or secondary— meaning]. My work borrows from those commentators who led the way in offering the simplest reading of Scripture. They include the great light Rashi and his grandson Rashbam who delved deeply into the *sensus literalis* of the text to the point that he even went too far. Rashbam's love for the *sensus literalis* steered him away from the ultimate point of truth.[92]

With respect to nonlegal philosophical material Mendelssohn parted ways with the rabbis of the Talmud (in favor of universal reason), but with regard to legal material he defended their interpretations.[93] For Mendelssohn, philosophy was something universal and could not contradict natural reason. Aggadic (narrative or philosophical) sections of rabbinic literature should be radically reinterpreted to conform to universal principles. Jewish particularity and difference resided in Jewish law; thus it was crucial to uphold and defend the uniqueness of rabbinic exegesis. By demonstrating the biblical origins of Jewish law, Mendelssohn wished to ensure that Judaism remained distinct and yet legitimate in the eyes of Christianity. For Mendelssohn, Rashbam's words were reminiscent of critiques issued by the German biblical scholars cited earlier, inasmuch as they provided an opening to dismiss the rabbinic tradition.

Contrary to popular and scholarly sentiment, Mendelssohn was not the only figure to have resurrected Rashbam from oblivion.[94] Isaac Satanov, a Polish-born Maskil who traveled to Berlin, was so enthralled with the medieval rabbi's exegetical approach that he forged a whole commentary on Psalms under Rashbam's name.[95] Likewise, the Gaon had access to a copy of Rashbam's commentary on the Bible and employed it as a source for his own understanding of the Bible's legal sections. In particular, the Gaon embraced those writings of Rashbam that contested rabbinic traditions. The phrase "and see the Rashbam" punctuates his commentary of the legally oriented Torah portion of *Mishpatim*. He explicitly cites Rashbam in his comments to Exodus 21:6 (the case of the slave and the doorpost). In other instances, such as Exodus 21:22 ("an eye for an eye"), the Gaon follows the interpretation adopted by Rashbam without citation.[96] Unlike Mendelssohn, who was ambivalent and ultimately rejected Rashbam, the Gaon not only adopted the early medieval rabbi's exegetical approach, but also extended it to other Jewish texts. The Gaon interpreted the *mishnayot* (early rabbinic rulings) against the Talmud (later rabbinic statements),[97] and the *Zohar* against later kabbalistic interpreters.[98] In addition, "unlike those who came before him, who quietly interpreted in such a manner, the Gaon did so in a formal way and passed his approach on to others as a principle [of interpretation]."[99] The Gaon's relatively unconstrained method and Mendelssohn's more apologetic one permeated all aspects of their respective exegetical projects.

Ultimately, the Gaon's critical exegetical practices went well beyond not only Mendelssohn's but even the parameters set by Rashbam. According to the Gaon, even the Bible contradicts itself. The precept in Exodus 21:6 that an indentured slave must serve his master forever, for instance, opposes the injunction in Leviticus 25:40 that the indentured slave must work only until the Jubilee year. Furthermore, following Nachmanides, the Gaon argues that the book of Deuteronomy was written later than the other four books of the Bible. As the Gaon opens his commentary to Deuteronomy: "This book alone Moses prophesized on his own."

Mendelssohn, meanwhile, shied away from invoking historical reasons for textual discrepancies. He could not even concede that Joshua (and not Moses) wrote the last eight verses of the Bible.[100] In so doing, Mendelssohn defended the most anti-historical position adopted by certain medieval rabbis and Talmudic sages. As one scholar remarks, "In Mendelssohn's unequivocal support for [Moses's authorship of the last eight verses,] one senses a conscious desire to reject interpretations that could be easily misconstrued as concessions to critical scholarship."[101] If Mendelssohn feared angering his more conservative co-religionists, he could easily have relied on the sages of the Talmud, who saw these verses as being composed by Joshua.

The Gaon, in contrast, builds on the historical position laid down by Ibn Ezra that the last verses, though inspired by Moses, were actually "arranged" by Joshua. In other places the Gaon likewise invokes a historical method to explain discrepancies between the plain sense of scripture and rabbinic law. For example, in his gloss to Leviticus 16:2, the Gaon explains how the *sensus literalis* of the biblical text allows a priest to enter the Temple's *sanctum sanctorum* whenever he pleases. (According to the rabbis of the Talmud, the high priest could enter only once a year.) The Gaon makes a simple but critical historical distinction: during the time of Scripture, biblical law permitted Aaron to go in when he pleased; his access to the *sanctum sanctorum* was restricted only later in history, when the law changed.

The Christian anti-rabbinic bias in Germany handicapped Mendelssohn from admitting, even to himself and to his co-religionists, that rabbinic interpretation did indeed sometimes fail to live up to the *sensus literalis* of the biblical text. To his Christian interlocutors, such an admission would have been tantamount to acknowledging that the Jewish tradition was inauthentic or unworthy of recognition alongside Protestantism. But apologies aside, for Mendelssohn rabbinic law was the essence of Judaism, and the state's claims to tolerance turned precisely on its ability to recognize Jewish law as a valid religious expression.

The Gaon, however, was not threatened by the nascent theories of Michaelis and other Christian exegetes. Nor was he interested in matters of Jewish political or social emancipation. It is doubtful that the Gaon was even bothered by the most pressing intellectual question facing Mendelssohn's world, namely the permissibility of studying philosophical or non-Jewish knowledge. The Gaon's disinterested posture has little to do with issues of "openness" and "insularity" toward non-Jewish knowledge, as has long been thought. Rather, it had everything to do with issues that were socially and intellectually pertinent to him as the intellectual leader of a majority Jewish culture.[102]

Operating as a leader of a majority culture allowed Elijah to challenge and diverge from the rabbinic tradition that Mendelssohn felt compelled to defend at all costs. Thus although these two towering figures of late eighteenth-century eastern and western European Jewish culture represent two poles of the modern Jewish experience, it is not for the reasons that historians and sociologists often cite. That is, they represent two poles not because one is traditional and the other modern, but rather because one embodies the political confidence, intellectual comforts, and creativity of someone who lived as part of a Jewish culture, while the other put forth a pluralistic and acculturated worldview that spoke to the experiences of being a minority.

The Gaon and the "Jewish Socrates" express two very different types of Jewish genius. Mendelssohn provided a model for nineteenth-century western European Jews, who lived as minorities—assimilating and acculturating into their host countries' majority traditions. The Gaon's intellectual legacy, like Mendelssohn's, initiated deep structural changes in eastern European Jewish life, but in most cases these changes were not based on the challenges of mass acculturation experienced by western European Jewry.

Mendelssohn and the Gaon towered intellectually above their respective Jewish contemporaries. Each would have been seen as a genius in any age and in any locale. The form, content, and style of their respective types of genius, however, were indelibly shaped by the great cities they inhabited. Mendelssohn fought against the social and political hegemony implicit in the universalism of the idealist tradition. Judaism (which he understood as law) was not the basis for universal truth, but a test case for demonstrating the importance of ethnic and religious difference in the state. As Michael Mack has noted, "In shifting the emphasis from religion to legislation, Mendelssohn underlined the sociopolitical aspect of Judaism, as he understood it. This aspect describes a particular way of life that does not purport to be a sine qua non for the salvation of the rest of the world."[103]

The Gaon does not express the least bit of worry about Polish authorities or ideas associated with western European Enlightenment circles. Living in Vilna, Elijah focused on matters pertaining to the upkeep of Jewish life and on battling rival Jewish worldviews. Most notably, Elijah would spend his political energies on opposing a new Jewish group that was just then spreading throughout Poland and Lithuania, a movement that would challenge his spiritual authority in Vilna and his worldview more generally.

4

The Gaon versus Hasidism

NOT ONCE DID ELIJAH DENOUNCE MOSES MENDELSSOHN, NAFTALI HERZ Wessely, or any other contemporaries for their Enlightenment sentiments. His silence toward the Berlin Haskalah, however, contrasts sharply with the ire he displayed toward the eighteenth-century eastern European Hasidic movement. As it swept through Podolia and Volhynia, the Hasidic movement challenged local and established Jewish governing structures before meeting stiff opposition from rabbinic authorities in Shklov, Brody, and Vilna. Mendelssohn's Haskalah posed far less of a threat to Elijah than did the rise of Hasidism. Elijah unequivocally and repeatedly condemned leaders of the Hasidic movement and accused them of Sabbatian tendencies.[1]

The Hasidic movement is said to have originated around the charismatic spiritual master Israel ben Eliezer, the Baal Shem (Master of the Name, 1698–1760). After years of wandering about, Israel settled in the town of Międzbórz, where he was given free residential rights as a rabbinic leader. He was known as someone who could heal the sick, perform miracles, and access the Divine. Eventually there gathered around him a group of disciples who saw in their master's ideas the seeds of a new spiritual movement.

Hasidism emerged in the mid-eighteenth century—an age of religious revivalism across Europe. It appealed to a growing group of young people in the Jewish population. It minimized the legalistic, elite intellectual, and ascetic elements in the Jewish tradition and promoted God's imminence, prayer, spiritual ecstasy, and popular social practices (songs, dance, and merrymaking). It put significant emphasis on the role of the rebbe, someone like the Baal Shem, who had a special relationship to the Divine. Though the position of the rebbe was less pronounced in the early years of the movement, it came to occupy a central place in Hasidic theology and political life. This development began when students of the Baal Shem went out across eastern Europe and became leaders of their own communities, each offering a unique interpretation of the master's teachings. Hasidic courts began sprouting up in towns and cities throughout Poland, often upending communal institutions, challenging local leaders, and pushing out ensconced rabbinic figures. The Hasidim demanded new prayer rituals, slaughter practices, and allocations of communal funds. According to Moshe Rosman, Hasidism was not simply a folk-pietistic movement. Its leaders occupied important political positions at the center of Jewish communal life. During the late eighteenth century, eastern European Jewish towns were consumed and eventually drained by battles between followers of the new group and their opponents.[2]

The meteoric rise of Hasidism prompted historians to depict its protagonists as "revolutionary" and its detractors as old-guard "traditionalists." The twentieth-century Jewish historian Simon Dubnow, for instance, wrote that the Mitnagdic movement spearheaded by the Gaon of Vilna consisted of those "who remained true to the doctrines espoused by classical rabbinism."[3] Dubnow's position, and for that matter Jacob Katz's, make Elijah the chief representative of a crumbling worldview. They reduce Elijah's contributions to Jewish history to his political "opposition" vis-à-vis the Hasidic movement. In their portraits, Elijah futilely tries to block the rise of Hasidism by upholding the medieval institutions of power.

Elijah was undoubtedly the central figure in the opposition to Hasidism, and he wielded his power unsparingly against the movement. But his historic role should not be reduced to its "Mitnagdic" (oppositional) elements. Elijah's social and theological concerns differ from those expressed by communal elites, who opposed Hasidism because of the threat it posed to their political leadership. Elijah's theology matured well before his public opposition to the new movement, and included the view that humanity could access the Divine only through the medium of the Torah. This clashed with what he took to be Hasidism's dangerous overestimation of the individual's ability to experience direct communion with God through prayer, nature, and other acts of devotion.

Elijah failed to coercively stem the tide of Hasidism. Contrary to common depictions of Elijah as a "reactionary," however, his worldview was if anything more innovative than Hasidism—and exerted an influence on Jewish history that was not only as powerful, but also much broader.[4] By framing his opposition to Hasidism within his larger ideas on the centrality of Torah study, we can understand why his more general theological framework eventually emerged victorious and transformed Jewish intellectual and cultural history.

Elijah versus Hasidism

Elijah's first public condemnations of Hasidism are found in a 1772 letter issued by the Vilna community that bears his signature. Published that summer in an anonymously edited pamphlet "Zemir Aritzim ve-Chorvot Tzurim" ("Song of the Ruthless and Sharp Knives of the Flint"),[5] it appeared alongside five other documents: (1) an anonymous letter of condemnation sent from a Vilna resident to communal leaders in Brody, (2) a statement of excommunication issued by Brody communal leaders, (3) an anonymous essay on the evils of Hasidism written by the editor of the pamphlet, (4) a letter from the Vilna communal leadership, signed by Elijah, informing Brisk (Brest-Litovsk) communal leaders of the excommunication issued against the Hasidim, and (5) an essay documenting the rise of Hasidism and Elijah's opposition to the movement.

"Zemir Aritzim ve-Chorvot Tzurim" is a one-sided polemical tract circulated by the political leadership of Vilna and Brody. While its observations on Hasidism are historically questionable, the letters express the perception and fears of its signatories, including Elijah. Neither Elijah nor his children challenged the letter's veracity, lending value to its historical worth in documenting Elijah's position and involvement in the struggle against Hasidism. The pamphlet was issued in the wake of the growing popularity among Vilna youth of the Hasidic rabbi Menachem Mendel of Vitebsk (1730–1788), political upheavals in Shklov, and rumors about Hasidic antinomian behavior throughout eastern Europe.[6]

According to Menachem Mendel's opponents, he started his own "prayer groups and was popular in the eyes of the youth and among the town's religious functionaries."[7]

The pamphlet describes how in the winter of 1772 Menachem Mendel attempted to visit Elijah in Vilna to calm his fears about the new group.[8] Shneur Zalman of Liadi offers a firsthand version of events in a letter he wrote to his Vilna followers in 1797.[9] There Shneur Zalman claims that he accompanied Menachem Mendel to the Gaon's home. "Before any real fight broke out between the two camps," he explains, "we went to visit the Gaon at his house, hoping to argue our case before him and remove his complaints against us." Their visit was a colossal failure; sadly, Shneur Zalman recalls, "the Gaon slammed his door on us numerous times." The pamphlet's anonymous editor claims that in the course of these events, Elijah labeled Shneur Zalman and his ilk "heretics, deserving the rabbinic punishment of death." The Vilna leadership's first letter to Brody asserts that Elijah instructed his followers to "catch them, run after them, minimize their influence, and banish them with full vigor."[10] Elijah expressed similar sentiments when endorsing the Shklov community's ruling to excommunicate Hasidim.[11]

Not everyone greeted Elijah's denunciation and snubbing of Shneur Zalman with applause. Rabbi Hayyim of Vilna and a certain Issar charged that "the Gaon was a liar, his Torah is full of lies, and his belief system is a lie."[12] Hayyim and Issar were respected authorities among Vilna's elite,[13] but demeaning Elijah in this way enraged Vilna leaders, who viewed their Gaon as "the crown of our city, our teacher and master, shining light, our right pillar, strong hammer, true genius, great kabbalist whose name is known all over and whose name brings honor and praise filling up and enlightening the land."[14]

A "*beit din*"—a Jewish court tribunal consisting of leading rabbinic authorities usually chosen in conjunction with both parties—was convened against Hayyim, Issar, and the Karlin Hasidim with whom the defendants were associated. The court demanded that the Karlin sect cease its independent prayer services. Rabbi Hayyim was forced to go before the ark in the town's main synagogue and publicly beg forgiveness for his actions and words.[15] Soon thereafter, he was also made to bring a quorum of men to Elijah and personally apologize for his disparaging remarks. Unlike when he snubbed Shneur Zalman, Elijah greeted Hayyim and was prepared to forgive him for the personal slight, although he would not grant him forgiveness for his heretical Hasidic leanings.

Regarding Issar, however, Elijah proved less kind. The court ruled that the rabble rouser was to be imprisoned, excommunicated, and his books burned. Issar spent a full week imprisoned under the Vilna community's jurisdiction. On a Friday before Shabbat, he was transferred to the *kehilah*'s meeting room, where he was greeted by the *kune*, a shaming device similar to the pillory that was used by their Christian neighbors to punish those who transgressed the community's statutes. With his head locked in its wooden arms, Isser was whipped, then held in its clutches overnight. Finally he was made to stand before the congregation at Shabbat morning services (with his fellow Hasidim), where he too asked for forgiveness.[16]

This would not be the last time the pillory was used to defend Elijah's honor. A few years later, Vilna leaders threw one Joel Spektor into the torture instrument for brazenly asserting that the town was wasting its money on employing Elijah, someone who rendered no communal service in return for his stipend.[17]

Elijah was outraged at the court's sentencing of Issar. "Why have you [the Vilna *kehilah*] ruled so leniently? If it was in my hands I would have done to him what Elijah had done to the false prophets of ba'al [and smite them]."[18] Elijah, it is said, demanded that Issar remain in the pillory after his overnight punishment had ended. The Vilna leadership, however, denied the Gaon's request and simply excommunicated the offender.

Elijah was not the only one issuing threats. One of the members of the circle led by Hayyim of Amdur (d. 1787), Rabbi Isaac Manishes (also known in polemical literature as "Sar Shalom" "General of Peace"), reportedly issued a death threat. If he saw the Gaon, Manishes warned, he "would stab a knife into his stomach!"[19] Likewise, in a letter written by the Vilna community to Brody, it was reported that the pamphlet "was publicly burned in Grodno."[20] While it is unclear if these acts were truly perpetrated or these fighting words were ever indeed proclaimed, such unconfirmed reports were commonplace, and they helped stoke the flames of the controversy.

The book burnings, beatings, and excommunications, all sanctioned by Elijah, only momentarily quieted the Hasidim. The 1781 publication of *Toldot Ya'akov Yosef* by the Hasidic rabbi Ya'akov Yosef of Połonne

(1710–1784) set off another spate of indictments and book burnings.[21] Again Elijah lent his name to a denunciation issued by Vilna communal leaders, which cited as precedent the excommunications distributed earlier in "Zemir Aritzim ve-Chorvot Tzurim"[22] and called on Jews to uproot the proliferating Hasidic ideas.[23]

The denunciation of *Toldot Ya'akov Yosef* signals a shift in Elijah's line of attack. In his first letter confronting the publication, written in 1772, he focuses on the social and spiritual disturbances caused by the new sect in the greater Vilna area, including local communities like Brody and Brisk. The ban against the Hasidim issued in 1781, which Elijah also supported, addresses the general growth of the movement throughout eastern Europe. The publication of *Toldot Ya'akov Yosef* allowed Hasidism to sprout up even in areas that lacked a charismatic Hasidic leader. The indictment published in 1781 does not address specific Hasidic practices as such; rather it focuses on the troubling spread of Hasidic ideas.

The various excommunications had only a short-term effect.[24] Writing in 1792, the vagabond intellectual Solomon Maimon (1753–1800) thought the Hasidim (whom he described as a "secret society") had met their demise. This was brought about, he conjectured, "by the authority of a celebrated rabbi, Elias of Wilna, who stood in great esteem among the Jews, so that now scarcely any traces of this society can be found scattered here and there."[25]

Maimon was only partially correct. Elijah's opposition was fierce, but Hasidic leaders were not dissuaded: instead of bowing to Elijah, they worked to neutralize his authority and influence. Shneur Zalman of Liadi suggested that Shklov leaders had unfairly "hung" their opposition on the "large tree" of the Gaon.[26] In doing so they had erred, "for one great individual does not overrule the majority." In contrast to Elijah's supporters, who saw him as embodying the characteristics of the prophet whose name he shared, Shneur Zalman compared him to the revered sage Rabbi Eliezer, who in the Talmud was excommunicated for refusing to follow the will of the majority. Shneur Zalman even kept his temper in check when Elijah was rumored to have burned the recently published teachings of Israel baal Shem, *Tzava'at ha-Rivash* (Zolkiew: 1793).[27] Instead of throwing invectives at the sage, Shneur Zalman shrewdly used the very panegyrics bestowed on Elijah to marginalize him. He charged that Elijah was indeed unique, not only in terms of his learning and piety, but also in his positions vis-à-vis the masses of Hasidim. If the Gaon was "one in his generation" (*yachid be-doro*), Shneur Zalman argued, he could not possibly represent the broader community's needs or interests.

Another Hasidic tactic was to deny Elijah's antagonism altogether. Some spread rumors that he had rescinded his ban against the new group. Not only was Elijah prepared to tolerate the sect, it was suggested, but in fact he had begged Hasidic leaders for forgiveness. Before 1782, Hasidim across eastern Europe concocted stories that Elijah had experienced a change of heart and now hoped to be pardoned for his unwarranted assaults. In one letter circulated in rabbinic circles, Elijah is said to have been prepared to "join with a congregation of men and nullify the excommunications issued against the Hasidim."[28]

One biographer of the Gaon, the Warsaw journalist and Zionist Shmuel Ya'akov Yatzken (1874–1936), also reports that according to Isaac Manishes, Elijah once asked Hayyim of Amdur for forgiveness. "Originally, Rabbi Hayyim was disinclined to accept Gra's overtures. Though God was able to purify the impure and save the lives of sinners, this soul [Elijah's] could not be saved, due to it being filled with strange forms of knowledge that blocked him from seeing the truth."[29]

In 1784, Vilna leaders and Elijah actively sought to dispel rumors "that Gra [and they] had lifted their ban."[30] They issued a letter to their Pińsk counterparts, supporting their firing of the Hasidic rabbi Levi Yitzchak (1740–1809) from his position as head of the Pińsk rabbinic court. They also sent word that all reports about a lifting of the ban were unfounded and unequivocally reaffirmed their excommunications.[31]

Yet the rumors persisted. Some were fueled by the antics of a charlatan wandering around Europe claiming to be Elijah's son and possessing firsthand knowledge that his "father" now embraced the Hasidic movement. According to a 1796 letter written by the Vilna community and widely disseminated, the man traveled with a little child. Upon entering a town, the boy would raise his voice to declare, "This man is the son of the Gaon of Vilna."[32] When questioned about his "father's" position regarding the Hasidim, the imposter would reply, "I am embarrassed to repeat the words of my father who has said, 'Woe is me, for it will take a great deal to repent for what I have wrought against these Hasidim. If I were younger, I would fast, eulogize, cry, and pray before God and ask Him to forgive me for opposing them.'" The Vilna communal leaders were even more enraged after learning that these rumors were being circulated with the

hope of collecting funds from European Jews to support newly established Hasidic communities in Palestine. But when Elijah finally
responded to the rumors, his letter focused strictly on theological and
social issues. It ignored entirely the concerns of the communal leaders,
namely the political and economic matter of fund distribution.[33]

The Vilna dispute soon became a cause célèbre. What had started as
criticism directed at the Hasidim of the Vilna, Brody, and Shklov communities turned into a large-scale theological war against the Hasidim
waged throughout eastern Europe. During the summer and fall of 1797,
Elijah signed two documents denying the claim that he had softened his
position and detailing his theological objections to Hasidism. Elijah
lambasts the Hasidim for transgressions ranging from theological heresy
to sexual lasciviousness. He reiterated that it was "binding upon everyone
who feared God to chase after and catch [the Hasidim]. With any means
available, they [the Hasidim] should be brought before Jewish authorities
who have the capacity to deal with them."[34] But as we will see, Elijah
refused to involve state authorities in pursuing the Hasidim, a stand that
reveals his larger sociotheological orientation.

Much earlier, prior to 1781, Elijah's responses to Hasidism were in large
measure colored by rumors and stories told about the new movement. But
by 1797, when Elijah signed the two documents, numerous Hasidic tracts
had been published and the movement's ideology had crystalized,
allowing Elijah and others to craft a more concrete intellectual rebuttal to
the movement. In Elijah's final letters on the subject, then, he mounts his
most incisive criticisms against Hasidism, by going beyond social
pronouncements to address Hasidism's theology. That is, he identifies the
theological assumptions animating the social and spiritual deviancy
documented in his earlier letters, and in so doing, offers a succinct formu-
lation of his philosophy developed over the course of a lifetime.

The Torah as Mediator

What lies at the heart of the Hasidic movement's distinctiveness?
"Every discussion of Hasidic doctrine," Gershom Scholem wrote, "has to
start with a basic question, namely: Is there a central point on which
Hasidism is focused and from which its special attitude can be devel-
oped?"[35] Scholem maintained that there was such a point, namely,
Hasidism's notion of *dvekut*, or cleaving to the Divine (*unio mystica*).

According to Scholem, the doctrine of *dvekut* rests on several assumptions: (1) humans have the capacity to commune with God, (2) this communion can take place anywhere, through any means, and (3) God's holiness resides within nature. For the early Hasidic masters, God's immanence meant that He was accessible at all times through any medium—such as prayer, contemplation, dancing, and feasting. Moreover, even the material or the mundane outside of the traditional purview of the Torah—eating and idle talk, for instance—could be used to access God.

Scholem's description of *dvekut* and understanding of Hasidism have been hotly debated for a generation.[36] In hindsight, it has been shown that Scholem was not describing the mainstream Hasidic notion of *dvekut* per se but the most extreme elements of *dvekut*, in a way that matches how the Mitnagdim and Maskilim understood the Hasidic interpretation of the concept.[37] In other words, irrespective of the milder ways that the term *dvekut* was actually invoked by early Hasidic masters, Elijah perceived them as radical. In Elijah's eyes *dvekut* was, as Scholem would later describe it, a theologically dangerous concept pregnant with antinomian and revolutionary possibilities.[38]

Scholem's treatment of Hasidism almost totally ignored Elijah.[39] As noted earlier, historians such as Dubnow and Katz also gave short shrift to Elijah's ideas, depicting him as purely reactive. Their lack of attention, however, glosses over the ways in which Elijah's opposition expressed a much more sophisticated worldview that outlived the Hasidic-Mitnagdic debate to animate nineteenth-century Jewish life and thought.

A more fruitful approach toward understanding the Hasidic-Mitnagdic debate within the larger framework of modern Jewish history begins by asking the same question about Elijah that Scholem posed toward Hasidism: Is there a central point on which his theology is focused and from which his worldview developed? Here I propose that the most outstanding feature of Elijah's doctrine is his conception of a world, humanity, and religion mediated by strict adherence to values contained in the Torah. Put in a modern idiom, Elijah's ideas are neither theocentric (focusing on the nature and role of the Divine) nor anthropocentric (centered on the human elements of religious life), but are focused on the Torah, the relational medium between these two poles. Like *dvekut*, Elijah's Torah-centric worldview did not sprout from barren ground. It has strong roots in rabbinic literature dating back not just to the medieval Ashkenazic rabbinic tradition, but even to Talmudic times.

For centuries, Jewish thinkers made the study of biblical and rabbinic texts central components of Jewish life. At the dawn of the Second Temple period, Jews were already emphasizing text and commentary as central religious components. As Moshe Halbertal has explained, "During this period text-centeredness manifested itself more forcefully and affected the nature of authority, the basic institutions of society, and spiritual life as a whole."[40]

At the risk of oversimplification, we can identify two opposing positions on the centrality of Torah texts in Jewish history. Already in the Tannaitic era,[41] some asserted that true knowledge was restricted to Torah literature, while others posited that other sources of knowledge, such as philosophy, science, and math (collectively termed "Greek knowledge") were acceptable subjects for study.[42] The tensions between these two approaches emerged in full force in the Middle Ages. Figures such as Moses Maimonides (1135–1204), Jacob Anatoli (1194–1256), and Joseph Ibn Kaspi (1280–1340) promoted a more open canon of Jewish learning; whereas Rabbi Jacob Meir Tam (1100–1171) and the Tosafist school of Talmudic interpretation in northern France argued for the exclusive study of rabbinic literature.

Historically, varying degrees of openness and insularity surrounded what constituted "accepted" religious works.[43] But even the rabbinic authorities of medieval Ashkenaz such as the Tosafists, who limited their canon to a Talmudic-centered curriculum, never saw Jewish texts themselves as being the sole arbiters and criteria for human understanding. On the contrary, for the Tosafists, societal custom (*minhag*) was a central value in adjudicating legal disputes and in guiding proper religious behavior.[44] The primary feature of Ashkenazic halakhic adjudication was its emphasis on the way local communities behaved. For the Tosafists, law was determined by contemporary legal authorities and, even more importantly, by communal practice and custom. Texts certainly accounted for much of what constitutes "Jewish knowledge," but they were considered just one thread in the rich tapestry of Jewish life and thought.

Some have suggested that Elijah's greatest contribution to Jewish history was the great religious value that he—and his student Hayyim of Volozhin—placed on the act of studying the Torah. Such a claim is at best meaningless and at worst inaccurate, inasmuch as it misses the revolutionary aspect of his philosophy.[45] Elijah's uniqueness derived neither from his emphasis on the act of learning, nor from the stress he placed on classical sources. Such ideas can found in the works of Solomon Luria and were adopted by leading eighteenth-century eastern and central European rabbinic figures like Ezekiel Landau.[46] Even elements of Elijah's radical break with accepted customs can be found in other eighteenth-century rabbinic and Hasidic circles.[47] Rather, what truly distinguishes Elijah is the way that he crowned texts—and the ideas they express—as the ultimate arbiters of Jewish life. For Elijah, the study and redemption (editing and clarification) of the text was the primary religious act. *Minhag* (Jewish custom), consensus, and personal spiritual insights and yearnings were irrelevant as guides to the ideal way to behave and think. Elijah accepted as authoritative an unusually expansive canon of texts. But that canon only represented and defined (at least consciously) his universe's theological, political, and social contours. Likewise, Elijah was not simply arguing for the centrality of Torah study in the context of a broader Jewish community in which some devote themselves to study while the overwhelming majority labor as tradesmen and merchants. Instead, Elijah proposed that Torah study offered the sole means through which one could cultivate a spiritual relationship with the Divine.

> What is the concept of covenant [*brit*]? It is similar to one who loves another but is unable to embrace him. Because of this situation, the [lover] gives the beloved something that expresses his feelings for his beloved. This gift keeps them connected and bound together. And even though he is not present, all of his thoughts are placed in this object. This is what is meant by the term "*brit*," for it is a promise based on this object that he will not "leave" his beloved. This metaphor also explains what is meant by "he cut" [a covenant]. He "cut" a part of himself and gave it to his beloved. The concept of covenant is based on this form of dependence. And all the philosophers and rabbinic exegetes who followed in these philosophers' footsteps were mistaken. For He is beyond comprehension. Thus, Torah and circumcision are mediating bodies that exist between God and the children of Israel. For it is impossible for one to comprehend God independently.[48]

In the act of revelation, God circumscribes his relationship with his people. God offers the Torah as a relational medium between Himself and humanity. In this world God is defined by the Torah. One cannot speak of or encounter God independently from the Torah.

A relationship, however, demands that each body experience a change. Man cuts off part of himself for God, and God cuts off part of Himself for the Jewish people. God in His original form cannot coexist with or relate to the world; likewise man in his original form cannot properly interact with God. The type of relationship that Elijah describes stands in marked contrast to a God-man encounter determined by the Hasidic concept of *dvekut*, a direct and ever-accessible cleaving to God.

This contrast can be seen in Elijah's interpretation of Proverbs 3:6, "and in all thy ways acknowledge Him and he will smoothen your paths." Elijah limits "all thy paths" to only those paved by the written and oral law.[49] What people take to be "nature" is not necessarily inherently holy; the world is "full of vanities, empty and devoid of any inherent meaning."[50] Its status is determined by the way it conforms or deviates from the rules and paths marked by the ideal Torah. In the same manner in which man circumcises and thereby perfects himself, nature, as explained in Chapter 2, must be worked on in order to bring it back to its original holy and sacred state of being. Nature, like God and each human being, is fashioned through its encounter with the ideal Torah.

Elijah vehemently objects to the Hasid who sees "*dvekut* [as] the starting point, not the end."[51] Holiness is not, as some Hasidic masters would have it, lying in the bushes waiting to be found. Rather, it is accessible only to those who have properly prepared themselves through study.

For Elijah, the Torah is the filter through which the materiality of the world must be passed. The world runs through the Torah, and in the process becomes more refined. The Torah relates critically to what it encounters, removing impurities. Likewise, the Torah's call to transform the self and society leads human beings to a critical relationship with their surroundings.

For the Hasid, God was not to be found solely within the Torah but also in nature and in material objects. According to Shneur Zalman of Liadi, the Torah is described as "water that falls from above to down below . . . reaching and infusing the material aspects of life."[52] For Dov Ber, the Maggid (preacher) of Międzyrzecz (1710–1772), "God has placed Himself in everything in nature, everything in one's household which is both pure and impure."[53] Seeing inherent spiritual value in material objects was a form of *unio mystica*, the absorption of God into this world, a position with distant echoes of ideas notably advanced by Spinoza.[54]

Elijah strenuously rejected the Hasidic notion that God could be found in all material things as they were. Elijah's 1797 condemnation of the Hasidim, for instance, admonishes them for seeing God "in every tree and every rock."[55]

Elijah's privileging of text and knowledge over theological communion contrasted not only with Hasidism, but also with prophetic models of authority. The Gaon famously rejected divine intermediaries, and his commentaries are based strictly on reason and interpretation. Consequently, he would have looked askance at the approach adopted by his Hungarian contemporary Moses Sofer, who invokes divine inspiration as a source of authority and legal justification.[56]

At least two consequences flow from Elijah's Torah-centric program. One was the shaping of a major tradition of hermeneutics as the study of principles of interpretation (notably of classical texts). The other was the insistence that access to the Divine, which comes about from understanding God's word, is determined by one's rational, interpretive abilities.

Prayer and Epistemic Humility

Elijah's views on the impossibility of an unmediated encounter with God draw on a notion of epistemic humility that he develops in his understanding of prayer and the kabbalistic *sefirot* (the Jewish mystical enumerations that comprise the Godhead). In creating the world, Elijah argues, God contracted Himself, as it were. This act of self-limitation, which the kabbalists metaphorically describe as *tzimtzum*, made it impossible for humans to fully comprehend God's essence.[57] The contraction splits the Godhead. "Gra's opposition [to the Hasidic movement]," Alan Brill writes, "reflects his mysticism which emphasized the split of the top three *sefirot* from the lower seven."[58] According to Elijah, the top three *sefirot*—*keter* (crown), *chokhmah* (wisdom), and *binah* (knowledge)—collectively also known as the realm of *atzilut*, are beyond human comprehension. Above all this means that humans can never claim a direct relationship to the Divine.[59]

Followers of the Baal Shem Tov countered Elijah's epistemic humility by pointing to the biblical Moses, who spoke with God "face to face." But for Elijah, Moses was an exception to the rule, someone unique in the annals of human history—and further, Moses mastered only the second of the three levels.[60] The Hasidic master Ya'akov Yosef acknowledged that

Moses was unique, but suggests that this was only because "God [the Shekheinah] spoke through him. This status may also be acquired by every Israelite after he sanctifies himself in God's holiness."[61] Ya'akov Yosef was understood to be promoting prayer as a means for every human being to become Moses-like and enter into the higher realms of *atzilut*.[62] But even though he may have been referring only to certain spiritually elite members of each generation, any such nuance was lost on the Mitnagdim. Fearing that every simpleton might now believe that he or she had the power to attain the spiritual and intellectual heights scaled by Moses, they banned Ya'akov's book for its dangerous hubris.

Elijah and his followers had reason to be concerned about those who believed prayer could be a gateway for the kind of direct God-human encounter that Moses had attained. The emphasis on *dvekut* and prayer implied a shift in the hierarchy of religious values. According to Shneur Zalman of Liadi, "even though normally the study of Torah is of greater value than prayer, in this time prayer is of greater importance."[63] The Krakow Hasidic master Kalonymus Kalman Epstein (1754–1823) claimed as well that while "there is no doubt that a man who studies Torah for its own sake can attain great sanctity provided always that he studies for its own sake . . . the only way he can attain real fear and love of God, the longing for worship, and comprehension of His divinity is through prayer offered with self-sacrifice and burning enthusiasm."[64]

Some Hasidic masters went even further. The eighteenth-century Hasidic rabbi Mendel of Przemyśl (1711–1781), for instance, suggests that textual study might actually hinder one's spiritual quest. "As a general rule," he writes, "one ought not to engage overly much in study." He explains, "We, whose intellects are limited, if we remove our thoughts from *dvekut* with God may He be blessed, and study too much, we may, heaven forefend, forget the fear of God."[65]

Elijah had no patience for this newfangled emphasis on prayer. At the same time that the Hasidim were promoting prayer and *dvekut* over study, Elijah was downgrading prayer's stature in his hierarchy of spiritual practices.[66] Take, for example, this passage in his commentary to Proverbs 13:12:

> Our Sages have said: What is the cure for unanswered prayers? The study of the Torah. This is because prayer is concerned with matters of this world and is therefore temporary. But Torah study is the path to

eternal life and the world to come. It can happen that God will not provide man with his requests in this world, such that he has only heartache. Thus, they advised that its cure is the study of Torah, which bestows eternal life; and through Torah study, man will most certainly attain his requests and desires. For this reason they call the Torah a tree of life.[67]

According to Elijah, prayer is subservient to the act of studying the Torah. These sentiments are affirmed in the first letter written by the Vilna rabbinate and Elijah against the Hasidim (in 1772), chiding them for "always spending hours in preparation for prayers." Furthermore, "they do away with the set times for the recitation of Shema and the Amidah," the central prayers in the daily liturgy.[68] Elijah's criticisms of the Hasidim reflect his more general contention that "it is prohibited for one to spend more than three hours a day in the act of praying."[69]

For Elijah, the excessive Hasidic accentuation of prayer suggests a wrong-headed view of both human-Divine and human-human relations. As we have seen, Elijah's metaphor of the lover and beloved describes the study of the Torah as God's sole connection to the Jewish people.

Contrast Elijah's vision with the picture of intimacy expressed by Rabbi Pinchas of Korzec (1726–1791): "Prayer is like intercourse with the Divine Presence. At the beginning of intercourse there are motions. Similarly, there is a need for motion in prayer. One should move when beginning to pray. Later on, one can stand without moving, attached to the Divine Presence with a powerful bond. As a result of the motions alone one can attain *dvekut*."[70]

While Pinchas's comparison of prayer to intercourse could be understood as part of the traditional trope of describing Israel and God as two lovers, he extended the metaphor considerably. The early nineteenth-century Mitnagdic polemicist David Maków would later associate Pinchas's position with that of one Leib Melamed, who is said to have believed that "to reach the highest spiritual level, it was productive to fantasize about a naked woman while praying."[71]

In the end, Elijah feared that by allowing God to be divorced from the ideal of the Torah, by loosening constraints on the God-human encounter, Hasidic theology opened the way to zealots, charlatans, and false prophets plotting to lead people astray. Piety, he argued, could become a pathway for spiritual and even social anarchy. While Elijah may not have been concerned about the upkeep of the *kehilah* system, he did worry about preserving Jewish social values. By threatening to destabilize those values, Hasidic pietism seemed poised to follow in the footsteps of other spiritually potent movements in Jewish history that had wrought havoc in the Jewish community.

Sabbatianism and Sexual Polemics

Elijah's polemical depiction of the Hasidim as initiating a radically different worldview is surprising given that the Hasidic masters' views were very similar to those held by many of the most revered medieval rabbinic authorities. Nachmanides (1194–1270), for example, had an understanding of *dvekut* that was remarkably similar to the one espoused by eighteenth-century Hasidim.[72] In essence, the Maggid of Międzyrzecz's notion of nonpetitionary prayer mirrors the one maintained by Elijah himself.[73] Was Nachman of Bratslav's idea of repentance—with its stress on the gradual process of returning to God—very far from the one put forth by Elijah?[74] Why then did Elijah see the Hasidim as being heretical enough to create one of the greatest schisms in Jewish history?[75]

There are two schools of thought on why the Hasidim so profoundly provoked the Mitnagdim. One stresses the political, economic, and social dimensions of the conflict—questions involving, for example, licenses for the slaughtering and selling of kosher meat, positions on local Jewish governing boards in Shklov, and changes in the style of prayer.[76] The other identifies Elijah's criticisms—which were not political or economic but theological—as the epicenter of the conflict and as the main fuel for the increasing contentiousness.[77]

But recent scholarship on the history of heresy offers a third way to understand the deep divide between the Gaon and the Hasidic movement.[78] We are tempted to think that major religious schisms occur when one group adopts a doctrine that had always been unacceptable to the mainstream. Charges of heresy, however, more often stem from beliefs and practices that were once widely accepted. Elijah and his followers identified the most troubling theological deviancy not in something strange and fundamentally "other," but precisely in that which was intimate and internal. Elijah was far less concerned with the radicalism of the Enlightenment, for example, than with the views of the Hasidic camp—which reminded him of another dangerous messianic movement, Sabbatianism.

Founded in the seventeenth century around the charismatic leader Sabbatai Tzvi (1626–1676?), Sabbatianism was a messianic movement that spread with astonishing speed from Salonika to the Netherlands, Italy, Germany, and Palestine. Sabbatai's opponents portrayed him as a ringleader for strange antinomian behavior and deviant sexual practices. As it happens, however, Sabbatai Tzvi 's meteoric rise was matched only by the speed of his downfall. After proclaiming that he was the messiah, he set out to Constantinople, where he was immediately arrested at the Sultan's command and soon thereafter converted to Islam under the threat of execution.[79]

Following Sabbatai's apostasy, the majority of his supporters died out, converted, or became disillusioned. Still, some prominent rabbinic figures continued secretly to believe that he was the messiah. Even in mid-eighteenth-century Vilna, there were some religious leaders suspected and known to be Sabbatians. In 1769, just three years before Elijah's first public protestations against the Hasidim, Jacob Emden, the best-known Sabbatian hunter, recorded the outing of Sabbatians residing in Vilna.[80] Emden singled out Shimon Rogoler (d. 1777),[81] a student of Emden's nemesis Yonatan Eibeschuetz, accusing him of secretly urging colleagues "to believe that Sabbatai Tzvi is the Messiah." Shimon was eventually exposed and in the end deposed from his position on the Vilna Jewish court (*beit din*). Furthermore, Emden maintained that "Rabbi Elijah openly objected to Rabbi Shimon Rogolar, claiming that Rabbi Shimon forged a letter using his [the Gaon's] name in support of the sinners who had sided with Eibeschuetz [against Emden's charges]."[82] Emden's accusation turned out to be at least partially correct: Eibeschuetz's Sabbatian proclivities were revealed when his son Wolff was unmasked as a closet Sabbatian. But in 1755 Eibeschuetz worked tirelessly to prove his innocence. Eibeschuetz published part of a letter in which Elijah cryptically remarks that Eibeschuetz's "words are true." The tone of the letter attributed to Elijah, however, is highly apologetic. Writing as "a very humble youth from a far-away land," Elijah, just thirty-five at the time, apologizes frequently and states that he wishes he could make peace between the feuding camps. Fourteen years later, Emden would claim that the letter was a forgery. Regardless of whether the letter was truly Elijah's, it seems that Elijah either passively supported Eibeschuetz or more likely did not want to involve himself in the nasty debate.

It is very likely that when Elijah weighed in on Hasidism, it was still unclear whether Hasidism would follow the path of Sabbatianism. In 1772 there were no Hasidic books or documents, and no centralized authority to speak of. To further complicate matters, Elijah's opinion of Hasidism was formed during the rise of the antinomian Frankist movement, which was led by the charismatic leader Jacob Frank (1726–1791), who had Sabbatian roots. Elijah's first impressions of the Hasidim were set against the backdrop of these other heresies.

Already in 1762, Elijah endorsed Shmuel ben Eliezer's work *Darkhei Noam* (Königsberg: 1764), which warned dilettantes against engaging in kabbalah. The Gaon worried that those who prematurely delved into esoteric matters without the proper background could become followers of Tzvi.[83] Elijah's denouncements cryptically, but repeatedly, express fears of the Sabbatian undercurrents beneath the surface of the new Hasidic movement. That such charges were oblique did not mean they were secondary. Adopting an allusive style was part of the genre of the condemnation letter. For example, Elijah's objections to the Hasidic emphasis on *dvekut* consist of just a few words without citations. His 1781 condemnation of Ya'akov Yosef's *Toldot Ya'akov* never even mentions the book's name. Thus it is not surprising that Elijah's statements on the sexual deviancy and Sabbatian tendencies lurking within Hasidism appear encoded. In his 1796 letter of excommunication, for example, Elijah alludes to rampant masturbation in Hasidic circles: "And they [the Hasidim] have made a new covenant. They have dirtied the masses in the house of the Lord. And they allow holy flesh to be let go. And they reveal parts of Torah that go against the law, such as when they read the letters Y'K'R."[84] The letters Y'K'R comprise the root for both the Hebrew words "dear" and "semen" (KRY). Elijah was likely referring to a remark made in the name of Israel Baal Shem Tov (by his disciple Dov Ber of Międzyrzecz) to the effect that the spilling of semen (when unintentional) was something "sweet" in the eyes of God.[85] Furthermore, Elijah's and the Vilna community's first letter of condemnation records testimony that the new sect's members had been "sleeping with men."[86]

Elijah's claims were echoed by Solomon Maimon, who described the Hasidim as latter-day followers of the Greek Cynic Diogenes of Sinop, known to have been fond of pleasuring himself in public. According to Maimon, "These [Hasidim were] genuine Cynics who violated all the laws of decency, wandering about naked in the public streets and attending to the wants of nature in the presence of others."[87] These charges echo Moshe of Satanów's claim in 1746 that "homosexuality and bestiality" were being practiced in pietistic groups based in Satanów:

> On occasion they engage in homosexual relations and bestiality. There is no limit to their sins, and even after maturing they are not able to repent because in the days of their youth their souls became attached to this worldly pleasure. All of this I saw and heard directly from an individual who in his youth was fervently observant, walked in God's path and prayed with great attachment [*dvekut*] to God. Then one day he was lured into following a group and they defiled him. From that day onwards he left his studies and followed these ne'er-do-wells. . . . He now tells me that it is impossible for him to come back and sit under the canopy of the Torah.[88]

Moshe perhaps unconsciously draws a connection between theological and social deviance: While *dvekut* is not pernicious in itself, those who begin praying with *dvekut* end up engaging in illicit sexual practices.

There is more to Moshe's claims and to Elijah's insinuations than meets the eye. In the second half of the eighteenth century, when Elijah wrote his first letter of condemnation (1772), there were no Hasidic books articulating the new movement's objectives and theology. Most of Elijah's knowledge of Hasidism was obtained by word of mouth and from testimony by people living in places like Satanów, which in the mid-eighteenth-century was a well-known refuge for Sabbatians. The charge that Hasidism promoted masturbation and sexual illicitness appears prominently in criticisms made against Sabbatians a century earlier.[89] It is probable, then, that Moshe and Elijah confused the two groups.[90]

Accusations of Sabbatianism were directed not only at deviant sexual behavior but also at Hasidic prayer rituals. Elijah accused the Hasidim of screaming Sabbatian chants such as "Ba-Ba" (a refrain invoked by the followers of Sabbatai Tzvi that switched the sequence of the letters *aleph* and *bet* as a way of symbolizing the randomness and antinomian nature of language).[91] The charge of Sabbatianism can be found in at least four of the six letters contained in the 1772 pamphlet. According to Mordekhai Wilensky, the fourth such letter, signed by Elijah and the Vilna community, draws an implicit connection between Hasidism and another messianic movement that left the fold, the Frankists: "Painful and disgusting [*mekhuarim*] things were explained in testimony given to us by honest and believable people. They informed us of the group's disgusting actions and crooked ways. And at this time they bring the youth of Zion to sin and cause others to sin."[92]

The last sentence references the biblical word *yinkor*. In its biblical context the word means misjudge, but in the mid-eighteenth century the word had another meaning, "conversion" (most often associated with conversion to Christianity). The sentence perhaps alludes to followers of Jacob Frank who from 1759 onward had started converting to Christianity.[93]

The association of Hasidic sects with Sabbatians and sexual deviancy reached its apex in polemics composed by later Mitnagdim. Examples include David Maków's *Shever Poshim* (1798) and Avigdor ben Hayyim's 1800 theological-political treatise written to Tsar Paul I of Russia, Pavel Petrovitch (1754–1801). Unlike these later polemicists, however, Elijah did not throw out such charges carelessly. In fact, he was known to have been very positively inclined toward the ideas of the controversial philosopher, and rumored Sabbatian, Moses Hayyim Luzzatto. While it is doubtful that Elijah endorsed or defended Eibeschuetz's or Luzzatto's Sabbatian tendencies, he never publicly condemned their works.

Barely a hundred years after the death of Sabbatai Tzvi, it seems that Elijah genuinely believed that Tzvi's movement still posed a theological and social threat.[94] Elijah's harsh reaction to Hasidism, then, was part of a broader concern, not a knee-jerk political response to a group of upstarts. The nature of this well-considered resistance becomes all the more evident when we consider the way that Elijah's attacks reflected his interpretation of the theological category of *erev rav*.

Hasidism as *Erev Rav*

Erev rav, or mixed multitude, is the biblical term for those Egyptians who, during the Exodus from Egypt, latched onto and then spiritually poisoned the Israelites (see Exodus 12:38).[95] The Talmudic rabbis blamed all of Israel's sins in the desert on this minority. In the kabbalistic tradition, the *erev rav* continue to plague the house of Israel. A cause of exile and sin, they are the bane of Israel's existence—the devil that lurks within.[96] To the traditional reading of *erev rav* as the epitome of evil, Elijah adds a political layer: "The continuation and promulgation of arguments not for the sake of Heaven emanate from those identified with *erev rav*. [The *erev rav*] jump at the opportunity to instruct others and constantly attempt to usurp the mantle of leadership."[97]

Elijah identifies *erev rav* with haughty, intellectually superficial, and divisive ersatz leaders. In his commentary to Deuteronomy, he writes: "There are five kinds of *erev rav*. The first kind are divisive people who speak evil of others; the second type is comprised of those who pursue their passions such as fornication; the third kind are made up of those who project in deceitful ways, who pretend to be righteous but whose hearts are disingenuous. The fourth kind pursue honor with the hope of memorializing their name; the fifth kind pursue money."[98]

The traits that Elijah attaches to *erev rav* are listed in the final letter he signed against the Hasidim (1797); they include "deceit," "sexual lascivi-ousness," "those who pretend to be righteous," and those who employ "wealth and influence to pursue their own religious agenda." For Elijah, *erev rav* not only is comprised of a few marginal troublemakers, but also includes leaders or others who may be an integral part of the community. In his *Peirush al-Kamah Aggadot* he writes: "And *erev rav* remains very much connected to Israel . . . like chaff attached to wheat . . . , and Israel learns from their ways. In the same way in which it is nearly impossible to separate the bran from the flour until you have beat and thrashed the flour, so it is impossible to get rid of the *erev rav*. And here the *erev rav* refers to those who are men of wealth. And they exist only because at this point Torah is dependent upon wealth [*im ein kemach, ein Torah*]."[99]

Erev rav, then, is associated with two distinct groups: certain types of pietists, and the wealthy establishment. As explained earlier, Elijah's problem is less with those operating on the outskirts of Jewish society than with malignant influences in its midst. In Elijah's third letter of condemnation in 1797, he claims that the Hasidim had managed to enlist the assistance of the communal leaders and the wealthy: "They desecrate God's name. Assisting in their evil is the hand of communal representa-tives and the wealthy [men] of the nation, who contribute to their deceitful behavior."[100]

Elijah's criticisms of Hasidism have been understood as expressing an unspoken fear, as one scholar has put it, "that the Hasidic movement [had] the ability to reveal the weaknesses and susceptibilities of the tradi-tional religious establishment. In the eyes of Elijah and the Mitnagdim, this was perhaps as dangerous a threat as the Hasidim's willful advocacy of heresy."[101] Yet Elijah's condemnations of the broader Jewish community (both its pseudo-pietistic and financial establishments) suggest otherwise. Those who diverge from Elijah's path, after all, included not only Hasidim but also large segments of the communal establishment.

Elijah responded to the political chaos that engulfed eighteenth-century Vilna by insisting that individuals detach themselves from their social, cultural, and institutional moorings and follow him in standing apart from mainstream Jewish society. The public square was no longer safe for the spiritually sensitive. Elijah's condemnation of Hasidim in 1781 expresses his concern regarding public spaces and his own reluctance to participate in the public sphere.[102] He prefaces his signature by noting, "I am not accustomed to go out beyond my courtyard." Elijah's 1781 letter against the Hasidim specifically invokes the distinction between public and private spheres. He warns his followers, "One should not leave the private sphere [*reshut ha-yachid*], the place of God, to the public sphere, where many have transgressed and fall to their graves."

Elijah's distinction between a pristine private sphere of Torah study and a decadent public sphere accounts for his devaluing of *mitzvot* (social deeds and actions obligated by God).[103] As he remarks in his commentary to Proverbs: "Torah is like bread, upon which man's heart is nourished . . . and is needed constantly like bread; therefore, 'You shall meditate upon them day and night' [Joshua 1:8]. But the *mitzvot* are like a confection, which is good periodically and at the proper time."[104]

Elijah's saw Torah study as the telos of Jewish life. *Mitzvot*, on the other hand, force one to come in contact with the corrupted masses who have fallen prey to the false spirituality both of the Hasidism and of the economic elite he identifies as *erev rav*. Elijah's antipathy toward the broader Jewish community is displayed vividly in another admonishment, this time to his wife:

> Most important is the fence you erect around yourselves. Do not, God forbid, leave the doorstep of your home. And even in the synagogue spend as little time as possible. Better to pray at home, for in the synagogue it is impossible to avoid jealousies, meaninglessness, and libelous speech. . . . And even on Sabbath and Holidays, when people are known to congregate, better that you do not pray at all . . . and regarding your daughters they should not go to the synagogue at all, for there they will grow jealous of the clothing others wear and will come home and talk about such matters.[105]

Here, exiting the public sphere is a precondition for re-creating it.[106] According to Elijah, "In order to criticize a wicked person, one must desist from being part of his group. Better one should sit alone and study, for if he joins with those who have gone astray and tries to teach them, he will be unsuccessful and will become engulfed by wickedness."[107] As Adam Teller notes, Elijah's "withdrawal from public office and devotion to full time study . . . was aimed at establishing a new source of spiritual authority in the Jewish community."[108]

Elijah's answer to the social and political problems plaguing Jewish life was to create an alternative universe, whose borders were Torah text and whose hierarchy—and economy—was based on knowledge and mastery of those texts. Establishing such a world was ideally the business of all Jews, not just scholars and rabbis.[109] In other words, Elijah's attack on Hasidism not only was directed at preventing the rise of a new group but also, like Shmuel ben Eliezer's attack against the new pietists,[110] pointed to larger problems facing eighteenth-century eastern European Jewry. Elijah's opposition to Hasidism, his own Torah-centric theology, and his notion of *erev rav* amounted to an indictment of public Jewish social structures—related to governance, observance of laws, and communal life. The way these various positions were played out can only be properly understood in the context of late eighteenth-century Vilna, and the fall of the Polish Commonwealth and the rise of the Russian state.

Elijah's Death, Jewish Political Autonomy, and the Russian State

Elijah's harsh words against the public sphere were expressed during social and intellectual upheavals brought about by the Polish king Stanisław-August Poniatowski (1732–1798). Crowned in 1764, King Stanisław immediately enacted a number of economic reforms. Chief among them was ordering that the Jews disband the Council of the Four Lands—the de facto Jewish parliament that had governed much of eastern European Jewry. Other reforms angered Polish noblemen, who saw in them an attempt to centralize the monarchy's power. Their challenges to the king's edicts contributed to the erosion of the Polish state and ultimately to the partitioning of Polish territories in 1772, 1793, and 1795.[111]

Among other consequences, the partitions split Polish Jewry among Russia, Austria, and Prussia. Russian authorities returned political power to local and regional Jewish leaders, including court jurisdiction and control over civil affairs.[112] These powers were curtailed again only a few years later, but local communities still retained a good deal of authority over religious and civil life.[113] In any case, the give and take of power on the part of Polish and then Russian officials undoubtedly left people uncertain about the authority wielded by Jewish communal leaders.[114]

Meanwhile, rampant corruption pervaded Jewish councils and courts. Rabbinic appointments were sold to the highest bidder. Members of the Vilna *kehilah* challenged the leadership of the chief rabbi, Shmuel ben Avigdor. By all accounts, Shmuel had been receiving an exorbitant salary and engaging in a host of quasi-criminal activities, ranging from bribery to informing on people whom he disliked to Polish officials.[115] In 1785, after recourse to local non-Jewish authorities, the rabbi was officially deposed, but the brouhaha left the community crippled.[116]

Many connected the disbanding of the Council of the Four Lands to the rise of Hasidism. Shneur Zalman of Liadi explicitly argued to Russian authorities, "When Poland was being divided [1772], the governing rabbinic councils were also disbanded and the nation became free. And each person is allowed to pray for as long as he pleases."[117] Writing eight years after the council's demise, Brody leaders used its downfall to justify their inability to prevent the spread of Hasidism. Idealizing earlier days, Brody leaders sighed with pity when remembering how the council once "pursued and made known the conduct of the previous generations' wicked and evil men [read: Sabbatians and Frankists]; this generation has been stripped of such power."[118] Some in the Mitnagdic camp suggested that the rise of Hasidism had brought on the council's disbanding. According to Avigdor ben Hayyim, "When King Poniatowski sat on the throne of Poland, the sect's actions were such that he rescinded the governing authority granted to Jews."[119]

To be sure, many local Jewish governing bodies functioned well into the latter part of the nineteenth century and were in some instances taken over by Hasidic leaders.[120] Yet the letters, excommunications, and proclamations issued by the Mitnagdim and sent to various communities indicate the weakened state of centralized Jewish governing institutions.

Elijah adamantly rejected taking any actions against the movement that would involve circumventing "Jewish authorities, who have the capacity to deal with them."[121] Elijah's reservations about involving state actors come through in a conversation recorded by the chief rabbi of Pińsk, Avigdor ben Hayyim. Around 1786, Avigdor solicited Elijah's

support for banning new Hasidic books and enlisting the Polish government in fighting the Hasidim. "I had hoped by speaking with him [the
Gaon]," Avigdor bemoaned to Tsar Paul I years later, "the actions of this
group would reach the high authorities of the State and then we would be
relieved of them."[122] Elijah rebuffed Avigdor's request, probably out of
respect for the Talmudic taboo against resorting to non-Jewish courts and
authorities to settle internal Jewish affairs.

Elijah's insistence on not involving non-Jewish authorities was known
even in Hasidic quarters. Shneur Zalman of Liadi, who was arrested and
jailed twice after Elijah's death, admitted: "We know for a fact that my
imprisonment was not the Gaon's doing, for in all of his days he never
once took these matters before the State authorities, heaven forbid."[123]

Elijah's insistence that all disputes be settled by Jewish bodies should
not be taken to mean that he supported the medieval *kehilah*, a structure
built around wealthy men with ties to noblemen and governmental officials. Rather, in his view, going to non-Jewish authorities threatened the
upkeep of Judaism. The institution of the *kehilah* was a means of
preventing the growth of Hasidism, not an end in itself.

As Immanuel Etkes has noted, Elijah's motives in opposing the Hasidim
differed from those of the *kehilah* leadership.[124] Dubnow mistakenly depicts
Elijah as a religious front man for the *kehilah*. The mistake results from the
way the Gaon was miscast in town feuds involving the chief rabbi. The
dispute put the chief rabbi, the populists, and Bishop Ignacy Massalski (who
faced charges similar to those brought against the chief rabbi, eventually
being charged with embezzling church funds) on one side, and the *kehilah*
leaders on the other. The *kehilah* leaders were thus perceived as lacking
rabbinic leadership, while Elijah was seen as the *kehilah*'s de facto religious
authority (though it is doubtful that he ever took a side in the controversy; if
he did, it would have been only after there emerged a rabbinic consensus
that the chief rabbi was not behaving in accordance with the expectations of
his position).[125] Over the course of his life, Elijah himself opposed the
dictates of the *kehilah* when he believed they had violated the rules of the
Torah. When the *kehilah* leaders banned members from donating directly to
the poor, for instance, Elijah admonished them and instructed that their
ruling be ignored. His student Avraham Danzig relates that Elijah himself
offered to distribute charity without asking the *kehilah*'s permission. The
early twentieth-century Vilna librarian, Chaikel Lunski, claims that Elijah
actually rejected outright the authority of the *kehilah*.[126]

Elijah's relationship to the *kehilah* is also reflected in his endorsement of Shmuel ben Eliezer's work *Darkhei Noam*. Although Shmuel concedes that rabbinic law requires individuals to obey the statutes of the *kehilah* (provided its members are properly elected and behave in an upright manner), *Darkhei Noam* as a whole offers a blistering criticism of the rampant abuses of power by wealthy leaders and by *kehilah*-appointed rabbis like Shmuel ben Avigdor. "In many instances the *kehilot* appoint rabbis who do not behave in an upright fashion," notes Shmuel. "These rabbis curry favor with wealthy men, dining and drinking with them to the point that they no longer have the independence to assert what is good and what is evil."[127] The relationship between the *kehilah* and the rabbi, he asserts, should be "turned on its head."[128] The rabbi should be supported by the *kehilah*, but given full autonomy so as not to compromise his religious authority.

Elijah's positions vis-à-vis the *kehilah*, Hasidism, and, as we will see, the establishment of the modern yeshiva grew out of his fundamental insistence on study as the primary locus of Jewish authority and identity. This meant that taking communal matters outside the world order of Torah was illegitimate. Evidence for this interpretation of Elijah's behavior can be gleaned from his refusal to speak with state investigators regarding the kidnapping of a young man who had converted to Christianity.[129] When confronted, it seems that all the Gaon said to the investigators was the phrase from the Talmud "yihareg u-bal ya'avor, u-bal yumar," though "he did not wish to explain [its] meaning."[130]

Elijah's mysterious (and perhaps misquoted) words invoke two different, but related Talmudic concepts. The phrase "yihareg u-bal ya'avor" refers to the commandment of martyring oneself rather than commit murder, idolatry, or grave sexual misconduct. "Bal yumar" perhaps refers to the prohibition against conversion to another faith. It is also possible that it was transcribed incorrectly and should read "bal yomar," referring to a prohibition against speaking to non-Jewish governmental authorities.

The prohibition against involving the state in Jewish matters has a long tradition. Elijah's theological rationale is most clearly articulated in his gloss to Yosef Karo's prohibition in *Choshen Mishpat* 21:1 against going to non-Jewish courts. Quoting from the rabbinic work *Midrash Tanchuma*, Elijah states, "[The phrase] God 'put before you the law,' teaches that it was 'put before you' and not the gentiles. For whoever

THE GAON VERSUS HASIDISM

ignores Jewish courts and goes to those administered by gentiles denies God and denies His Torah. As it says [Deuteronomy 32:31], 'our Rock is not their Rock [our God is not their God].'" Contrary to his grandfather Moses Rivkes, who claimed that Jews and gentiles share the same God, Elijah argued that Jew and gentile do not share the same deity, and thus it would be heretical for a Jew to seek justice in a gentile court. It is unclear what actual issue, if any, Elijah was referring to when writing these words. At any rate they were composed in his later years while the Vilna Jewish community was in turmoil.[131]

Elijah's insistence that Jewish affairs be resolved within a Jewish context was severely compromised in 1795 when Russian authorities curtailed Jewish self-governing privileges. Jews were now obligated to submit to Russian law and could no longer wield the power of excommunication.[132]

Elijah's prohibition against the use of gentile courts seems to have been ignored after his death on October 9, 1797, which could not have been more untimely. It fell on the festival of Sukkot, when it is customary for observant Jews to partake in carnival-like celebrations (*Simchat beit ha-Shoevah*).[133] Chaos erupted on the streets of Vilna upon the news of his death. On one side of town, Elijah's followers wailed and mourned the loss of their towering leader. On the other side, Hasidim continued to celebrate the holiday (one imagines with enhanced exuberance). In the eyes of the Mitnagdim, the Hasidim seemed to be celebrating the demise of their great antagonist: "The Hasidim perpetrated the most grave and evil of sins. Immediately following the Gaon's death they gathered, partied, drank, slaughtered cattle, and danced into the night."[134]

The Hasidim's reported behavior confirmed for many the accusations that had been made about them over the previous thirty years—that they were socially disruptive, irresponsibly enthusiastic, and demonic desecrators of the Torah and its scholars. According to the historian Simon Dubnow, some testified that by the next morning three Hasidim had been killed and the Mitnagdim had sworn on the Gaon's grave that they would avenge the desecration of their master's honor.[135] While it seems farfetched that blood was shed against the Hasidim, a day later the Vilna leadership issued its most forceful ban of the sect. A year later they went even further, invoking the concept of *rodeph*—a situation in which a would-be murderer is setting upon his victim—in order to empower "each and every member of the community who is able to hunt down" anyone associated with the Hasidic sect to use all means available to prevent them from practicing their beliefs.[136] In theory, at least, the pronouncement empowered individuals to take violent measures to ensure the excommunication and eradication of the Hasidim residing in Vilna.

Not surprisingly, the threats of violence were accompanied by a full-scale polemical war conducted by the Mitnagdim. Over a single year, the war of words escalated to a feverish pitch. David Maków and Israel Loebel published caustic treatises condemning the Hasidim. It would not be long before both sides competed for the ear of the Russian authorities.

Dubnow points his finger at the Mitnagdim for being the first to seek outside political assistance. But Klausner and Wilensky uncovered a trove of documents clearly demonstrating that in March 1798 the Hasid Yehudah ben Eliyahu first informed Russian governmental officials of the excommunications and punishments being inflicted on the Hasidim by the Mitnagdim in Vilna. A few months later, Hirsch ben Yosef filed another complaint, this time in Russian.[137] He charged the Mitnagdim, and the Vilna leadership in particular, with rampant corruption and theological oppression. In April 1798, the authorities outlawed the use of all coercive measures by the Vilna *kehilah*. The Mitnagdim's appeals were met with silence.[138] Next the Mitnagdim began secretly contacting Jewish regional councils with the hope of marginalizing the Hasidim in communities throughout eastern Europe. But before they could make much headway, the Hasidim got wind of the plan and informed the Russian government. The government in turn mobilized its resources to contain a situation that threatened to spiral out of control.

Thus was opened a Pandora's box of recriminations. Over the next two years numerous groups and individuals were jailed and questioned by police for a host of reasons. Documents found in Russian archives by Israel Klausner reveal the dysfunction and contradictory responses that plagued the various Russian governments' approaches to Jewish affairs throughout the nineteenth century.[139] Moreover, officials in Vilna and St. Petersburg were often at cross-purposes when trying to adjudicate the myriad allegations.[140]

All this came to a head in 1800 when the deposed chief rabbi of Pińsk, Avigdor ben Hayyim, submitted a political-theological treatise to Tsar Paul I. The treatise called on the tsar to outlaw Hasidism and to compensate the rabbi for the financial losses he had incurred as a result of the Hasidic coup that had ousted him. The document also charged that followers of the Hasidic leader Ahion of Karlin (1736–1772) had now appeared in Vilna and were showing antinomian and anarchical tendencies. Invoking Elijah's rhetoric, Avigdor alleged that the group posed not only a Sabbatian threat to Judaism, but equally important, a Sabbatian threat to the interests of the state. Finally, Avigdor suggested that whereas the Mitnagdim and the tsar worshipped the same God, the same could not be said of Sabbatians (that is, the Hasidim). Avigdor's language signaled a shift from Elijah's earlier excommunications, which had focused on Jewish interests, to a vocabulary of state interests. Avigdor translated Elijah's complaints into a political idiom to argue that the Mitnagdim and the tsarist regime shared a theological orientation and that a threat to one translated into a threat to the other.

Avigdor's letter and the flurry of Hasidic counter-complaints passed through various governmental offices until finally making their way to the desk of Mikhael Kutuzov (1745–1813), then governor of Lithuania. In only five years Kutuzov would earn worldwide fame as the general who defeated Napoleon. Leo Tolstoy in *War and Peace* etched his name into western literature as the wily old General Kutuzov, who at Russia's greatest moment of peril saved the Motherland. But before his military feat, he found himself the arbiter in the debate between the Hasidim and the Mitnagdim. Kutuzov's biographers pass over his time spent in Lithuania as an "eventless period" in his career. Though he is said to have "felt great affection for Vilna . . . his duties [there] had been dreary," one biographer remarks.[141]

Kutuzov, who was responsible for assessing the conflict and offering policy recommendations to the prosecutor-general, succeeded two other Russian governor-generals who had unsuccessfully tried to settle the matter. Avigdor's theological arguments forced Kutuzov to undertake a close investigation of the theological underpinnings of the Hasidic movement. The governor-general's office had some resources at its disposal for such a study. The last document the government had commissioned was a tendentious anti-Semitic tract by the Russian poet Gabriel Romanovich Derzhavin (1743–1816).[142] Previous governor-generals, too, with the help of local Russian officials, had compiled large amounts of data by asking both groups to reply to each other in print through a translator. But these documents were not arranged in any kind of useful order and those who had supplied the information in them disputed their value. At one point, for instance, Shneur Zalman was given the opportunity to respond to charges of heresy brought against him by Avigdor, but Avigdor loudly complained that he was being denied the opportunity to refute Shneur Zalman's answers.[143]

Remarkably, none of these handicaps prevented Kutuzov from proceeding diligently and (for all we know) in good faith. His analysis is the first (apparently) nonpartisan examination of the Hasidic-Mitnagdic dispute.[144] His task, which began in 1798, was no simple matter. Kutuzov begins his report to the prosecutor-general by noting that in light of the seriousness of the accusations, it is astonishing that no serious governmental documentation existed prior to 1798. "Not only was there nothing in our own files," Kutuzov confesses, "but even in my predecessor's files there is no mention of the matter." He continues by denying Avigdor's suggestion that the Russian government supported the burning of the Hasidic work *Tzava'at ha-Rivash*. "The local officials stationed in Vilna never heard about any book burnings."[145] Nonetheless, Kutuzov concedes that Shneur Zalman's book was burned in Elijah's lifetime—and according to the rabbi's decree.

Kutuzov then identifies all major leaders and groups, and their respective roles. While his approach is bureaucratic and objective, his assessment of the situation is based mainly, but not exclusively, on Hasidic testimony. Take, for example, his remarks regarding Elijah:

> Concerning Elijah, whom Rabbi ben Hayyim mentions as having asked to raise the issue with governmental officials, there was such a Jew in Vilna. He was a sage and outstanding in his knowledge, who through his machinations and fanaticism acquired for himself honor and the trust of the people of Israel who popularized him as a Saint. Almost all of the Jews believed everything he said, except for the Karlin Hasidim, as if he were a prophet. He was given a large house and had all of his needs fulfilled, which cost the Jews dearly.[146]

Kutuzov's exaggerated claims of donated wealth and posh living conditions for Elijah parrot criticisms (mentioned earlier) by Vilna residents in the context of the scandal involving the Vilna chief rabbi. Kutuzov seems to have used complaints expressed to governmental officials in 1786 by the Vilna thug Isaac ben Leib,[147] who charged the *kehilah* with engaging in financial misconduct by continuing to support Elijah—complaints that were probably in files available to Kutuzov.[148] As for Elijah's "large house," both Isaac Leib and Kutuzov seem to be referring to Elijah's *kloiz* (study house).

Kutuzov's letter goes on to address the veracity of Avigdor's charges of Sabbatianism. The issue, as Kutuzov saw it, boiled down to whether the Hasidic movement was a dangerous Sabbatian offshoot or a legitimate child of "traditional" Judaism. From Elijah's first writ of excommunication onward, this claim of Sabbatian leanings was invoked repeatedly.

After all the major rabbinic figures who had weighed in on this debate, it is ironic that the individual ultimately ruling on the matter would be a Russian governor. Kutuzov unambiguously asserted that the Sabbatians were distinct from the Hasidim. The heirs of the Sabbatians were not the Karlin Hasidim living in Vilna, he found, but the Frankists in Satanów (whom Kutuzov claims that the Jews called "Edom"). Kutuzov writes, "There is nothing here [with regard to the Hasidim] that would qualify them as the offspring of the sect of Sabbatai Tzvi, as Avigdor claims. Furthermore, if the group Avigdor refers to is the Karlin Hasidim, they do not threaten the state." In the coup de grâce to the Mitnagdim, Kutuzov adds, "In terms of the religion of Israel, the Hasidim correct some of the mistakes that have crept into the religion of late." The governor's assessment called for a full cessation of violence, with the hope that the Hasidim would be free to express their religious views, even within the confines of the Vilna Jewish community. Although Avigdor still would not put down his arms, and appealed in vain to Kutuzov and various other parties, the Hasidim were allowed to worship as they pleased.

The repercussions of the Hasidic-Mitnagdic debate extended to the Jewish Reforms of 1804 issued by Alexander I.[149] The reforms included the following provision: "If in any place there arises a separation of sects and a split occurs in which one group does not want to be in a synagogue with the other group, then it is possible for each to build its own synagogue and to establish their own rabbinic dynasties."[150] A few paragraphs earlier, Jewish communal leaders were stripped of their power to excommunicate, and all Jews were granted the right to petition tsarist courts. These rules were not the result of the Hasidic-Mitnagdic feud, but the feud certainly contributed to the impression that Jewish life had become unruly and in need of being brought under the state's aegis. The Russian edicts may have been a "hodgepodge of unsystematic provisions" that were never fully implemented,[151] but by the first decade of the nineteenth century the fight had subsided, and Hasidim in Vilna could hold their own services.[152]

In hindsight, Elijah's responses to the Hasidic movement seem extreme. His refusal to be distracted from his studies—a trait celebrated by his biographers—became his Achilles' heel the moment he was finally compelled to make a critical public-policy decision. Elijah's inability to properly categorize and understand the Hasidim resulted not merely from his theological worldview, but also from his reluctance to engage with anyone who might disagree with him. When Elijah shut out the world, he ensured that no one impinged on his judgment, wasted his time, or put him in a comprising situation. His determined isolationism, however, also contributed to a deep schism in Jewish life.

The Gaon's confusion and alarm are more understandable when we consider the context of his life in eighteenth-century Vilna. After all, Elijah was born only two generations after Sabbatai Tzvi's messianic antinomianism had led to a Jewish catastrophe of biblical proportions. He was also not the only one who had difficulty deciphering the nature of the new group. For example, the Russian government expended a great deal of effort before ruling unequivocally that there were no ties between the Sabbatians and the Hasidim.

The triumph of Hasidism is often seen as the final chapter in Elijah's life. (The last of Elijah's condemnations against the new group were issued only a few months before his death.) But such a narrative unjustly truncates Elijah's influence and the implications of his worldview. Hasidism, after all, would garner only a small following in Elijah's Vilna. Furthermore, it might well be argued that Elijah's harsh condemnations of Hasidism's most radical elements forced Shneur Zalman and other early Hasidic leaders to purge the movement of any Sabbatian residue. Shneur Zalman used Elijah's condemnations as a way of consolidating his own power and marginalizing more radical voices within Hasidism.[153] More importantly, the campaign that Elijah led against Hasidism's crude God-intoxicated theology and against its diminution of Torah study also created the conditions needed for the birth of the modern yeshiva. Next we will look at this most enduring expression of Elijah's intellectual legacy through the lens of his magnum opus.

5

The *Biur* and the Yeshiva

THE INEFFECTIVE BANS ISSUED BY ELIJAH AND THE VARIOUS *KEHILOT* ON the Hasidim reveal the declining strength of public religious institutions during the late eighteenth and early nineteenth centuries. But even though Elijah and his students failed to stem the tide of Hasidism, in 1802 Elijah's students succeeded in establishing the modern yeshiva.[1] Over the next century, the yeshiva would replace the legal institution of the *kehilah* as the locus of centralized authority for non-Hasidic rabbinic Jewry. This shift was encouraged by Elijah's commentary (*Biur*) to the *Shulchan Arukh*, the sixteenth-century Jewish legal code. Indeed this pathbreaking commentary, Elijah's magnum opus, contributed to the transformation of eastern European Jewish intellectual life away from a code-based culture that reflected the governing institution of the *kehilah* toward a modern religious one revolving around the model of persuasive education adopted by the Volozhin yeshiva.

The Code and *Pilpul*

Understanding the unique qualities and influence of the Gaon's *Biur* requires an appreciation of the text on which it comments. The *Shulchan Arukh* (Hebrew for "the set table") was composed by Yosef Karo

(1488–1575) and included a gloss, or *"mapah"* (covering) by Moshe Isserles (also "Ramah," 1530–1572). The joint printing of Karo's code and Isserles's gloss in 1587 forever altered the educational and religious landscape of world Jewry. Although earlier figures, including Maimonides and Jacob ben Asher (1269–1340), also wrote codes, Karo and Isserles's work coincided with the rise of the printing press, ensuring that it would have wider distribution. More importantly, these works established a strong shared legal discourse between the Sefardic community (composed of Jews originally from Spain and Portugal) and the Ashkenazic community (made up of Jews originally from Germanic lands and northern France).[2]

Publication of the Karo-Isserles code paralleled a more general trend of codification that was sweeping across Europe during the sixteenth century.[3] During this period, jurists and intellectual elites across Europe focused their energies on "applying a single model or schema to everything and everybody . . . to eliminate anomalies, exceptions, marginal populations, and all kinds of non-conformists."[4] Codes, catechisms, and detailed manuals proliferated.

More specifically, argues Moshe Halbertal, the publication of Karo's code was "a response to an overabundance of opinions and their too facile dissemination; the code serves to stanch the flow of legal opinions at a moment when the authority of the law is threatened."[5] In his view, Jewish codes were formed in order to end the unruly conflict and dissonance brought on by differing rabbinic positions. John Mathews, however, offers a different explanation. These works, he argues, do more than solve textual and hermeneutic problems. They limit the range of legal opinions, consolidating power in the face of a perceived threat either from within or from outside a particular body politic. "The question why, given the general case for it, codification should be undertaken at any particular time relates in part to the juristic and general intellectual culture of an age, and also the political climate."[6] Mathews's theory is drawn from the issues surrounding the publication of the Theodosian code, where we "have to reckon with a historical perception of the role and importance of law. The law is not just a facility for resolving problems and attributing responsibility . . . it stands for something significant in the ideology of the State . . . it forms a part of the perceived aims of a state or [is codified] because these aims are threatened."[7] Codes are produced by states and entities charged with governance, not just by scholars focused on creating textual harmony. Codes bring together various groups and exclude others. They are tools not only for adjudication, but also for consolidating authority and demarcating sociopolitical boundaries.

Karo's code was not without precedents. Many have suggested that the Mishnah produced by Yehudah ha-Nassi (200 C.E.) was the first rabbinic attempt to create a code.[8] The Mishnah, however, came to be eclipsed by the Talmud—a text defined by its editors' commitment to open-ended debate, narrative, and deferment of judgment. In the Geonic period (850–1050), code emerged once again as a privileged form of exposition. But it was the publication of the *Mishneh Torah* (1170–1180) by Maimonides (1135–1204) that raised code to a prominent position in Jewish intellectual life. That is, Maimonides and others in Sefardic lands laid the groundwork for Karo's project.

By contrast, Isserles's gloss was exceptional in Ashkenaz—a culture historically known for its antipathy toward codes, and preference instead for locally produced law. Isserles's work signaled to his Ashkenazic brethren that the code was not only an acceptable halakhic medium, but a preferred one.[9] Following Isserles, the next generation of eastern European scholars—including Mordekhai Jaffe (1530–1612), Joshua Falk (1555–1614), and Solomon Luria (1510–1574)—composed their own codes, which differed slightly in style and substance from those written by Karo and Isserles.[10] Isserles's students tweaked the *Shulchan Arukh* by buttressing their rulings with rationales and textual proofs. For a brief period their works competed with the *Shulchan Arukh* for the position of ultimate legal authority.[11] In the sixteenth and first half of the seventeenth centuries, the *Shulchan Arukh* enjoyed only a modest readership, but from the mid-seventeenth century until the end of the eighteenth century, code study was a permanent fixture in European houses of learning.[12]

As the wave of codification crested, the Talmud was never obliterated from the Jewish curriculum. But its position shifted. Once a primary text—even *the* primary text—the Talmud was in some circles relegated to the status of a secondary source, a handmaiden of Karo's authoritative code. Accordingly, Isaac Wetzlar (b. 1680) from the town of Celle in Germany writes in his Yiddish book *Libes Briv* (*Love Letter*, 1749) that "the ideal for a student is to learn those tractates of the Talmud that are applicable to the study of the *Shulchan Arukh*."[13]

Some rejected the study of the Talmud outright in favor of learning only Karo's code. In 1736, Abraham Rakvice of Frankfurt expressed frustration with his students who assumed that "in our generation the study of the Talmud is no longer necessary. For the legal decisor has already ordered all of the laws and ordinances in the *Shulchan Arukh*. In the *Shulchan Arukh*, one finds all that he needs to know without losing time by studying the Talmud."[14] In many Sefardic and Ashkenazic curricula, the clarity and practicality of the *Shulchan Arukh* was preferred over the meandering complexities of the Talmud.[15] Even in western Europe, where the study of codes had been resisted, scholars eventually succumbed to the ascendancy of code learning.

The rising influence of legal code was not the only factor that contributed to the diminished role of the Talmud in sixteenth- and seventeenth-century curricula.[16] Some suggest that after the burning of the Talmud in Rome in 1553, Talmudic texts were simply too rare to be studied en masse.[17] When the Talmud was studied, its students employed a distinctive method known as *pilpul*, a word meaning pepper and used in this context to denote fiery Talmudic debate. Originating among the most elite Sefardic scholars in the fifteenth century, *pilpul*'s characteristic style was formulated by Isaac Campanton (1360–1463) in his work *Darkhei ha-Gemara*.[18] The method assumes that each *sugya* (a section that comprises the basic unit of Talmudic composition) progressed according to a clear set of formal and logical rules. Unlike the seemingly ad hoc manner in which members of the early medieval Tosafist school commented on Talmudic texts, proponents of *pilpul* argued that each word, sentence, and page of the Talmud could be understood through an a priori philosophical scheme. Every dot on the page had a purpose that merited—even demanded—explanation.[19] According to Campanton, studying a page of the Talmud requires readers "to place their minds in a state of passivity because all those who appear in the text—the questioner and the respondents—are masters of knowledge. All of their words are full of wisdom, intelligence and knowledge. Their words do not have anything wrong or problematic . . . therefore you should delve into everything . . . and see how they are 'all words of the living God.' If anything is lacking, it is with you."[20]

By the sixteenth century, *pilpul* had spread from Sefardic to Ashkenazic centers of learning in Augsburg, Regensburg, and Nuremburg.[21] The term *pilpul* became associated with a range of learning methods, many of which diverged greatly from Campanton's description. Differences aside, these schools all justified and explained each word written by the rabbis of the Talmud and their commentators.[22] In sixteenth- and seventeenth-century Ashkenaz, *pilpul*'s detractors claimed that pilpulists were studying Talmud, Rashi, and Tosafot as though each bore responsibility for the other. For pilpulists, every opinion in the Talmud not only had to cohere with all other opinions on the page of the Talmud, but also had to account for questions and challenges posed by commentators writing hundreds of years later. Furthermore, instead of focusing on the text of Talmud (as emphasized by its earlier medieval followers), sixteenth- and seventeenth-century *pilpul* was perceived as being both highly abstract and hyper-textual. Nathan of Hannover's historical work *Yeven Metzulah* (1653) offers a colorful description of the way some saw *pilpul* in seventeenth-century Ashkenaz: "[One who engages in *pilpul*] starts out asking a question on the Talmud or on Rashi or Tosafot. He then points out a contradiction between them. He then shows how all the answers to the contradiction still lead to contradictions in some other texts. Finally, after asking a few different kinds of questions, he provides an answer that explains all of the seeming contradictions."[23]

Hannover's depiction is echoed by Shmuel ben Eliezer, who in his youth embraced the casuistic approach to study, but later (1764) criticized those whom he referred to as "insane" practitioners of *pilpul*:

> Such is the method adopted by those who study [*pilpul*]. . . . At the beginning of their discourse they ask a question, answer the question, then ask another question, and follow it by answering the question. They continue to ask and answer up to ten or so questions. After they have built up a whole tower based on these questions and answers, a learned man then comes to them and overturns the bedrock upon which they built this conceptual tower. And if a third person comes he will proceed to do the same and undermine everything the second person said and take the side of the first person. . . . In other words, they miss at getting at any truth of the issue. By learning Talmud in such a way they have wasted precious time.[24]

Shmuel compares pilpulists "to cantors who drone on for hours singing Greek melodies ruining peoples' prayer experience." His sharp denunciation of *pilpul* was shared by, among others, the Gaon of Vilna, who gave his approbation to the book *Darkhei Noam* in which Shmuel's comments appear.

The Gaon and Shmuel were responding to the curricula of elite Ashkenazic sixteenth- and seventeenth-century Jewish study houses (*kloizim*), which were divided over two semesters (or two parts of the day), with one part being spent on the study of *halakha* (Jewish legal codes) and the other spent on *pilpul*.[25] *Pilpul* complemented *halakha*—with *pilpul* being highly theoretical, and *halakha* insistently practical. But in their critics' eyes, both approaches (in their sixteenth- and seventeenth-century Ashkenaz iterations) were guilty of limiting the role of the Talmud.

Chief among those who lamented the neglect of the Talmud during this period was the Maharal of Prague, Rabbi Judah Loew (1525–1609).[26] Together with his brother Bezalel, he contested the very nature and purpose of legal codes.[27] Some rabbinic figures criticized *pilpul* but stopped short of condemning the study of codes. Others disapproved of the emphasis placed on code without commenting on *pilpul*. The Maharal, however, questioned both reigning systems of learning. His critique of code was primarily an attempt to hold on to the early medieval Ashkenazic preference for local custom as the decisive factor in legal adjudication. His voice was ultimately ignored: *pilpul* and code study remained the dominant modes of learning in European study houses for the next two hundred years.[28]

The influence of *pilpul* and legal codes waned in the early to mid-eighteenth century.[29] Some ascribe this to the republication of early Sefardic Talmudic commentaries such as those written by Nachmanides (1194–1270), Zerachia ha-Levy (1125–1186), and Yom Tov Asevilli (1250–1330). These medieval commentaries had fallen out of use in the heyday of *pilpul* but were reprinted in the eighteenth century, encouraging a revolution in "rational" text-based learning. For these interpreters, the Talmud was a text that had multiple and often conflicting opinions. In many instances, the medieval Sefardic commentators presented semi-historical or typographic explanations in their analysis of Talmudic literature.

This theory, however, leaves a number of questions unanswered: What were the currents that carried medieval Sefardic commentaries into early modern rabbinic learning circles? Why were these texts republished in the eighteenth century? If their dissemination prompted a "revolution," why did the Gaon, someone who leveled the strongest and most penetrating critique of sixteenth- and seventeenth-century *pilpul* and code learning, either have minimal access to these newly published texts, allow them to have only a negligible influence on him, or simply never think it important enough to harness them to his interpretive project?[30] If they are to exert influence, new texts need institutions to house them, a public to purchase them, elites capable of teaching them, and social and political conditions that will encourage their publication. The republication of these medieval commentaries, then, is more a symptom of the transformation of eighteenth-century Jewish intellectual history than its cause. More correctly, at the heart of this shift from code to commentary was the larger sociopolitical transformation of late eighteenth-century eastern European Jewish life and specifically the Gaon's commentary to Karo's great code.

The *Biur:* Its History and Sources

The Gaon's commentary to Karo's code, based on notes that the Gaon penned,[31] is so boldly idiosyncratic in its methodology and legal conclusions that his most prized student, Hayyim of Volozhin, claimed that the *Biur* was intended only for its author's own eyes.[32] The *Biur* is a four-volume commentary on the four volumes of Karo's *Shulchan Arukh: Yoreh De'ah, Even ha-Ezer, Choshen Mishpat,* and *Orach Chayyim.* To these four volumes the Gaon added, later in life, three volumes of supplementary comments. The supplementary comments occasionally contradict the original commentary, leading students of the *Biur* to ponder the Gaon's true position.

The politics surrounding the publication and reception of Elijah's writings deserve their own study, but a word is needed regarding the printing of the *Biur.*[33] Yisrael of Shklov, along with Menachem Mendel of Shklov and Elijah's children, published the *Biur* on *Orach Chayyim* in 1803 and the *Biur* on *Yoreh De'ah* in 1806. These printings announced a revolution in rabbinic history. The editors brazenly took the liberty of changing the *tzurat ha-daf*—"the page layout"—of Karo's and Isserles's code. For over a century, Karo's *Yoreh De'ah* code had been usually encased by *Siftei Kohen (The Lips of the Priest),* a commentary by Sabbatai ben Meir ha-Kohen (1621–1662), and by *Turei Zahav (Rows of Gold),* written by David ha-Levi Segal (1586–1667). These two works sat on opposite sides of each page of the *Shulchan Arukh, Yoreh De'ah,* and (in Segal's case also) Karo's *Orach Chayyim,* so as to present explanations and arguments concerning Karo's and Isserles's opinions. The first editors of the *Biur* replaced these and all other commentaries with the Gaon's commentary, suggesting with their aesthetic change that Elijah's commentary was more valid and relevant than those of his predecessors.

Thirteen years later, Ya'akov Moshe of Słonim (1779–1849) edited and published the *Biur* on *Even ha-Ezer*. Ya'akov Moshe followed Menachem Mendel's example and eliminated the established commentaries on *Even ha-Ezer* by the mid-seventeenth-century commentators Moshe Lima (*Chelkat Michokek*) and Shmuel ben Uri Shraga Feivush (*Beit Shmuel*). During the printing of this volume, many complained that once again Elijah's students were recklessly doing away with large tracts of the rabbinic tradition. Critics charged that Elijah's editors had replaced the accessible sixteenth- and seventeenth-century commentaries with a difficult text that only the elite could study. But the early editors ignored such complaints. For instance, in his introduction to *Yoreh De'ah* (Grodno: 1806), Menachem Mendel mocked "the masses who claimed that Elijah's *Biur* is too dense." Rebuffing his adversaries, Menachem Mendel remarked that prior to Elijah, Jewish learning had languished in the "dark ages." Elijah's commentary, he asserted, had "enlightened" a new generation of scholars. Ya'akov Moshe, however, was not permitted to be so flippant. In his introduction he reveals how, during the *Biur*'s printing, Hayyim of Volozhin had ordered that the Gaon's commentary should share the page with the earlier commentaries. This typographical alteration limited the revolution engendered by Elijah's work, but also made his ideas seem more "mainstream" and canonized them in rabbinic literature.

The fourth and final volume, the *Biur* on *Choshen Mishpat*, was edited and printed in 1856 by Meir Ya'akov Gintsburg (who purchased from Elijah's descendants all of Elijah's manuscripts on *Choshen Mishpat*).[34] Meir Ya'akov followed Ya'akov Moshe by leaving the original commentaries in place. He likewise adopted Ya'akov Moshe's editing style, which differed substantially from that used in the first two volumes. To explain: the first volumes, edited by Menachem Mendel, had merged Elijah's three-volume supplementary comments together with the original four-volume commentary. Sometimes the merging involved placing the supplemental comments immediately after the topically relevant text of the original commentary; in other cases, it entailed combining the original and supplemental commentaries into a single argument. This method, which made an already confusing work even more cryptic, drew harsh criticism from rabbinic figures.[35] Moreover, Menachem Mendel and other first editors of Elijah's material feared altering "one dot or letter of his [Elijah's] golden words."[36] They tried to copy Elijah's personal scribbles word for word and weave them into a commentary made for mass consumption. Their abundance of caution, however, turned into a fool's piety. Rather than preserving the clarity of Elijah's commentary, they made their teacher's writings incoherent. Ya'akov Moshe and later on Meir Ya'akov, by contrast, took pains in the third and fourth volumes to distinguish Elijah's original from his supplementary commentary.

In 1884, Avraham Kleinerman in essence sided with Meir Ya'akov and Ya'akov Moshe when he re-edited *Yoreh De'ah*, lambasting its first editors for creating a text "filled with mistakes and errors." He suggests that in straining so hard not to alter Elijah's language, they had distorted Elijah's original meaning. In his edition, Kleinerman put Elijah's commentary alongside writings by the earlier commentators and distinguished between Elijah's original and supplemental commentaries.[37]

But even after Kleinerman had polished the Gaon's "golden words," appreciating their beauty remained a pastime for only the most trained scholars. A typical comment made by the Gaon in the *Biur* assumes a familiarity with Talmudic texts from three or four very different tractates. The reader would be expected to know the positions of each Tanna (early sages recorded in the Mishnah) and Amora (later sages recorded in the Talmud) cited in the relevant Talmudic passages, as well as the medieval commentaries of Rashi, Tosafot, Asher ben Yechiel (1250 or 1259–1328), and Maimonides. Only then would he be able to turn his attention to the *Shulchan Arukh* and finally to Elijah's *Biur*.

The Gaon explains these source documents sometimes with only a ten-word statement that might cite three or four different authorities. For example, when Karo interprets the biblical injunction against sacrificing an animal with its child as referring to specific animals, Elijah comments: "See there [*Chullin*] 79b and in the Midrashic work *Torat Kohanim* [*Emor*, section 8, chapter 7]. But Rabbi Isaac Alfasi [*Chullin* 27b] and Rabbi Asher ben Yechiel [*Chullin* chapter 4, topic 3] say it also refers to a bull and not a non-domesticated animal, a sheep nor chickens." In other cases, he uses only six words to clarify folios upon folios of Talmudic text.

Elijah's concise prose typifies the art of commentary, surpassing in certain ways even the indispensable Rashi.[38] Rashi's commentary on the Talmud focuses on the text at hand, skillfully paraphrasing and at times quoting pertinent sources. But his comments seldom reach beyond the immediate text. He keeps readers focused, but denies them a sense of the vast textual fields from which the primary text draws its energy. Elijah's commentary, by contrast, ambitiously assumes that his readers have at their disposal the entire rabbinic canon. While explaining the primary text (Elijah almost never paraphrases or fully cites a secondary source), he provides the reader with a comprehensive, bird's-eye view of the subject.

The style of Elijah's commentary is unique in three respects: its economy of language, its sharp clarity of conception, and its profound originality. His frugality of language reveals more than the cribbed nature of note taking; it conveys his masterful control over his predecessors and his exacting mode of expression. Elijah himself thought that there were two styles of writing—an "explanatory" style, which is verbose and used to express ideas to the masses, and a "visionary" style. Elijah privileged the "visionary" style, claiming that it was the one adopted by the "knowledgeable and wise." For the intellectual elite, "linguistic verbosity leads the reader astray and is a stumbling block."[39]

The stylistics of Elijah's commentary reflects his privileging of an elite "visionary" approach. In his commentary to Karo's code, Elijah distills the arguments of Isserles and Maimonides. He explicates their positions in just three or four words, then marshals the very sources they employed to render a new reading.

Elijah's reading of the tradition is expressed with unrivaled certainty and clarity. He is undoubtedly the strongest commentator in the annals of rabbinic history, so strong that only codifiers such as Maimonides and Karo compete with his clarity of conception and certainty of position. This feature of Elijah's work is most remarkable given the nature of the genre he chose to employ. Unlike a code, a commentary bears the burden of interpreting myriad texts and ideas and of assembling background information. Too much information and the reader grows tired; too little and the reader may be left puzzled. Elijah's commentaries never tease with rhetorical questions, tip over with weighty introductions, tire readers with background texts, or test one's patience.

Hayyim of Volozhin once described Elijah's words as "stars that seem small from our perspective, yet the whole world stands beneath them." Hayyim realized the drawbacks to Elijah's style, admitting that "had we wanted people to appreciate them, we would have had to enlarge them. But we did not want to change the words that we found in his manuscript."[40]

Readers of the *Biur* are forced to play a game of intertextual connect the dots. Each source explains the other. Taken together they create a constellation that illuminates the interpretive history of the texts employed by Karo or Isserles. Most importantly, Elijah's comments usually lead the reader back to the way the law is discussed in the Talmud.

The Gaon's emphasis on the Talmud was only one of the ways in which his commentary differed from its predecessors. The *Biur*'s terse and compact prose breaks decisively with the verbose, long-winded style of the pilpulists. Even more noticeable is the markedly different nature of the questions and issues consuming his attention. The pilpulist traditionally starts an exposition of a Talmudic passage with the following query: "How can the text say x if we already know y (from another place)?" In one characteristic pilpulistic commentary on the Talmudic discussion of "The Merchants of Lud" (Baba Metziah 50a–50b), we are informed that "the first thing this commentary will do is offer an opening superficial explanation of the text followed immediately by posing a question that contradicts the assumptions of our explanation."[41] The anonymous medieval pilpulist answers his own question by proposing a *sevara mi-bachutz*, or "an implicit logic . . . that can be grasped by the reader and that is not explicitly stated in the text."[42]

By contrast, Elijah's glosses never pose questions, and rarely digress. Elijah's commentary plows through the thicket of rabbinic literature in the most direct course, undeterred by tertiary questions, until it reaches its conceptual destination. His interpretation of the primary text and his own thesis reinforce one another.

Unlike the practitioners of *pilpul*, Elijah does not assume that sacred texts must agree or even complement one another. Neither does he subscribe to the pilpulists' assumption of textual infallibility. In contrast to Elijah, for Campanton, the burden of biblical and rabbinic interpretation is placed on the reader. All rabbinic texts (Talmudic and even post-Talmudic) are *already* perfect, textual inconsistencies are illusory, and seeming contradictions emanate from the reader's limitations. Elijah, however, assumes that different texts have different levels of canonicity and thus require distinct interpretive lenses.

At the top of this hierarchy is the Bible, which Elijah considered a fully divine and thus errorless text. In his view, however, Talmudic texts can be emended (and thus perfected) by the human hand, an act that shows both that a particular text is worthy of the investment of attempting to perfect it, as well as that it has errors to fix. Karo's sixteenth-century *Shulchan Arukh*, for instance, was deemed neither quasi-divine nor worthy of emendation. The Gaon treats Karo (and other medieval interpreters) as an equal, so when Elijah disagrees with a position taken in the *Shulchan Arukh*, he does not emend its words—he rejects its authority. Menachem Mendel of Shklov claims that "he heard from Gra's holy mouth . . . that whereas for the Tosafot it was difficult to understand a certain section of the Talmud in tractate Shabbat, for him [Gra] it was absolutely clear." In case one might assume such statements were uttered rarely and in hushed tones, Menachem asserts that "many such statements were hurled from the Gaon's mouth on numerous occasions."[43] For medievals such as Campanton, the human reader is subservient to the text; for the Gaon, humanly authored texts are subservient to human wisdom and understanding.[44] And unlike the pilpulists, who sought to smooth over contradictions, Elijah considered it "well known that the author of the *Shulchan Arukh* contradicts himself, and there is nothing unique about this [*eyn ba-zeh klum*]."[45]

Responding to Elijah's habit of ignoring or rejecting medieval rabbinic authorities, the famed early twentieth-century rabbi Avraham Yeshaya Karelitz (1878–1953) remarked: "We relate to Gra in the following historical trajectory: Moses our teacher, Ezra the prophet, Rabbi Yehudah ha-Nasi [the redactor of the Mishnah], Rav Ashi [the redactor of the Talmud], Maimonides, and Gra. And he should be seen as one of the medieval sages and therefore he can strongly differ with them and specifically Rabbi Isaac Alfasi and Maimonides in a number of places. . . . Therefore one should not be surprised when he disagrees with the *Shulchan Arukh*."[46]

Karelitz's praise is more than a piece of mere reverence; it recognizes Elijah's power to reorganize the historical pecking order of rabbinic authority. To justify how Elijah could challenge even the most renowned of his medieval predecessors, such as Karo, Karelitz fashioned a new historical trajectory and dating system that treated the Gaon as though he belonged to the early medieval period.

Elijah's main point of contention with Karo had to do with the misreading of classical rabbinic sources, most notably the Talmud. Yisrael of Shklov noted that the Gaon often criticizes the *Shulchan Arukh* for failing to list—and sometimes even to follow—opinions expressed in Talmudic sources.[47] For this reason, the *Biur* can leave the impression that it is a commentary on the Talmud as much as on Karo's code. Elijah seeks in the *Biur* diachronically to attach Talmudic sources to the halakhic issue at hand, while at the same time synchronically to open new interpretive spaces for positions not mentioned in the codes of Karo and Maimonides. In his commentary on Proverbs, the Gaon writes: "One who studies without understanding the source of knowledge, but rather only to have a cursory knowledge of the material so that he may claim that he knows a great deal, makes himself poor. In the end, such a person will also forget even the cursory knowledge that he thinks he has acquired. This individual does not understand the source of his knowledge. However, those who understand the source of knowledge and know each law and its true origin will become wealthy in knowledge."[48]

Elijah's emphasis on the Talmud can be seen throughout his commentary and lies at the heart of his critique against Karo. For example, in *Yoreh De'ah* 46:1 Karo presents a list of various blessings one recites upon awakening, ranging from praising God for the ability to hear when one is awakened by the rooster's crow to thanking God for strength when putting on one's belt. Karo's list is roughly 110 words. Elijah's comments to Karo's list comprise no more than fifteen words, "and this list was arranged by Rabbi Asher ben Yechiel and Jacob ben Asher, but Alfasi and Maimonides compiled another list, and our version is different [than both lists] and is based on the Gemara [Berachot 60b]."

Elijah was far from the first to connect Talmudic sources to the *Shulchan Arukh*. The seventeenth-century Lithuanian rabbi Moses Rivkes (1590–1671), author of the *Be'er ha-Golah* and Elijah's ancestor, made such an undertaking his life's work. But familial ties were about the only thing the two scholars shared. Rivkes cites only the sources used by the *Shulchan Arukh* (which he found in Karo's other work, the *Beit Yosef*). Elijah, by contrast, wants to show the Talmudic basis for every law and textually justifiable custom. As Moshe Petrover explains, "Gra was not content with simply presenting the sources of laws to which he agreed with the *Shulchan Arukh* and Ramah [Isserles]. Rather, he reveals the sources to the places he disagrees with them [Karo and Isserles]."[49]

Against Maimonides

Elijah criticized not only Karo but also the originator of the medieval halakhic code, the great sage Maimonides (Moshe ben Maimon). He repeatedly points to places where Maimonides's interpretations are *dachuk* (forced) and *tamuha* (implausible).⁵⁰ Elijah's harsh words did not go unnoticed. Some have argued that the *Biur ha-Gra* on the *Shulchan Arukh* may be more accurately thought of as a *Biur* on Maimonides: "At times, even when the *Shulchan Arukh* did not adopt Maimonides's position and does not even make mention of it, Gra ignores the *Shulchan Arukh*'s comments and attempts to explain the opinion of Maimonides."⁵¹ So pervasive was this sentiment that the editors of the most recent and authoritative edition of Maimonides's code (published by the Frankel publishing house in 1982) lifted the *Biur* from the *Shulchan Arukh* and placed it beneath Maimonides's text.

Elijah's objections to Maimonides's legal rulings, however, reflect his more general criticisms of the medieval philosopher's inability—in his philosophical and legal writings alike—to take seriously the totality of the Jewish canon. Take, for example, this passage from the *Biur* (*Shulchan Arukh, Yoreh De'ah*, 179:6):

> All those who came after Maimonides differed [because they did not use his rational allegorical interpretive technique]. For many times we find magical incantations mentioned in the Talmud. Maimonides and philosophers claimed that such magical writings and incantations, and devils, are all false. However, he [Maimonides] was already reprimanded for such an interpretation. For we have found many accounts in the Talmud about magical incantations and writings. . . . Philosophy is mistaken in a majority of cases when it interprets the Talmud in a superficial manner and destroys the *sensus literalis* of the text. But one should not think that I in any way, Heaven forbid, actually believe in them or in what they stand for. Rather, [what I mean] is that everything written follows according to its *sensus literalis* but all of these things have within them a hidden essence [that must be interpreted]. Not the meaning of the philosophers who toss [the *sensus literalis* of the text] into the refuse, but the [inner essence] of the masters of truth.

Scholars from the past century have interpreted this passage as a denunciation of philosophy.⁵² Jacob Dienstag, for example, has argued that Elijah criticized Maimonides for his reliance on philosophy even as he fully supported Maimonides's legal outlook. Claiming that this was also the opinion of the young J. B. Soloveitchik,⁵³ Dienstag insisted that Elijah opposed the study of philosophy.

Yet Dienstag's view fails to account for passages elsewhere in which Elijah invokes Aristotelian terminology and philosophical vocabulary borrowed from Maimonides's *Biur Milot ha-Higayon*.[54] In his commentary to Proverbs, for example, Elijah employs Aristotelian terms like material cause, formal cause, efficient cause, and finite cause. More importantly, in his *Aderet Eliyahu* (Genesis 1:2), Elijah himself quotes Maimonides's *Guide of the Perplexed*. Finally, Elijah went out of his way to procure a copy of Aristotle's *Ethics*. This evidence has led some to suggest that Elijah objected to a materialistic or epicurean lifestyle often associated with philosophy, but not to philosophy's heuristic value.[55]

It is most likely, however, that Elijah is concerned with philosophical essentialism. As I have shown elsewhere, his comments are directed not at studying philosophy,[56] but rather at the way a philosophical approach may ignore linguistic nuance. Elijah's words quoted earlier seem to refer to Maimonides's position on parables. Maimonides writes: "Parables are of two kinds. In some of these parables each word has a meaning, while in others the parable as a whole indicates the whole of the intended meaning. In such a parable very many words are to be found; not every one adds something to the intended meaning. They serve rather to embellish the parable and to render it more coherent or to conceal further the intended meaning; hence the speech proceeds in such a way to accord with everything required by the parable's intended meaning."[57] Maimonides here distinguishes two types of parables: in some, specific words are to be taken seriously and examined carefully, whereas in others, the gist can be discerned without paying close attention to each word.

Elijah objects to Maimonides's distinction and more generally to his philosophic hermeneutics.[58] With regard to Talmudic texts (as opposed to medieval rabbinic literature), Elijah argues that each word must ultimately have both a specific "external" and "internal" meaning. Ultimately, no word in a Talmudic text is solely aesthetic or poetic.

In particular, Elijah maintains that Maimonides ignored texts that did not conform to his notion of rationality. In Elijah's view, references to demons, magic, charms, and other irrational objects and ideas cannot be ignored—though not per se because he thinks they actually exist. (Elijah's admirer Menashe Illya [1767–1831] recalled "that according to his memory," Elijah actually "criticized those who interpreted Midrash according its literal sense when the Midrash went against reason."[59]) Rather Elijah's criticism against Maimonides was based on the belief that one cannot simply deny or gloss over the anti-rational elements that consistently appear in rabbinic literature. Either they belong in the text or they do not; if they do belong, they must be explained. By not including or explaining them, Elijah contends, Maimonides and "philosophers" fail to take seriously the very words and signs that make up the rabbinic tradition.[60]

In short, Elijah's problem with Maimonides revolves around issues of linguistics, interpretation, and hermeneutics and not whether it is permissible to read secular philosophy. This distinction highlights the profound difference between two of Jewish history's most important intellectual tendencies: medieval scholasticism and what might be broadly termed modern rabbinic textuality.[61]

Elijah's religious identity is rooted less in whether he accepts philosophy as a valid religious discipline than in the responsibility he feels toward the Jewish canon.[62] In Elijah's view, Maimonides's code and philosophic worldview fail to express this responsibility. That is, Maimonides's code (the *Mishneh Torah*) and his philosophic treatise *Guide of the Perplexed* essentialize biblical and rabbinic texts, omitting those opinions that Maimonides deemed marginal or legally insignificant.

Maimonides was a careful reader of the Talmud, but he was unapologetic about his essentialism. In a letter to Pinchas ha-Dayan, he writes:

> You should know that every book . . . always adopts one of two ways (structure and styles): either that of a monolithic code (*chibbur*) or that of discursive commentary (*peirush*). In a monolithic code, only the correct subject matter is recorded without any questions, without answers, and without proofs, in the way Rabbi Judah adopted when he composed the Mishnah. The discursive commentary, in contrast, records both the correct subject matter and other opinions which contradict it, as well as questions on it; on all its aspects, answers, and proofs as to why one opinion is proper and another improper; this method, in turn, is that of Talmud.[63]

Even here, in a letter where Maimonides attempts to refute charges that he has made the Talmud unnecessary, he still defends the ways his *Mishneh Torah* departs from the Talmud's style, legal theory, and worldview.

In sum, whereas Maimonides's code favors the style of the Mishnah, featuring only "correct" rulings, Elijah's writings highlight the method of Talmudic commentary that accounts for "both correct statements and other statements that contradict them." Elijah challenges followers of Maimonides who used the monolithic style of code to downplay Talmudic study.[64] In so doing, he reintroduces texts and positions that Maimonides's code had disregarded.

The Gaon was perhaps the first great halakhic authority whose writings on the *Shulchan Arukh* were not produced for mass consumption nor to be enacted as public policy. Why Elijah stopped short of presenting his own halakhic opinions and never offered his own code is a question that confounds his biographers and later scholars. According to his son Avraham, Elijah cryptically claimed that "the heavens were not prepared" and that he was unwilling to compromise "his own understanding."[65] Still, it is puzzling that Elijah composed a commentary on the *Shulchan Arukh* but not on the Talmud itself. One possible reason may be that in the eighteenth century it was much easier to purchase a set of Karo's code than to acquire a full set of the Talmud.[66] When Elijah wrote his commentary on Karo, the *Shulchan Arukh* had already become an essential work in rabbinic circles.[67] Attaching his words to this authoritative text guaranteed Elijah a wide readership.[68] Scholars of Karo's work were forced to contend with Elijah's pervasive criticisms of code-based learning.

In the end, Elijah's critiques turned his students away from Karo's work and toward the Talmud itself. Whereas code study and commentaries on the *Shulchan Arukh* flourished in seventeenth and the eighteenth centuries, during the early nineteenth century Talmudic study rose to prominence in Jewish learning circles. Though difficult to ascribe such intentions to Elijah himself, by challenging the code movement from within its own textual confines, on its own terrain, the Gaon's *Biur* ushered in a new era.

Nineteenth-Century Rabbinic Life

"Massive and swift." That is how the historian Haym Soloveitchik describes the influence and dissemination of Elijah's *Biur* in the nineteenth century.[69] Hayyim of Volozhin was the first to note the *Biur*'s significance. He suggested that prior to Elijah,

> Many tried to throw away the burden and importance of studying Talmud. They attempted to extrapolate only legal rulings [from the Talmud]. For they said, "for study which is practical it is worth studying the *Shulchan Arukh*." Even when they learned Gemara, it

was only for intellectual purposes. There were those who stopped learning Talmud altogether and were satisfied with studying the *Shulchan Arukh* alone. Anyone who will read this work written by our holy teacher Rabbi Eliyahu the Hasid will see that his approach is to reveal and make note of the Talmudic origins of the study of the *Shulchan Arukh*.[70]

To be sure, these remarks should be tempered somewhat, given that among the masses of nineteenth-century Jewry, pictures and paintings of Elijah sold better than did Elijah's dense writings.[71] Difficult texts like the *Biur* demand great amounts of time and energy from publishers and even more effort from readers. The *Biur*'s readership should instead be compared to that of other imposing works published in the late eighteenth century. Immanuel Kant's *Critique of Pure Reason*, for instance, was at first met with deafening silence. If we were to judge the influence of Kant's philosophy based purely on the immediate reception of his *Critique*, we would have to conclude, like Frederick Beiser has, that "no one had the time, energy, or interest to read, let alone review, such an imposing tome."[72] Indeed, it would take seven years after its publication until virtually anyone even understood Kant's arguments.[73] In terms of these works' immediate reception, there certainly were more students of the *Biur* than there were early readers of the *Critique*.

The ban placed by Elijah's children on publishing his notes attests to the demand for the Gaon's writings. A "Kol Koreh" (a call announcing a prohibition) attached to the 1799 first printing of *Shenot Eliyahu* (Elijah's commentary to *Mishnah Zeraim*) is telling in this respect:

> We have found people who are repeating laws, customs, and commentaries in the name of our master and teacher, the Gaon and true Hasid, who has been laid to rest. As we can attest from his writings and notes in both halakhic [*nigleh*] and kabbalistic [*nistar*] spheres, it is well known that the Gaon never issued these incorrect words. We suspect that there are those who would like to halakhically enforce these statements and to put them on paper and bring them to a printing press. In order to prevent this from occurring, it should be publicized in all the houses of study that one should not listen or believe any statement said in the name of the Gaon without proper authorization.[74]

As Elijah's notes circulated rapidly and broadly, his students recognized immediately the intellectual transformation that was being ushered in by their teacher's method of Talmud study. Hayyim of Volozhin's grandson Avraham Simcha explained:

> For more than two hundred years, the whole universe of learning was mistaken in its approach to study, except the great one of his generation [Gra] . . . who suddenly brought the light of God upon us. . . . He focused his efforts on producing new ideas but according to a straight way of learning . . . and he only set his eyes on what was true. His style of learning was publicized in all our provinces. It is known in all provinces that from him onwards we have been given light to study according to the correct path.[75]

These sentiments are seconded in the candid intellectual autobiography of Rabbi Yehudah Epstein (d. 1879), which describes the Gaon's influence on the earliest curricula of the Volozhin yeshiva. In his work *Minchat Yehudah* (Warsaw: 1877), Epstein documents *pilpul*'s saturation of late eighteenth-century eastern European learning. He also bemoans that code study had dulled eastern Europe's sharpest and wisest rabbinic minds. As he explains, "The corrupted system of learning reigned supreme even in the works of great scholars who spent their days immersed in pilpulistic study, first studying codes then studying Talmud." He mentions how Moshe Ze'ev Alshikh from Białystok, author of *Ma'arot Tzvaot* (Minsk: 1810), once visited Yehudah's childhood hometown in Hulsk (eighty-four miles from Minsk), where he stopped to lunch with Yehudah's father. Alshikh told Yehudah's father explicitly "that he learned the *Tur* [an early code written prior to Karo's] before he would study a page of the Talmud." "Had Alshikh learned Talmud before the codes," remarks Yehudah, "he would have been three times as knowledgeable as he was." Those like Alshikh bore responsibility for the "thousands who came to study and the miracle it would take for one to emerge with any teaching ability." In the very first years of the nineteenth century, Yehudah continues, "only in Vilna and its surroundings did people adopt the style of learning developed by our teacher Rabbi Eliyahu the Gaon, the Hasid." Yet soon thereafter, Elijah's approach took other eastern European learning centers by storm. Yehudah notes, "After Rabbi Hayyim of Volozhin arranged and institutionalized the Gaon's approach within the curricula of the Volozhin Yeshiva, students began studying the Talmud first and codes second." Subsequent commentaries ceased to be treated as primary literature.[76]

During the first decade of the nineteenth century, Elijah's method (as presented in the *Biur*) garnered followings well beyond his home base of Vilna. Yosef Grueaver from Słutzk (1796–1864), Belarus, who studied in Volozhin, visited Yehudah's home and "had already adopted the Gaon's approach to learning." Yosef followed Elijah's approach presented in the *Biur*. "He taught me tractate *Berakhot* with the commentary of *Rashi*, *Tosafot*, and the Rabbi Asher ben Yechiel," Yehudah recalls. "Now I was able to study the *Shulchan Arukh Orach Chayyim* with the commentaries of the *Magen Avraham*, the *Turei Zahav*, and the *Biur ha-Gra* and now I understood each one of the commentators and each of their interpretations and how they read the Talmud and how they ruled." Yehudah specifically mentions that his teacher, Yosef, showed him that each commentator "had their own way of reading the Talmud."[77] Finally, in 1817 Yehudah's father invited Hayyim of Volozhin's student Rabbi David Tevel ben Moshe Ruben (1790–1861) to his house to study with his son.[78] For a year and half, they studied together in the manner laid out by Elijah, eventually reading through all the tractates of the Talmud in a cursory style in order to improve their general knowledge of Talmudic literature.[79]

Epstein's education represents in a microcosm the way that Elijah's *Biur* shifted rabbinic study away from codes back to the text of the Talmud. Epstein's claims regarding the *Biur*'s place in the Volozhin curriculum are supported by documents attesting to its founder's own involvement in editing Elijah's works.[80] According to Yosef Zundel of Salant (1786–1866), Hayyim "instructed his students to review what they had learned in the *Shulchan Arukh* and to study intensely the *Biur ha-Gra*."[81] Yisrael of Salant (1810–1883), founder of the Mussar (ethical) movement, writes in his introduction to his journal *Tevunah* (Königsburg: 1861) that his teacher Yosef of Salant placed special emphasis on studying the *Biur*.[82]

As we have seen, Epstein, Salanter, and Hayyim of Volozhin made practice the telos of study. Even as they followed the *Biur* in identifying the Talmud as their primary text, they were still, like Elijah, born into a world where *halakha* was a critical component of learning. "In Volozhin at the beginning of the century," Etkes notes, "students also studied *poskim* (legal decisors). . . . Later on, students stopped studying *poskim* at the Volozhin Yeshiva."[83]

Elijah's *Biur* encouraged a dramatic shift away from the codes of law and toward Talmud study as the locus of Jewish life. But such a shift could not have occurred in the absence of a set of social and political developments, chief among them the emergence of the modern yeshiva.

From *Kehilah* and Code to Yeshiva and Talmud

The Volozhin yeshiva once again placed the Talmud atop the pedestal of privileged texts. While Elijah did not found the yeshiva, his students saw in his worldview a path leading to its creation.[84] Studying the Talmud, distancing oneself from the public sphere, and creating a universe around the act of learning—practices central to Elijah's approach to scholarship and to life—formed the ideological bedrock of the Volozhin yeshiva. While rabbinic learning institutions had existed for fifteen hundred years, the modern yeshiva, as exemplified in Volozhin, distinguished itself from its predecessors in significant ways—all of which were related to a weakening of the centralized *kehilah* structure, the delegated communal governing system that was responsible for the social, political, and religious upkeep of European Jewry from the sixteenth through the eighteenth centuries.

As mentioned earlier, the *kehilah* functioned almost as a Jewish state within a state. Though each town and district had its own unique structure of authority and degrees of political autonomy, in most instances *kehilot* were comprised of lay and rabbinic arms whose responsibilities ranged from judging civil disputes, to collecting taxes for local authorities, to allotting residential rights. For example, in 1741 the Dubno community noted that "our lord the prince has commanded that all civil suits between Jew and Jew be brought before a *beit din* and damages cases shall be brought before the judgment of the chiefs of the *kehilah*, sitting together with the rabbi."[85]

Local rabbis, however, were hired by the local lay-controlled governing boards, which also set rabbinic contracts and determined the extent of rabbinic authority. Rabbinic duties primarily consisted of serving the community and adjudicating disputes, not running large-scale learning institutions. Such communal handicaps did not stop rabbis from trying to broaden their intellectual and spiritual authority. In some instances rabbinic contract negotiations hinged on the number of students that the local *kehilah* admitted into the city.[86] Those granted entry learned side by side with local townspeople in study houses funded by the community. Eventually, students who were given residential rights were encouraged to move out of their host towns to take public rabbinic posts elsewhere.[87] Such measures ensured both that a town was not overrun or impoverished by students and that the local chief rabbi would not establish an alternate base of support. Rabbis were beholden to the community, not to their students.

Many of the lay-controlled bodies considered their learning institutions to be service providers for their own local needs. Study houses, according to this view, were not just the domain of the learned elite, but in some instances also functioned as "courts of law, and gathering houses for the *kehilah* leadership."[88] They were often attached to the main synagogue and the *kehilah*'s meeting place, thereby providing intellectual substance to the community and spiritual legitimacy to the *kehilah*. The Italian rabbi Simcha Luzzatto (1582–1663) notes how in his day "there are yeshivot and houses of study where numerous students sit and study the local laws and Jewish laws, because in these lands Jews are given autonomy to judge their own disputes in all disagreements, in civil and criminal matters."[89] Thus from the sixteenth century through the late eighteenth century, when an Ashkenazi community appointed a rabbi it was customary, although not always possible, to also offer him the positions of "head of the town's legal court" and leader of its "house of study."[90]

These local *kehilot* were autonomous; in certain instances, however, they reported to larger regional councils such as the Va'ad of Lita (the Lithuanian Council) or the Va'ad Arba Artzot (Council of the Four Lands), which also possessed two governing arms—rabbinic and lay. As Edward Fram notes, the Council of the Four Lands gave rabbis governing authority. For example, it threatened to close any printing press that dared to publish a book without approbation. The rabbis also recognized the council's right to regulate the marketplace with ordinances that supplemented halakhic decrees to allow for the free flow of credit.[91] Both of the rabbinic and lay arms, according to Adam Teller, at least originally derived their authority from the Polish king, who used the council to help collect taxes and used the appointed rabbis as a means to consolidate power and exert social control.[92] This symbiotic relationship between laity and the rabbinate on the one hand and the Polish government on the other led historians like Jacob Katz to conclude that the *kehilah* provided at least the trappings of a somewhat centralized halakhic body: "It sought . . . to create permanent institutions of justice with authority over broader areas, and, indeed, did so in all regions where the secular government did not specifically prevent this development."[93] On average, the council was convened twice a year. It was attended by local leaders, rabbis of the main *kehilot* and the districts, and sometimes by judges elected for the purpose of settling quarrels between the leaders and the districts.[94]

It should thus come as little surprise that those rabbinic authorities most instrumental in the founding and upkeep of the council were also some of the strongest proponents of code study. One of the council's founding members, if not the founder, was Mordekhai Jaffe, author of the legal code *Levush*. In 1572, almost immediately after he once again began working on his code, "he returned to Poland where, for the next forty years he served as . . . the head of [what was then still] the Council of the Three Lands."[95] That Jaffe, Falk, and Horowitz (all students of Isserles) served on the rabbinic arm of the council signified a harmonious relationship between civil and religious law throughout the eastern European Jewish communities.[96]

In 1764, the Council of the Four Lands was abolished by the enlightened Polish king Stanisław-August Poniatowski (1732–1798). According to Richard Butterwick, Stanisław's rule was marked by repeated attempts to transform the Polish Commonwealth into a modern state like England, where he had studied.[97] Stanisław's decision to eliminate Jewish self-rule coincided with other widespread reforms. These included mandating that all taxes would be paid directly to the crown treasury (bypassing established mediating corporate bodies), and reducing the nobility's power by consolidating all forces under his domain.

Stanisław's measures further eroded the centralized institutions capable of enforcing *halakha*.[98] By the late eighteenth century, notes Moshe Rosman, Lithuanian Jews were increasingly seeking out gentile courts.[99] As we saw in our discussion of the Hasidic-Mitnagdic battle, even rabbinic figures sought out non-Jewish authorities to arbitrate their disputes.

Some have suggested that the deterioration of centralized legal authority inspired the Gaon of Vilna to attempt to establish a privately funded learning institution. According to Samuel Joseph Fuenn (1819–1891), "Gra realized early on that the sanctions against the Hasidim would not be implemented. He set out to found a *beit midrash* (house of study) in 1780."[100] The *beit midrash* mentioned by Fuenn was the Slutzki house that stood outside the courtyard of the main synagogue and was purchased by Elijah with funds that he had raised from his own supporters.[101] While it seems that Elijah set up a learning operation in the Slutzki house,[102] it was not formally recognized as a *kloiz* (an elite learning house), perhaps due to resistance from community leaders.[103]

Hayyim of Volozhin likely spent time in the Slutzki house during his frequent visits with Elijah. Yet Hayyim would succeed where the Gaon, for all his influence, could not: he would create the first modern yeshiva.[104] Hayyim would build his institution not in bustling Vilna, but in the more sparsely populated town of Volozhin. Hayyim's yeshiva functioned independently of any communal governing structure, and it recruited both students and funds from across European Jewry. Rather than submit to the whims and control of an organized legal and political body (the *kehilah*), the yeshiva distributed monies as it saw fit. As Stampfer argues, "The method of fund distribution of the Volozhin yeshiva differed fundamentally from the relationship that existed between localized houses of study and the *kehilah* organization. Those who learned in study houses were dependent on the benevolence of the *kehilah*. . . . Now in Volozhin the monies from private funders were given directly to the yeshivot, without any *kehilah* intermediary."[105]

The new methods for raising and distributing money accompanied more profound changes in both content and culture. At Volozhin the relationship between the communal leadership and the hundreds of students who spent their days learning on the yeshiva's benches "was neither good nor bad; it was simply non-existent."[106] Volozhin cut the financial and social cord between the yeshiva and the public organ of the *kehilah*, which made study a private religious initiative, independent of public structures and communal demands. This transformation signaled not so much a decentralization of authority as the creation of an entirely new center of authority. Students were no longer beholden to their parents or to communal leaders; they were "children of the Yeshiva."

Volozhin also granted students newfound freedoms in their studies. It was "focused on being a place of study and not a place that promoted the teaching of law—and certainly not a place that groomed communal rabbis."[107] While in the sixteenth and seventeenth centuries the *kehilah* had forced students from across central and eastern Europe to study the same tractate of Talmud,[108] the Volozhin curriculum allowed each student to create his own Talmudic curriculum.

In the modern yeshiva the Talmud was no longer seen as merely a text subservient to law and governance; it became once again a primary text.

Later in the nineteenth century this freedom and individuation of the Talmud (vis-à-vis law) encouraged an ethos of *chidush* (innovation) in study. In the new ethos, one was not only permitted but encouraged to offer new insights into passages, even if those insights radically contradicted accepted social and legal norms. While the idea of *chidush* has been present in all stages of rabbinic history, it became most prominent during the rise of the modern yeshiva at Volozhin. The emphasis there on originality, brilliance, and intellectual achievement as its own end, unfettered by public or instrumental demands, reinforced the yeshiva's independence from communal financial resources and further alienated the yeshiva from the public.[109]

Well into the twentieth century, taking a public rabbinic position was looked down on by the yeshiva leadership. In imitation of Elijah, yeshiva students sought to unburden themselves from the weight of familial and public duties, so a rabbinic role was thought to be a step in the wrong direction.[110] In fact, according to Meir Berlin (Bar-Ilan), a communal rabbinic appointment was considered a fallback option for those who failed to secure the funds needed to stay within the yeshiva system. The study of both practical rabbinics and (to a lesser degree) practical *halakha* was made secondary to the study of the most obscure and non-practical sections of the Talmud—such as those detailing the temple sacrifices.[111] This distancing of the practical and scholarly spheres extended to the enforcement of established laws. In the modern yeshiva what was at stake was no longer practical *halakha*, but the cogency and creativity of one's learning. The coercive power invested in the *kehilah* was replaced by a linguistic *milchamta shel Torah* (war of Torah). In such a battle, parties "fought" each other not with police forces, economic sanctions, pillories, or communal excommunications, but with the thrusts and parries of verbal sparring.

The sparring sometimes had very real consequences. The fight between the students of Naftali Tzvi Yehudah Berlin and those of Hayyim Soloveitchik (1853–1918), for example, led to great consternation and distress within the yeshiva. In some cases, students or teachers felt compelled to break away from the yeshiva and set up their own intellectual fiefdoms.

Hayyim of Volozhin's invention of the yeshiva has often been understood as a two-edged response that addressed both a Hasidic movement that eschewed structured learning and (later) the Maskilim who mocked the study of rabbinic texts as pilpulistic. But the rise of the yeshiva, like other major movements of the period, might also be attributed to the weakening of the centralized *kehilah* structure that governed pre-modern European Jewish life, and more generally to the privatization of religion in the modern state. Gershon Hundert has rightly observed that local *kehilot* continued to hold sway over various eastern European Jewish communities—as seen in the Vilna community's ability to prevent the spread of Hasidism within Vilna. Still, the fall of the centralized *kehilah* contributed to wholly new models of centralized leadership and governance.

The pattern of this transformation conformed to what Charles Taylor calls the modern "internalization" of religious life. In the modern period, religion did not simply die off or adopt certain liberal principles, but rather was structurally transformed. The inward turn didn't only mean a turn to the self, as we see in certain Protestant theologies. On the contrary, the turn inward was something that affected various institutions in different sectors of society.[112] Just as the centralized *kehilah* system gave way to the yeshiva as a centralized body for traditional Jewry, practical code-oriented learning gave way to the theoretical study of the Talmud. The yeshiva became the center of authority for rabbinic Jews in modernity—a place for re-engagement with a Talmudic corpus that privileged learning over adjudication, and pedagogic persuasion over coercion.[113] This development in rabbinic learning is most strikingly formulated in a footnote by an editor or censor that marks every other page of Yisrael Salanter's halakhic and homiletic journal, *Tevunah* (1861). The note reads:

> All laws concerning monetary transactions have absolutely no practical authority. For we follow the law of the land. And this is the meaning of the great principle of "the law of the land is final." We study, analyze, and debate monetary topics in the same way in which we study the laws of donations to the temple, tithes, sacrifices and purities, which are not practiced today. They are discussed only in terms of fulfilling our duty to study the Torah.

While one cannot discount the pressures of governmental censorship that may have contributed to this position, still it marks an important development in rabbinic history. As Elchanan Reiner correctly notes, "Diverting attention from the actual ruling to the text itself, namely to the very practice of interpretation, constitutes a dramatic shift in the history of knowledge."[114]

That shift mirrors an even more dramatic transformation in Jewish social history. Privatized religious institutions, persuasion, polemics, and study replaced political bodies and public legal coercion as the defining centripetal forces for modern non-Hasidic Jews. The Volozhin yeshiva was founded not in opposition to the cultural and intellectual upheavals of the nineteenth century. It was itself built on the most modern of assumptions, the separation of public and private spheres. This privatization of religious life, however, created the conditions for what would become a hostile relationship between the yeshiva and the followers of the Mussar movement. Hayyim of Volozhin, for instance, did not see his yeshiva as standing in opposition to modernity or the world at large.[115] But Yosef Yoizel Hurwitz (1849–1919), in founding the Novardok yeshiva, adamantly asserted otherwise:

> We cannot connect with the world because the world has distanced itself from us. . . . The world and the Yeshiva are diametrically opposed to one another. . . . In these dangerous times, we need to further contract ourselves into the four cubits of Torah. We need to create a spirit of privatization that calls upon us to distance ourselves from the outside world and choose the life of the yeshiva as a place for learning and acting.[116]

For Hayyim, the privatization of religion provided him with a means for establishing a yeshiva, not fighting against an outside world. In contrast, Hurwitz's words, written nearly a century later, succinctly describe the eventual radicalization of religious life engendered by this privatization.

Hurwitz's disengagement from the public sphere does not necessarily indicate a diminution of rabbinic political leadership. In many ways, the strident tones he and others used indicate that rabbinic authorities enjoyed more power (over a much narrower sector of Jewry) than they possessed during the seventeenth and eighteenth centuries, when they had been subservient to the dictates of communal leaders. From Hayyim of Volozhin and his son Isaac (d. 1849), on through the family Sofer, to Isaac Elchanan Spector (d. 1896), rabbinic figures were revered by broad swaths of nineteenth-century eastern European Jewry for their knowledge and piety. These figures were not inclined to reestablish anything like the *kehilah* structures that had governed pre-modern Jewish communities.[117] To their flocks they were towering giants, even if they barely appeared on governmental radars.[118]

The sources of authority for eastern European rabbinic leaders also changed during this transition. During the late nineteenth and early twentieth centuries the Va'ad Arba Artzot, the Council of Four Lands, was replaced by the Va'ad ha-Yeshivot, the Council of the Yeshivot, which covered the myriad learning institutions throughout eastern Europe. In addition, the pre-modern title "rosh va'ad arba artzot" (head of the Council of the Four Lands) was replaced by that of "rosh va'ad ha-yeshivot" (head of the Council of the Yeshivot), the title held by Chaim Ozer Grodzinski (1863–1940). Traditional Jewry, no longer functioning as a state within a state, was creating a universe revolving around study.

The privatization of nineteenth-century religious life was a twofold process, with "Hasidim refocusing the center of religious life towards the rebbe's court, [while] the Mitnagdim refocus[ed] the center of religious life around the Yeshiva."[119] For the greater part of the nineteenth and early twentieth centuries, the yeshiva struggled to remain standing next to the Hasidic court and the secular university.[120] In his well-known poem *Ha-Matmid* (1898), the poet and ex-Volozhin student Hayyim Nachman Bialik offered a lyrical romantic description of the tired, disheveled, and hunchbacked yeshiva *bachur* (boy). There was more than a kernel of historical truth in the poem. The emptying and closing of yeshivot such as Volozhin and the rise of Hasidic courts throughout Russia might imply that Elijah's worldview, at least by the middle of the nineteenth century, had lost out to the Hasidic model. Indeed, for nearly a century, the yeshiva model was rejected by an increasing number of Jews.

But starting with the establishment of the first Hasidic yeshiva in Polish lands in 1880 by Shlomo Halberstam (1847–1906), Hasidism began to adopt elements of the Mitnagdic ethos.[121] Indeed, over the following decades, the yeshiva became a central organizing institution for much of the Hasidic world. Already by the first quarter of the twentieth century, "every important Hasidic court organized study for young people within the framework of yeshivot."[122] Elijah's legacy would endure.

6

The Genius

JEWISH HISTORY'S GREATEST INTELLECTUAL FIGURES ARE IMMORTALIZED BY their masterpieces: Rashi by his *Commentaries*, Maimonides his *Mishneh Torah* and *Guide of the Perplexed*, Mendelssohn his *Jerusalem*, Freud his *Interpretation of Dreams*, Einstein his theory of relativity. Some rabbinic figures became known by the very name of their magnum opus, as Moses Sofer did after writing the *Hatam Sofer*.

Elijah of Vilna wrote perhaps with greater breadth and variation than any other figure in Jewish history. There is hardly a biblical, rabbinic, or kabbalistic text on which he did not comment. Yet in popular lore, the legend of Elijah's genius eclipses anything he penned. The Gaon's celebrity was less the fruit of any particular writings (which were tremendous but little appreciated by the masses) than the result of his reputation for intellectual brilliance. Before Einstein, Freud, and Marx, the Gaon inspired modern European Jews who saw intellectual achievement as a means to attain upward social mobility.

The concept of the Jewish genius is often thought to have originated with nineteenth-century western European race scientists and Jewish intellectuals' internalization of their theories.[1] From Francis Galton's blatantly anti-Semitic *Hereditary Genius* (London: 1869), to Anatole Leroy-Beaulieu's philo-Semitic *Israel among the Nations* (Paris: 1893), to Joseph Jacob's chauvinistic "The Comparative Distribution of Jewish Ability" (London: 1891), the legend of Jews' superior intelligence is often discussed in the context of modern western European history. Among Jews themselves, however, it originated in a very different cultural milieu—eastern Europe in the first half of the nineteenth century—and with very different connotations.

Following Elijah's death in 1797, a dedicated coterie of students began transmitting stories of his life, learning, and genius to a wide audience of scholars. In particular, the Gaon's children and students sprinkled the introductions to Elijah's commentaries with personal testimonies.[2] In time, biographers patched together these firsthand testimonies into a portrait of intellectual excellence. The most famous of these biographical monographs was Yehoshua Heschel Levin's *Aliyot Eliyahu* (Vilna: 1856), which was the first to offer lay people a discursive picture of the Gaon's life, beliefs, and contributions to Jewish history. Levin's book was not simply a hagiographical paean but a carefully composed work with specific institutional and ideological commitments. According to its author, the book aimed to "understand Gra's traits and actions"[3] by detailing his behavior "in his home, in his neighborhood, in his town, and with all of Israel."[4] It was read not only by those taking advantage of new educational opportunities but also by lay people who were attracted to these new opportunities. Levin composed the work only a few years after leaving the Volozhin yeshiva, which was founded by his grandfather-in-law and Elijah's prize student, Hayyim.[5] *Aliyot Eliyahu* was the product of a large-scale collaborative project involving leading rabbis across eastern and western Europe. Among those intimately involved in its production were David Luria (1798–1857) and Ya'akov Tzvi Mecklenburg, the rabbi of Königsberg.[6] These Boswells, however, had never even seen their Johnson; born after the Gaon's death, they relied heavily on written and eyewitness testimony from his immediate students and children.

Aliyot Eliyahu was republished three times over the next twenty-five years (Stien: 1860, Vilna: 1874, Vilna: 1875), and appeared in numerous forms throughout the second half of the nineteenth century. In May 1857, Abraham Mapu (1806–1867), the nineteenth-century Lithuanian Maskil and Hebrew novelist, bemoaned the sales of his own work, *Ayit Tzavua* (*The Hypocrite*, 1858): "Until now I have been able to secure only 600 subscriptions for my work *Ayit Tzavua*. . . . That said, what am I supposed to do? They have printed the book *Aliyot Eliyahu* that tells lies about the great man, Gra. The boors of our people have become wealthy through its publication."[7]

Levin's work followed a less popular *Ma'aseh Rav* (Vilna: 1832), in which Yissaschar ben Tanchum (1769–1846) had accentuated the Gaon's pietism.[8] The publication of *Aliyot Eliyahu* and *Ma'aseh Rav*, respectively, was followed by the increased printing of the Gaon's most popular works: his Passover Haggadah used by lay people at their seders,[9] and his farewell letter to his wife, "Alim li-Terufah" ("Leaves for Healing"), which was written to her from Königsberg during a failed trip to the Land of Israel. Originally published in Vilna in 1800, the letter is a concise and clear statement of a select set of the Gaon's beliefs and values, highlighting his learning, piety, and positions on child rearing and domestic life. Its simple style and subject matter made it accessible to a broad audience.[10]

The mass printing of "Alim li-Terufah" in the second half of the nineteenth century coincided with the mass production of the Gaon's portrait. Most Gaon iconography is based on an 1825 drawing by the Polish painter Józef Hilary Głowacki (1789–1858). To be sure, Głowaki's painting was not an actual portrait, but rather an imagined picture of the master. Today a lithograph of it is housed in the Polish National Museum in Kraków. Elijah sits upright with his left hand folded over the top edges of a large tome, his right hand gently arched on a quill. It "emphasizes the scope of his erudition, which encompassed, in addition to Torah knowledge, a broad knowledge of the sciences."[11]

By 1827, Jews as far away as Amsterdam were requesting the Gaon's portrait.[12] Improvements in printing and the popularization of the Gaon's biography in the second half of the century in western Europe only multiplied such requests. After virtually all of the Gaon's commentaries and all the formative biographies of him had been published, the Gaon's picture and letter to his wife began to be consumed en masse.[13] Some pictures cast him as an "enlightened" figure dressed in Polish garb, with a clock hanging above his head and an inscription beneath him testifying to his mastery of the seven sciences. Other homes, however, were decorated by what Rachel Schnold calls the folk-traditional portrait, in which Elijah appears in phylacteries and draped in a prayer shawl; no indication is given of his knowledge of the seven sciences.[14] In still other residences, such as the one depicted in Yehudah Pen's painting *Divorce*,

Jewish children grew up looking at a portrait of Elijah hanging beside one of Moses Montefiore, the "Gaon" (as it were) of philanthropy and communal leadership.[15]

Still, the differences between these depictions of Elijah are not as great as the similarities. Nearly all of the portraits show the Gaon with features identical to Głowacki's original painting, and in the same left profile. "The original local artist," postulates Zusia Efron, "saw the prototype and it remained in their visual memory for generations to come."[16] The valuation of Elijah's iconography mirrored a trend witnessed among educated Russians, who following the Napoleonic Wars saw icons not as objects of worship but as works of art to be treasured as a "cultural legacy" that "was itself a modern enterprise."[17] The mechanical reproduction of Elijah's picture in the second half of the nineteenth century brought the Gaon spatially and humanly closer to European Jews. If *Ma'aseh Rav* and *Aliyot Eliyahu* made the Gaon's ideas accessible to those who were not equipped to study the Gaon's kabbalistic and legal commentaries, then "Alim li-Terufah," his Passover Haggadah, and his portraits made the Gaon an intellectual hero to those who were illiterate in the rabbinic tradition.[18]

These popular texts and images marked a migration of the Gaon's reputation from the rarified confines of the study house to the home. That is, during the nineteenth century—an age when people's "sense of the universal equality of things" had increased exponentially—the Gaon's writings and legacy ceased to be restricted to scholars and began to move the masses (with whom he had never engaged in his lifetime).[19] By the centennial of the Gaon's death in 1897, it was observed that there is "not a single Jew in Russia, be he ever so ignorant, who did not know something of the 'Wilnaer Gaon'—[and] pictures him as an old man, bending his *talith* and *t'philin* over a large scroll, in which he studies Mishnah, Talmud, Poskim, and all other branches of knowledge."[20] By means of these popular representations, even those who never entered into a study house could identify with the Gaon's legacy of intellectual excellence.

Defining the Gaon

The term *gaon* has a long history with various meanings. In biblical literature, *gaon* connotes majesty, dignity, or exaltedness, as in the phrase "u-pri ha-aretz le-gaon u-le-tiferet" ("and the splendor of the land [will give] dignity and majesty," Isaiah 4:2). But it also connotes arrogance, as in the phrase "ge'ah ve-gaon ve-derekh ra" ("pride, arrogance, and the evil way," Proverbs 8:13). In the ninth century, Gaon was a title bestowed on Babylonian scholars who occupied positions of political and intellectual leadership.[21] Like the Catholic Church's idea of "Magisterium" (the authoritative teaching of the pope or bishops),[22] the title Gaon designated an official role as teacher and leader. Marina Rustow argues that originally "embedded in the title *Gaon* . . . was a claim to jurisdiction over all of Israel."[23] The title, she adds, contained "powers and prerogatives that were the bearer's exclusive preserve . . . including dispensing titles, stipends and shares of tax revenue."[24] In the medieval period, *gaon* was used as an adjective to describe the exaltedness of a rabbi's political position.[25] The title Gaon modified those of rabbi and head of court, as in "the exalted rabbi." In the medieval period, a rabbinic leader was referred to as Gaon not because of his intellectual abilities alone, but rather because of a combination of knowledge and political leadership.[26]

For much of the medieval period the honorific was extended only to those who held an official rabbinic appointment and performed a communally sanctioned function.[27] Menachem ben Shlomo, also known as Meiri (1249–1310), explains the origins and meaning of the title:

> What is the Talmud referring to when it mentions three orders? It refers to the order of the Holidays (*Mo'ed*), Women (*Nashim*), and Damages (*Nezikin*); and one who is familiar with each of them was referred to by the title *Chakham*. And what does the Talmud mean when it mentions four orders? It includes the order of Sacrifices (*Kodshim*); and one who is familiar with these four orders is called *Rav*. And what does the Talmud mean when it mentions six orders? It includes the orders of Agriculture (*Zeraim*) and Purities (*Taharot*); and one who is familiar with these six orders is considered to be a *Gaon*, and this term GAO"N numerically alludes to the sixty tractates of the Talmud found in these six orders. That said, the term was never invoked unless one was officially appointed as the head of a yeshiva.[28]

For Menachem, the title Gaon connotes a specific level of mastery of the Talmud. Even so, knowledge alone is not sole criteria for designating someone a Gaon. Only those appointed as the head of a yeshiva could rightfully bear the honorific.

Meiri's requirements seem to have waned by the end of the sixteenth century. In a legal query sent from Crete to the distinguished Safed rabbi

David ben Zimra, known as Radvaz (1479–1573), a petitioner wants to know whether a wealthy Cretan family may put their coat of arms on the synagogue and attribute the title of Gaon to one of their ancestors. While Radvaz is heavy-handed about blocking the coat of arms from being etched onto the synagogue, a helpless sigh accompanied his response to the family's devaluing of the title Gaon. "In previous generations," reflects Radvaz, "it was restricted to only those who knew all the six orders by heart, but in the past few generations it has been the custom [to crown undeserving individuals with the title]."[29] The practice of assigning the title Gaon to one who has mastered sixty tractates appears again in *Sefer ha-Tishbi*, written in 1541 by the controversial Renaissance scholar Elia Bachur (1468–1549).[30] Elia's words are echoed in turn by the seventeenth-century rabbi David Conforte (1617–1678?),[31] and by the eighteenth-century bibliophile and traveler Hayyim Joseph David Azulay (1724–1807) in his work *Shem ha-Gedolim* (Livorno: 1774–1788).[32] In the seventeenth and even eighteenth centuries, a theoretical consensus still existed on the meaning of the term *gaon*, but practically speaking such definitions were being ignored.

Some claim that by age twenty Elijah was referred to as Gaon; certainly by age thirty-five he was addressed in this way,[33] even by his brother.[34] After his death his students struggled to explain why their teacher, who never occupied an official communal position, warranted the title. To do so, they redefined the term to conform to Elijah's intellectual prowess. Thus a seemingly banal panegyric to the Gaon by Menachem Mendel of Shklov in his introduction to Elijah's commentary to *Pirkei Avot* (Shklov: 1804) opens with the following words:

> In the introduction to his work the *Mishneh Torah*, Maimonides wrote:
> "all those wise men that followed the publication of the Talmud,
> adding to it, whose names were known based on their knowledge,
> were called Geonim." I heard from the holy mouth of our teacher the
> "Gaon olam"[35] that they gave the honorific "Gaon" to all those leaders
> who came after the Talmud because of what it says in Song of
> Songs 6:8: "sixty is kingship"; this refers to the sixty tractates of law.
> And in the early generations people would not allow someone to be in
> a position of political leadership until they knew by heart all sixty
> tractates of the Talmud. . . . Thus, they called the head of each genera-
> tion GAO"N which numerically translates into sixty which alludes to
> the sixty tractates [he had mastered].[36]

In this commonly quoted but oft-misunderstood passage, Menachem Mendel of Shklov attaches the "exaltedness" of the title Gaon first and foremost to intellectual achievement, not political standing. Political leadership, in this view, is merely a function of one's fund of knowledge. Becoming a "Manhig Yisrael" (a political leader of Israel) is the result of *geonut* (intellectual stature) and not vice versa. Knowledge, not political position, determines whether one merits the title Gaon.

More importantly, Avraham Danzig (1748–1820), in his eulogy for Elijah, homiletically redefines the very nature of the term *gaon:*

> And he was the Gaon of Israel. For all would say: "praiseworthy is this Gaon in your town [of Vilna]." The name Gaon numerically alludes to a mastery of all spheres of knowledge. The letter *gimel* is numerically equivalent to the three parts of the Bible: Torah, Prophets, and Writings. The letter *aleph* is numerically equivalent to the study of one God [metaphysics]. The letter *vav* is numerically equivalent to the six orders of the Talmud. The letter *nun* is equivalent numerically to the fifty gates of wisdom. And the Gaon of Israel mastered all of these spheres of knowledge.[37]

In this reading, the Talmud is subsumed under a much larger canopy of knowledge. Elijah's *geonut* includes all forms of wisdom, ranging from the Bible to metaphysics, to the fifty gates of wisdom. Entirely ignoring the original usage of the term, Avraham defines Elijah's *geonut* as something akin to genius, an overflowing intellectual capability that cannot be contained by any one discipline.[38]

In what must have sounded to his audience as the most impolitic of comparisons, Avraham goes on to demonstrate Elijah's *geonut* by contrasting him to two other recently deceased scholars, "Rabbi" Shaul Shiskas and "Rabbi" Hayyim, the *moreh tzedek* of Vilna. Unlike those rabbis' "public beauty" (*hadar*), "our Gaon" was so special that "his body was an ark" within which rested "a Torah scroll . . . and all of the Torah was set before him."[39] Avraham also compares Elijah to "a Menorah, symbolizing his mastery of the seven branches of wisdom. For who knew more," Avraham asks, "than the Gaon in grammar, mathematics, and metaphysics?"[40]

This description of Elijah as genius was promoted throughout Europe by Głowacki's 1825 picture, which bore a caption in Hebrew and Polish: "For who knows more than the genius (*gaon*) and greatest wonder of his generation and light unto Israel? Who knew more than any other person in the seven sciences? Rabbi of the Diaspora Elijah of Vilna." The central importance of Elijah's legacy in redefining the term *gaon* as genius was first noted by the linguist Ya'akov Kana'ani in his *Otzar Lashon ha-Ivrit*. The entry for "Gaon" reads: "The Gaon of Vilna; (from a foreign influence, genius); a term given to someone with exceptional intellectual or creative abilities."[41]

The Gaon's students were impressed by two aspects of their master's genius. They were awed, first, by the sheer range of his intellectual abilities. Elijah commented on what was considered at that time to be every major intellectual discipline: kabbalah, Talmud, science, geography, engineering, mathematics, and music. Second, they were mesmerized by his intellectual fecundity: he was able to learn and generate novel ideas at an astonishing rate.

Accentuating Elijah's genius entailed downplaying other biographical tropes. For example, Elijah's biographers could have adopted the narrative that Peter Brown describes as the "holy man" (referring to remarkable piety),[42] or what Pierre Hadot terms a "sage" (noting profound wisdom),[43] or what Peter Burke describes as "great men" (identifying the ability to wield great social power).[44]

The decision to stress Elijah's genius developed in tandem with two other trends: the Hasidic usurpation of the mantle of piety in eastern European Jewish culture, and the emergence of various opportunities of higher learning for eastern European Jews, first in the modern yeshiva and later in the university. When the Volozhin yeshiva opened its doors in 1802, it was the first time that young men from all economic and social backgrounds were afforded the opportunity to study. One of its students, the nineteenth-century Zionist writer Zalman Epstein (1860–1936), explains, "Our teacher Eliyahu of Vilna was known in Volozhin as a shining model and the right pillar of traditional Judaism. From the yeshiva's inception, [Elijah's] splendor and spirit radiated, not however under the title 'the Pious One,' as they called him in Vilna, but only under the heading of 'Gaon.' "[45]

In Vilna, Epstein relates, Elijah was referred to by both of his titles ("Gaon" and "Hasid") as late as 1875. But in Volozhin, eastern European Jewry's Oxford, his *geonut* was emphasized. Epstein's perceptive linguistic point is echoed by Levin, who sought to consolidate Elijah's legacy around his *geonut* rather than his *hasidut*. "All those living in the Diaspora," Levin claims, "know him simply by the name 'Gaon,' which expresses the wonderment of his knowledge, which towered over all those of his generation. Only a few called him by his other name 'Hasid.'" To support this claim, Levin points to the very titles given to the master's work by his students: "Biurei ha-Gra, Hidushei ha-Gra."[46] By 1888, even the *moreh tzedek* of Vilna, Shlomo ben Yisrael Moshe (1828–1905), would be forced to admit that contrary to those who were still trying to claim the Gaon's pietism as a model of true *hasidut*, "the Gaon ha-Geonim, the leader of the Diaspora, the Gaon and Hasid, our teacher Rabbi Elijah, may his memory be blessed, is now simply referred to by the name 'the Gra of Vilna.'"[47] Even though only relatively few attended yeshivot, the idea of the genius provided the means through which the yeshiva ideal was popularized—in other words, the means through which people identified with a specific nineteenth-century educative movement centered on the yeshiva.

As Levin and Epstein intimate, Elijah's extreme lifestyle could be understood as stemming from his piety (*hasidut*) rather than from his genius per se. In other words, Elijah could be viewed as having two distinct personas—Genius and Hasid. Elijah himself drew from both models of religious scholarship. On the one hand, Elijah follows those sixteenth to eighteenth century eastern European rabbinic authorities whose customs express the early German pietists' sectarian impulses, critical social tendencies, and emphasis on man's internal state of being.[48] On the other hand, his practices derive from a tradition of Aristotelian virtue ethics as reinterpreted in the work of Maimonides and others.[49] Like Maimonides, the Gaon believed that practice and habituation contributed to ethical edification.[50] According to the Gaon, "There are two types of human characteristics: those that have been given to one at birth and those that one acquires through practice." Sages, he writes, "transform themselves by dressing in a different manner . . . even when their original actions and nature point in an opposite direction."[51]

The Gaon's students, however, saw his pietistic behavior not simply as "endowing the self with certain kinds of capacities that provide the substance from which the world is acted upon,"[52] but also as reinforcing traits uniquely befitting a master of knowledge.[53] For example, his biographers consistently stress the intellectual aspects of Elijah's Talmudic interpretation,[54] while downplaying or ignoring the pietistic elements associated with reciting sacred texts, such as those displayed by Hasidic masters "who emphasize the importance of the recitation, the oral performance, and even the orality itself involved in reading."[55] The Gaon's son tells us that his father read "Talmud out loud in a pleasant and awesome manner."[56] Yisrael of Shklov's introduction to *Pe'at ha-Shulchan* (Safed: 1836) records that the Gaon reviewed the entire Talmud every month. Menachem Mendel of Shklov reports that the master read each tractate "many hundreds of times." The Gaon's grandson claimed that his grandfather read at least a hundred pages of Talmud every day.[57] According to the authors of *Aliyot Eliyahu*, by the time Elijah reached his mature years he could recite seventy pages of Talmud in half an hour.[58] These testimonies reflect the Gaon's stated belief that "understanding entails knowing something through and through. To have such knowledge requires one to read out loud."[59] But such testimonies ignore the long-standing kabbalistic, spiritual, and pietistic dimensions involved in the act of study and the recitation of sacred texts.

The triumph of Hasidism in the first half of the nineteenth century coincided with the transformation of Elijah from "the Gaon" and "the Hasid" into simply "the Gaon." Elijah's biographers did not merely ignore his pietistic behavior; they reinterpreted it so that the explanation of how he achieved his genius would fit contemporary ideas about intelligence and achievement. Thomas Carlyle, for instance, defined genius as "the infinite art of taking pains," suggesting that genius results from a regimented set of extreme practices, habituations, ergonomic structures, and a retraining of senses. This kind of genius is best exemplified in Roland Barthes's description of Einstein as a "genius so lacking in magic that one speaks of his thought as a functional labor analogous to the mechanical making of sausages, the grinding of corn, the crushing of ore: he used to produce thought, continuously, as a mill makes flour."[60] Genius was not a quality endowed, but a labor to be pursued.

The Gaon's disciples quantified and measured their teacher's genius in terms of hours spent studying, techniques employed to maximize one's intellectual potential, and abilities to manage one's relationships emotionally. Elijah certainly possessed gifts that only nature could bestow, but these biographers maintained that it was only by taking painful measures that he was able to actualize those gifts. These measures included unfettering himself from his predecessors, contemporaries, family members, and the general public, thereby assuring that his individuality was never compromised by any outside source.

Starting with the comments of Hayyim of Volozhin (in his introduction to *Sifra di-Tzniuta*) and continuing in the writings of Luria and Levin, the Gaon is depicted as refusing all *genii* (protective spirits), or *maggidim* (divine intermediaries).[61] Neither his students nor his biographers saw his genius as something bestowed on him by the accidents of nature or as a form of divine inspiration. Elijah did not follow the poets or prophets and *have genii*; Elijah *was* a genius.[62] Instead of being overcome by a *furor poeticus*, Elijah is depicted as being in control of his own intellectual capacities. In taking this approach, Elijah's biographers were rejecting notions of genius still prevalent in eastern European Jewish life. These folk notions were not only promoted by Hasidic masters, as one might expect; even Moses Hayyim Luzzatto (1707–1746) was still claiming in 1727 that his knowledge came from heavenly powers.[63]

This idea of self-generated genius reflects Jonathan Bate's observation that the very term "genius" drastically changed in the late eighteenth century. It no longer connoted a type of "tutelary deity" or even one's "horoscope." It now meant a unique kind of humanly endowed "capacity."[64] Indeed, the Gaon ushered in an age when genius was thought to be self-generated and self-contained. Scholars point to the Gaon's rejection of mystical intermediaries as indicative of his rationalist leanings. Elijah, they claim, did not believe in ghosts or otherworldly beings.[65] This is not so: the Gaon affirmed that one could theoretically receive knowledge through divine intermediaries, but he was adamant that none of *his* knowledge came from such sources.[66]

The same assumptions behind Levin's claim that Elijah rejected divine intermediaries account for his insistence that the Gaon rejected doctors. This claim does not reflect an attempt to convey "traditionalist" or anti-modern tendencies (although such tendencies do appear elsewhere in the Gaon's oeuvre). For only a few pages before Levin's assertion, he claims that the young Elijah aspired to become a doctor himself.[67] Furthermore, the authors of *Ma'aseh Rav* admit that the Gaon heeded doctors' advice and cut back on his use of candles.[68] *Aliyot Eliyahu*'s emphasis on the Gaon's reluctance to consult doctors was part of its agenda of affirming that Elijah's genius had nothing to do with outside help—divine, medical, or otherwise.

These claims are reinforced by a colorful story told by Hayyim of Volozhin.[69] A group once asked Hayyim for his opinion regarding miracle stories told about certain rabbis (probably certain Hasidic rebbes). "Do you believe in such things?" they asked. In response, he recalled a Talmudic tale (BT Shabbat 53b) about a man whose wife died after giving birth, leaving her husband to care for the newborn. This man lacked the means to pay for a wet nurse, but a miracle occurred and milk flowed from his own breasts. The Talmud records that some sages believed the man must have been very righteous to merit such a miracle. Hayyim, however, objected, echoing the other position recorded in the Talmud: "How awful is this man that God had to change the order of creation for him!"

The Gaon, Hayyim explains, did not have to rely on miracles or divine inspiration, nor did he need the help of any external sources, "for everything he achieved, he did on his own." Other geniuses in Jewish history, such as the Sefardic rationalist Maimonides, were celebrated as well, most notably in western Europe. But for those in eastern Europe, Elijah was a homegrown icon, a figure who appealed to rationalists, Jewish nationalists, and the religiously observant.

For the Gaon's biographers, achieving one's potential requires not only personal will, but also protection against outside threats, including received ideas—political, cultural, or scholarly—that could compromise one's individuality. These sentiments appear in the Gaon's own attempt to avoid the polluting societal influences of monetary and sexual pressures. Isaiah 28:9 reads: "To whom shall one teach the knowledge of instruction? To whom shall one explain a message? [To] those weaned from [mother's] milk, removed from the breasts." The Gaon comments:

"To whom shall [one] teach knowledge to provide instruction to others?" This refers to the teaching of the written law. And "to whom shall [one] explain a message?" refers to the oral law. And who is such a person? One who has been "weaned from the milk." This refers to one who has overcome desire. And one who has been "removed from the breasts"—this refers to one who has overcome lust. For there are two types of evil: desire and lust. Desire is located in the act of eating and drinking, and things that the body enjoys. Lust is located in things that one acquires through money, such as the purchasing of homes, fields, and vineyards. And in what ways are these things related to milk and breasts? When a child is breastfeeding he is doing so for the milk which is a source of life, yet once he has been weaned from them he still desires, not the milk, but the breasts themselves. This desire for the breast is the result of one misidentifying the breast as a life source, even though after one has been weaned the breast is merely being sought after as a form of lust. And the same is true regarding money which is a lust. And the mantle of Torah is not possessed until a man has detached himself from these two traits.[70]

In effect, Elijah describes how one achieves sovereignty over one's own existence—how one acquires the rights and possibilities that flow from independence. Sovereignty requires detachment from desire and lust.[71] Desire and lust are necessary; they move us to eat, drink, find shelter, and ultimately to serve God. Yet they can severely compromise a human being's individuality and moral fortitude.[72] The enslaved person misidentifies the means (the breast and money) as ends, whereas a sovereign individual overcomes the fetishes of material acquisition and sexual pleasure. Intellectual leadership requires absolute freedom, that is, total independence from all forms of influence.

Much in the same way that Ralph Waldo Emerson's essay "Self-Reliance" became a blueprint for a nineteenth-century romantic notion of genius,[73] the Gaon's biographers used his self-reliance and resistance to social conventions to create a model of *geonut*. The Gaon's biographers and students maintained that "Gra's achievements were not the products of any teacher or external forces."[74] The Gaon's later biographers stressed these elements too: "All of Gra's feats were produced only from himself."[75] By the mid-nineteenth century, he is described as "never fearing anything in this world even for a minute; all forms of indigence, sickness, and loss never saddened him."[76] Heinrich Graetz saw Elijah as "isolated" from all corrupting influences. "In point of fact," Graetz claims, "it seemed as though from his youth he had been afraid of following the errors of his compatriots, for he attached himself to no special school, but strange to say, was his own teacher of Talmud."[77] Shmuel Yosef Fuenn depicts him as "not having a teacher, nor studying in yeshivot." Rather his achievements "were generated by the very novelty of his own intellectual abilities; he was not fettered by accepted custom and practice."[78]

The fears that an external force might impinge on the Gaon's individuality, autonomy, and unique abilities—and might thereby compromise his genius—inform the Gaon's own writings, as well as those of his students and biographers.[79] Early biographers and students alike saw every aspect of Elijah's life as coming to bear on the formation of his genius. When his biographers report on his eating habits or familial relationships, they are not indulging their readers' curiosity about the mundane or pietistic practices he adopted. Rather they regarded his genius as a precious seed whose blossoming depended on very specific social conditions and intellectual freedoms.

Discipline and Distance

The Gaon's anti-social tendencies color many of the stories told about him. He did not have friends in the common sense of the term, and his involvement in political and social affairs was limited to the most pressing of matters. His taciturn nature inscribed itself, too, in his commentaries. Rarely does he cite anyone in his kabbalistic works; his legal writings mention only a select group of rabbinic figures and post-Talmudic texts; and his biblical commentary records mainly sources from the rabbinic period and a few medieval commentators. Unlike the eighteenth-century Hungarian sage Moses Sofer—whose lengthy responsa for contemporary rabbis, students, and lay people touched on a wide range of socially pertinent questions—the Gaon wrote no responsa, commented only on ancient texts, and cited none of his contemporaries. This left the impression of someone unengaged with his surroundings. His studies did not involve any kind of discourse ethics, where normative and ethical truths are discovered by engaging others and examining their arguments. Elijah counseled others to avoid situations in which they would have to confront those whom they knew had opinions different from their own.[80]

Elijah's students interpreted these sentiments not as their master's attempt to develop a closer relationship to God, but rather primarily as a way to ward off those who might upset the equilibrium necessary for intense study. Sometimes such interpretations entailed describing Elijah in anti-pietistic terms. The nineteenth-century rabbi Yosef Zundel of Salant, for example, maintained that Elijah "limited speaking in general to the point of only talking about matters pertaining to the performance of a mitzvah. On the Sabbath," he claimed, "Gra was of the opinion that one should not speak at all, but rather only study."[81] The Gaon himself said as much in a letter to his wife, Hannah, written before his failed trip to Israel. He warned her that "only reluctantly did the law allow one to express greetings on Shabbat. . . . Train yourself to sit alone."

Sitting alone, however, was not to be confused with mystical silences or "speaking fasts" (*ta'anit dibbur*) that were intended to draw one closer to

THE GENIUS

God. Rather, the Gaon is portrayed as refraining from speaking so that he could increase his learning potential. Yisrael of Shklov describes the Gaon "sitting all day in his study with the window shades closed, studying by candle light so as not to be disturbed by any individual."[82] Levin has the Gaon sitting "in a room alone with the shades shut, lighting candles to allow him to read and see only what was before his eyes."[83] The darkness beyond the candle's light acted as a barrier between the Gaon and the rest of the world.[84] In at least one popular nineteenth-century picture, the Gaon sits in front of a table with a book and candle. The portrait is captioned: "Good is the eye that sees him, a candle was put in front of us, the great Rabbi the Gaon, the great one of the generation, light of Israel, like an angel in his knowledge of the seven sciences, the teacher of the Diaspora Elijah ben Solomon."[85] Here the candle no longer functions as a pietistic prop as it did in medieval kabbalistic rituals—or even in the way it appears in a story told about the Gaon's candle-lighting ritual when completing a commentary—but rather as a means to focus on the books before his eyes and block out everything else around him. The Gaon, Hayyim Volozhin recalled, did "not look beyond four handbreadths in front of him."[86]

This willed contraction of space finds a parallel in the Gaon's privileging of the present over both the weight of the past and the endless possibilities of the future. The Gaon, it might be said, favored the moment closest to him. David Luria explains that according to the master,

> Time is man's friend and lover. Time can be broken up into three parts [past, present, and future]. And one should never say, "Oh, how great were the days of old." For all of time is only experienced in the "present." For the past has passed and can only be employed to teach or instruct us. Regarding the future, one should not worry about the troubles of tomorrow. And one should not think about the future for it is not his; as it is written, "one should not worry about the world" for you do not own it. . . . Thinking about the future is like one who desires to eat meat but the meat is not his.[87]

The Gaon equates time and desire. Those looking into the future seek worlds, objects, and events beyond their ken and thereby lose focus on their studies. The "now" reins in one's appetites, training one to appreciate strictly what is necessary to master knowledge. One befriends time, living with it, not for it (in the future) or against it (in the past). In explaining how the Gaon's notion of space, time, and self was brought to bear on his accumulation of knowledge, the nineteenth-century rabbi Yissaschar Ber Meritova claims that the Gaon said, "Each man must be mindful that he is the only person in the world; he should live as if he had only one day; and that in this whole world there is only one page and nothing more."[88]

Gastronomy, Ergonomics, and Circadian Rhythm

The Gaon's students saw his eccentric and extraordinary lifestyle as but another opportunity to describe the practices that cultivated his genius. The Gaon's intellectual achievements, they claimed, required an ascetic diet. We are told that his daily food intake consisted of "a thin slice of stale bread no larger than a measurement of two olives soaked in water." This miserable portion was reportedly served to him "once in the morning and then again in the evening."[89] More disturbing, the Gaon was said to have "ingested spoiled food."[90]

These testimonies reflect the Gaon's belief that there is no greater "need" in this world than "bread."[91] Food's functional value is often forgotten in gastronomic excess, where one eats not to satiate or survive but to indulge oneself.[92] His students claim that Elijah worried so much about bread's unrecognized "evil" ingredients that he even questioned the well-established custom of partaking in delicacies during Sabbath meals.[93] Miniscule portions guarded his appetite against enslavement to any particular "taste."

Even the act of swallowing was described by his children to be a regimented process, consisting of "quickly pushing anything he ingested to the back of his throat so as not to savor any enjoyment."[94] Savoring the taste only delays the inevitability of ingestion and ultimately, loss. Unfulfilled desire creeps to the fore after conquering or consuming. As the Gaon's quasi-fictional follower Reb Hersh Rasseyner stated so bluntly to his disputant, the writer Chaim Grade, "all the pleasures of life are like salt water: the more a man drinks, the thirstier he becomes. That's why we want a Torah that will leave no room in us for anything else."[95] By curbing his appetite and minimizing his dependencies, Elijah could consume greater quantities of information. As the authors of *Aliyot Eliyahu* describe it, the Gaon worked hard at "devising strategies against his passions" for his "war against the predispositions of his body." The Gaon's discipline was attributed to an attempt to restrict enjoyment to the realm of knowledge. Whereas the morsels of bread were made to be bland at best, the "*ta'am*" (taste/reason) of the Torah was full of tang.

The Gaon's children and Hayyim of Volozhin also invoke the metaphor of taste to describe their master's circadian cycle, writing, "He almost never tasted sleep."[96] Unlike the Byzantine monk Alexander the Sleepless, who stayed awake in order to enter prayer trances, the Gaon limited his sleep in order to maximize study time.[97] We are told that Elijah adopted a polyphasic sleep cycle, dividing his rest time into four half-hour intervals, three during the night and one during the day. While the Gaon himself claims that "anger and pain are what prevent a person from falling asleep,"[98] his students claim that his lack of sleep was carefully calibrated. Similarly, the Gaon was known to arise at midnight to take part in the ancient pietistic custom of mourning for the destruction of the Temple. Yet later biographers claim that the Gaon awoke at midnight strictly for the purpose of studying the Talmud, for "at these hours it is most appropriate to study the oral Torah in depth."[99]

What we would today call "time management" features prominently in biographies on the Gaon as well as in those drawings of him with a clock in the background over his left shoulder. In some pictures the clock is attached to a bookshelf; in others it is suspended in a kind of halo. While the clock suggests scientific tendencies and modern time, it also symbolizes a maximization of every minute for the sake of study.[100] By studying full-time, with a candle lit and the shades drawn, Elijah made his body "think" that "nights were days,"[101] mastering his zeitgebers, the signals that normally tell the body when it requires sleep.

In case the Gaon's eyes did not fall for his tricks, he is said to have stayed awake by taking advantage of the harsh Vilna winters, where temperatures could drop as low as −30 Celsius. His children remember their father refusing to purchase a furnace for his study house. Yisrael of Shklov offered a dramatic description of the Gaon "dipping his legs in a bowl of ice water" to ensure that he would remain awake while studying.[102] This extreme practice can be traced back to certain medieval pietistic circles with which the Gaon was familiar. As Ivan Marcus documents, Judah the Hasid, a medieval Jewish pietist (d. 1217), told penitents that to be forgiven, "if it is winter . . . break the ice [on a river] and sit in the water up to your nose." In other texts, one is instructed to "put his legs into a container filled with water until his legs became stuck in the ice."[103] It is not clear to what extent the Gaon actually performed these practices;

what is significant is his students' claim that Elijah employed these techniques to help him attain his intellectual goals.

Sentimentality and Emotion

The Gaon's children and his students also interpreted his idiosyncratic familial behavior and pietistic practices as necessary for his genius. "You will see," Avraham explains, that "everything my father accomplished over the course of his life, from beginning to end, was the result of diligence, wholeness, and dangerous practices."[104] Avraham and Yehudah candidly admit that their father swore off all forms of sentimentality and natural emotional ties with his immediate family. Their father, they report, "was never disturbed by any worry or sadness."[105] In one startling vignette, they recount that as their father was preparing to leave on a journey of self-reflection, his favorite child, Shlomo Zalman, fell gravely ill. Elijah refused to change his plans. Only after a month away "not thinking about his family or his children" did the Gaon find himself on the toilet one day wondering about the boy's well-being (for one is not supposed to think thoughts of Torah then). He immediately returned home.[106]

The episode was not anomalous. His children divulge that Elijah never once wrote a letter to any of them. Nor when he saw them, once every year or two, "did he ever ask about their work or their well-being." His sons note that their father did not even think to inquire after their homes, their children, or their livelihoods. After a very enjoyable hour of speaking with them, the Gaon would hurry back to his studies so as not to waste time.[107] The Gaon made the same impression on his favorite grandchild, Ya'akov Moshe of Słonim, who confirms his father Avraham's impressions: "I was in Vilna for over three years and when I visited Gra, he did not inquire after my household or my children until a few weeks into our meetings."[108]

Elijah's students and children reveal these painful memories to highlight the high cost exacted by the Gaon's genius. David Luria in *Aliyot Eliyahu* records a story about the Gaon's grandchild (and Luria's in-law) Zalman Ber. When Zalman's mother, Pesia Bassia (Elijah's daughter), was pregnant with him, she traveled to Vilna. Because "numerous children she previously bore had died in their youth, she sought compassion (*rachamim*) from her father." Elijah granted his distraught child only a few words: "It will be a positive omen if you name your next child after the last one who died." Otherwise, the Gaon "did not waste time speaking

160   THE GENIUS

with her."[109] Luria justifies the Gaon's behavior, noting that his advice bore out fruitfully: Zalman Ber survived and had children himself.

Similar overtones can be heard in the Gaon's *Peirush al-Kamah Aggadot* (Vilna: 1800), where he suggests that one should follow the Babylonian Talmud's injunction (Tractate Eruvin 22a) to "blacken" oneself toward one's children as a "raven" does to her fledglings. The "raven," the Gaon explains, is "an allegory for the scholar who becomes cruel to his children [so that] he can spend all of his time studying the Torah." In almost Nietzschean terms, the Gaon claims that though this "cruelty" goes against the grain of human nature, such unfettering must be carried out if one is to soar to higher intellectual heights.[110]

We might say, generously, that the Gaon was heeding Plato's advice in the *Symposium* that eternal ideas are more desirable than ephemeral children. The Gaon himself argued that "students are better than children . . . for children only fulfill a physical commandment of procreation, but students fulfill a spiritual commandment attached to the soul of the Torah."[111] Still, the seemingly callous nature of the Gaon's relationships is striking.

Commenting on these emotional sacrifices, Levin claims that the Gaon believed "what his heart desired was not the ultimate good; it was better to resist yearnings."[112] The Gaon writes as much in his letter to his wife: "I know you are aware of how my heart moans for having left my children and my books." The Gaon, they say, "was very happy to see his children" but was simply unable to fit them into his life of study. Painfully, or perhaps wishfully, *Aliyot Eliyahu*'s authors note that "To love the path of God and His Torah . . . he [Elijah] had to fight against his human instincts, pause, and let go of his own love for his own children."[113] Precisely such accounts led the late nineteenth-century scholar Solomon Schechter (1847–1915) to fault *Aliyot Eliyahu*'s authors with "being incapable of marking the line between monster and hero."[114] To be charitable, however, the Gaon's children, students, and early biographers were clearly also documenting the immense self-sacrifice required for Elijah ben Solomon to transform himself into the Gaon of Vilna.

"Vil-nor Goen"

In his 1798 essay "Whether Genius Be Born or Acquired," William Jackson wrote: "Of late it has been thought that a child just born may be anything you please. If you wish your child should speak like Cicero, write like Homer, paint like Apelles, or compose like Timotheus, set the models before him which he is to imitate, keep him intent on his subject, put his thoughts in the train they should go, and, if accidents do not interrupt their progress, they will proceed onwards towards the goal, until they successfully reach it."[115] Nineteenth- and early twentieth-century Jewish parents had a pithy version of Jackson's adage. Playing on the Yiddish vocalization of the Gaon's name, they bade their children, "Vil-nor Goen": "if you will it, you too can be a Gaon." The Gaon's students and his mid-nineteenth-century biographers produced, packaged, and eventually sold this impression of genius to a European Jewry just then experiencing heady new educational opportunities. By the end of the nineteenth century, the Gaon's image and legacy were widely celebrated in modern European Jewish popular culture.[116]

What is said of Shakespeare's genius might equally describe the Gaon's—namely, that it was only after he was "known as a 'genius' [that] he became infinitely exportable, infinitely reappropriable."[117] The rise of the modern yeshiva in eastern Europe provided students from various economic and social backgrounds access to higher educational opportunities and yielded a new cadre of scholars who liberally showered on each other the title "Gaon." Students drawn to secular intellectual pursuits likewise celebrated the Gaon's genius. But more socially important than the thousands of young students who flocked to secular or religious institutions of higher learning was the way in which Gaon iconography, *pushkes* (charity boxes) for various yeshivot,[118] and lower-brow books such as *Aliyot Eliyahu* became a part of Jewish households throughout eastern Europe. These artifacts allowed those living far away from institutions of higher learning to identify with the ideologies those institutions promoted.

Though representing only a small fraction of eastern European Jewry, the new yeshivot promoted a novel religious discourse—one that became more widely known in the nineteenth century in part by terms used to distinguish the various degrees and kinds of student knowledge. There was "the *lerner*, or studious one; *ben Toyreh*, son of the Law; *baal Toyreh*, master of the Law; *lamdan*, erudite one; *talmid chokhem*, wise scholar, *masmid*, one who is always bending over his books; *kharif*, acute; *illuy*, genius [more correctly prodigy], superior or accomplished person; *oker horim*, 'uprooter of mountains,' one who excels in competitive scholarly pyrotechnics; *gaon*, genius."[119]

The poem "Kotso shel Yud" ("The Tip of the Yud," 1871) by Yehudah Leib Gordon (1830–1892) places this phenomenon in the context of a powerful indictment of the way some individuals used their brilliance to keep women chained (*agunaot*) to their husbands. In a satirical aside, Gordon keenly observes the proliferation of the title among nineteenth-century rabbis:

Not a spade to dig with, not a pedigree of bravado,
Geonim [Torah geniuses] were only very few in number out of
  each generation,
All of them were holy individuals whose reputations preceded them;
Now the number of geonim has equaled the number of rabbis.
So much so that even our young rabbis laud themselves with this title,
We even have geonim of various and sundry varieties; "True geonim"
  and "formidable geonim,"
And "the greatest of all geonim," to the second and third degree,
As well as "luminaries" and "eagles," "pillars," "hammers."[120]

Gordon, the classic nineteenth-century Vilna Maskil, expresses in bold relief the way in which the Gaon's legacy had become popularized to the point of absurdity. In his idyllic view of yesteryear, the poet notes that the designation "genius" was restricted to a select few whose characters were as refined as their minds. In the nineteenth century, bemoans Gordon, the term was handed out for free to any young scholar who thought his advanced studies made him a genius. Young scholars trained in yeshivot claimed the title Gaon, even though in most instances they adopted only the most superficial elements of the severe practices that were believed to have nurtured Elijah's exceptional intellectual abilities.

The grueling lifestyle associated with the Gaon's genius developed alongside the eighteenth- and early nineteenth-century German idea of *Bildung*, according to which "the aesthetic and moral examples contained in classic sources affect [one] deeply and totally."[121] But Elijah's hermetic and anti-social lifestyle was very different than the model of intellectual achievement that was connected to a socially conscious western European experience and that was often identified with bourgeois Jews and German *Kultur*.

The critical perspective of hindsight reveals the blemishes and imperfections of Elijah's intellectual achievements. But attentiveness to them ought not tarnish Elijah's image or diminish the originality of his genius, just as documenting the poverty, stench, and frugal living conditions of

Vilna should not diminish its significance in the annals of Jewish history. The Gaon himself, after all, never concealed the price that his genius exacted. He no doubt would have vehemently objected to the notion that Jonathan Richardson advanced in his pioneering work "An Essay on the Theory of Painting" (1715): "The way to be an Excellent Painter, is to be an Excellent Man." *Geonut* had nothing to do with his nineteenth-century cousin, the *mensch* (one who lives with honor and integrity).[122] In an emendation to a passage from the early rabbinic work "Teachings of the Fathers," the Gaon explicitly admits that there is nothing socially palatable about the acquisition of knowledge. Chapter 6, Mishnah 8, records that the sage Shimon ben Yehuda said in the name of Shimon bar Yochai that "beauty, strength, wealth, honor, knowledge, sagacity, old age and children are pleasant to the righteous and to the rest of the world." This saying assumes that the righteous and the worldly share a similar love and respect for knowledge. The Gaon, however, comments: "One should delete from this passage the trait of knowledge, for knowledge is not related to what is normally considered pleasant. For one who is stupid does not fear sin. For that reason there is no biblical proof adduced later in the text to justify this trait being included among those traits that are good for the righteous and the rest of the world."[123] There is no manuscript support for the Gaon's emendation. While he justifies himself, claiming that no biblical proof exists for the statement in question, the Gaon's ideological leanings push his hand. The Gaon argues that only ignorance allows people to live "pleasant" lives. Those dedicating themselves to the acquisition of knowledge confront challenges that more "worldly" chaps do not have to bear. What constitutes pleasantness is not always the same for the "worldly" as for the "wise."

While the Gaon had little to do with the worldly, his children and students went out of their way to paper over any tensions that may have existed between him and his social surroundings.[124] According to the Gaon's children, their father, who for fifty years lived and studied in the middle of the bustling town of Vilna, enchanted the townspeople with the spectacle of his genius:

> The elders and pious ones living in Vilna during Gra's lifetime understood Gra's holy lifestyle. They recognized that his being was an absolute wonder. They also knew that their actions were not the same as his, neither was their lifestyle the same as his. Still, they never ceased to be interested in his doings. They greatly looked forward to

seeing him once a day or once a week. . . . When he appeared, they hoped he would lay his eyes upon them.[125]

The Gaon's sons heap praise on the town for its "partnership" with their father, which was believed to lay the groundwork for the legacy and ethos of "Vil-nor Goen." According to his children, Vilna in the late eighteenth and early nineteenth centuries was a religious Athens of sorts, "a community overflowing with those spreading Torah, punctilious in their observance of the commandments, abhorring political rabbis, God fearing, and packed with those who made study their life's work. For such individuals, chores were only occasional, and their livelihood was the concern of other family members."[126] By the mid-nineteenth century, Vilna was perceived as "a town so great that even God himself could have dwelled there. . . . And one great man was born in this town. He stood above all of its greatest scholars and that man was Rabbi Eliyahu."[127] In contrast, the townspeople of Frankfurt excommunicated the Gaon's contemporary Nathan Adler (1741–1800) for, among other infractions, his jarring pietistic behavior, establishing independent prayer services, and walking about in white garb.[128] The Gaon's biographers claim that "Every time Gra was seen outside, throngs of people would fill up the Vilna streets watching his every move. There was no room to see the majesty of his greatness."[129]

By the nineteenth century, the Gaon and Vilna were virtually synonymous; thinking about one conjured up the image of the other. Recalling 1860s Vilna, Abraham Cahan, one of America's preeminent Yiddish novelists and newspapermen (1860–1951), summed up the relationship between the town and the man: "Even as a child I knew this was the city of the Vilna Sage . . . one of the greatest geniuses of all generations."[130] The Gaon and the Jewish metropolis of Vilna would become the pride and joy of modern eastern European Jewry. "Vilna," as one of its biographers remarked, was "more than simply a city, it was an idea."[131] That idea was genius, and the man most responsible for fashioning it and then burnishing it to high polish was the Gaon.

Conclusion

THE EXPERIENCE OF JEWISH MODERNITY TENDS TO BE SEEN AS A PROCESS OF secularization—an arc starting with Jews living under static corporate governing structures and ending with their becoming citizens of nation-states, congregants of reformed synagogues, and acculturated members of civil society.[1] In the familiar narrative, this transformation was inaugurated by Moses Mendelssohn and his Berlin circle and eventually spread to Jews living in various Protestant lands. Over the course of the nineteenth century, this wave moved eastward toward the Russian Pale of Settlement. But the farther it traveled from Berlin, the more the wave of modernity trailed off, barely registering in eastern European Jewry's religious expressions, intellectual institutions, and political movements. Given the vast terrain of eastern Europe and the unique, varied experiences of the Jewish people living there, historians have been forced to reconsider their notion of modernity by either attenuating the western European categories they employ, reinterpreting the phenomenon these categories are supposed to explain, or simply ignoring broad swaths of eastern European Jewry.

Instead of relegating eastern European Jewry to the margins of modernity or reinterpreting western European categories, Gershon Hundert has tried to offer a new understanding of modern Jewry based on the eastern European experience. He argues that "the basic values and patterns of behavior by which most Jews [living in eastern Europe in the modern period] lived their lives were unexamined and unself-conscious."[2] But

166

Hundert's emphasis on the "traditional" elements of eastern European Jewry has led some of the most distinguished historians once again to dismiss this segment of Jewry as simply being part of a "relatively insular and unchanging cultural landscape well into the twentieth century."[3] Hundert himself has provoked this misunderstanding of his otherwise groundbreaking thesis by employing a category, "tradition," that he defines by a Weberian framework that describes such groups as static and unchanging—a framework created as the straw man for the very definition of "modernity" he seeks to overturn. In so doing, Hundert implicitly allows a conception of modernity rooted in the dynamic western European categories of acculturation, emancipation, and religious reform to define Jewish "modernity." This misnomer has allowed historians to once again either ignore, reject, or selectively document the development of eastern European Jewry in the modern period.

Late eighteenth- and early nineteenth-century eastern European Jews, like their western European counterparts, produced considerable intellectual and political ferment. Vilna alone was host to a group of influential Maskilim,[4] political upheavals engendered by the continued spread of Hasidism,[5] harsh reactions to conscription and state involvement in Jewish education,[6] the rise of the Mussar movement, the Yiddishist movement, and of course Zionism.[7] It was anything but an "insular and unchanging cultural landscape" or an unconscious extension of pre-modern Jewish life.[8] But these happenings cannot be generically classified as eastern European movements that followed established patterns of religious reform, acculturation, or emancipation. The majority of Jews living in Russian and Polish lands did not undergo a process of embourgeoisement,[9] did not attend secular universities, and did not enjoy political emancipation until the end of the nineteenth and beginning of the twentieth centuries. Any theory that attempts to explain the transformation of late eighteenth- to early twentieth-century modern eastern European Jewry must account for its unique political landscape, demographic conditions, and intellectual movements.

The modern transformation of eastern European Jewry began in the late eighteenth century with the rise of the state and the fall of the centralized *kehilah* structure, which created the privatized space necessary for various religious and intellectual expressions of nineteenth-century eastern European Jewry to flourish. The Russian government's role in ending the Hasidic-Mitnagdic feud inaugurated a long and socially tumultuous process of religious privatization (which took a very different course from the religious privatization commonly associated with the Reform and Orthodox movements in western Europe). The privatization of eastern European Jewry is reflected in Y. L. Gordon's demand that a Jew be "a man on the outside and a Jew in one's tent."[10] Some took his dictum so seriously that they secluded themselves in the four walls of the Volozhin yeshiva; others confined themselves within a Hasidic court.

Conversely, religious privatization did not prevent Maskilim, Mitnagdim, and Hasidim from trying to use local governing structures (local *kehilot* and those offered by the Russian state) to enforce policies sympathetic to their causes.[11] In many cases Hasidim actually took over local Jewish communal institutions. The futility of coercive political measures to impede the rise of Hasidism (as opposed to the Mitnagdim's success in harnessing private resources to establish the yeshiva) confirms José Casanova's argument that privately controlled religious initiatives have fared better in the modern age than have those that rely on state or communal power structures.[12]

The privatization of late eighteenth- and nineteenth-century eastern European Jewry was shaped by a unique demographic situation in which Jews lived as virtual majorities. This condition structured all encounters with ideas associated with emancipation, religious reform, and acculturation. So although the Englishman Sir Moses Montefiore was dumbfounded to learn that Vilna Maskilim wanted to study German and not the language of their host country, it should have come as no surprise that the majority of Vilna's Jews had little desire to become Russians or Germans; instead, empowered by their majority status, they aspired to be Torah scholars or intellectuals. Unlike their counterparts in western Europe, who felt a gravitational pull toward their host countries' dominant French, German, and English cultural reference points, the Jewish community in the east felt these cultural influences as a centripetal force that pushed them to produce their own art, music, poetry, and literature. That is, as majorities in their respective locales, eastern European Jews developed a sense of agency rooted in a deep and pervasive investment in Jewish life and ideas.

In this context, the role of the Gaon takes on new meaning. Elijah was undoubtedly influenced, at least indirectly, by a host of seventeenth- and eighteenth-century philosophical and religious sources. But to gauge his contributions to modern Jewish history in terms of how he was influenced by Enlightenment tendencies or the struggle for Jewish emancipation is to miss the central role he played in the trajectory of modern Jewish history.

The Gaon was the pride of Vilna and modern eastern European Jewry much in the same way that Moses Mendelssohn was the pride of Berlin and German Jewry. The Gaon and the Jewish Socrates embodied the ethos and values of each city's Jewish community. Whereas Mendelssohn translated the Bible into German, Elijah encouraged the translation of *Euclid* into Hebrew. Elijah's life and legacy functioned as the *ingenium*— the intellectual seed—for various and conflicting groups. His Torah-centered worldview, which downplayed medieval scholastic and theosophic knowledge, influenced not only nineteenth-century rabbinic Jews who rejected the study of metaphysics, but also the founders of the modern yeshiva at Volozhin,[13] Maskilim like Isaac Ber Levinsohn (1788–1860) who focused on humanistic elements in the Jewish tradition, and even those Hasidim who in light of the Gaon's critiques eventually established their own yeshivot.[14] Likewise, his spiritual investment in the idea of *Eretz Yisrael* and disinterest toward integrating into Polish society inspired his students to take bold political actions. They heard in their teacher's writings a clarion call for their own immigration to Safed and Jerusalem.[15]

To be sure, each of these movements selectively adopted certain elements of the Gaon's worldview. They all could claim him precisely because he never affiliated with any movement. He was an aloof eighteenth-century rabbinic figure, not a nineteenth-century Maskil, Mitnaged, or Zionist. The differences between Elijah and his disciples, even his most dedicated, illustrate perfectly the differences between eighteenth- and nineteenth-century Jewry. For example, Maskilic students at the nineteenth-century state-sponsored school in Vilna read the Gaon's commentary to the Bible, a text expressing universalistic sentiments.[16] Their counterparts in yeshivot, meanwhile, were engrossed in his more particularistic glosses to Karo's code. But both groups were equally distant from the Gaon, who learned by himself and spent most of his time focused on the kabbalah, a subject that neither institution expressed much interest in. The Gaon, the most learned and innovative kabbalist since Luria, would probably never have recognized the way his ideas were employed by these groups. Similarly, the Gaon's understanding of *Eretz Yisrael* was crafted in a different context from the national-political ideology of nineteenth-century secular and religious Zionists who took up his mantle.[17] Although substantial parts of nineteenth-century Jewry's aesthetic and secular worldviews differed radically with the Gaon's more ascetic and religious one, and although nineteenth-century Jews knew little of his writings, still the most ardent twentieth-century secular Vilna resident could assert that "the Vilna Yiddishist and secular movements, as well as modern poetry . . . were proud to continue the tradition of the Vilna Gaon."[18]

In describing the most influential rabbinic figure in modern Jewish history, it is essential to understand modernity as a condition as opposed to a movement. Focusing on the condition of modernity—a condition constituted by the rise of the state and the subsequent division of public and private spheres—challenges both those who have seen modernity as a monolithic liberal ideology as well as those who "complicate" the term by proposing a theory of multiple modernities that ultimately empties the term of any defined ideological or political core. The management of public and private spheres is the locus for understanding both the formation of modern liberal and radically conservative religious groups as well as the deep structural shifts that affected all sectors of European Jewry during the eighteenth and nineteenth centuries. Namely, for European Jews intellectual achievement became an avenue to greater social and economic opportunities, Judaism became privatized, and various ideological commitments replaced local communal identity markers. Yet these conditions played out in radically different ways in eastern and western Europe.

It might be suggested that the differences between eighteenth-century eastern and western European Jewry express in embryonic form the differences between two great modern Jewish traditions. Many have already described the path that leads from Mendelssohn to Jewish emancipation, acculturation, and religious reform. It is now becoming increasingly clear that such a story represents at most only half of the modern Jewish experience. The tradition defined by the "Jewish Socrates," Mendelssohn, fails to account for the most dynamic aspects of contemporary Jewry. In particular, it cannot render intelligible the religious and political proclivities of the fastest growing religious group, the Orthodox Jewish community; the breakdown of denominational Judaism; the phenomenon of gentiles converting to Judaism in order to marry desirable Jewish partners; the establishment in majority Jewish neighborhoods of charter schools that teach Hebrew to Christians; and the strong national element in Israeli politics.

Indeed, these developments emerge from the other great current in modern Jewry, inspired by the Genius of Vilna. In this other tradition, Jews, who made up a virtual majority, focused on developing their own cultural infrastructure. They developed their own Jewish languages. Some produced great works of rabbinic scholarship. Many embraced new religious models, while others rejected religion entirely. Few, however, thought it was necessary to reform Judaism in line with Protestant sensibilities. Instead, the movement embodied by the Genius of Vilna was reflected in various anti-bourgeois political expressions ranging from Zionism and Bundism to the Mussar movement.

When pogroms became oppressive, eastern European Jews did not reaffirm their ties to the Motherland. They stopped beseeching the tsar for mercy and gave up on any appeal for a Russian-Jewish symbiosis. When they came to Palestine and the United States they once again tried to live as virtual majorities, moving to New York City's Lower East Side and Newark, the poorer geographic ancestors of Beverly Hills and Long Island. They lived among other Jews not because they were forced to but because that was what felt comfortable. They created strong Jewish organizations and influenced the American Reform Movement with their Zionist leanings, although some continued to be wary of the state and of bourgeois life.

The Genius of Vilna is embodied in those residents of Tel Aviv and New York who live as though they are majorities. The Genius of Vilna tradition represents the protean nature of a Jewish people that has arisen out of the horrors of modernity. Modern Jews have not simply whiled away their days negotiating their identity vis-à-vis those who have excluded them. From the birth of the State of Israel, to the Jews' involvement in radical anti-statist modern political movements, to the creation of a robust, vibrant Jewish life in the United States, Jewish modernity derives much of its intellectual dynamism, social confidence, and political assertiveness from an astonishing source: the brilliant writings and untamed personality of Elijah ben Solomon, who first captured the imagination of eastern European Jewry in the eighteenth century.

Notes

Introduction

1. See the wall plaque entitled "Geonei ve-Gedolei Yisrael," collected and arranged by Israel Wiesen (Kettwig: 1881). For other nineteenth-century pictures of Elijah, see Dov Eliakh, *Sefer ha-Gaon: Le-Toldot Chayav u-Verur Mishnato shel Morenu ve-Rabenu ha-Gaon Eliyahu mi-Vilna* (Jerusalem: Moreshet Yeshivot, 2002), 3:319–328; Rachel Schnold, *Aderet Eliyahu: Ha-Gaon mi-Vilna, Demuto ve-Hashpa'ato* (Tel Aviv: Beit ha-Tefutsot al shem Nahum Goldmann, 1998), 48–55; and Zusia Efron, "Portrait of the Gaon of Vilna: Two Centuries of Imagination," in *The Gaon of Vilnius and the Annals of Jewish Culture* (Vilnius: Vilnius University Publishing House, 1998), 164–168. On portraits of rabbinic figures in the nineteenth century, see Richard Cohen, *Jewish Icons: Art and Society in Modern Europe* (Berkeley: University of California Press, 1998), 114–154.

2. See the introductory approbation of Yisrael Lifshitz, the author of the rabbinic work *Tiferet Yisrael*, to *Biur ha-Gra al Shulchan Arukh Choshen Mishpat* (Königsberg: 1856).

3. On the image of the Gaon as the founder of contemporary Haredi society, see Eliakh, *Sefer ha-Gaon*, 2:594–625. On the debate over the Gaon's relationship to Zionism, see Arie Morgenstern, *Meshichiyut ve-Yishuv Eretz Yisrael: Ba-Machatzit ha-Rishonah shel ha-Meah ha-19* (Jerusalem: Yad Yitzchak Ben Tzvi, 1985), 94–99, 205, translated by Joel Linsider in Arie Morgenstern, *Hastening Redemption: Messianism and the Resettlement of the Land of Israel* (New York: Oxford University Press, 2006), 77–83, 17; and Israel Bartal, *Galut ba-Aretz* (Jerusalem: Ha-Sifriyah ha-Tzionit, 1994), 236–295. On the

debate over the Gaon's opposition to Maskilic thought, see Allan Nadler, *The Faith of the Mithnagdim: Rabbinic Responses to Hasidic Rapture* (Baltimore: Johns Hopkins University Press, 1997), 128–131; and Immanuel Etkes, *The Gaon of Vilna: The Man and His Image* (Berkeley: University of California Press, 2002), 44–83.

4. See Jacob Katz, *Tradition and Crisis: Jewish Society at the End of the Middle Ages*, trans. Bernard Dov Cooperman (New York: New York University Press, 1993), 8–9, "the crises that affected traditional society . . . seemed to be primarily a crisis of the rabbinate" (75). On his general social-historical methodology, see Jacob Katz, "The Concept of Social History and Its Possible Use in Jewish Historical Research," in Roberto Bachi, ed., *Scripta Hierosolymitana* (Jerusalem: Magnes Press, 1955), 3:292–312.

5. On the prevalence and importance of Katz's model for understanding traditionalism, see David Ellenson, "A Disputed Precedent: The Prague Organ in Nineteenth-Century Central-European Legal Literature and Polemics," *Leo Baeck Institute Yearbook* 40 (1995): 251–264, reprinted with the same title in *After Emancipation: Jewish Religious Responses to Modernity* (Cincinnati: Hebrew Union College Press: 2004), 121–138 (chapter 5). On Katz's influence in medieval historiography, see most recently Ivan G. Marcus, "Israeli Medieval Jewish Historiography: From Nationalist Positivism to New Cultural and Social Histories," *Zion* 74 (2009): 122–131; and on modern Jewish historiography see Paula Hyman, "Jacob Katz as Historian," in Jay M. Harris, ed., *The Pride of Jacob: Essays on Jacob Katz and His Work* (Cambridge, Mass.: Harvard University Press, 2002), 87–88. See also Elisheva Carlebach's critique of Katz's notion of "Ashkenaz" and traditional society in Elisheva Carlebach, "Early Modern Ashkenaz in the Writings of Jacob Katz," in Harris, *The Pride of Jacob*, 65–66.

6. See Paul R. Mendes-Flohr and Jehuda Reinharz, eds., *The Jew in the Modern World: A Documentary History*, 2d ed. (Oxford: Oxford University Press, 1995), 6.

7. Ibid.

8. See Michael A. Meyer, "Tradition and Modernity Reconsidered," in Jack Wertheimer, ed., *The Uses of Tradition: Jewish Continuity in the Modern Era* (New York: Jewish Theological Seminary of America, 1992), 465. See also Meyer, "Reflections on Jewish Modernization," in his *Judaism within Modernity: Essays on Jewish Historiography and Religion* (Detroit: Wayne State University Press, 2001), 34–36.

9. See David Gross, *The Past in Ruins: Tradition and the Critique of Modernity* (Amherst: University of Massachusetts Press, 1992), 79.

10. On Silber's disproval of those who commonly refer to ultra-Orthodoxy as an "unchanged and unchanging remnant" of traditional society, see Michael K.

Silber, "The Emergence of Ultra-Orthodoxy: The Invention of a Tradition," in Wertheimer, *The Uses of Tradition*, 24–25. For Silber's retrospective on Katz, see Silber, "A Hungarian Rhapsody in Blue: Jacob Katz's Tardy Surrender to Hagar's Allure," in Harris, *The Pride of Jacob*, 141–161. On Sofer see also Jacob Katz, "Towards a Biography of the Hatam Sofer," in his *Divine Law in Human Hands: Case Studies in Halakhic Flexibility* (Jerusalem: Magnes Press, 1998), 403; Katz, "Towards a Biography of the Hatam Sofer," trans. David Ellenson, in Frances Malino and David Sorkin, eds., *Profiles in Diversity: Jews in a Changing Europe, 1750–1870* (Detroit: Wayne State University Press, 1998), 223–266; and Katz, "Introduction," in Katz, ed., *Toward Modernity: The European Jewish Model* (New Brunswick, N.J.: Transaction, 1987), 8. On Sofer as a reactionary, see Moshe Samet, *He-Chadash Asur min ha-Torah* (Jerusalem: Merkaz le-Cheker Toldot Yisrael, 2005), 15, 22–23. For definitions of Orthodoxy see Mordechai Breuer, *Modernity within Tradition: The Social History of Orthodox Jewry in Imperial Germany*, trans. Elizabeth Petuchowski (New York: Columbia University Press, 1992), viii–xv.

11. Jacob J. Schacter, "Editor's Introduction," *Torah u-Madda* 2 (1990): 5–6.

12. In many cases, rabbinic figures living in nineteenth- and twentieth-century Germany can be adequately understood in this way. For example, see David Ellenson's *Between Tradition and Culture: The Dialectics of Modern Jewish Identity* (Atlanta: Scholars Press, 1994), where he "centers on those people who consciously affirm the worth of modern culture and engage in the effort to mediate between that culture and its values and those of the Jewish past" (xiii). What makes German rabbinic figures unique is the strong emphasis they placed on the issues of emancipation, religious reform, and secular knowledge, as can be seen in Marc B. Shapiro's *Between the Yeshiva World and Modern Orthodoxy: The Life and Works of Rabbi Jehiel Jacob Weinberg* (Oxford: Littman Library, 1999), in particular the passages focusing on Weinberg's conscious adoption of academic methodologies in his relationship to *Wissenschaft* (76–99), state-based politics (175–180), and acculturation (150–157, 205–221).

13. The journals *Bekhol Derakhekha Daehu (BDD)* and *Torah u-Madda* contain numerous articles focusing on what connection Elijah and his circle had to Jewish secularization. See for example Aaron Moses Schreiber, "Hashkafato Shel ha-Gra: Al Chashivut ha-Haskalah ha-Kelalit ve-al ha-Kesher le-Yemot ha-Mashiach," *Bekhol Derakhekha Daehu* 9 (Summer 1999): 5–28; and Yisrael Shapira, "Askolot Chalukot be-She'elat Torah u-Madda'im be-Veit Midrasho shel ha-Gra," *Bekhol Derakhekha Daehu* 13 (August 2003): 5–53. In *Torah u-Madda* see Jacob J. Schacter, "Haskalah, Secular Studies, and the Closing of the Yeshiva in Volozhin in 1892," *Torah u-Madda* 2 (1990): 76–133; Raphael Shuchat, "The Debate over Secular Studies among the Disciples of the Vilna Gaon," *Torah u-Madda* 8 (1999): 283–294; Aaron M. Schreiber, "The Hatam Sofer's Nuanced

Attitude towards Secular Learning, Maskilim, and Reformers," *Torah u-Madda* 11 (2003): 123–173; and Gil S. Perl, "No Two Minds Are Alike: Tolerance and Pluralism in the Work of Netziv," *Torah u-Madda* 12 (2004): 74–98.

14. See Shmuel Feiner and David J. Sorkin, eds., *New Perspectives on the Haskalah* (Oxford: Littman Library, 2001), 3; Shmuel Feiner, *The Jewish Enlightenment*, trans. Chaya Naor (Philadelphia: University of Pennsylvania Press, 2003); and Andrea Schatz, "Review Forum on Shmuel Feiner's *The Jewish Enlightenment:* An Incomplete Revolution," *Jewish Quarterly Review* 97, no. 1 (Winter 2007): 143–147. In recent years, Feiner has reclaimed the older paradigm of secularization as the decisive factor in the development of modern Jewish history. See Feiner, *The Origins of Jewish Secularization in Eighteenth-Century Europe*, trans. Chaya Naor (Philadelphia: University of Pennsylvania Press, 2010). By contrast, Jonathan Garb has further developed the paradigm of "multiple modernities" to include the study of kabbalah in modern Jewish history. See Jonathan Garb, "The Modernization of Kabbalah: A Case Study," *Modern Judaism* 30, no. 1 (2010): 17–19.

15. See most recently David J. Sorkin, *The Religious Enlightenment: Protestants, Jews, and Catholics from London to Vienna* (Princeton, N.J.: Princeton University Press, 2008); Sorkin, *The Berlin Haskalah and German Religious Thought: Orphans of Knowledge* (London: Valentine Mitchell, 2000), 5–9; and Sorkin's earlier study, *Moses Mendelssohn and the Religious Enlightenment* (Berkeley: University of California Press, 1996), xxiii–xxv. Whereas Sorkin asks how eighteenth-century religious thinkers contribute to the creation of the Enlightenment, this work not only addresses the minority of eighteenth- and nineteenth-century Jews who identified with Enlightenment-inspired movements, but also accounts for other genealogies in modernity: namely, how eighteenth-century figures like Elijah of Vilna contributed both to what is commonly understood as modern secular Jewish life and to the creation of modern religious movements such as Evangelicalism, Pietism, and ultra-Orthodoxy. See more generally David J. Sorkin, "The Early Haskalah," in Feiner and Sorkin, *New Perspectives on the Haskalah*, 9–26.

16. See Max Weber, *General Economic History*, trans. Frank H. Knight (New Brunswick, N.J.: Transaction, 1981), 360. Weber's description of rabbinic Judaism (the religion) as traditional has been glossed over by many of those who have written about his understanding of Judaism. On Weber's understanding of the role of Jews (the people) in modern European economic structures, see Hans Liebeschutz, "Max Weber's Historical Understanding of Judaism," *Leo Baeck Institute Yearbook* 9 (1964): 41–68; and Arnaldo Momigliano, "A Note on Max Weber's Definition of Judaism as a Pariah Religion," *History and Theory* 29, no. 1 (1980): 313–318. See also David Ellenson, *After Emancipation, Jewish Religious Responses to Modernity* (Cincinnati: Hebrew Union College Press, 2004), 81–95.

17. Edward Shils explicitly admitted that he and Talcott Parsons in their earlier work ignored the shortcomings of Weber's notion of traditional society: see Shils, *Tradition* (Chicago: University of Chicago Press, 1981), 8; and David Gross's broad thematic analysis of "tradition" in modern thought in his *The Past in Ruins*, 1–19.

18. See Max Weber, *The Theory of Social and Economic Organization*, trans. and ed. Talcott Parsons (New York: Free Press, 1964), 341. On the use of the term "traditional society" in sociological and historical studies, see Shils, *Tradition*, 19–21. For an overview of Weber's types of authority, see David Little, *Religion, Order, and Law: A Study in Pre-Revolutionary England* (Chicago: University of Chicago Press, 1984), 6–33.

19. Shils, *Tradition*, 294.

20. See Eric J. Hobsbawm and Terence O. Ranger, *The Invention of Tradition* (Cambridge: Cambridge University Press, 1992), 5. There Hobsbawm reveals how nation-states and nationalist movements dressed themselves up with "authentic traditions" in order to legitimate certain political institutions. Hobsbawm claims that his exposé astonished his readers by suggesting that the modern nation-state fabricated certain "traditions" (and thus succeeded in establishing their authority not because of its own independent claims to reason).

21. See Max Weber, *The Protestant Ethic and the Spirit of Capitalism*, trans. Talcott Parsons (New York: Courier Dover, 2003), 95–155.

22. On Weber's selective reading of eighteenth-century pietists see Michael Walzer, *The Revolution of the Saints: A Study in the Origins of Radical Politics* (Cambridge, Mass.: Harvard University Press, 1965), 301–304.

23. See Karl Mannheim, "Conservative Thought," originally published in 1927 and reprinted in *Karl Mannheim*, ed. Kurt Wolf (New York: Oxford University Press, 1971), 157.

24. See Dean C. Tipps, "Modernization Theory and the Comparative Study of Societies: A Critical Perspective," *Comparative Studies in Society and History* 15, no. 2 (March 1973): 213. For a parallel discussion on Chinese history, see Paul A. Cohen, *China Unbound: Evolving Perspectives on the Chinese Past* (New York: Routledge, 2003), 54. See also Talal Asad's study *Genealogies of Religion: Discipline and Reasons of Power in Christianity and Islam* (Baltimore: Johns Hopkins University Press, 1993). There, in his essay "The Limits of Religious Criticism" (200–236), Asad explains the social and cultural infrastructure behind certain forms of "traditional" Islamic social criticism. In order to explain his subject, however, Asad first disentangles his project from "those who tended to evaluate and measure traditions according to their distance from Enlightenment and liberal models" (200).

25. See Raphael Shuchat, *Olam Nistar be-Memadei ha-Zeman* (Ramat Gan: Bar-Ilan University Press, 2008), 15–24; and Etkes, *The Gaon of Vilna*.

26. My understanding of modernity draws on Ulrich Beck's *Risk Society: Towards a New Modernity*, trans. Mark Ritter (London: Sage, 1992), 10–14. While Beck uses the term "reflexive modernity" to explain the risks inherent in and unintended consequences of industrial society, I argue that the same processes, risks, and unintended consequences are at play in the formation of secular ideologies. More theoretically, it might be suggested that the movements and ideologies that emerged from the division of public and private spheres came to undermine the very principles and structures that made them possible. This undermining was not expressed as a reaction to modernity, but rather points to a seminal tension inherent within modern secularism itself—a tension that makes it impossible for secularism to achieve itself fully in all spheres of life. In other words, secularism has always maintained what some might call a schizophrenic, and what others see as a healthy, division of society as half-secular and half-religious. This division is not created ex post facto but rather in the very semantic definition of the term. The religious side cannot be understood simply as a relic of tradition or be in strict opposition to the secular. Rather it is the foundation, built into the institutional plan of the modern liberal state. As a result, secularism becomes divided against itself whenever it separates religion from the state. Secularism gives religion a demarcated private field where it may act as it pleases provided that it does not break any of the state's laws or coerce individuals to follow its dictates. But in freeing religion from the social responsibilities of governance, secularism creates a privatized version of religion that sows the seeds for religion's ideological radicalization and the actualization of its exclusivist tendencies.

27. See for example Yehoshua Heschel Levin, *Aliyot Eliyahu* (Vilna: 1856); Shmuel Joseph Fuenn, *Knesset Yisrael* (Warsaw: 1886), 106–110; Shmuel Joseph Fuenn, Matisyahu Strashun, and Hillel-Noah Maggid Steinschneider, *Kiryah Ne'emanah: Korot Adat Yisrael be-Ir Vilna* (Vilna: Yitzchak Funk, 1915), 292–333; Bezalel Landau, *Ha-Gaon ha-Hasid mi-Vilna* (Jerusalem: 1964); Yehudah Leib Maimon, "Toldot ha-Gra," in his *Sefer ha-Gra* (Jerusalem: Mossad ha-rav Kook, 1953), 1:1–199; and Eliakh, *Sefer ha-Gaon*, vols. 1–3.

28. On the reception of the Gaon see Shuchat, *Olam Nistar be-Memadei ha-Zeman*, 15–24; and Etkes, *The Gaon of Vilna*. For a general overview of reception theory see Robert C. Holub, *Reception Theory: A Critical Introduction* (London: Methuen, 1984). On reception history, see Martyn P. Thompson, "Reception Theory and the Interpretation of Historical Meaning," *History and Theory* 32 (1993): 248–272; and Lorna Hardwick and Christopher Stray, *A Companion to Classical Receptions* (Malden, Mass.: Blackwell, 2008). For a general discussion on the reception of modern Hasidic masters, see David Assaf, *The Regal Way: The Life and Times of Israel of Ruzhin* (Palo Alto, Calif.: Stanford University Press, 2002), 9–126.

29. Chapter 1 includes immediate impressions of Elijah's students and detractors. These statements are historical eyewitness accounts of how people experienced Elijah during his lifetime. Immediate impressions differ from what are usually called hagiographies in that they can be positive or negative. Certainly the exactness of their testimonies, such as the number of pages that Elijah could read in an hour, could be questioned (although highly fluent Talmudic scholars would claim that it certainly is plausible that someone could theoretically read 140 folios in under an hour given that some folios of the Talmud contain no more than twenty-five words; likewise it is not unfathomable to believe that Elijah literally shut the door on Hasidic leaders who came to visit him). Such eyewitness experiences, however, are critical for understanding why Elijah's students spent the rest of their lives toiling to edit and publish his work, following his lead in excommunicating the Hasidim, settling in Palestine, and building institutions that would allow people to mimic Elijah's lifestyle. Chapter 6 addresses the way these immediate impressions were used and recast by scholars later in the century in order to construct a legacy of genius.

30. In the introduction to his work *Shemoneh Perakim*, Maimonides reminded his readers that the ideas presented in these chapters "are not my own invention. . . . I have gleaned them from the words of the wise occurring in the *Midrashim* and Talmud, and in other of their works, as well as from the words of the philosophers, ancient and recent, and also from the works of various authors, as one should accept the truth from whatever source it proceeds." Maimonides cautiously conceals his sources, "since the mentioning of the name of the authority drawn upon might lead one who lacks insight to believe that the statement quoted is faulty, and wrong in itself." This translation is taken from Isadore Twersky, ed., *Maimonides Reader* (New York: Behrman House, 1972), 363.

31. While originally Bloom limited his argument to nineteenth-century Romantic writers, he has since broadened his theory to include earlier figures such as Shakespeare. See the preface to Harold Bloom's updated version of *The Anxiety of Influence: A Theory of Poetry* (New York: Oxford University Press, 1997), xxiv.

32. In a lecture given at Yeshiva University on May 10, 1988, Haym Soloveitchik questioned Israel Ta-Shma's article "Seder Hadpasatam shel Chidushei ha-Rishonim le-Talmud: Perek le-Toldot ha-'Pilpul,'" *Kiryat Sefer* 50, no. 2 (1975): 325–326, which suggested that in the eighteenth century a shift occurred in eastern European learning circles in the wake of the proliferation of newly published medieval rabbinic texts such as the writings of Nachmanides and Rabbi Zerachia ha-Levi. More specifically, Ta-Shma's article argues that these texts promoted a more rational and text-based approach to the study of Jewish law. Soloveitchik claimed that based on the Gaon's writings, it is unclear to what degree he was influenced by these emerging internal bibliographic

developments. For a discussion of various influences on rabbinic history see Haym Soloveitchik, "Halakhah, Hermeneutics, and Martyrdom in Medieval Ashkenaz (Part I of II)," *Jewish Quarterly Review* 94, no.1 (Winter 2003): 77.

33. The shift described here did not translate into non-Hasidic rabbinic Jews' ceasing to employ legal and public policy sanctions as social control mechanisms. Indeed, Elijah lent his name to three bans against the Hasidim. But as demonstrated by Elijah's impotence in banning the new Hasidic groups, by the late eighteenth century such measures no longer conjured up the same fear and deterrence. See Mordekhai Wilensky, *Hasidim u-Mitnagdim: Le-Toldot ha-Pulmus she-Beineihem ba-Shanim, 5532–5565* (Jerusalem: Mossad Bialik, 1990), 1:37–44, 106–109, 187–190. The bans' inability to squelch the rising Hasidic movement points to the political weakness of non-Hasidic rabbinic Jews. While the Gaon's words were powerful enough to create a strong and vibrant rabbinic world, the coercive measures he wielded against the new group were ultimately ineffective in stemming the tide of Hasidism.

34. On the local Jewish study halls of seventeenth- and eighteenth-century eastern Europe, see Elchanan Reiner, "Temurot be-Yeshivot Polin ve-Ashkenaz be-Meot ha-16–ha-18 ve-ha-Vikuach al ha-Pilpul," in Israel Bartal, Ezra Mendelson, and Chava Turniansky, eds., *Ke-Minhag Ashkenaz ve-Polin: Sefer Yovel le-Chone Shmeruk* (Jerusalem: Merkaz Zalman Shazar, 1993), 9–80. For how these study halls differed from the modern Lithuanian yeshiva, see Shaul Stampfer, *Ha-Yeshiva ha-Litait be-Hithavutah* (Jerusalem: Merkaz Zalman Shazar, 1995), 14–20.

35. See Israel Klausner, *Toldot ha-Kehilah ha-Ivrit be-Vilna* (Vilna: 1938), 126.

Chapter 1. Elijah and Vilna in Historical Perspective

1. For the most recent bibliography on the history of the Jews in Vilna in the eighteenth and nineteenth centuries, see the introduction and bibliography written by Mordekhai Zalkin accompanying Hillel Noah Maggid Steinschneider, *Ir Vilna*, ed. M. Zalkin (Jerusalem: Magnes Press, 2002), 21–26; see also Israel Klausner, *Toldot ha-Kehilah ha-Ivrit be-Vilna* (Vilna: 1938), 186. On early modern Vilna see the bibliography compiled by David Frick, "Jews and Others in Seventeenth-Century Wilno: Life in the Neighborhood," *Jewish Studies Quarterly* 12, no. 1 (2005): 11 fn.4. In general see the exhaustive bibliography listed in *Yerushalayim de-Lita: Ilustrirt un Dokumentirt*, collected and arranged by Leyzer Ran (New York: Vilna Album Committee, 1974), 3:282–467.

2. See Joshua Fishman, "The Gaon of Vilne and the Yiddish Language," in Izraelis Lempertas, ed., *The Gaon of Vilnius and the Annals of Jewish Culture* (Vilnius: Vilnius University Publishing House, 1998), 18–19.

3. Some claim that Elijah was born in Słutzk. See the testimony of Elijah's descendent Eliyahu Landau in his introduction to *Sefer Minchat Eliyahu* (Jerusalem: 1927). For those who claim he was born in Vilna, see Bezalel Landau, *Ha-Gaon ha-Hasid Mi-Vilna* (Jerusalem: 1964), 15 fn.15.

4. On the dire conditions of early eighteenth-century Vilna, see Danutė Blažytė, "The Vilnius Magistracy and the Jewish Community in the Eighteenth Century," in Lempertas, *The Gaon of Vilnius*, 309. Vilna's central synagogue was almost confiscated by local officials due to the large-scale debt of the Vilna *kehilah*. See Israel Klausner, *Vilna, Yerushalayim de-Lita: Dorot Rishonim, 1495–1881* (D.N. Western Galilee, Israel: Ghetto Fighter's House, 1988), 1:50. On the ransacking of the town by the Muscovites, see Laimondas Briedis, *Vilnius: City of Strangers* (Budapest: Central European University Press, 2009), 55–58.

5. Rivkes inherited his wealth from his wife's father, Rabbi Asher ben Yehudah. The surname "Rivkes" came from his mother whose name was Rivka. See Bezalel Landau, "Rabbi Moshe Rivkes-bal Be'er ha-Golah," *Yeshurun* 5 (1999): 688–690. Rivkes describes himself fleeing from the troops of Muscovy (who invaded Vilna in the mid-seventeenth century) with a pair of phylacteries in one hand and the astronomical work *Sefer Evronot* in the other. Rivkes typified sixteenth- and seventeenth-century Polish-Lithuanian rabbinic scholars who, due in part to an indirect influence of Copernicus, embraced studying the celestial calculations of the Jewish calendar. On Ashkenazic rationalism in seventeenth-century Vilna, see Joseph Davis, "Ashkenazic Rationalism and Midrashic Natural History: Responses to the New Science in the Works of Rabbi Yom Tov Lipmann Heller," *Science in Context* 10, no. 4 (1997): 608, and David Ruderman, *Jewish Thought and Scientific Discovery in Early Modern Europe* (Detroit: Wayne State University Press, 1995), 61–62. While the troops invaded Vilna and burned down his library, Rivkes worked in Amsterdam on his monumental *Be'er ha-Golah*, a commentary that provides the Talmudic sources to Joseph Karo's and Moses Isserles's code of Jewish law, *Shulchan Arukh*. His interest in codifying ritual practice aligned with the interests of other seventeenth-century Vilna rabbis such as Moshe ben Isaac Lima (d. 1670) and Sabbatai ben Meir ha-Kohen (1621–1662). See the introduction to *Be'er ha-Golah* (Amsterdam: 1661); and Avraham ben ha-Gra, *Sa'eret Eliyahu* (Warsaw: 1877), 2.

6. On Moses Kraemer see the remarks of Yosef ben Ya'akov in his introduction to *Rosh Yosef* (Kitin: 1717). Piously, or perhaps shrewdly, Moses refused a salary. As his surname, Kraemer, suggests (it translates from the German "kram" as shopkeeper), he and his wife were proprietors of a local shop. On Kraemer's role in Vilna, see Klausner, *Toldot ha-Kehilah ha-Ivrit be-Vilna*, 108. On Elijah's brothers see Chaikel Lunski, *Legendes: Vegn Vilner Goen* (Vilna: 1924), 6.

7. See the introduction to *Biur ha-Gra al Shulchan Arukh Orach Chayyim* (Shklov: 1803).

8. See the recollection of Shaul of Vilna in Yehoshua Heschel Levin, *Aliyot Eliyahu* (Vilna: 1856), 57 fn.16.

9. See the introduction of Yisrael of Shklov to *Pe'at ha-Shulchan* (Safed: 1836).

10. See Yehudah Leib Margoliot, *Atzei Eden* (Frankfurt am Main: 1802), 15b.

11. On the *cheder* system, see Shaul Stampfer, "Heder Study, Knowledge of Torah and the Maintenance of Social Stratification in Traditional East European Jewish Society," *Studies in Jewish Education* 3 (1988): 271–289.

12. See *Pinkas Medinat Lita*, ed. Simon Dubnow (Berlin: 1925), 223.

13. On the miserable conditions and popular perceptions of the *cheder*, see Steven Zipperstein, *Imagining Russian Jewry: Memory, History, and Identity* (Seattle: University of Washington Press, 1999), 41–63.

14. See the irreverent statements recorded in the Gaon's name by the Av-Beit Din of Kiedan in Levin, *Aliyot Eliyahu*, 74.

15. On Elijah's study partner see the Gaon's children's introduction to *Aderet Eliyahu* (Dubrovna: 1804) and Aryeh Leib Tshanavith's introduction to Tzvi Hirsh ben Shmuel Zanvil Segal's *Margolit ha-Torah* (Fritzk: 1788). Elijah's studies with the famed Rabbi Moshe Margolit could not have lasted more than three months; see Dov Eliakh, *Sefer ha-Gaon: Le-Toldot Chayav u-Verur Mishnato shel Morenu ve-Rabenu ha-Gaon Eliyahu mi-Vilna* (Jerusalem: Moreshet Yeshivot, 2002), 1:73. According to his sons, Elijah stopped studying with teachers at the age of six. See his childrens' introduction to *Biur ha-Gra al Shulchan Arukh* (Shklov: 1803).

16. See for example, Jacob Raisin, *The Haskalah Movement in Russia* (Philadelphia: Jewish Publication Society Press, 1913), 73–75.

17. David Strashun claims that he moved to Kiedan at the behest of Rabbi Abraham Katzenellenbogen (one of the first objectors to the Hasidic movement) to study with the rabbi's brother, David. See comments made to Levin in *Aliyot Eliyahu*, 55.

18. Hannah is said to have been the daughter of a wealthy man, known as Rabbi Yehudah of Kiedan. While Elijah's marrying of a wealthy man's daughter suggests that he was thought of as a budding scholar deserving of financial support, it is unclear to what extent her "wealthy" father was ever able to provide for the newlyweds. See Levin, *Aliyot Eliyahu*, 65; and Bezalel Landau, *Ha-Gaon ha-Hasid mi-Vilna* (Jerusalem: 1964), 22. On the possibility that Elijah may have been engaged to Hannah at an even earlier age, see Peter Wiernik, "Der Vilner Goen," in *Lebens-beshraybungen fun ale Goenim un Gdoylim fun Yiddishen Folk*, ed. Philip Krantz (New York: International Publishing Co., 1910), 3:226–227.

19. On Elijah's travels, see Arie Morgenstern, *Mysticism and Messianism: From Luzzatto to the Vilna Gaon* (Jerusalem: Meor, 1999), 263–306.

20. In none of the tales told about Elijah's journeys is his wife mentioned as being by his side. On Rabbi Hayyim of Sereje, see David Kamenetsky, "Lehavdil bein Hayyim le-Hayyim," *Yeshurun* 22 (2010): 886–887 fn.34.

21. See Elijah's son Avraham's recollection in his introduction to *Yoreh De'ah* (Grodno: 1806) about the time his father left home when his brother Shlomo Zalman fell ill.

22. For an overview of the practice of self-imposed exile in Jewish pietistic circles, see Arthur Green, *Tormented Master: A Life of Rabbi Nahman of Bratslav* (Tuscaloosa: University of Alabama Press, 1979), 229. On the tradition whereby rabbis leave their homes to study in seclusion, see Daniel Boyarin's discussion of Rav Ada in "Internal Opposition in Talmudic Literature: The Case of the Married Monk," *Representations* 36 (Autumn 1991): 93–94.

23. On the various channels through which Jews registered complaints, see Frick, "Jews and Others in Seventeenth-Century Wilno," 8–9; and on the general structure of government in the Grand Duchy of Lithuania see Daniel Stone, *The Polish-Lithuanian State: 1386–1795* (Saint Louis: Washington University Press, 2001), 63.

24. Wiernik, "Der Vilner Goen," 216.

25. Briedis, *Vilnius: City of Strangers*, 173.

26. See Israel Klausner, *Toldot ha-Kehilah ha-Ivrit be-Vilna*, 28–29. On the seventeenth-century social and legislative background that preceded the eighteenth-century residential restrictions see Frick, "Jews and Others in Seventeenth-Century Wilno," 19–24.

27. See Avraham's eulogy for his father in his *Sa'eret Eliyahu*, 13b.

28. See the story told in the name of Yehudah Edels in Levin, *Aliyot Eliyahu*, 66 fn.45.

29. See the story recorded by Ya'akov Tzvi Mecklenburg in ibid., 60 fn.31.

30. See the stories recorded by Dov Eliakh in his *Sefer ha-Gaon*, 2:771–776, 3:1185–1189.

31. These texts and manuscripts, which became the foundation for his library, included "various early rabbinic midrashim, aggadot, ancient tosafot, and the books of the geonim." See Shmuel Luria's letter published in *Rav Pe'alim* (Warsaw: 1894), 9. There Luria explains how Elijah's library provided the books and manuscripts necessary for Avraham to compose his bibliographic work on rabbinic literature.

32. See Israel Cohen, *Vilna* (Philadelphia: Jewish Publication Society, 1943), 177.

33. On the fires and the anti-Semitic backlash, see Klausner, *Toldot ha-Kehilah ha-Ivrit be-Vilna*, 23–24. Actually, many of the fires probably were caused by housing complexes built in the seventeenth century that lacked chimneys,

resulting in smoke-filled homes. On the construction of homes in Vilna, see Briedis, *Vilnius: City of Strangers*, 51.

34. On the Mariavite mission and order see Elena Keidosiute, "Missionary Activity of Mariae Vitae Congregation," *PaRDeS: Zeitschrift der Vereinigung für Jüdische Studien* 16 (2010): 57–72.

35. See Magdalena Teter, "Jewish Conversions to Catholicism in the Polish-Lithuanian Commonwealth of the Seventeenth and Eighteenth Centuries," *Jewish History* 17, no. 3 (2003): 261–262. Many of these converts were probably part of the Mariavite missionaries, which targeted young women from financially distressed homes. From 1758 to 1764 there seems to have been a second wave of conversions, perhaps associated with the Frankist movement. The rash of conversions is alluded to in the first statements of condemnation against the Hasidim published in 1772 and reprinted in Mordekhai Wilensky, *Hasidim u-Mitnagdim: Le-Toldot ha-Pulmus she-Beineihem ba-Shanim, 5532–5565* (Jerusalem: Mossad Bialik, 1990), 1:59. On the Frankists see Majer Bałaban, *Le-Toldot ha-Tnuah ha-Frankit* (Tel Aviv: Devir, 1935); Gershom Scholem, "Jacob Frank and the Frankists," in his *Kabbalah* (New York: Dorset, 1987): 287–310; and most recently Paweł Maciejko, *Jacob Frank and the Frankist Movement, 1755–1816* (Philadelphia: University of Pennsylvania Press, 2011), 129–130. After 1764, however, the number of converts in Vilna decreased due to the Polish government's decision to take away the advanced societal status previously given to Jewish converts, as well as because the local bishop of Vilna, Ignacy Massalski, opposed the forced Jewish conversions. See Jacob Goldberg, *Ha-Mumarim be-Mamlekhet Polin-Lita* (Jerusalem: 1985), 38–40. More generally, on Jewish conversions to Christianity in Lithuania see Gershon Hundert, *Jews in Poland and Lithuania in the Eighteenth Century: A Genealogy of Modernity* (Berkeley: University of California Press, 2004), 59–79; and Edward Fram, "Perception and Reception of Repentant Apostates in Medieval Ashkenaz and Premodern Poland," *AJS Review* 21, no. 2 (1996): 299–339.

36. See Klausner, *Toldot ha-Kehilah ha-Ivrit be-Vilna*, 22. On Vilna Jews complaining to the pope that Catholic officials were abducting their children, see Stasys Yla, *Šiluva žemaičių istorijoje* (Boston: Krikščionis gyvenime, 1970), 1:261, cited by Vytautas Kavolis, "The Devil's Invasion: Cultural Changes in Early Modern Lithuania," *Lituanus* 34, no. 4 (Winter 1989): fn.23, available at www.lituanus.org/1989/89_4_01.htm (last accessed March 14, 2012).

37. Klausner, *Toldot ha-Kehilah ha-Ivrit be-Vilna*, 61.

38. Ibid., 66.

39. See Alfonsas Tamulynas, "Demographic and Social Professional Structure of the Jewish Community of Vilnius," in Lempertas, *The Gaon of Vilnius and the Annals of Jewish Culture*, 335.

40. Klausner, *Toldot ha-Kehilah ha-Ivrit be-Vilna*, 44.

41. See Avraham ben ha-Gra, introduction to *Yoreh De'ah*.

42. On Elijah giving money to the poor, see Avraham Danzig, *Chokhmat Adam* (New York: Yudaika Press, 1991), ruling 147:24; the introduction of Yisrael of Shklov, *Pe'at ha-Shulchan;* and Levin, *Aliyot Eliyahu*, 66–67.

43. These comments were recorded by Hannah's grandson Ya'akov Moshe of Słonim and published in Morgenstern, *Mysticism and Messianism*, 260.

44. See the letter Elijah wrote to his wife while traveling to Palestine. The letter, sent from Königsberg, was originally published under the title "Alim li-Terufah" (Vilna: 1800). Elijah spends the last three paragraphs of the letter pleading with his wife and mother not to anger one another. See "Letter of Elijah (Gaon) of Wilna," in *Hebrew Ethical Wills*, ed. and trans. Israel Abrahams (Philadelphia: Jewish Publication Society, 1926), 311–325.

45. See the introduction of Yisrael of Shklov, *Pe'at ha-Shulchan;* and Avraham ben ha-Gra, *Sa'eret Eliyau*, 8b.

46. Zwi Werblowski, *Joseph Karo: Lawyer and Mystic* (Philadelphia: Jewish Publication Society, 1977), 311–312.

47. See Avraham ben ha-Gra's claims in *Rav Pe'alim*, 58.

48. On the publication history of the Gaon's kabbalistic writings, see Yosef Avivi, *Kabbalat ha-Gra* (Jerusalem: Eliyahu, ha-Makhon le-hotsa'at sifrei ha-Gra, 1992), 14–28.

49. Ibid., 30–31.

50. *Rav Pe'alim*, 58.

51. See Menachem Mendel of Shklov's introduction to Proverbs (Shklov: 1798).

52. On Elijah's brother, see Abraham's introduction to *Ma'alot ha-Torah* (New York: 1946), xiii–xxiv.

53. On Elijah's ability to break with his predecessors and even his family members, see Levin, *Aliyot Eliyahu*, 41.

54. See Yisrael of Shklov's introduction to his *Pe'at ha-Shulchan*.

55. Elijah's name appears in at least one major eighteenth-century debate. He is known to have written a letter on behalf of Eibeschuetz that was published by Eibeschuetz in *Luchot Edut* (Altona: 1755). Fourteen years later, Emden, in his work *Hitavkut* (Altona: 1769), claimed that the letter to Eibeschuetz was a forgery. For a translation of the Gaon's letter and the possibility that it may have been forged or tampered with, see Sid Z. Leiman, "When a Rabbi Is Accused of Heresy: The Stance of the Gaon of Vilna in the Emden-Eibeschuetz Controversy," in Ezra Fleischer, Gerald Blidstein, Carmi Horowitz, and Bernard Septimus, eds., *Me'ah She'arim: Studies in Medieval Jewish Spiritual Life in Memory of Isadore Twersky* (Jerusalem: Magnes Press, 2001), 253–254.

56. On Pesseles and his relationship to the Gaon, see Israel Klausner, *Vilna be-Tekufat ha-Gaon* (Jerusalem: Reuben Mass, 1942), 60–61 fn.1. On Pesseles's relationship to Elijah's father, Shlomo Zalman, see Levin, *Aliyot Eliyahu*, 53 fn.3.

57. See the personal records of Eliyahu Pesseles listed in Kamenetsky, "Lehavdil bein Hayyim le-Hayyim." On Elijah's daughter see Hillel Noah Steinschneider, *Ir Vilna* (Vilna: 1900), 152.

58. See Levin, *Aliyot Eliyahu*, for the testimony by Hayyim of Volozhin (81 fn.95) and for more on those who wanted to censor this story from being published (2).

59. See the story told in ibid., 82 fn.96. On the fear of death in Mitnagdic writings see Allan Nadler, *The Faith of the Mithnagdim: Rabbinic Responses to Hasidic Rapture* (Baltimore: Johns Hopkins University Press, 1997), 103–126.

60. On the eastern wall of the Gaon's *kloiz* there was a plaque that read: the study house of the Gaon founded in his life in the year 1758 and renovated in 1768. See the reflections of Asher Katzman in his "Zikhronot mi-Kloiz shel ha-Gaon mi-Vilna," *Yeshurun* 6 (1999): 687.

61. Pesseles transferred the dowry to Elijah's father, Shlomo Zalman, to cover his expenses during the remaining two years of his life. See the records of Eliyahu Pesseles recorded in Chaim Freedman, *Eliyahu's Branches: The Descendents of the Vilna Gaon and His Family* (Bergenfield, N.J.: Avotaynu, 1997), 58.

62. There may have been even less room in the Fatel house, given that Elijah's family had grown and that by 1759 the *kehilah* was trying to liquidate its holdings in the housing complex. On the liquidation of the Fatel house, see Klausner, *Toldot ha-Kehilah ha-Ivrit be-Vilna*, 71–72.

63. See Mark Wishnitzer, "Die Geschichte fun Yiddin in *Lita*," in Wishnitzer, ed., *Lita* (New York: Futuro Press, 1951), 1:72.

64. See Zdzisław Budzyński, *Ludność Pogranicza Polsko-Ruskiego w Drugiej Połowie XVII Wieku* (Prezymśl and Rzeszów: 1993), 1:102–108, cited by Hundert, *Jews in Poland-Lithuania in the Eighteenth Century*, 24.

65. On the deep economic ties between Jews and Catholics in Vilna, see Hundert, *Jews in Poland-Lithuania in the Eighteenth Century*, 32–56.

66. See Klausner, *Vilna, Yerushalayim de-Lita*, 1:56–57.

67. William Coxe, *Travels in Poland, Russia, Sweden, and Denmark* (London: J. Nicholas, 1784), 148, cited by Briedis, *Vilnius: City of Strangers*, 69.

68. Jacob Goldberg, *Ha-Mumarim be-Mamlekhet Polin-Lita* (Jerusalem: 1985), 37.

69. Ibid., 38–39.

70. Briedis, *Vilnius: City of Strangers*, 43.

71. On the history of Vilna's cosmopolitan literary and social character, see Tomas Venclova, "Vilnius/Wilno/Vilna: The Myth of Division and the Myth of Connection," in Marcel Cornis-Pope and John Neubauer, eds., *History of the Literary Cultures of East-Central Europe: Junctures and Disjunctures in the Nineteenth and Twentieth Centuries* (Amsterdam: John Benjamins Publishing, 2004), 2:11–28.

72. On the cultural role played by Vilnius University, see Briedis, *Vilnius: City of Straugers*, 84–85.

73. See Jacob Shatzky, "Kulture-Geschichte fun der Haskole bei Yidden in Lita," in Wishnitzer, *Lita*, 1:694. Regarding the Gaon's relationship to the university see the historically unverifiable but interesting story told in Chaikel Lunski, *Legendes: Vegn Vilner Goen* (Vilna: 1924), 23.

74. See Danzig, *Chokhmat Adam*, ruling 89:1.

75. Among other things, the Vilna leadership charged Chief Rabbi Shmuel ben Avigdor of engaging in questionable business dealings and turning individuals over to local authorities. On the dispute, see most recently the documents collected by Yehoshua Mondshine in his "Kinat ha-Mitnagdim le-Minhagei Ashkenaz," *Kerem Habad* 4, no. 1 (1992): 158–181; Hundert, *Jews in Poland-Lithuania in the Eighteenth Century*, 113; and Klausner, *Vilna be-Tekufat ha-Gaon*, 59–60, 79.

76. Elijah's supporters were divided between two camps (Abba ben Zeev Wolf and Noach Mindas supported the *kehilah*, and Yosef ben Eliyahu Pesseles supported the chief rabbi). Klausner, in his *Toldot ha-Kehilah ha-Ivrit be-Vilna*, 86, claims that begrudgingly and belatedly Elijah lent his name to a petition against Shmuel ben Avigdor. But Klausner does not list any source for this assertion, leading one to question the extent to which Elijah took any side.

77. Stanisław Lorentz, *Jan Krzysztof Glaubitz, Architekt Wileński XVIII wieku* (Warsaw: 1937).

78. On Elijah's complaints and the community's response, see the sources compiled in Kamenetsky, "Lehavdil bein Hayyim le-Hayyim," 880–881 fn.17. See also the statements recorded in the "Pinkas Kloiz ha-Gra," printed in "Kitaim mi-Pinkas ha-Kloiz shel ha-Gaon mi-Vilna," *Yeshurun* 6 (1999): 691 (specifically, "Pinkas Kloiz ha-Gra," 9). On Elijah's living quarters and study, see Klausner, *Toldot ha-Kehilah ha-Ivrit be-Vilna*, 78–80; and most recently Arie Morgenstern, "Bein Banim le-Talmidim: Ha-Ma'avak al Moreshet ve-al ha-Ideologia," *Dat* 53 (2004): 86–87.

79. On the possibility that Elijah traveled through Amsterdam in 1778, see Arie Morgenstern, "An Attempt to Hasten the Redemption," *Jewish Action* 58, no. 1 (Fall 1997): 38–44. For more in-depth discussions, see Morgenstern, *Mysticism and Messianism*, 263–306; Arie Morgenstern, *Hastening Redemption: Messianism and the Resettlement of the Land of Israel*, trans. Joel Linsider (Oxford: Oxford

University Press, 2006), 53–57; and Shuchat, *Olam Nistar be-Memadei ha-Zeman*, 75–88.

80. It is still very difficult to decipher exactly when Elijah made his trips to the Land of Israel. On reports that he traveled through Berlin and Amsterdam, see statements made by Yonatan Eibeschuetz in *Luchot Edut* (Altona: 1755); and Morgenstern, *Mysticism and Messianism*, appendix 18.

81. On the publication and history of the letter, see Yeshayahu Winograd's introduction to his *Otzar Sifrei ha-Gra* (Jerusalem: Kerem Eliyahu, 2003), 18.

82. See Elijah's commentary to Proverbs, *Mishlei im Biur ha-Gra* (Petach Tikvah: 1991), 11:18.

83. On Barukh Schick of Shklov, see David Fishman, *Russia's First Modern Jews: The Jews of Shklov* (New York: New York University Press, 1995), chapter 2; and Fishman, "A Polish Rabbi Meets the Berlin Haskalah: The Case of R. Barukh Schick," *AJS Review* 12, no. 1 (Spring 1987): 96–97.

84. See Cohen, *Vilna*, 177.

85. See my discussion of Wessely and the Gaon in Chapter 3. Wessely incorrectly asserted that the Gaon opposed the printing of Mendelssohn's *Biur*. See Moritz Güdemann, "Die Gegner Hartwig Wessely's Divrei Shalom ve-Emet," *Monatsschrift für Geschichte und Wissenschaft des Judentums* 19, no. 10 (1870): 479.

86. See the letter of Saul Berlin to the heads of the Altona community, documented in Winograd, *Otzar Sifrei ha-Gra*, 224.

87. See Klausner, *Toldot ha-Kehilah ha-Ivrit be-Vilna*, 52–53.

88. See Klausner, *Vilna, Yerushalayim de-Lita*, 1:59.

89. On Elijah's brother Abraham, see *Ma'alot ha-Torah* (New York: 1946), xv–xvi.

90. The Gaon hoped to turn the "Slutzki" home into a study house. On the "Slutzki" house, see Klausner, *Toldot ha-Kehilah ha-Ivrit be-Vilna*, 81; and Frick, "Jews and Others in Seventeenth-Century Wilno," 12–13.

91. See, for example, Manashe ben Yosef, *Alfei Menashe* (Vilna: 1822), chapter 67.

92. Shraga's words appear in his introduction to Gaon's biblical commentary *Aderet Eliyahu* (Dubrovna: 1804). On the publication history of Elijah's commentary on the Bible, see "Aliyat Kir," published in Levin, *Aliyot Eliyahu*, 109–110.

93. See the testimony of Hayyim of Vilna recorded in Levin, *Aliyot Eliyahu*, 76 fn.77.

94. See the description of Menachem Mendel's editorial practices in Chapter 5.

95. On Elijah's brothers Avraham and Yissaschar Ber, see Shuchat, *Olam Nistar be-Memadei ha-Zeman*, 37.

96. On the nature of Elijah's relationship to his children, see Avraham's and Yehudah Leib's introductions to *Biur ha-Gra al Shulchan Arukh Orach Chayyim, Yoreh De'ah* (Grodno: 1806), and *Aderet Eliyahu* (Dubrovna: 1804).

97. The Gaon's earliest disciples include Shlomo Zalman of Volozhin and Moshe Shlomo of Tołoczyn (both of whom died in the Gaon's lifetime), Moshe Shlomo of Vilkomer, Shlomo of Mohylów, and Menachem Mendel of Lublin. See the statements made about Shlomo Zalman (Hayyim's brother) and Moshe Shlomo of Tołoczyn by Elijah's children in their introduction to *Biur ha-Gra al Shulchan Arukh Orach Chayyim.* For more on Shlomo Zalman, see Yechezkel Feivel, *Toldot ha-Adam* (Dyhernfurth: 1801). On Moshe Shlomo of Vilkomir and Shlomo of Mohylów see Levin, *Aliyot Eliyahu*, 71–72. On Menachem Mendel of Lublin, see the sources and manuscripts listed in Winograd, *Otzar Sifrei ha-Gra*, 277. On the politics surrounding who was considered a first-tier versus a second-tier student of Elijah, see Morgenstern, "Bein Banim le-Talmidim," 83–125.

98. The Gaon's beadles included Sa'adya ben Natan Nata, Pinchas of Połock, and Tzvi Hirsch of Zeimis. On Sa'adya ben Natan Nata, see the introduction to *Ma'aseh Rav* (Jerusalem: 2009), 7–22; David Kamenetsky, "Sefer 'Ma'aseh Rav,' " *Yeshurun* 21 (2009): 774–827; and Levin, *Aliyot Eliyahu*, 87. On Tzvi Hirsch of Zeimis see Levin, *Aliyot Eliyahu*, 72–73. On Pinchas of Połock, see the introduction of Pinchas of Połock's work *Midrash Chachamim* (Minsk: 1809); and Allan Nadler, *The Faith of the Mithnagdim: Rabbinic Responses to Hasidic Rapture* (Baltimore: Johns Hopkins University Press, 1997).

99. The Gaon studied with Ya'akov Moshe of Słonim (his grandson), Noach ben Avraham Lifshitz (Mindes, the Gaon's grandson-in-law), Gershon ben Avraham (the Gaon's nephew), Shraga Feivush ben Shlomo Zalman (the Gaon's son-in-law), Moshe of Pińsk (a nephew), and Avraham Yechiel Danzig (the Gaon's granddaughter's in-law). On Ya'akov Moshe, see his introduction to *Shulchan Arukh Even ha-Ezer* (Vilna: 1819). On Mindas and Elijah see Israel Klausner, *Vilna be-Tekufat ha-Gaon* (Jerusalem: Reuben Mass, 1942), 287. On Gershon's relationship to Elijah, see David Luria's comments recorded in "Aliyat Kir," in Levin, *Aliyot Eliyahu*, 112. On Shraga Feivush's connection to Elijah, see Shraga's comments recorded at the end of the Gaon's commentary to Leviticus in *Aderet Eliyahu* (Dubrovna: 1804). On Moshe of Pińsk, see the introduction to *Shenot Eliyahu* (Lvov: 1799). On Avraham Danzig, see his introduction to *Chayyei Adam* (Vilna: 1819) and *Chokhmat Adam* (Vilna: 1825); and his eulogies about Elijah in *Mussar Adam* (repr. Jerusalem: Hadrat Yerushalayim, 1994), 97–103.

100. His most illustrious students from Shklov include the brothers Simcha Bunim and Menachem Mendel, and others such as Benjamin Rivlin and Yisrael of Shklov. On Simcha Bunim see Elijah's children's introduction to *Biur ha-Gra al*

Shulchan Arukh Orach Chayyim. On Menachem Mendel see his introduction to the Gaon's commentary to *Pirkei Avot* (Shklov: 1804) and comments made about him in the introduction to Yisrael of Shklov, *Pe'at ha-Shulchan* (Safed: 1836) and Levin, *Aliyot Eliyahu*, 74. On Yisrael of Shklov see his introduction to *Taklin Chadatin* (Minsk: 1812) and *Pe'at ha-Shulchan*.

101. On Hayyim of Volozhin's relationship to the Gaon, see Hayyim's introductions to Elijah's commentaries to *Biur ha-Gra al Shulchan Arukh Orach Chayyim*, *Shenot Eliyahu*, and *Sifra di-Tzniuta* (Vilna: 1820); as well as Levin, *Aliyot Eliyahu*, 70.

102. See Levin, *Aliyot Eliyahu*, 74 fn.83.

103. See Menachem Mendel of Shklov's introduction to *Mishlei* (Shklov: 1798).

104. See the description offered by his student Meir of Vilna in his introduction to *Taharat ha-Kodesh* (Zolkiew: 1804).

105. See the reflection on the way the Gaon's words were seen as "God-like" in *Sefer Toldot Adam* (Dyhernfurth: 1801), 83b.

106. See, for example, the story recorded in the name of Yehudah Edels, in Levin, *Aliyot Eliyahu*, 65 fn.46.

107. See the testimony of Yehudah Leib Margolit recorded in ibid., 76, 77.

108. See Hayyim of Volozhin's reflections recorded in ibid., 80 fn.94.

109. See the testimony of Hillel of Shklov in ibid., 68 fn.54.

110. See the introduction of Yisrael of Shklov to *Pe'at ha-Shulchan*.

111. See Yehudah (Yudel) Epstein's letter to Shmuel Yeven printed in Avraham ben ha-Gra, *Sa'eret Eliyahu*, 20b.

112. The one exception to this general rule seems to have been the letter of support that Elijah wrote for Meir of Vilna when Meir finished studying in Vilna. In Meir's introduction to *Taharat ha-Kodesh*, he records a letter that Elijah wrote attesting to Meir's impeccable character and his struggle to earn a livelihood to pay for his children's dowries.

113. See, for example, stories about the Gaon's consoling Rabbi Zalman of Volozhin recorded in *Sefer Toldot Adam*, 83a; and about his attempt to reconcile with the Menashe of Illya recorded in *Porat Yosef* (Vilna: 1858), 13.

114. The letters sent by Elijah to Kranz first appeared in *Brit Avot* (Breslau: 1839). On Kranz's relationship to Elijah, see Levin, *Aliyot Eliyahu*, 87.

115. On Raphael's relationship to Elijah see Levin, *Aliyot Eliyahu*, fn.11. On Raphael's involvement in Elijah's battle against Hasidism see Wilensky, *Hasidim u-Mitnagdim*, 1:182.

116. See Levin, *Aliyot Eliyahu*, 87; and Landau, *Ha-Gaon ha-Hasid mi-Vilna*, 279. According to Levin, the Gaon focused on reading Scripture in his later years (40).

117. See Levin, *Aliyot Eliyahu*, fn.41; Klausner, *Vilna be-Tekufat ha-Gaon*, 57.

118. It is not surprising that Elijah remarried quickly. In so doing, he followed most Jewish males of his era, who took second wives. In 1784 Vilna widowers comprised only 0.7 percent of the Jewish population. Second marriages were common due to high infant mortality rates, the financial benefits of marital life, and of course the desire for sexual fulfillment. On the importance of second marriages in eastern European Jewry, see Shaul Stampfer, "Remarriage among Jews and Christians," in his *Families, Rabbis and Education: Traditional Society in Nineteenth-Century Eastern Europe* (Oxford: Littman Library, 2010), 56–85, esp. 69–72; and Tamulynas, "Demographic and Social Professional Structure of the Jewish Community of Vilnius," 343.

119. Shaul Stampfer calls attention to the Gaon's salary but it must be noted that this sum can only be verified from 1784 onward (after Elijah was sixty). See Shaul Stampfer, "On the Creation and the Perpetuation of the Image of the Gaon of Vilna," in Moshe Hallamish, Yosef Rivlin, and Raphael Shuchat, eds., *Ha-Gra u-Veit Midrasho* (Ramat Gan: Bar-Ilan University Press, 2003), 45. See also Yehoshua Mondshine, "Parnasei Vilna ve-ha-Gra ve-Milchamtam be-Hasidut," *Kerem Habad* 4, no. 1 (November–December 1992): 184–185.

120. See Stampfer, "On the Creation and the Perpetuation of the Image of the Gaon of Vilna," 44; and more recently Shuchat, *Olam Nistar be-Memadei ha-Zeman*, 50.

121. On Mechotievitz, see the comments made by Menashe of Illya in Levin, *Aliyot Eliyahu*, 68; and Shmuel Joseph Fuenn, Matisyahu Strashun, and Hillel-Noah Maggid Steinschneider, *Kiryah Ne'emanah: Korot Adat Yisrael be-Ir Vilna* (Vilna: Yitzchak Funk, 1915), 162, 270–271.

122. On those who objected to the community supporting the Gaon, see Klausner, *Vilna be-Tekufat ha-Gaon*, 153–155, 164; and Stampfer, "On the Creation and the Perpetuation of the Image of the Gaon of Vilna," 43–45.

123. See the accounts of the Vilna *kehilah* documented in Klausner, *Toldot ha-Kehilah ha-Ivrit be-Vilna*, 160–161.

124. Wiernik, "Der Vilner Goen," 234.

125. See Klausner, *Toldot ha-Kehilah ha-Ivrit be-Vilna*, 171–185; and Yehudit Kalik, "Patterns of Contact between the Catholic Church and the Jews in the Polish-Lithuanian Commonwealth: The Jewish Debts," in Adam Teller, ed., *Studies in the History of the Jews in Poland in Honor of Jacob Goldberg*, published as a special edition of *Scripta Heirosolymitana* 38 (1998): 102–122.

126. Klausner, *Toldot ha-Kehilah ha-Ivrit be-Vilna*, 83, 97–99.

127. On the kidnapping and conversion of the young Jewish boy Edgardo Mortara, see David Kertzer, *The Kidnapping of Edgardo Mortara* (New York: Alfred Knopf, 1997).

128. Klausner, *Vilna be-Tekufat ha-Gaon*, 230.

129. See ibid., 271.

130. See *Sefer Ma'aseh Rav*, number heading 72. On the importance to the Gaon of the practice of sleeping in the sukkah, see Levin, *Aliyot Eliyahu*, 43.

131. See Klausner, *Vilna be-Tekufat ha-Gaon*, 267–269.

132. Ibid., 290.

133. Elijah's trip probably took place sometime before 1791. Yisrael of Shklov's statements in his introduction to *Pe'at ha-Shulchan* suggest that the Gaon studied in Sereje with Menachem Mendel, who was known to have studied with Elijah for a year and a half. According to Morgenstern, "Bein Banim le-Talmidim," the Gaon's studies with Menachem Mendel took place prior to 1791 (118). Further support for the notion that the Gaon moved briefly to Sereje is located in a document written in 1881 by Hayyim Reznik, located in YIVO archives, and printed by Dov Eliakh in *Sefer ha-Gaon*, 1:90, suggesting that at some point Elijah was forced to leave Vilna for a time. Elijah's connections to Sereje are further confirmed by his son Yehudah Leib's marriage to the daughter of the chief rabbi of Sereje.

134. See Klausner, *Vilna be-Tekufat ha-Gaon*, 237.

135. See the introduction of Menachem Mendel of Shklov to *Avot de-Rebbe Natan* (Shklov: 1804).

136. This is a rough estimate based on the 1798 census (the actual numbers might have even been higher). See Shaul Stampfer, "The 1764 Census of Lithuanian Jewry and What It Can Teach Us," *Jewish Population Studies, Papers in Jewish Demography 1993* 23 (1997): 97.

137. See Danzig, *Chokhmat Adam*, ruling 141:18.

138. See Levin, *Aliyot Eliyahu*, 89.

139. Shnayer Z. Leiman, "Who Is Buried in the Vilna Gaon's Tomb? A Mysterious Tale with Seven Plots," *Jewish Action* 59, no. 2 (Winter 1998): 36–41.

140. On the connection between Elijah and "the capital city of Vilna," see Hillel ben Shahar's eulogy republished in *Genuzot ha-Gra* (Jerusalem: Y.D. Kroizer, 2000), 313. On Elijah's connection to Vilna, "a city of glory," see Avraham Danzig's eulogy republished in *Mussar Adam* (Jerusalem: Hadrat Yerushalayim, 1992). On Elijah's connection to Vilna, a "city worthy of praise," see his children's introduction to *Yoreh De'ah* (Grodno: 1806); and Morgenstern, *Mysticism and Messianism*, 176–178.

141. On Vilna's and more generally eastern European Jewry's having characteristics of a virtual "majority" culture, see Adam Teller, *Koach ve-Hashpa'ah: Hayehudim be-Achuzot Beit Radzhivil be-Lita ba-Meah ha-18* (Jerusalem: Merkaz Zalman Shazar, 2005), 33–45; and Hundert, *Jews in Poland-Lithuania in the Eighteenth Century*, 21–31.

142. See the description of Vilna as a "metrapolin rabbati ba-goyim" recorded by the Va'ad Medinat Lita of 1594 in *Pinkas Medinat Lita*, ed. Simon Dubnow (Berlin: 1925), 63.

143. See the reflections of William Coxe in Coxe, *Travels in Poland, Russia, Sweden, and Denmark*, 211.

144. On these three groups involved with the Gaon's legacy, see Morgenstern, "Bein Banim le-Talmidim," 83–125.

145. See Akiva Eiger's letter printed in Avraham ben ha-Gra, *Sa'eret Eliyahu*.

146. See their introduction to the Gaon's commentary to the Bible, *Aderet Eliyahu*.

147. Ibid.

148. See the ban they placed against unlawful publication of the Gaon's writings—a ban first issued in 1798, then reaffirmed and published in 1799—in the "Kol Koreh" (a call announcing a prohibition) attached to the 1799 printing of *Shenot Eliyahu* (the Gaon's commentary to *Mishnah Zeraim*); see also the Gaon's sons' introduction to *Peirush al Kamah Aggadot* (Vilna: 1800).

149. See Tuviah Gutmann, *Kol Nehei* (Warsaw: 1797), republished in *Genuzot ha-Gra* (Jerusalem: Y.D. Kroizer, 2000), 304.

Chapter 2. Elijah's Worldview

1. Paul Franks argues in his work *All or Nothing: Systematicity, Transcendental Arguments, and Skepticism in German Idealism* (Cambridge, Mass.: Harvard University Press, 2005), 13–51, that German idealism is rooted "in a family of philosophical programs" that are first expressed in the work of Leibniz and fully developed by Immanuel Kant. Franks identifies two theses that distinguish their respective philosophical programs: the "Monistic Thesis" (the argument that all arguments can be traced back to one absolute and final source), and the "Dualistic Thesis" (the argument that "ideal" world based on the relational mediums of space and time allows us to distinguish between the physical and metaphysical world). On idealism and Leibniz, see most recently Paul Redding, *Continental Idealism: Leibniz to Nietzsche* (New York: Routledge, 2009), 1–35; Jonathan Israel, *Radical Enlightenment: Philosophy and the Making of Modernity, 1650–1750* (New York: Oxford University Press, 2001), 501–502; Rachel Albeck-Gidron, *Ha-Meah shel ha-Monadot: Ha-Metafizikah shel Leibniz ve-ha-Moderniyut shel ha-Meah ha-Esrim* (Ramat-Gan: Bar-Ilan University Press, 2007), 46–85; Matthew Stewart, *The Courtier and the Heretic: Leibniz, Spinoza, and the Fate of God in the Modern World* (New York: Norton, 2006), 17; and Ernst Cassirer, *The Philosophy of the Enlightenment* (Princeton, N.J.: Princeton University Press, 1979), 22.

2. Leibniz in *Philosophische Schriften*, ed. C. I. Gerhardt (Hildesheim: Olms, 1960), 5:560 points to Plato as the source of his understanding of the "ideal."

3. On Raphael Levi of Hannover's connection to Leibniz see Steven Schwarzschild and Henry Schwarzschild, "Two Lives in the Jewish Frühaufklärung–Raphael Levi Hannover and Moses Abraham Wolff," *Leo Baeck Year Book* 29 (1984): 229–258.

4. On the circulation of Levi's manuscripts throughout eastern Europe in the 1720s and 1730s, see ibid., 42 fn.III. See the introduction by Elijah's sons Avraham and Yehudah Leib to *Aderet Eliyahu* (Dubrovna: 1804), and Yehoshua Heschel Levin, *Aliyot Eliyahu* (Vilna: 1856), 22b, 24b. On the possibility of intellectual affinities between Elijah and Leibniz, see Alan Brill, "Auxiliary to 'Hokhma': The Writings of the Vilna Gaon and Philosophical Terminology," in Moshe Hallamish, Yosef Rivlin, and Raphael Shuchat, eds., *Ha-Gra u-Veit Midrasho* (Ramat Gan: Bar-Ilan University Press, 2003), 9–37.

5. Levin, *Aliyot Eliyahu*, 22b.

6. On Leibniz and Luzzatto, see Rivka Schatz-Uffenheimer, "Moshe Hayyim Luzzatto's Thought against the Background of Theodicy Literature," in Henning Graf Reventlow and Yair Hoffman, eds., *Justice and Righteousness: Biblical Themes and Their Influence* (Sheffield: JSOT Press, 1992), 173–199. See also Jonathan Garb, "Ha-Model ha-Politi be-Kabbalah Modernit be-Kitvei Ramchal," in *Al Da'at ha-Kahal*, ed. Benjamin Brown, Menahem Lorberbaum, Avinoam Rosenak, and Yedidyah Stern (Jerusalem: The Zalman Shazar Center and Israel Democracy Institute, forthcoming 2012), 21–25. On Elijah's relationship to Luzzatto, see Isaiah Tishby, *Messianic Mysticism: Moses Hayyim Luzzatto and the Padua School*, trans. Morris Hoffman (Oxford: Littman Library, 2008), 407 fn.8. Elijah received manuscripts of Luzzatto's writing from Yekutiel Gordon of Vilna. Tishby notes that "the position of the Gra and his pupils with regard to the teachings of kabbalah, and their attitude to messianic ideas and aims in general and to Luzzatto's messianic kabbalah in particular, are still tabula rasa so far as concerns scholarly research. Without clarification of these matters our picture of the Gra's personality and historical influence remains defective." Tishby's call first appeared in the Hebrew addition of his book published in 1993. Since then, important work has been produced that charts out the overlap and intellectual relationship between Luzzatto and Elijah. Specifically, see Raphael Shuchat's in-depth discussion in his *Olam Nistar be-Memadei ha-Zeman* (Ramat Gan: Bar-Ilan University Press, 2008), 113–151. On Yekutiel Gordon, see Jacob Shatzky, "Kulture-Geschichte fun der Haskole bei Yiddin in Lita," in Mark Wishnitzer, ed., *Lita* (New York: Futuro Press, 1951), 693; and Israel Klausner, *Vilna, Yerushalayim de-Lita: Dorot Rishonim, 1495–1881*, ed. Shmuel Barantchok (D.N. Western Galilee, Israel: Ghetto Fighter's House, 1988), 1:74–75. On the

issue of periodization and the secular aspects of Luzzatto's work, see Israel Bartal, "On Periodization, Mysticism and Enlightenment: The Case of Moses Hayyim Luzzatto," in David B. Ruderman and Shmuel Feiner, eds., *Jahrbuch Des Simon Dubnow Instituts*, vol. 6 (Leipzig: Vandenhoeck and Ruprecht, 2007), 201–214.

7. On the myriad statements made by Elijah's children and other descendants regarding the decisive influence that Luzzatto had on their master's worldview, see Shuchat, *Olam Nistar be-Memadei ha-Zeman*, 132–141.

8. On the relationship between kabbalah and philosophy in western thought see most recently Hava Tirosh-Samuelson, "Philosophy and Kabbalah: 1200–1600," in Daniel H. Frank and Oliver Leaman, eds., *The Cambridge Companion to Medieval Jewish Philosophy* (Cambridge: Cambridge University Press, 2003), 218–258. On the connection of kabbalah and idealism more generally, see Eliot Wolfson, *Language, Eros and Being: Kabbalistic Hermeneutics and Poetic Imagination* (New York: Fordham University Press, 2005), 200–212.

9. On the kabbalistic influences in Leibniz's work, see Allison P. Coudert, *Leibniz and the Kabbalah* (Boston: Kluwer Academic, 1995), 8. For an overview of the many seventeenth- and early eighteenth-century scientists and philosophers who were influenced by kabbalah, see Amos Funkenstein, *Theology and the Scientific Imagination: From the Late Middle Ages to the Seventeenth Century* (Princeton, N.J.: Princeton University Press, 1986), 79–80.

10. See *Aderet Eliyahu*, Genesis, 1:34. Elijah's commentary to Genesis first appeared in *Aderet Eliyahu* (Dubrovna: 1804). His commentary to the first chapter of Genesis is taken from the notes of his son Avraham, who adds, "These are the exact words I heard from my father's holy mouth." On the editing of Elijah's commentary to Genesis see David Luria's bibliographic notes in "Aliyat Kir" published by Yehoshua Heschel Levin, *Aliyot Eliyahu* (Vilna: 1856), 109–110. I am using the edition published in Warsaw in 1887 with Abraham's version of Elijah's commentary (which also appeared in the 1804 edition). My decision to rely on Abraham's notes is based on Luria's endorsement and the way Elijah describes "form," "matter," and "motion" in his other writings.

11. See Allison Coudert's translation of Leibniz's notes, "Concerning Man, Blessedness God and Christ," in Coudert, *Leibniz and the Kabbalah*, 129.

12. See Luzzatto, *Da'at Tevunot* (Jerusalem: 1943), 89.

13. Elijah contends that matter is "evil" in the sense that it is "unintelligible." Elijah in *Aderet Eliyahu*, Genesis 1:4, equates unintelligibility with both "night" and "matter." Unlike Maimonides who believes that darkness was simply a covering up of light, or Manicheans who believe that evil exists independently of the Creator, Elijah argues that light (good) and dark (evil) were in fact different creations, both with purpose, and both emanating from the same source. See

Elijah's comments to Genesis 1:4 on the creation of light and darkness and how he reinterprets Maimonides (*Guide of the Perplexed*, 2:30) in order to address the issue of theodicy.

14. On the concept of error in Leibniz's thought and in the early Enlightenment, see David William Bates, *Enlightenment Aberrations: Error and Revolution in France* (Ithaca, N.Y.: Cornell University Press, 2002), 41–72. Bates shows how Leibniz's notion of error was adopted across Europe in the eighteenth century. Specifically, he points out that Condillac, among other French Enlightenment thinkers, was in this respect "more indebted to Leibniz then to Locke in many ways" (57).

15. Gottfried Wilhelm Leibniz, *Philosophical Papers and Letters*, ed. and trans. Leroy E. Loemker, 2d ed. (Dordrecht: D. Reidel, 1970), 124.

16. Coudert, *Leibniz and the Kabbalah*, 153.

17. See Ernst Cassirer, *The Philosophy of Symbolic Forms*, trans. Ralph Mannheim (New Haven: Yale University Press, 1953), 3:362.

18. On the ancient sources animating Leibniz's ideas on math and kabbalah, see Stuart Brown, "Some Occult Influences on Leibniz's Monadology," in Allison Coudert, Richard Popkin, and Gordon Weiner, eds., *Leibniz, Mysticism, and Religion* (Dordrecht: Kluwer Academic, 1998), 1–21; and Coudert, *Leibniz and the Kabbalah*, 54.

19. See Elijah's commentary to *Sefer Yetzirah*, in Elijah ben Solomon, *Sefer Yetzirah* (Vilna: 1828), 2c. This statement is based on Moshe Shlomo of Tołoczyn's interpretation of Elijah's writing (which he tells us was related to him *peh le-peh*, "mouth to mouth," from Elijah). Yosef Avivi adopts Moshe Shlomo's interpretation. Avivi's and Moshe Shlomo's reading is correct; Elijah invokes the word *sefar* as a kind of "code," comprising both elements of a "book" and "math." As explained by Yosef Avivi, Moshe Shlomo's testimony is essential for making sense of Elijah's commentaries. Moshe Shlomo's version corresponds to the way Elijah's invokes the act of *zivug* (pairing) and *binah* (understanding) in his other writings. See Avivi, *Kabbalat ha-Gra* (Jerusalem: Kerem Eliyahu, ha-Makhon le-hotsa'at sifrei ha-Gra, 1992), 34–37. Avivi's and Moshe Shlomo's version is supported by Elijah's writings, where he privileges the act of speech. See, for example, Elijah's comments to Proverbs 8:33 in Elijah ben Solomon, *Sefer Mishlei im Biur ha-Gra*, ed. Moshe Philip (Petakh Tikvah: 2000). Eliot Wolfson, in his essay "From Sealed Book to Open Text: Time, Memory, and Narrativity in Kabbalistic Hermeneutics," *Interpreting Judaism in a Postmodern Age*, ed. Steven Kepnes (New York: New York University Press, 1996), 145–181, esp. fn.14 contests Avivi's reading. Wolfson argues that the exact wording and word ordering should follow Menachem Mendel of Shklov's version, namely, *Sefer, ve-Sefer, ve-Sippur*. Wolfson (and by extension Menachem Mendel) argues that instead of a

mathematical basis for Elijah's hermeneutic (*be-sefar*), the first word should be read as *sefer*, symbolizing an unknowable sealed book, and that the second book (*ve-sefer*) should be understood as an open book (two books). But Elijah's mathematical writings, especially his interpretation of the letters *sfr* in his commentary to *Sifra di-Tzniuta* (Shklov: 1820), draw a distinction between "*be-sfr*" and "*ve-sfr*." The first *sfr* connotes a mathematical code (*sefar*), and the middle *sfr* means an actual book comprised of a specific language (*sefer*). The first book is "sealed" not because one cannot know anything about it, but because numbers, according to Elijah, do not have any specific content (Elijah in *Sifra di-Tzniuta* actually compares *sefar* to "water"). *Sefar* is a universal blueprint, while the middle term, *sefer*, represents a contraction of this theoretical mathematical code into a specific content (speech). Wolfson also challenges Moshe Shlomo/Avivi on the word ordering, noting that virtually all versions of Elijah's writings have *sippur* in the third, not the middle, position (*be-sefer, ve-sefer, ve-sippur* as opposed to *be-sefar, ve-sippur, ve-sefer*). Wolfson contends that by placing *sippur* at the end, Elijah is showing that he sees writing as preceding speech (*sippur*). While Wolfson is correct that throughout *Sefer Yetzira* and *Sifra di-Tzniuta* Elijah lists *sippur* in the third position, there is a difference between the way the terms are listed and the way they interact with one another in the genesis of the world. Elijah sees *sippur* acting as a mediator between *sefar* (numbers) and *sefer* (writing), between the sealed code and the open text. In the genesis of the world the spoken word of *sippur* (*da'at*) negotiates the mathematical world of *sefar* (*chokhmah*) and the written world of *sefer* (*binah*). Elijah actually invokes the image of a scale (*mishkal*), with *sefar* and *sefer* on opposing ends and *sippur* acting as the scale in the middle holding up the two arms (see also Elijah's commentary to *Tikkunei ha-Zohar im Tikkunim mi-Zohar Chadash im Biur ha-Gra* [Vilna: Rosenkranz, 1867], 27a, "de-alin telat" and 33b "de-taman chokhmah"). Elijah in his commentary to *Tikkunei ha-Zohar* 54a states "and *da'at* comes in between *chokhmah* and *binah*." Though *sippur* is listed in the third position (perhaps in terms of cosmological importance), Elijah saw it as playing a "middle" role, like *da'at* (which is why Moshe Shlomo explains the text accordingly). In terms of their chronological genesis, *sippur* comes in the middle (the second position) of these two spheres. Putting *sippur* in the middle position is further corroborated by Elijah in *Tikkunei ha-Zohar*, 54a, where he claims that "*da'at hu ha-emtzaei*," the category of "knowledge," stands for "speech," and "*sippur*" comes between *chokhmah* (wisdom) and *binah* (understanding). In other words, according to Elijah the text reads *sefar, sefer, sippur*, but the genesis of these categories for what is in God's mind (*sefar*) is translated into the idiom of this world through a story (*sippur*), thereby producing the text read by all (*sefer*). Most of Elijah's kabbalistic writings are in large measure based on the notes of Menachem Mendel and Moshe Shlomo. It seems that Moshe Shlomo's notes are more reliable, however; on a number of occasions the early nineteenth-century editors of Elijah's work criticize Mendel's work. See, for example, David Luria's remarks in "Aliyat Kir" in Levin, *Aliyot Eliyahu*, regarding Menachem Mendel's editing of Elijah's *Sefer Yetzirah* (15). Finally, even Menahem Mendel in his work *Sefer Derekh ha-Kodesh* (Jerusalem: Kolel Torat ha-Chakham, 1999), not yet published when Wolfson wrote his article, admits that his teacher Elijah believed "that the word math [*cheshbon*] comes from thought [*machshava*] and this is what constitutes the first form" (4).

20. According to Elijah, in kabbalistic discourse, mathematics and pure thought exist within the realm of *chokhmah* (wisdom). On the kabbalistic implications of Elijah's hermeneutics, see Brill, "Auxiliary to 'Hokhma,' " 19.

21. For a parallel text, see Elijah ben Solomon, *Sefer Yetzirah* (Grodno: 1806), 166a, where Elijah describes the act of writing and creation as follows: "When someone writes a *Sefer Torah* [a Torah scroll], he bases his ideas on a text which he neither writes nor speaks. Afterwards, he reads [the Torah he is copying from] and then writes [it down]."

22. The World-Book trope was still heavily invoked by eighteenth-century thinkers and specifically by Leibniz. On this point, see Hans Aarsleff, *From Locke to Saussure: Essays on the Study of Language and Intellectual History* (Minneapolis: University of Minnesota Press, 1982), 42–69. On the history of this trope more generally, see Ernst Robert Curtius, *European Literature and the Latin Middle Ages*, trans. Willard R. Task (Princeton, N.J.: Princeton University Press, 1967), 302–347. According to Eliot Wolfson, "In the Jewish context, the [World-Book] metaphor is not to be understood metaphorically but hyperliterally, that is, Torah, the prototype of all books, the hypertext, if you will, informs us about the semantic character of nature." See Wolfson, *Language, Eros, Being: Kabbalistic Hermeneutics and Poetic Imagination* (New York: Fordham University Press, 2005), 202.

23. Robert S. Leventhal, *The Disciplines of Interpretation: Lessing, Herder, Schlegel and Hermeneutics in Germany, 1750–1800* (New York: Walter de Gruyter, 1994), 36.

24. For Elijah the concepts of speech, communication, and ethics are interlocked within the kabbalistic *sefirah* of *binah* (human knowledge/understanding). Ethics is directly attached to the concept of speech (inter-human communication) and not writing. Also, Elijah's rigorous classification of speech in the *sefirah* of *binah* again points to the position occupied by *binah*. Namely, *binah* (the spoken word) stands directly beneath the most privileged *sefirah* of *chokhmah* (wisdom).

25. See for example, Elijah's comments in *Mishley im Biur ha-Gra*, ed. Moshe Philip (Petach Tikvah: 1991) 3:13, 20; as well as his comments to *Tikkunei ha-Zohar*, 38b–39a.

26. See Elijah's comments in *Mishlei im Biur ha-Gra*, 2:3.

27. According to Elijah, "The poet does not use any extra words. For the poet each and every utterance is for a specific reason" (comments to Proverbs 8:6, in *Mishlei im Biur ha-Gra*).

28. Georg Friedrich Meier, *Versuch einer Allgemeinen Auslegungskunst* (Düsseldorf: Stern-Verlag, 1965), 57.

29. These are Moshe Shlomo of Tołoczyn's words, heard directly from Elijah. See the citation in Elijah ben Solomon, *Sefer Yahel Or* (Vilna: 1882), 16a.

30. Elijah ben Solomon, *Sefer Yetzirah*, 2b.

31. On attempts in the seventeenth century to create a *mathesis universalis*, see Funkenstein, *Theology and the Scientific Imagination*, 28–29. On Leibniz's notion of *mathesis universalis*, see Jan C. Westerhoff, "Poeta Calculans: Harsdörffer, Leibniz, and the *Mathesis Universalis*," *Journal of the History of Ideas* 60, no. 3 (1999): 449–467. On *mathesis universalis* and its connection to kabbalistic thinking, see Marcia Keith Scuchard, "Leibniz, Benzelius, and the Kabbalistic Roots of Swedish Illuminism," in Coudert, Popkin, and Weiner, *Leibniz, Mysticism and Religion*, 84–106. On eighteenth-century attempts to create a universal language, see Thomas Schlereth, *The Cosmopolitan Ideal in Enlightenment Thought: Its Form and Function in the Ideas of Franklin, Hume, and Voltaire, 1694–1790* (Notre Dame, Ind.: University of Notre Dame Press, 1977), 42–44; and David Wellbery, *Lessing's Laocoon: Semiotics and Aesthetics in the Age of Reason* (Cambridge: Cambridge University Press, 1984), 29.

32. Elijah's investment in mathematics is expressed in his own geometrical work *Ayil Meshulash*. The title, which translated means "A Ram in Three Parts," was named by Rabbi Shmuel Luknik and plays on the words and story of Genesis 15:9. There Abraham is said to have made a "covenant between the parts (*meshulash*) of a ram." The word *meshulash* also contains the root for the Hebrew/rabbinic word for geometry. Published in 1833 by Lukink, the book focuses on engineering and algebraic principles. It does not explicitly invoke any kabbalistic images and only tangentially touches on some rabbinic concepts. See Elijah ben Solomon, *Sefer Ayil Meshulash: Al Chokhmat ha-Meshulashim ve-ha-Handasah* (Vilna: 1833).

33. Catherine Wilson, *Leibniz's Metaphysics: A Historical and Comparative Study* (Manchester, Eng.: Manchester University Press, 1989), 147.

34. Coudert, *Leibniz and the Kabbalah*, 145.

35. See G. W. Leibniz, *Dialogus de Connexione inter Reset Verba* (1677), cited and translated in Joseph Politella, "Platonism, Aristotelianism and Cabalism in the Philosophy of Leibniz," Ph.D. diss., University of Pennsylvania, 1938, 30.

36. See Coudert, *Leibniz and the Kabbalah*, 155.

37. See G. W. Leibniz, *A New System*, trans. Jonathan Bennett, para. 11, available at www.earlymoderntexts.com/f_leibniz.html (last accessed March 28, 2012).

38. See Moshe Idel, "Bein ha-Kabbalah Nevush le-Kabbalat R. Menachem Mendel mi-Schklov," in Moshe Hallamish, Yosef Rivlin, and Raphael Shuchat, eds., *Ha-Gra u-Veit Midrasho* (Ramat Gan: Bar Ilan University Press, 2003), 173–194.

39. Menachem Mendel of Shklov, *Sefer Derekh ha-Kodesh* (Jerusalem: Kolel Torat chakham, 1999), 4.

40. On Abulafia's kabbalah see Moshe Idel, *Kabbalah: New Perspectives* (New Haven: Yale University Press, 1988), 200–208; Idel, *Language, Torah, and Hermeneutics in Abraham Abulafia*, trans. Menachem Kallus (Albany: State University of New York Press, 1989), 1–11; and Idel, *The Mystical Experience in Abraham Abulafia*, trans. Jonathan Chipman (Albany: State University of New York Press, 1988), 9.

41. Avraham ben ha-Gra, *Sefer Rav Pe'alim*, 62.

42. The letter can be found in Tzvi ha-Levi Horowitz, *Kitvei ha-Geonim* (Warsaw: 1938), 3–10. Regarding Aristotle's *Ethics* it is unclear if the Gaon was requesting a Latin edition or more likely a copy of Meir Alguadez's Hebrew translation (*Sefer ha-Middot*) of the Latin text, composed in 1400.

43. Leibniz's reflections on Maimonides can be found in his posthumously published "Observationes ad Rabbi Mosis Maimonidis librum qui inscribitur Doctor Perplexorum," in Alexandre Foucher de Careil, *La philosophie juive et la cabale* (Paris: 1861). For English readers see Lenn E. Goodman, "Maimonides and Leibniz," *Journal of Jewish Studies* 31, no. 2 (1980): 214–236.

44. Wilson, *Leibniz's Metaphysics*, 271.

45. See Goodman, "Maimonides and Leibniz," 220–221.

46. See Elijah's comments in *Aderet Eliyahu*, (Dubrovna: 1804), Genesis 1:3. Elijah explicitly lists "*ha-heder*" (ether) and "*ha-yuli*" (primordial matter) as existing prior to creation in his "Seventy Forces of Nature." Elijah's Great Chain of Being theory first appeared in *Aderet Eliyahu* (Vilna: 1820) as an interpretation of Isaiah 11:1. On the history of this often censored text see Ya'akov Greenwald, *Kuntres Shivi'im Kochot ha-Adam* (Jerusalem: 1991), 123, and my more detailed discussion in "Philosophy and Dissimulation in Elijah of Vilna's Writings and Legacy," *Revue Internationale de Philosophie* (forthcoming).

47. While it may be argued that Maimonides in fact never subscribed to the belief in Creation ex nihilo, such issues require their own study. The literature on Maimonides's understanding of this passage of *Pirkei de-Rabbi Eliezer* and Plato is extensive. See most recently Kenneth Seeskin, *Maimonides on the Origins of the World* (New York: Cambridge University Press, 2007), 16–60; Lawrence Kaplan,

"Maimonides on the Miraculous Element in Prophecy," *Harvard Theological Review* 70, nos. 3–4 (1977): 233–256; Herbert Davidson, "Maimonides' Secret Position on Creation," in *Studies in Medieval Jewish History and Literature*, ed. Isadore Twersky (Cambridge, Mass.: Harvard University Press, 1979), 16–40; and Warren Zev Harvey, "A Third Approach to Maimonides' Cosmogony-Prophetology Puzzle," *Harvard Theological Review* 74, no. 3 (1981): 287–301.

48. On Plato and the kabbalistic understanding of creation, see Moshe Idel, "Jewish Kabbalah and Platonism in the Middle Ages and Renaissance," in Lenn E. Goodman, ed., *Neoplatonism and Jewish Thought* (Albany: State University of New York Press, 1992), 320–321.

49. See also Elijah's comments on creation ex nihilo in his commentary to *Mishnat Hasidim*, an edited version of which appears in Raphael Shuchat, "Peirush ha-Gra mi-Vilna le-Mishnat Hasidim: Mashal ve-Nimshal be-Kitvei ha-Ari," *Kabbalah* 3 (1998): 297.

50. See G. W. Leibniz, *Textes inédits*, ed. G. Grua (Paris: 1948), 98.

51. On Leibniz's views regarding creation, see Reginald O. Savage, *Real Alternatives: Leibniz's Metaphysics of Choice* (Dordrecht: Kluwer Academic, 1998), 99–130; and Daniel Cook, "Leibniz on Creation: A Contribution to His Philosophical Theology," in Marcelo Dascal, ed., *Leibniz: What Kind of Rationalist? Logic, Epistemology, and the Unity of Science* (Tel Aviv: Tel Aviv University Press, 2008), 449–460.

52. See Elijah's comments in *Aderet Eliyahu*, Genesis 1:1; see also Elijah ben Solomon, *Imrei Noam Berachot* (Warsaw: 1899), 60b. The radical nature of Elijah's comments on creation ex nihilo have been noted as well in Yehudah Lifshitz, *Nachal Yehudah* (Kovno: 1920), 4–5.

53. See Seymour Feldman, "Synopsis of Book Six" in Levi ben Gershom, *The Wars of the Lord*, trans. and ed. Seymour Feldman (New York: Jewish Publication Society and Jewish Theological Seminary of America Press, 1999), 195.

54. See Mejeris Šubas, "The Gaon's Views on Philosophy and Science," in Izraelis Lempertas, ed., *The Gaon of Vilnius and the Annals of Jewish Culture* (Vilnius: Vilnius University Press, 1998), 65–74, esp. 69.

55. See Feldman, "Synopsis of Book Six," 208. More generally, see Jonathan Goldstein, "The Origins of the Doctrine of Creation Ex-Nihilo," *Journal of Jewish Studies* 35 (1984): 127–135.

56. On Occasionalism and Descartes, see most recently the volume edited by Steven Nadler, *Occasionalism: Causation among the Cartesians* (New York: Oxford University Press, 2011). Descartes and the overwhelming majority of early modern kabbalists adopted neo-Platonic notions of how form precedes and remains independent of matter. See Israel, *Radical Enlightenment*, 16–19. On early modern kabbalah and Platonism, see Idel, "Jewish Kabbalah and Platonism

in the Middle Ages and Renaissance," 319–351; and Goodman, "Maimonides and Leibniz," 214–236.

57. Elijah ben Solomon, *Aderet Eliyahu*, Genesis 2:2, 2:6, and Ezekiel 1:51.

58. See Elijah ben Solomon, *Sifra di-Tzniuta*, *likkutim* 38b; for parallels and similar comments see 17a and 28b. See also Elijah's statements in Elijah ben Solomon, *Sefer Yetzirah*, 8c.

59. See Elijah ben Solomon's comments to *Mishlei im Biur ha-Gra*, 1:1.

60. See Leibniz, *Theodicy*, ed. Austin Farrar, trans. E. M. Huggard (New Haven: Yale University Press, 1952), section 395, and Elijah ben Solomon, *Aderet Eliyahu*, Genesis 1:1.

61. Elijah argues, in his comments to *Shulchan Arukh, Orach Chayyim*, 5:1 and in *Sefer Yetzira* 1:1c, that God is a philosophic category: "the necessary being" (*nimtzah kayam*).

62. See Elijah ben Solomon, *Aderet Eliyahu*, Genesis 1:2.

63. On this point see Nachmanides's comments to Genesis 1:1.

64. On the debates surrounding Elijah's position on the kabbalistic concept of the divine contraction, *tzimtzum*, see Shuchat, "Peirush ha-Gra mi-Vilna le-mishnat hasidim," 265–274.

65. On Leibniz's understanding of creation and human-produced evil, see Jeffrey K. McDonough, "Leibniz: Creation *and* Conservation *and* Concurrence," *Leibniz Review* 17 (2007): 35–37.

66. Leventhal, *The Disciplines of Interpretation*, 53.

67. See Elijah's comments to Deuteronomy 1:1 in Elijah ben Solomon, *Aderet Eliyahu*.

68. Hans W. Frei, *The Eclipse of Biblical Narrative: A Study in Eighteenth- and Nineteenth-Century Hermeneutics* (New Haven: Yale University Press, 1974), 78.

69. See Christian Wolff, *Logic; or, Rational Thoughts on the Powers of the Human Understanding, with Their Use and Application in the Knowledge and Search of Truth*, trans. Baron Wolfius, vol. 77 of Wolff, *Gesammelte Werke, Materialien und Dokumente* (Hildesheim: Olms, 2003), 172–192.

70. On the use of the term *takhlit ha-sefer*, see Moses Hayyim Luzzatto, *Derekh Tevunot* (Jerusalem: Eshkol, 1973), 52. Even when Luzzatto invoked the term *kavanah*, intent, he references the intent of the words of the text, not the writer (18). It should be noted with respect to the issue of authorial versus textual intention that Moses Mendelssohn was one of the first eighteenth-century interpreters to place primary emphasis on the author of the text. The historical singularity of Mendelssohn's approach has been noted by Edward Breuer, who writes that "Mendelssohn's terminology, and his particular notion of primary and secondary notions of meanings as expressions of intentionality, also appear quite

novel when examined in the context of contemporary German exegesis and literary theory." See Breuer, *The Limits of Enlightenment: Jews, Germans, and the Eighteenth-Century Study of Scripture* (Cambridge, Mass.: Harvard University Press, 1996), 192.

71. See Elijah's comments to Proverbs 1:2 in *Mishlei im Biur ha-Gra*; his comments to Deuteronomy 1:1 in *Aderet Eliyahu*; and his comments to Isaiah 1:1 in *Biur ha-Gra le-Nevi'im* (Jerusalem: Mossad ha-Rav Kook, 2002).

72. Robert Leventhal claims that "the author within Enlightenment theory thus cannot be equated with the modern notion of the author as . . . meaning-endowing. [Likewise,] the notion of "intention" (*Absicht*) should not be identified with a modern notion of intentionality as it appears in phenomenology or pragmatics." See Leventhal, *The Disciplines of Interpretation*, 53.

73. Johann M. Chladenius, *Einleitung zur Richtigen Auslegung Vernünftiger Reden und Schriften* (Düsseldorf: Stern-Verlag Janssen, 1969), para. 157.

74. As suggested by Harry Fox, "[Elijah's] philological approach is based on a *divinatio* [of text]. . . . The majority of Elijah's emendations do not have any possibility of being originally present, and each comes to offer a corrective by inserting material that he thought [made] better [sense] than what stood before him in the text." See Menachem Tzvi Fox, "Hagahot ha-Gra le-Midrashei Halakha ke-Yesod le-Tfisat Olamo ha-Ruchani," *Sidra* 15 (1999): 115.

75. Martin Heidegger, *Being and Time*, trans. J. Macquarrie and E. Robinson (New York: Harper & Row, 1962), 194.

76. David Couzens Hoy, *The Critical Circle: Literature, History, and Philosophical Hermeneutics* (Berkeley: University of California Press, 1978), 2–5.

77. See Kurt Mueller-Vollmer, *The Hermeneutics Reader: Texts of the German Tradition from the Enlightenment to the Present* (New York: Continuum, 2006), 4.

78. See the comments by Elijah recorded in the *likkutim* to Isaiah 2:1 in *Biur ha-Gra le-Nevi'im* (Jerusalem: Mossad ha-Rav Kook, 2002).

79. See Luzzatto, *Derekh Tevunot*, 64–66.

80. See the comments of Shlomo Zalman of Zamosc in his *Beit Avot* (Berlin: 1889), 101b–102a. Shlomo Zalman argues (based on Elijah's ideas in Deuteronomy 1:1 and Proverbs 1:1–7) that Elijah's theory of interpretation was based on his notions of nature and the Aristotelian four causes. On Elijah's employment of Aristotelian language in his interpretive practices see also Brill, "Auxiliary to Hokhma," 25–27.

81. Avraham ben ha-Gra, *Sa'eret Eliyahu* (Warsaw: 1877), 3b.

82. See Elijah's comments to Psalms 5:10 in *Peirush ha-Gra le-Tehilim* (Prague: 1812).

83. Joseph Albo argues: "Before the syllogism is constructed, the thing is known potentially in the premise." See Albo, *Sefer ha-Ikarim*, ed. and trans. Isaac

Husik (Philadelphia: Jewish Publication Society, 1946), 1:139–140. Albo's textual "preformation" theory is repeated and stressed by those identified with the late medieval *pilpul*-based Iyyun School. In his work *Darkhei ha-Gemara*, Isaac Campanton, the leader of the Iyyun School, uses language almost identical to that of Elijah in explaining that one should "always keep in mind the general concepts, which [one] originally derived from the section. Then, go over it again to see if what [one has] derived fits into the language." At that point, he writes, "one is ready to delve into the roots and reasoning of the subject, investigating all of its details and sources. . . . This means that in the beginning [one] should look at it generally."

84. Wolff, *Logic*, 185.

85. Ibid., 179.

86. Hidé Ishiguro, *Leibniz's Philosophy of Logic and Language* (Ithaca, N.Y.: Cornell University Press, 1972), 57–62.

87. On this point, see Moses Hayyim Luzzatto's distinction between empirical knowledge and logic in the interpretation of texts, described in his *Derekh Tevunot*, 34–37.

88. On the role of subject-predicate propositions in Leibniz's thought, see Bertrand Russell, *A Critical Exposition of the Philosophy of Leibniz* (Boston: Longwood Press, 1989), 4–11. Ishiguro, in his *Leibniz's Philosophy of Logic and Language*, criticizes Russell for pushing Kantian definitions onto Leibniz's use of the terms subject and predicate (171–176).

89. See Leibniz's letter to Arnauld in *The Correspondence between Leibniz and Arnauld*, ed. and exp. Jonathan Bennet (2010), vi.1686, available at http://www.earlymoderntexts.com/pdfbits/leiba2.pdf, p. 30 (last accessed May 1, 2011).

90. There is a unique corollary between Elijah's and Leibniz's preformation theories. See the statement reported in the name of the Gaon by his brother Rabbi Abraham ben Solomon in Abraham ben Solomon, *Ma'alot ha-Torah*, ed. Michael Feinstein and Nissan Waxman (New York: Peninim, 1946). "In truth there are an infinite number of *mitzvot* (commandments): And with regard to this teaching it is said in the name of David, 'I have seen that all things have a limit but your commandments are beyond limit'" (Psalms 119:96). With regard to the 613 *mitzvot* these are only roots, for their branches spread out infinitely. In truth this distinction between leaves and roots is hidden from us. And it is not critical that we even know which one is which. For in every *mitzvah*, in every word of Torah, there is encompassed the entirety of Torah and all the *mitzvot*, all of their principles, specifics, and details. It is in this regard that Torah is described as a Tree of Life (Proverbs 3:18). Torah is just like one trunk of a tree that spreads out into many branches, and each branch spreads out in many sticks, and each stick

spreads out in fruit, and within each fruit there are seeds that possess the force of creation to produce a full tree, ad infinitum. And as the philosophers argue, within each branch there are contained all the elements that embody a tree, so too it is with the words of the Torah. Each word and commandment has within it all other words and commandments (6)." Similarly, Leibniz in *The Monadology* writes, "The Author of nature has been able to employ this divine and infinitely wonderful power of art, because each portion of matter is not only infinitely divisible, as the ancients observed, but is also actually subdivided without end, each part into further parts, of which each has some motion of its own; otherwise it would be impossible for each portion of matter to express the whole universe. . . . Each portion of matter may be conceived as like a garden full of plants and like a pond full of fishes. But each branch of every plant, each member of every animal, each drop of its liquid parts is also some such garden or pond. . . . Philosophers have been much perplexed about the origin of forms, entelechies, or souls; but nowadays it has become known, through careful studies of plants, insects, and animals, that the organic bodies of nature are never products of chaos or putrefaction, but always come from seeds, in which there was undoubtedly some preformation; and it is held that not only the organic body was already there before conception, but also a soul in this body, and, in short, the animal itself" (paras. 65–74).

91. See the example Luzzatto gives of "Nashim chayavot be-kiddush ha-yom" in his *Derekh Tevunot*, 13. It should be noted, however, that in *Derekh Tevunot*, Luzzatto never crosses the threshold of calling for the emendation of sacred or rabbinic texts. Ultimately, he falls back into the older Iyyun School model discussed earlier, which gave the reader the ultimate responsibility for justifying the logic of the text under examination (43–44). On Elijah's relationship to the ideas expressed by Luzzatto in *Derekh Tevunot*, see the statements recorded by Rabbi Avraham Simcha in a letter that appears in Luzzatto's *Derekh Tevunot*, 38b.

92. Luzzatto, *Derekh Tevunot*, 18.

93. Some medieval and modern scholars emended rabbinic texts based on oral tradition and manuscripts; others did so based on textual reasoning. Yet compared to even the most daring of these medieval and early modern interpreters, Elijah's emendations to *Midrash Halakha* are extraordinary. Early students of Elijah and followers of the nineteenth-century *Wissenschaft des Judentums*, like M. S. Zuckermandel, argued that Elijah's radical emendations of rabbinic literature were drawn from his own manuscripts. Later scholars and intellectual descendants of Elijah, like Saul Lieberman, claim that Elijah's emendations of rabbinic texts such as the early Tannaitic work *Tosefta*, were not based on manuscripts, but rather on his own interpretive sense. See Lieberman, *Tosefet*

Rishonim (Jerusalem: Bamberger Vahrman, 1937), 1:2. More recently, Dov Eliakh re-entertained the possibility that Elijah did, in fact, possess manuscripts and employed them when emending and commenting on texts. See Dov Eliakh, *Sefer ha-Gaon: Le-Toldot Chayav u-Verur Mishnato shel Morenu ve-Rabenu ha-Gaon Eliyahu mi-Vilna* (Jerusalem: Moreshet Yeshivot, 2002), 2:771–776, 3:1185–1189. Yet regarding Elijah's emendations to *Midrash Halakha*, almost all scholars agree that even if Elijah did possess manuscripts, he ignored them and relied on his own interpretive abilities. The majority of emendations attributed to Elijah come from notes he wrote in the margins of his books. On this point, see Ya'akov Shmuel Spiegel, *Amudim be-Toldot ha-Sefer ha-Ivri: Hagahot u-Megahim* (Ramat Gan: Bar-Ilan University Press, 1996), 407. Spiegel quotes Rabbi Ya'akov Bachrach as saying that "[Elijah] emended by himself on the margins of the books he studied from. Therefore, we are not informed of the logic or basis behind his emendations. He does not leave a note regarding the source for his emendation. And who knows if those who copied them did so with good faith and understood his writings."

94. Many different hands were involved in the publication of Elijah's emendations of *Midrash Halakha*. Irrespective of the editor, Elijah's basic approach toward emendation and synonymy of Midrash remains consistent. Elijah's emendations of *Mekhilta* were first edited by Yitzchak Eliyahu Landau and published in Vilna in 1844. This edition was followed by the publication in 1877 of a different set of his notes edited by Meir Leibush. Elijah's emendations of *Sifrei* were originally in the hands of Hayyim of Volozhin and Rabbi David Luria. See Luria, "Aliyat Kir," 106. These emendations were published in Vilna in 1866 and edited more carefully by Shachne Koledetzki in Jerusalem in 1950. David Luria in "Aliyat Kir" also claims to have had a copy of Elijah's emendations of *Sifra* (106). These emendations, however, were not published until 1911 by Yisrael Meir Kagan. On the complete publication history of Elijah's emendations to *midrash halakha* texts, see Yeshayahu Winograd, *Otzar Sifrei ha-Gra* (Jerusalem: Kerem Eliyahu, 2003), 50–54.

95. On the importance of *Midrash Halakha* in the modern period, see Jay M. Harris, *How Do We Know This? Midrash and the Fragmentation of Modern Judaism* (Albany: State University of New York Press, 1995), 103–105; see also Harris, "Modern Students of Midrash Halakha: Between Tradition and Wissenschaft," in Jack Wertheimer, ed., *The Uses of Tradition: Jewish Continuity in the Modern Era* (New York: Jewish Theological Seminary of America, 1992), 261–277. On the central role that *Midrash Halakha* played in Elijah's learning circle, see Yehudah Copperman, *Li-Feshuto shel Mikra: Kovetz Ma'amarim* (Jerusalem: Hotsa'at Haskel le-Yad Mikhlalah Yerushalayim le-Vanot, 1974), 86–90; and Yehudah Leib Maimon, *Sefer ha-Gra* (Jerusalem: Mossad ha-Rav Kook, 1953), 47.

96. Nachman Krochmal, *Moreh Nevukhei ha-Zeman*, 2d ed. (Lemberg: M. Volf, 1863), 163.

97. See, for example, Fox, "Hagahot ha-Gra le-Midrashei Halakha ke-Yesod le-Tfisat Olamo ha-Ruchani," 111–117. Fox argues that "the originality of Elijah's interpretive practices is based on his privileging of the Babylonian Talmud even over Tannaitic text, the earliest layer of rabbinic text" (114). Fox's "Bavlification" theory has been challenged on the following grounds. First, if such were the case then Elijah would never have emended and interpreted the Mishnah against the Babylonian Talmud. Compiled around 200 C.E., the Mishnah is the work on which the Babylonian and Palestinian Talmuds are based. While almost all medieval scholars see these two bodies of literature (Mishnah and Talmud) as inseparable and interpretively in line with one another, Elijah explained the Mishnah independently and in opposition to the Talmud. On this point see Maimon, *Sefer ha-Gra*, where Maimon claims that "we see from Gra's commentary that sometimes [his interpretation of the Mishnah] differed with the writers of the Gemara" (44). Finally Ya'akov Elman convincingly demonstrates in his "Methodology and Purpose of the Gaon's Commentaries to the Halakhic Midrashim in *Aderet Eliyahu* on Leviticus," in Hallamish, Rivlin, and Shuchat, *Ha-Gra u-Veit Midrasho*, 77, that "one should not assume that our teacher [Elijah] was compelled to merge the words of the *Sifra* with what is written in the Babylonian Talmud."

98. Jay Harris, *How Do We Know This? Midrash and the Fragmentation of Modern Judaism* (Albany: State University of New York Press, 1995), 236.

99. See Katriel Fishel Tchorsh, "Sirtutim le-Demuto shel ha-Gra," *Talpiyot* 4, nos. 1–2 (July 1949): 155–166. Though Tchorsh grossly oversimplifies Elijah's worldview, he was one of the first to address the concept of "harmony" in Elijah's writings. More recently, see the work of Yehudah Liebes, "Tzidkat ha-Tzadik: Yachas ha-Gaon mi-Vilna ve-Chugo Klapei ha-Shabta'ut," *Kabbalah* 9 (2003). Liebes explains how the concept of "mishkal" (scale) operates in Elijah's kabbalah, as that which will reestablish the "harmony" of the world (305). Liebes steers his findings in the direction of what influence, if any, Sabbatai Tzvi might have had on Elijah. Though not discussed by Liebes, it seems likely that Elijah's conception of "original harmony" might have been the result of reading Luzzatto's writings.

100. Specifically, the Gaon places two texts under the rubric of "Midrashei ha-Torah," *Sifra* and *Sifrei*. While numerous distinctions can be drawn between *Sifra* and *Sifrei*, Elijah sees them both expressing a similar exegetical orientation, bridging the chasm between the oral and written law. Surprisingly, he does not mention the other main Midrashic work, *Mekhilta*.

101. See Elijah's *Aderet Eliyahu*, Deuteronomy 33:1. A parallel to this interpretation is found in the Elijah's comments to *Tikkunei ha-Zohar*, 36b. There Elijah

argues: "Kabbalah is what connects both Torahs. For in the Torah there are the secrets of kabbalah. Therefore, the early Rabbis [*tannaim*] engaged in the study of *midrashei mekorot*. As found in the simple reading of the *Sifra* and *Sifrei* that reveal the scriptural sources of the oral law. It is for this reason that *Torat Kohanim* begins with the thirteen hermeneutic principles."

102. On Elijah's ideas regarding the present age of "tohu" see Leibes, "Tzidkat ha-Tzadik," 298–299.

103. *Sifra*, Parshata 7, 9: 1–3, reads: "(1) Represents a specific law directed only at those who err based on their own [mistake] and does not include those who err because of an incorrect legal ruling from a Jewish court. (2) What is the case being discussed? A Jewish court ruled [incorrectly] to transgress one of the commandments stated in the Torah, and an individual went and committed an inadvertent infraction based on the court's ruling. Irrespective of whether or not the members of the court and the individual carried out the ruling simultaneously or whether the individual followed their ruling, only after the members of the court practiced what they had ruled or even if they did not but he did, [the individual is exempt from any punishment]. And Rabbi Shimon adds that if the court ruled and they [its judges] realized it had erred and went back on their ruling, irrespective of whether they gave an atonement sacrifice or did not bring their atonement sacrifice, one who acted according to their [first incorrect] ruling is not liable for his actions. And Rabbi Meir said [such a person] is liable. And Rabbi Eliezer said it is questionable [as to whether or not he should be held liable]. Sumchos says it depends upon the circumstances surrounding this act, [namely it has been said that] if one acts [inadvertently] based on his own judgment he is liable, if he acts inadvertently because of an incorrect ruling of the court he is not liable. What are the conditions being discussed here? If a court ruled and one of them on the court knew that they had erred or there was an especially wise student in attendance before them who is worthy of giving judgments himself such as Shimon ben Azzai, and knew the court had erred and yet went out and followed their words based on the above logic, one could argue that he would be exempt. Therefore, the word in the verse 'when he shall do' comes to teach us that such an individual is liable." Halakha 8 reads as follows: " 'By doing:' One who acts incorrectly based on their own [inadvertent] judgment is liable. However, if one acts incorrectly because of a court's ruling, he is exempt. In what circumstances is this so? If the court ruled and one of the judges sitting on the court knew the court had erred or if there was someone present during the hearing who was capable of sitting on the court, such as Shimon Ben Azzai, who then practiced [the incorrect law] based on their ruling. Lest one think such an individual is exempt, Scripture teaches us 'by doing' to tell us such an individual is liable, while one who [does not know any better but to trust the court] is exempt."

104. Other examples of Elijah's emendation practices include: *Sifra*, Parshat Vayikra, Deibura Dechataot, Parshata 6, Perek 7, emendation 1; *Sifra*, Parshat Vayikra, Deibura Dechataot, Parshata 9, Perek 16, emendation 2; and *Sifra*, Parshat Vayikra, Deibura Dechataot, Parshata 10, emendation 1.

105. See Ya'akov Moshe of Słonim's discussion of Elijah's linguistic philosophy in his introduction to *Shulchan Arukh Even ha-Ezer* (Vilna: 1819).

106. See Elijah ben Solomon, *Aderet Eliyahu*, Deuteronomy 1:1.

107. The unique elements of Elijah's emendations are not recognized, although they are very nicely laid out, by Gil Perl in his dissertation on the nineteenth-century rabbi Naftali Tzvi Yehudah Berlin (Netziv). See Gil S. Perl, "'Emek ha-Neziv': A Window into the Intellectual Universe of Rabbi Naftali Zvi Yehudah Berlin," Ph.D. diss., Harvard University, 2006, 156–166. There Perl plots a chart comparing the emendations to the *Midrash Sifrei Ekev* of three different modern scholars: the twentieth-century historical-critical scholar Louis Finkelstein, the mid-nineteenth-century Lithuanian rabbi and head of the Volozhin yeshiva Naftali Tzvi Yehudah Berlin, and Elijah. Perl explains certain emendations made by Elijah by noting "deleted entire line" or "deleted entire passage." Perl's translation of the word *meyutar* as "deletion" misses the philosophic underpinnings behind the emendation. Unlike Elijah, Netziv's emendations are primarily focused on correcting copying and transmission errors (117–122). Finkelstein in trying to restore the historical text goes further than Netziv, employing a vast array of manuscripts and applying a full arsenal of historical and philological tools to reconstruct an original text.

108. Abraham Geiger, *Urschrift und Übersetzungen der Bibel in ihrer Abhängigkeit von der innern Entwicklung des Judenthums* (Breslau: J. Hanauer, 1857), appendix 1, 435.

109. See Yisrael of Shklov's introduction to *Taklin Chadatin* in *Masekhet Shekalim min Talmud Yerushalmi* (Minsk: 1812). Rabbi Yisrael's treatment of Elijah's interpretive legacy (and in his book *Pe'at ha-Shulchan*) highlights the radical nature of his teacher's interpretive legacy and emending practices. Although Yisrael was responsible for the publication of Elijah's emendations of Tractate *Shekalim*, Yisrael actually entertained the possibility of "burying" Elijah's emendations. He constantly feared that they would be misused and misunderstood. For a discussion of Yisrael and other eastern European rabbinic figures who expressed a great deal of apprehension about Elijah's emendations, see Eliakh, *Sefer ha-Gaon*, 3:1172–1189. Although Eliakh's treatment of the topic is apologetic, his discussion and the forced answers he offers for Elijah's emendations express the ambivalence toward Elijah's interpretive techniques in contemporary Haredi circles. See Eliyahu Stern, "Modern Rabbinic Historiography and

the Legacy of Elijah of Vilna: A Review Essay," *Modern Judaism* 24, no. 1 (February 2004): 79–90.

110. See Rabbi Yisrael's introduction to *Taklin Chadatin* in *Masekhet Shekalim min Talmud Yerushalmi*.

111. See Luzzatto, *Derekh Tevunot*, 58.

112. See ibid., 18.

113. See Leibniz, *Theodicy*, paragraph 124.

114. Spiegel, *Amudim be-Toldot ha-Sefer ha-Ivri*, 421.

115. See Jacques Derrida, *Writing and Difference*, trans. Alan Bass (Chicago: University of Chicago Press, 1978), 19.

116. See George MacDonald Ross, "Leibniz and the Origin of Things," in M. Dascal and E. Yakira, eds., *Leibniz and Adam* (Tel Aviv: University Publishing Projects, 1993), 242–243.

117. Gottfried Wilhelm Leibniz, *New Essays on Human Understanding*, ed. and trans. Peter Remnant and Jonathan Bennett (Cambridge: Cambridge University Press, 1981), 336.

118. Ibid., 497–498.

119. Ibid., 513.

120. See Elijah's comments to Proverbs 8:8 in *Mishlei im Biur ha-Gra*.

121. See Ishiguro, *Leibniz's Philosophy of Logic and Language*, 117–118.

122. See Leibniz, *Philosophical Papers and Letters*, 124.

123. Daniel Boyarin, *Ha-Iyyun ha-Sefaradi: Le-Farshanut ha-Talmud shel Megorshei Sefarad* (Jerusalem: Mekhon Ben-Tzvi le-Cheker Kehilot Yisrael ba-Mizrach, 1989), 49.

124. See Isaac Campanton, *Darkhei ha-Talmud*, ed. Isaac Sampson Langeh (Jerusalem: Yitzchak Shimshon Langeh, 1980), 22–23. On Campanton's more general hermeneutics see Sergey Dolgopolski, *What Is Talmud? The Art of Disagreement* (New York: Fordham University Press, 2009), 26–41, 85–126.

125. See Allan Arkush's discussion of Leibniz's notion of evil in his *Moses Mendelssohn and the Enlightenment* (Albany: State University of New York Press, 1994), 12–14. See also Wellbery, *Lessing's Laocoon*, which notes how for eighteenth-century thinkers, "errors and disputes follow from our inattention to the ideas signified by words" (38).

126. See Shuchat, *Olam Nistar be-Memadei ha-Zeman*, 147.

127. Alan Brill, in "The Mystical Path of the Vilna Gaon," *Journal of Jewish Thought and Philosophy* 3, no.1 (1993): 133 fn.7, argues that Elijah differs with Luzzatto by adopting a more dualistic position regarding evil. While Brill may be correct that Elijah has a slightly more dualistic position regarding good and evil, Yehudah Liebes, in his article "Tzidkat ha-Tzadik," 297–298, demonstrates that

Elijah still believes in the potential for the transformation of evil into good, which in turn gives human beings a purpose for being.

Chapter 3. Elijah and the Enlightenment

1. See Jacob Katz's placement of the Gaon under the rubric of a "bearer of the tradition" in Katz, *Tradition and Crisis: Jewish Society at the End of the Middle Ages*, trans. Bernard Dov Cooperman (New York: New York University Press, 1993), 210.

2. On Mendelssohn representing the start of "modernity," see Heinrich Graetz, *Geschichte der Juden* (Leipzig: 1870), 11:3; and in translation, Graetz, *The History of the Jews* (Philadelphia: Jewish Publication Society, 1949) 5:291–292. See also Graetz, *The Structure of Jewish History and Other Essays*, trans. Ismar Schorsch (New York: Jewish Theological Seminary, 1975), 130. On Mendelssohn's ties to modern thought, see Daniel O. Dahlstrom's introduction to his *Moses Mendelssohn: Philosophic Writings* (Cambridge: Cambridge University Press, 1997), ix–xxx; Moses Paul Spalding, "Toward a Modern Torah: Moses Mendelssohn's Use of a Banned Bible," *Modern Judaism* 19, no. 1 (1999): 67–82; David Sorkin, *Moses Mendelssohn and the Religious Enlightenment* (Berkeley: University of California Press, 1996), 5–14; Sorkin, *The Religious Enlightenment: Protestants, Jews, and Catholics from London to Vienna* (Princeton, N.J.: Princeton University Press, 2008), 177–180; and Allan Arkush, *Moses Mendelssohn and the Enlightenment* (Albany: State University of New York Press, 1994), 1–68. On the use of the term "modern" see Michael Meyer, "Tradition and Modernity Reconsidered," in Jack Wertheimer, ed., *The Uses of Tradition: Jewish Continuity in the Modern Era* (New York: Jewish Theological Seminary, 1992), 465. See also Meyer, "Reflections on Jewish Modernization," in *Judaism within Modernity: Essays on Jewish Historiography and Religion* (Detroit: Wayne State University Press, 2001), 34–36.

3. See Heinrich Graetz, *The History of the Jews* (Philadelphia: Jewish Publication Society, 1949), 5:329–336. On the printing of Mendelssohn's Pentateuch, see Alexander Altmann, *Moses Mendelssohn: A Biographical Study* (Philadelphia: Jewish Publication Society of America, 1973), 376–377; Peretz Sandler, *Ha-Biur le-Torah shel Moshe Mendelssohn ve-Siato* (Jerusalem: Reuven Mas, 1940), 85–89.

4. Heinrich Heine, *Zur Geschichte der Religion und Philosophie in Deutschland* (Frankfurt am Main: Insel Verlag, 1964), 9:230. To be sure, there were those nineteenth-century biographers of Mendelssohn such as Simon Bernfeld, *Dor Tapuchot* (Warsaw: 1897), who could "not fathom whether Mendelssohn truly believed what he said" regarding rabbinic interpretation (84–85).

5. Shraga's words appear in the Gaon's biblical commentary *Aderet Eliyahu*, originally published in *Chamisha Chumshei Torah* (Dubrovna: 1804). On the publication history of *Aderet Eliyahu*, see "Aliyat Kir," published in Yehoshua Herschel Levin, *Aliyot Eliyahu* (Vilna: 1856), 109–110, and Yeshayahu Winograd, *Otzar Sifrei ha-Gra* (Jerusalem: Kerem Eliyahu, 2003), 1–2. According to the nineteenth-century rabbi Yisrael of Shklov, the Gaon demonstrated how "all the words of the prophets, the writings, and the oral law were hidden inside the text of the Torah." See Yisrael's introduction to his work *Pe'at Shulchan* (Safed: 1836). Naftali Tzvi Yehudah Berlin, the head of the Volozhin yeshiva, likewise saw the Gaon as connecting rabbinic interpretation and the *sensus literalis* of Scripture; see his comments to Deuteronomy 33:2 in Berlin, *Ha-Emek Davar* (Jerusalem: 1999). See also the claims made about the Gaon's exegesis by the early twentieth-century exegete Barukh ha-Levi Epstein in his *Torah Temimah* (Jerusalem: Machon Ha-Torah, 2005), 1:1 fn.2.

6. On Jewish life in Berlin during Mendelssohn's lifetime, see Altmann, *Moses Mendelssohn*, 15–25, 272–286; and Steven Lowenstein, *The Berlin Jewish Community: Ennlightenment, Family, and Crisis, 1770–1830* (New York: Oxford University Press, 1994), 10–67.

7. Graetz, *History of the Jews*, 389.

8. On those who traveled between Berlin and Vilna and the modes of transportation they used, see Moses Shulvas, *From East to West: The Westward Migration of Jews from Eastern Europe during the Seventeenth and Eighteenth Centuries* (Detroit: Wayne State University Press, 1971), 104–108.

9. See Laimonas Briedis, *Vilnius: City of Strangers* (Budapest: Central European University Press, 2009), 41–43.

10. Shulvas, *From East to West*, 122.

11. On the unique social demographics of Berlin Jewry, see Lowenstein, *The Berlin Jewish Community*, 19–22; and Deborah Hertz, *Jewish High Society in Old Regime Berlin* (New Haven: Yale University Press, 2005), 23–28.

12. On the salons, see Hertz, *Jewish High Society in Old Regime Berlin*, 1–23; and Lowenstein, *The Berlin Jewish Community*, 163–182.

13. See the 1777 letter sent by Mendelssohn to his wife cited by Hertz, *Jewish High Society in Old Regime Berlin*, 49.

14. Ibid., 16.

15. Ibid., 123.

16. See ibid., 37; and Alexander Altmann's discussion of Mendelssohn's "maturity and fame" in his *Moses Mendelssohn*, 92–193.

17. See Moses Mendelssohn, *Gesammelte Schriften Jubiläumsausgabe*, ed. F. Bamberger, A. Altmann, et al. (Stuttgart: Frommann, 1971–1975) (hereafter *GSJ*), 4:1, 171–210.

18. Jonathan Sheehan, *The Enlightenment Bible: Translation, Scholarship, Culture* (Princeton, N.J.: Princeton University Press, 2005), 179–184.

19. Robert Lowth, *Lectures on the Sacred Poetry of the Hebrews* (Hildesheim: Georg Olms Verlag, 1969), 136.

20. Ibid., 7–8 n.4.

21. See the end of the introduction to Johann David Michaelis, *Mosaisches Recht* (Frankfurt am Main: Johann Gottlieb Garbe, 1770).

22. See Friedrich August Wolf, *Prolegomena to Homer, 1795,* trans. with introduction and notes by Anthony Grafton, Glenn W. Most, and James E. G. Zetzel (Princeton, N.J.: Princeton University Press, 1985), 18–26.

23. See Jonathan M. Hess, *Germans, Jews, and the Claims of Modernity* (New Haven: Yale University Press, 2002), 35–37.

24. See Mendelssohn, *GSJ*, 5:1, 48–50.

25. See Johann Jacob Rabe, *Mischnah oder der Text des Talmuds* (Ansbach: 1760–1763).

26. See Mendelssohn's letter to Elkhan Herz on July 22, 1770, *GSJ*, 20:2, 212, trans. in Altmann, *Moses Mendelssohn*, 250.

27. See Moses Mendelssohn, *Jerusalem; or, On Religious Power and Judaism,* trans. Allan Arkush (Hanover, N.H.: Brandeis University Press by University Press of New England, 1983). As Michah Gottlieb has argued in his excellent article "Mendelssohn's Metaphysical Defense of Religious Pluralism," *Journal of Religion* 86, no. 2 (2006): 205–225; Mendelssohn's philosophical argument for respecting metaphysical differences should be seen in conjunction with his defense of rabbinic authority and exegesis. Mendelssohn was not interested in German Jews' merely being accepted into German society as quasi-Christians but instead strove for mutual respect based on their similarities (natural religion) and differences (rabbinic Judaism). Thus defending the rabbis was not just an apologetic act but also essential to his philosophy of tolerance. On Mendelssohn's rejection of a universal religion and his plea for difference to be respected, see also Shmuel Feiner, *The Jewish Enlightenment*, trans. Chaya Naor (Philadelphia: University of Pennsylvania Press, 2003), 166–172. Mendelssohn's philosophical and political "pluralism" calls into question the dichotomy of his possessing "public" and "private" personas. On historiography dealing with "public" and "private" Mendelssohns, see Jeremy Dauber, *Antonio's Devils: Writers of the Jewish Enlightenment and the Birth of Modern Hebrew and Yiddish Literature* (Palo Alto, Calif.: Stanford University Press, 2004), 105–108.

28. See Mendelssohn, *GSJ*, 15:1, 40.

29. On those who claim that one should distinguish between Mendelssohn's Hebrew and German writings, see, for example, Tzemach Tzimrion, *Moshe Mendelssohn ve-ha-Ideologia shel ha-Haskalah* (Tel Aviv: Tel Aviv University

Press, 1984), 109–121; Allan Arkush, "The Questionable Judaism of Moses Mendelssohn," *New German Critique* 77 (Spring–Summer 1999): 29–44; and Arkush, *Moses Mendelssohn and the Enlightenment* (Albany: State University of New York Press, 1994), 229–231. Similarly, according to Michael Meyer, "It must have been clear to Mendelssohn that he would have lost all personal effectiveness as an educator and reformer of his people had he freed himself from the law." See Meyer, *The Origins of the Modern Jew: Jewish Identity and European Culture in Germany, 1749–1824* (Detroit: Wayne State University Press, 1967), 51.

30. See the first paragraph in Moses Mendelssohn, *GSJ*, 15:1, 41.

31. Steven Lowenstein, "The Readership of Mendelssohn's Bible Translation," *Hebrew Union College Annual* 53 (1982): 183.

32. See Altmann, *Moses Mendelssohn*, 386–389.

33. On Dubno's educational background see ibid., 354.

34. Many theories have been offered for Dubno's abrupt departure. Some claim that the breakup was due to a financial dispute with Mendelssohn's brother Saul. Still others contend that Dubno broke with Mendelssohn because Mendelssohn refused to print all of Dubno's introduction to the *Biur*. On this point see Edward Breuer, *The Limits of Enlightenment: Jews, Germans, and the Eighteenth-Century Study of Scripture* (Cambridge, Mass: Harvard University Press, 1996), 150. For Mendelssohn's response to Dubno's departure, see *GSJ*, 15:1, 40.

35. This letter is listed as "letter 13" in *Osef ha-Chakhamim* (1878), cited in Israel Zinberg, *A History of Jewish Literature*, trans. Bernard Martin (Cincinnati: Hebrew Union College Press, 1974), 44.

36. See Israel Klausner, *Toldot ha-Kehilah ha-Ivrit* (Vilna: 1938), 41. On the lack of a beckoning bourgeoisie see Gershon Hundert, "Re(de)fining Modernity in Jewish History" in Jeremy Cohen and Moshe Rosman, eds., *Rethinking European Jewish History* (Oxford: Littman Library, 2009), 139–140.

37. See the charts of subscribers to the *Biur* arranged according to locale printed in Lowenstein, "Readership of Mendelssohn's Bible Translation," 195.

38. See Nancy Sinkoff's chapter "The Linguistic Boundaries of Enlightenment" in her *Out of the Shtetl: Making Jews Modern in the Polish Borderlands* (Providence: Brown Judaic Studies, 2004), esp. 173–176; and Nehama Rezler Bersohn, "Isaac Satanow, the Man and His Work: A Study in the Berlin Haskalah," Ph.D. diss., Columbia University, 1975, 31–32. It is thus not surprising that Mendelssohn penned his first exegetical work, *Sefer Megillat Kohelet* (Berlin: 1770), on Ecclesiastes and that the Gaon's major exegetical work was his commentary to Proverbs (Shklov: 1798).

39. On Schick's enlightened tendencies and his relationship to the Gaon, see his introduction to *Euclid: Explanation of all the Geometric Sciences*, trans. Barukh Schick (The Hague: Leb Zusmensh, 1780; Hebrew), where he claims the

Gaon told him "that for every deficiency of knowledge a man has in general knowledge, he will have a hundred deficiencies of knowledge in the science of Torah. For Torah and science are closely related." Furthermore, Schick proffers that the Gaon "commanded me to translate everything possible of the sciences into our holy tongue." On the Gaon's meeting with Schick, see most recently Yisrael Shapiro, "Askolot Chalukot be-She'elat Torah u-Madda'im be-Veit Midrasho shel ha-Gra," *Bekhol Derakhekha Daehu* 13 (2003): 6–18; and David Fishman, "A Polish Rabbi Meets the Berlin Haskalah: The Case of R. Barukh Schick," *AJS Review* 12, no. 1 (Spring 1987): 96–97.

40. On Dubno, see the comments made by Menachem Zobel in "Bibliography," *Kiryat Sefer* 28, no. 2 (July 1941): 126–132. For other examples of the impact and impression that Dubno made on the Vilna community, see Shmuel Joseph Fuenn, Matisyahu Strashun, and Hillel-Noah Maggid Steinschneider, *Kiryah Ne'emanah: Korot Adat Yisrael be-Ir Vilna* (Vilna: Yitzchak Funk, 1915), 177, 225–227. See also Altmann, *Moses Mendelssohn*, 400–403.

41. In a letter that Dubno sent to Mendelssohn dated September 22, 1780, he suggests that Mendelssohn had objected to publishing his introduction due to its length. See Mendelssohn, *GSJ*, 19:258–260.

42. For a full list of all the rabbinic approbations to Dubno's project, see David Kamenetsky, "The Great Rabbis' Approbations of Rabbi Shlomo Dubno's Bible" (Heb.), *Yeshurun* 9 (2002): 711–754.

43. The approbation of Hayyim of Volozhin's brother, Zalman, a close student of the Gaon's, reads as follows: "Very dear to me are the words of Rabbi Shlomo Dubno whose commentary on the Torah provides us with two good things. First, his commentary brings together all of those who interpreted texts in a *peshat* manner. Secondly, . . . when [his] book [*Tikkun Sofrim*, which focuses on Scriptural and grammatical issues] came to my hand I realized that he had resolved problems that had perplexed me for ages. Therefore, I have given my approbation to his edition of *Tikkun Sofrim*, and I am prepared to buy a copy of the Bible from him. I implore all men who fear God in their hearts to purchase a copy of his Bible, so that Rabbi Shlomo Dubno will be able to finish his work and perhaps will be strengthened to write on the Prophets and Writings" (recorded in Fuenn, Strashun, and Steinschneider, *Kiryah Ne'emanah*, 165–166).

44. The books contained in Dubno's library are preserved in a catalogue published under the name *Reshimat Misparim* (N.p.: 1814). Israel Zinberg, in his *A History of Jewish Literature* (Tel Aviv: Y. Shreberk, 1959), 45 fn.62 refers to the catalogue as *Reshimat Sifrei Rashad*. Prior to his arrival in Berlin, Dubno worked for seven years in libraries throughout Amsterdam. Regarding Dubno's access and acquisition of books and manuscripts, see Zinberg, *A History of Jewish Literature*, 41. On his listing of Mendelssohn, Wessely, and Satanov, see *Reshimat*

Misparim, 6, 19, 46, 47, 51, and 53. The bibliographic connections among the Gaon, Dubno, and Mendelssohn are attested to in a bibliographical document recorded by Malachi Beit-Arié. The document, which is a manuscript version of the bibliographic work *Siftei Yeshenim* (Amsterdam: 1680) compiled by Rabbi Shabbtai Bass (1641–1718), contains emendations and additions made by the Av Beit-Din of Berlin, Rabbi Herschel Lewin (who wrote an endorsement to the *Biur*), Shlomo Dubno, and Rabbi Avraham, the Gaon's son. Beit-Arié suggests that when Dubno came to Vilna, among the texts he brought was this bibliography. See Malachi Beit-Arié, "Sefatim Dovevot: Hagahot ve-Hashleimut be-Ketivat Yad le-*Siftei Yeshenim*," *Kiryat Sefer* 40, no. 1 (December 1964): 132.

45. On a few occasions Rabbi Avraham refers to his library in the plural "etzleinu," suggesting perhaps a joint or family ownership. See Avraham ben ha-Gra, *Sefer Rav Pe'alim* (Warsaw: Shuldenberg, 1896), 28a–29b.

46. On Yosef ben Eliyahu Pesseles, see Fuenn, Strashun, and Steinschneider, *Kiryah Ne'emanah*, 224.

47. The letters sent between Pesseles to Friedländer are reprinted in Shmuel Yosef Fuenn, *Sofrei Yisrael* (Vilna: 1871), 138–143.

48. See Kamenetsky, "The Great Rabbis' Approbations of Rabbi Shlomo Dubno's Bible," 711 fn.1, 2.

49. Conflicting testimonies have been offered regarding the Gaon's position on Mendelssohn's work. Israel Zinberg claims in "Appendix 1" of his *History of Jewish Literature* that the Gaon did in fact see the *Biur* and was not disturbed by its contents. Zinberg cites a letter collected by Moritz Güdemann that attests to a letter written by N. H. Wessely, which, in turn, refers to three rabbis who objected to the publication of the *Biur*. Among those rabbis listed is Rabbi Eliyahu of Vilna. (See Moritz Güdemann, "Die Gegner Hartwig Wessely's Divrei Shalom ve-Emet," *Monatsschrift für Geschichte und Wissenschaft des Judentums* 19, no. 10 [1870]: 479.) Zinberg correctly points out, however, that at the time Wessely made this statement, the Gaon could not possibly have had access to the *Biur* let alone have made a public statement regarding its status. According to Zinberg, it was the Hasidic book *Toldot Ya'akov Yosef* (Korets: 1780), written by Rabbi Ya'akov Yosef of Połonne (d. 1782), that was condemned by the Vilna community. Because both books were published around the same time, many such as Wessely confused them and thought the Gaon objected to Mendelssohn's work. In reality, Zinberg notes that Graetz himself claims he saw a document attesting to a letter sent by the Gaon to Berlin indicating that he had refused to speak out against the *Biur*. Likewise, it is hard to believe that the Gaon would condemn a work that was supported by many in his most inner circle. Finally, the strongest but most dubious testimony supporting the claim that the Gaon had read and was impressed by the content of the *Biur* can be found in the statements made by the

nineteenth-century Maskil Kalman Shulman in the introduction to his reprinting of Wessely's work *Words of Peace and Truth* (Warsaw: 1886). There Shulman claims that "the Gaon praised Rabbi N.H. Wessely's commentary to Leviticus, for he appreciated his attempt to prove the plain sense of Scripture from the words of the Sages." On Kalman Shulman see also Harkavi's "Appendix" to *Divrei Yemei Yisrael* (Warsaw: 1893). On the Gaon's connection to the *Biur* see also Yehuda Friedlander, "Le-Birur Yachaso shel ha-Gaon mi-Vilna la-Haskalah be-Reishitah: Ha-Gaon ve-N. H. Wesseley," in *Ha-Gra u-Veit Midrasho*, ed. Moshe Hallamish, Joseph Rivlin, and Raphael Shuchat (Ramat Gan: Bar-Ilan University Press, 2003), 197–205.

50. See Briedis, *Vilnius: City of Strangers*, 61; and Israel Klausner, *Vilna be-Tekufat ha-Gaon* (Jerusalem: Reuven Mas, 1942), 226–227.

51. Compare the statistical analysis compiled in Lowenstein, *The Berlin Jewish Community*, 4, 16, with those figures compiled in Klausner, *Toldot ha-Kehilah ha-Ivrit*, 46–53. On Vilna's Jewish population and eighteenth-century Jewish Lithuania-Poland, see the data most recently compiled by Shaul Stampfer in his article "The 1764 Census of Lithuanian Jewry and What It Can Teach Us," *Jewish Population Studies: Papers in Jewish Demography, 1993* 23 (1997): 91–121, and Stampfer, "Some Implications of Jewish Population Patterns in Pre-partition Lithuania," in Adam Teller, ed., *Scripta Hierosolymitana* 38 (1998): 189–223.

52. See Adam Teller, *Koach ve-Hashpa'ah: Ha-Yehudim be-Achuzot Beit Radzhivil be-Lita ba-Meah ha-18* (Jerusalem: Merkaz Zalman Shazar, 2005), 33–45; and Gershon David Hundert, *Jews in Poland-Lithuania in the Eighteenth Century: A Genealogy of Modernity* (Berkeley: University of California Press, 2004), 21–31. On the implications of the demographic differences between sixteenth- and seventeenth-century eastern and western European Jewish communities, see Elchanan Reiner, "Aliyat ha-Kehilah ha-Gedolah," *Gal-Ed* 20 (2006): 31–34.

53. Jacob Goldberg, *Ha-Mumarim be-Mamlekhet Polin-Lita* (Jerusalem: 1985), 37–39.

54. On Elijah's deposition, see the transcription and translation of Israel Klausner, *Vilna be-Tekufat ha-Gaon*, 236.

55. See Moses Mendelssohn's introduction to *Sefer Megillat Kohelet* in *GSJ*, 14:149. On Mendelssohn's relationship to governmental authorities, see Chimen Abramsky, "The Crisis of Authority within European Jewry in the Eighteenth Century," in Siegfried Stein and Raphael Loewe, eds., *Jewish Religious and Intellectual History: Presented to Alexander Altmann on the Occasion of His Seventieth Birthday* (Tuscaloosa: University of Alabama Press, 1979), 18–19.

56. The Gaon in his commentary to *Sifra di-Tzniuta* (repr. Israel: 1969), writes that in the text of the Torah one sees "the past, present, and future. Everything is included in the Torah. . . . Not just its general rules but each and every particular thing, person and everything that will happen to a person from their birth until their death" (55a). Likewise, in the *Biur* on Genesis 2:8, *GSJ*, 15:2, 23, Mendelssohn claims that "all of the creation story and all that is told in Scripture about what happened to Adam and Eve to Cain and Abel all of it is true without question . . . within this story there is a hint of what will take place to every being. What is the case with Adam and his sons and what happened to them in particular will be the case for the entire species in general." The World-Book trope adopted by both figures goes back at least to Augustine and was still heavily invoked by eighteenth-century thinkers and specifically by Leibniz.

57. On the Gaon's influence in nineteenth-century exegetical circles, see Ya'akov Elman, "The Rebirth of Omnisignificant Biblical Exegesis in the Nineteenth and Twentieth Centuries," *Jewish Studies: An Internet Journal* 2 (2003): 222; Yehudah Leib Copperman, *Pirkei Mavo la-Peirush ha-Ketav ve-ha-Kabbalah al ha-Torah* (Jerusalem: Hotsa'at Haskel le-Yad Mikhlalah Yerushalayim le-Vanot, 1985), 86; and Edward Breuer, "Between the Haskalah and Orthodoxy: The Writings of R. Jacob Meklenburg," *Hebrew Union College Annual* 66 (1995): 273–279. On Mendelssohn's popularity in nineteenth-century rabbinic exegetical circles, see Meir Hildesheimer, "Moses Mendelssohn in Rabbinic Literature," *Proceedings of the American Academy for Jewish Research* 55 (1988): 79–133. On the *Biur*'s general readership, see Steven Lowenstein, "The Readership of Mendelssohn's Bible Translation," *Hebrew Union College Annual* 53 (1982): 179–213.

58. See Hans W. Frei, *The Eclipse of Biblical Narrative: A Study in Eighteenth- and Nineteenth-Century Hermeneutics* (New Haven: Yale University Press, 1974), 56–57.

59. While the term *PaRDeS* appears in Talmudic literature as a form of mystical knowledge, in the medieval period it is identified with a specific hermeneutic scheme. For an overview of the scholarship produced on the interpretive aspects of *PaRDeS* see Peretz Sandler, "On the Problem of *PaRDeS* and the Fourfold Method," in Arthur Biram, ed., *Sefer Urbakh* (Jerusalem: Kiryat Sefer, 1955), 222–235; and Frank Talmage, "Apples of Gold: The Inner Meaning of Sacred Texts in Medieval Judaism," in Talmage, *Apples of Gold in Settings of Silver: Studies in Medieval Jewish Exegesis and Polemics*, ed. Barry Dov Walfish (Toronto: Pontifical Institute of Mediaeval Studies, 1999), 114–116.

60. Edward Breuer, *The Limits of Enlightenment: Jews, Germans, and the Eighteenth-Century Study of Scripture* (Cambridge, Mass.: Harvard University Press, 1996), 69.

61. See Moses Mendelssohn, *GSJ*, 14:4. On Mendelssohn's introduction to Ecclesiastes and his use of *PaRDeS*, see Philip Culbertson, "Multiplexity in Biblical Exegesis: The Introduction to *Qohelet* by Moses Mendelssohn," *Cincinnati Judaica Review* 2 (Spring 1991): 10–18.

62. See *GSJ*, 15:1, 40.

63. See Moses Mendelssohn's introduction to *Sefer Megillat Kohelet* in *GSJ*, 14:148.

64. See Ibn Ezra's lengthy comments to Exodus 20:1, available in English in Ibn Ezra, *Commentary to the Pentateuch Exodus/Shemot*, trans. Norman Strickman and Arthur M. Silver (New York: Menorah Publishing Company, 1997). On Ibn Ezra's exegetical theory of synonymy, see Uriel Simon, "Le-Darko ha-Parshanit shel Ibn Ezra al-pi Shloshet Biurav le-Pasuk Echad," *Sefer ha-Shanah shel Universitat Bar Ilan* 3 (1965). On synonymy in medieval Jewish exegesis, see Ya'akov Elman, "'It Is No Empty Thing': Nahmanides and the Search for Omnisignificance," *Torah u-Madda* 4 (1993): 1–83; and Nechamah Leibowitz, *Iyyunim Chadashim be-Sefer Shemot* (Jerusalem: World Jewish Agency, 1969), 66–67, 445.

65. See David Halivni, *Peshat and Derash: Plain and Applied Meaning in Rabbinic Exegesis* (New York: Oxford University Press, 1991), 52–54. On Mendelssohn's notion of "literal meaning" and the role that "connectedness" plays in his exegesis, see Sorkin, *Moses Mendelssohn and the Religious Enlightenment*, 65–67.

66. See Sandler, *Ha-Biur le-Torah shel Moshe Mendelssohn*, 140 fn.10.

67. On the Gaon's concept of synonymy, see Moshe Philip's essay in *Sefer Mishlei im Biur ha-Gra*, ed. Moshe Philip (Petach Tikvah: 2001), 438–439; Levin, *Aliyot Eliyahu*, 16; Barukh ha-Levi Epstein's introduction to his *Torah Temimah* (Jerusalem: Machon Ha-Torah, 2005), 1 fn.2; and Yehudah Leib Copperman, *Li-Feshuto shel Mikra: Kovetz Ma'amarim* (Jerusalem: Hotza'at Haskel le-yad Mikhlalah Yerushalayim le-Vanot, 1974), 86.

68. Starting with the publication of Elijah's commentary under the title *Me'il Tzedek* (Berlin: 1856), there have been numerous attempts to publish Elijah's various commentaries to Esther. See Winograd, *Otzar Sifrei ha-Gra*, 27–31.

69. See the Gaon's comments to Proverbs 1:20 in *Mishlei im Biur ha-Gra*, ed. Moshe Philip (Petach Tikvah: 1991) and *Tikkunei ha-Zohar*, 61b.

70. The Gaon differs from those who describe the relationship of *peshat-remez-derash-sod* in a hierarchic manner (with *sod* at the top of the ladder and *peshat* on the bottom). See, for example, the Gaon's comments to Proverbs 24:11 (in *Mishlei im Biur ha-Gra*), where he describes the interpretive categories of *PaRDeS* in circular imagery with *peshat* and *sod* coming together full circle. In his commentary to Proverbs 23:23 the Gaon uses a horizontal diagram to describe the

relationship between these hermeneutic techniques—a relationship in which each category has equal footing and functions independently of the other "*zeh mul zeh*" [each one facing the other].

71. In the Gaon's commentary on Proverbs prepared by Menachem Mendel of Shklov (Shklov: 1798) those who study *peshat* are situated in a synagogue. But those learning in the synagogue are described as children and the knowledge they possess is characterized as "outside knowledge." The edition published by Shlomo Luria (*Chemdah Genuzah*) describes *peshat* in the same terms as those used by Menachem Mendel of Shklov. His description, however, leaves out any mention of *peshat* being located in a synagogue, or for that matter in any institution. Other versions of the Gaon's ideas, recorded in Moshe Philip, *Sefer Mishlei im Biur ha-Gra* (Petach Tikvah: 1991), attest to *peshat*'s being a hermeneutic that operates in an even more detached and autonomous position in relation to the rest of the "world" of Jewish knowledge.

72. See Elijah ben Solomon, *Aderet Eliyahu*, Genesis 1:1.

73. David Halivni argues that these two understandings of *peshat* can be found throughout rabbinic literature. See Halivni, *Peshat and Derash*, specifically chapter 3, where he stresses the idea of context as the defining element of *peshat*.

74. See Mendelssohn's comments to Exodus 21:1 in Mendelssohn, *GSJ*, 16:198.

75. Mendelssohn seems to be citing Ibn Ezra's citation of Sa'adya found in Ibn Ezra's commentary to Exodus 21:24.

76. See Mendelssohn, *GSJ*, 16:206.

77. The Gaon interprets Exodus 21:23–25 by invoking the interpretive scheme of general-specific, *klal u-frat*. This hermeneutic principle—which is one of the thirteen hermeneutic principles attributed to the Tannaitic sage Rabbi Ishmael—assumes that the biblical text offers general rules and applies those rules to specific cases. In this instance, the general rule is the payment of damages, while the specifics (stated in the next verse) are three particular occurrences of bodily damage. Ironically, the Gaon employs a rabbinic interpretive principle (general-specific) to interpret these verses against their rabbinic interpretation. The Gaon employs a select number of Rabbi Ishmael's thirteen interpretive principles (and perhaps some of the thirty-two by Rabbi Eliezer, the son of Rabbi Yosi), such as general-specific and *a fortiori*, for his own *peshat* readings. While he saw some of the rabbis' principles as uncovering the text's *sensus literalis*, he saw others as being more homiletic. According to Fuenn, Strashun, and Steinschneider, *Kiryah Ne'emanah*, for the Gaon "there are those [of the rabbis' thirteen] principles that [are to be considered] *peshat* and there are those that open up the doors to *derash*" (154). On Mendelssohn's use of Rabbi Ishmael's thirteen hermeneutic principles, see Sandler, *Ha-Biur le-Torah shel Moshe Mendelssohn*, 107; and Sorkin, *Moses Mendelssohn and the Religious Enlightenment*, 72–73. While one

may be tempted to say that neither exegete follows what contemporary scholars would deem the *sensus literalis* of the text, what is most striking is the Gaon's unbridled challenging of the rabbinic tradition, while Mendelssohn finds it necessary to justify the rabbis' views.

78. For other examples of the Gaon disagreeing with the rabbinic interpretation of Scripture, see Aviya Hacohen, "Be-Ikvei Biur ha-Gra le-Parshat Amah Ivriya," in Moshe Ahrend and Moshe Bar Asher, eds., *Sefer ha-Yovel le-Rav Mordekhai Breuer: Asufat Ma'amarim be-Maddaei ha-Yahadut* (Jerusalem: Akademon, 1992), 77–90. For a list of examples where the Gaon interprets Scripture in accordance with its plain and simple meaning, and against the interpretation offered by the rabbis, see Menachem Kasher, *Torah Shleima, Exodus* (Jerusalem: 1927), 17:302–303.

79. See the Gaon's comments in his *Aderet Eliyahu*, Exodus 21:6.

80. See *Tosefet Ma'aseh Rav* (Jerusalem: 1891), subject heading 240.

81. On the life of Elia Bachur (also known as Eliyahu Ben Asher Ashkenazi, Eliyahu Tishbi, and Eliyahu Levita), see the introduction in Christian D. Ginsburg, *The Massoreth ha-Massoreth of Elias Levita* (London: Longmans, Green, Reader & Dyer, 1867); and further, Salomon Buber, *Toldot Eliyahu ha-Tishbi* (Leipzig: C.L. Fritzsche, 1856). On Levita as a biblical exegete see Deena Arranoff, "Elijah Levita: A Jewish Hebraist," *Jewish History* 23 (2009): 17–40.

82. See the introduction to the second edition of Elijah Levita, *Sefer Masoret ha-Masoret* (Venice: 1538).

83. Like Levita, Shlomo Zalman Hanau (1687–1746) was a proto-Maskil who unabashedly challenged the canons of traditional rabbinic exegesis, a practice that earned him the ire of the rabbinic establishment. On Hanau see Andrea Schatz, " 'Peoples Pure of Speech': The Religious and Secular, and the Jewish Beginnings of Modernity," in David B. Ruderman and Shmuel Feiner, eds., *Jahrbuch Des Simon Dubnow Instituts*, vol. 6 (Leipzig: Vandenhoeck and Ruprecht, 2007): 183–185, and David Sorkin, *The Berlin Haskalah and German Religious Thought: Orphans of Knowledge* (London: Vallentine Mitchell, 2000), 44–45. Recent scholarship has demonstrated that specifically in his *Sha'arei Zimra*, Hanau borrowed ideas from seventeenth-century Christian exegetes, employing the principle of grading as the basis of his theory of accentuation. See Aron Dotan's "Prolegomenon" to William Wickes's writings in *Two Treatises on the Accentuation of the Old Testament: On Psalms, Proverbs, and Job, on the Twenty-one Prose Books* (New York: Ktav, 1970), xi.

84. See Avraham ben ha-Gra, *Sefer Rav Pe'alim* (Warsaw: Shuldenberg, 1894), 41a–b. Avraham further elaborates on his notion of the *masorah* in his "Introduction" to *Midrash Aggadat Bereishit* (Vilna: 1802). On the publication

history and subsequent plagiarism of Rabbi Avraham's edition of and notes to *Aggadat Bereishit*, see Fuenn, Strashun, and Steinschneider, *Kiryah Ne'emanah*, 210–221.

85. The Gaon's use of Bachur's work is further corroborated by a handwritten notebook of Rabbi Joseph Zundel of Salant (1786–1866), in which the author asserts that the Gaon was influenced by Bachur. The manuscript was shown to me by its owner, Ari Bergmann of Lawrence, N.Y., on January 5, 2007. See Yosef Avivi, *Kerakh Ktivat Yad ha-Kollel be-Tokho Shlosha Sefarim* (Jerusalem: Asufa Auction House, 2001). On Rabbi Joseph Zundel of Salant, see Immanuel Etkes, *Rabbi Israel Salanter and the Mussar Movement*, trans. Jonathan Chipman (Philadelphia: Jewish Publication Society, 1993), 57–68.

86. The nineteenth-century Vilna publisher Nachman ben Tzvi insinuates in Yehoshua Heschel Levin's *Aliyot Eliyahu* fn.111 that the Gaon read and borrowed from Bachur's work *Sefer ha-Tishbi*. Compare the Gaon's comments in *Tikkunei ha-Zohar im Tikkunim mi-Zohar Chadash im Biur ha-Gra* (Vilna: Rosenkranz, 1867), 44b; and Elia Bachur, *Sefer ha-Tishbi* (Bnei Brak: 1976), 9.

87. See the Gaon's comments in *Biur ha-Gra al-Shulchan Arukh, Even ha-Ezer* (Vilna: 1819), 129:32.

88. See Buber, *Toldot Eliyahu ha-Tishbi*, 10.

89. Mendelssohn, *GSJ*, 15:1, 30.

90. Ibid., 15:39.

91. In the seventeenth century the only extant manuscript of the Rashbam was owned by the famed bibliophile David Oppenheim (1664–1736). Eventually, the manuscript was acquired by the Christian Hebraist and biblical scholar Daniel Ernst Jablonski (1660–1741), who finally printed it in 1705. Subsequently, the text fell into the hands of the Fraenckel family and was kept in the Breslau Seminary library, before disappearing during World War II. Between Jablonski's publication and the Fraenckel family's procurement of it, the manuscript came into the possession of Moses Mendelssohn (see Mendelssohn's comments in *GSJ*, 15:1, 41), who included Rashbam along with Ibn Ezra, Rashi, and Ramban (Nachmanides) as the main exegetical sources for the *Biur*. See David S. Loewinger and Bernard D. Weinryb, *Catalogue of the Hebrew Manuscripts in the Library of the Juedisch-Theologisches Seminar in Breslau, a Publication of the Leo Baeck Institute, New York* (Wiesbaden: Harrassowitz, 1965), viii.

92. See Mendelssohn, *GSJ*, 15:1, 40.

93. Breuer, *Limits of Enlightenment*, claims that a contradiction exists in Mendelssohn's writings between the *Biur*, where Mendelssohn opposes the idea of dual hermeneutic truths, and his commentary on Ecclesiastes, where he embraces such a position (221–222). It might be suggested that no such contradiction exists. Rather, as Mendelssohn states (in his comments to Exodus 21:1), whenever *peshat*

goes against rabbinic law it must be abandoned; but where it does not go against rabbinic law, the *peshat* interpretation is allowed to stand (*GSJ*, 16:198). In Ecclesiastes, which is primarily a non-legal text, Mendelssohn was more amenable to the theologically more daring theory of multiple hermeneutic truths. In the *Biur*, however, where he faces the issue of rabbinic law being contradicted by *peshat*, he cannot adopt such an approach and therefore explains the limitations of the theory he had expressed in Ecclesiastes. The distinction between rabbinic law (*halakha*) and non-legal material (which is usually identified as *aggada*) is revealed in Mendelssohn's philosophy of tolerance expressed in his work *Jerusalem*. There Mendelssohn dismisses or argues with the Sages regarding matters of belief (*aggada*). Reason and belief are universal concepts that all human beings share, so the Sages' words are not to be taken as dogmas. For Mendelssohn, however, rabbinic law (*halakha*) is something particular to Judaism and highlights Judaism's distinctive features. Thus, *halakha* need not conform to reason or natural religion. Jewish emancipation requires German society to recognize and respect not only what it has in common with Jews, but also what makes Judaism unique.

94. See Martin Lockshin's introduction to Shmuel ben Meir, *Rashbam's Commentary on Leviticus and Numbers: An Annotated Translation*, ed. and trans. Martin Lockshin (Providence: Brown Judaic Studies Series, 2001).

95. David Rosin, *Peirush ha-Torah asher Katav Rashbam* (Breslau: S. Shottlender, 1881), xix.

96. See Elijah ben Solomon, *Aderet Eliyahu*, Exodus: 21:6, 21:22.

97. On the Gaon's and his students' approach to the interpretation of Mishnah and Gemara, see Chanan Gafni, "Hirsch Mendel Pineles and His Work *The Way of Torah*," master's thesis, Hebrew University, 1999, 34–37 fn.29.

98. Yosef Avivi notes that the Gaon applied the same hermeneutic to his reading of kabbalistic texts. For example, the Gaon explains mystical works such as the *Zohar* and *Sefer Yetzirah* in opposition to the manner in which Rabbi Isaac Luria (the famed Ari) interpreted these texts. The radical nature of the Gaon's kabbalistic hermeneutics drew criticism from a number of quarters. See Yosef Avivi, *Kabbalat ha-Gra* (Jerusalem: Kerem Eliyahu, ha-Makhon le-hotza'at sifrei ha-Gra, 1992), 28–30.

99. See Fuenn, Strashun, and Steinschneider, *Kiryah Ne'emanah*, 154.

100. On the last eight verses of the Bible, compare the Gaon's comments in *Aderet Eliyahu*, Deuteronomy 1:1 to Mendelssohn's commentary to Deuteronomy 34:5 in *GSJ*, 15:1, 21. The Gaon also limits the claim that the last eight verses of the Bible were written by Joshua: he argues that they only were arranged by him. Such a position, however, must be seen in light of the Gaon's belief that even Moses only arranged the words of the Torah.

101. See Breuer, *Limits of Enlightenment*, 165.

102. The terms "openness" and "insularity" express an embattled or minority discourse in which a group is being challenged by an outside force. Any reading of Elijah's writings reveals that these were simply not the conditions in which he operated. On the issues of openness and insularity in early modern Ashkenaz (whose Jewish communities were but a fraction of the size of those that existed by the end of the eighteenth century), see David Ruderman, *Jewish Thought and Scientific Discovery in Early Modern Europe* (Detroit: Wayne State University Press, 1995).

103. Michael Mack, *German Idealism and the Jew: The Inner Anti-Semitism of Philosophy and German Jewish Responses* (Chicago: University of Chicago Press, 2003), 82.

Chapter 4. The Gaon versus Hasidism

1. On the central documents regarding the bitter wars between the Hasidim and Mitnagdim, see Mordekhai Wilensky, *Hasidim u-Mitnagdim: Le-Toldot ha-Pulmus she-Beineihem ba-Shanim, 5532–5565* (Jerusalem: Mossad Bialik, 1990), vols. 1, 2. For the English reader see Wilensky, "Hasidic and Mitnaggdic Polemics in the Jewish Communities of Eastern Europe: The Hostile Phase," in *Tolerance and Movements of Religious Dissent in Eastern Europe*, ed. Bela K. Kiraly (New York: Columbia University Press, 1975), 89–113.

2. On the rise of Hasidism, see Simon Dubnow, *Toldot ha-Hasidut* (Tel-Aviv: Devir, 1967); also Jacob Katz, *Tradition and Crisis: Jewish Society at the End of the Middle Ages*, trans. Bernard Dov Cooperman (New York: New York University Press, 1993), 210. It should be noted that recent scholarship has challenged Dubnow's and Katz's interpretations of Hasidism as a revolutionary social group. Moshe Rosman has shown how the founders of Hasidism were not attempting to do away with the *kehilah* structure but rather capture its authority. See Rosman, *The Lord's Jews: Magnate-Jewish Relations in the Polish-Lithuanian Commonwealth* (Cambridge, Mass.: Center for Jewish Studies, 1990), 210–212; Shmuel Ettinger, "Hasidism and the Kahal in Eastern Europe," in Ada Rapoport-Albert, ed., *Hasidism Reappraised* (Oxford: Littman Library, 1996), 63–75; and most recently Glenn Dynner, *Men of Silk: The Hasidic Conquest of Polish Jewish Society* (New York: Oxford University Press, 2006), 1–5.

3. See Dubnow, *Toldot ha-Hasidut*, 3. See also Allan Nadler's critique of Hasidic and Mitnagdic historiography in Nadler, *The Faith of the Mithnagdim: Rabbinic Responses to Hasidic Rapture* (Baltimore: Johns Hopkins University Press, 1997), ix.

4. This point was first noted in Rivka Schatz-Uffenheimer, *Hasidism as Mysticism: Quietistic Elements in Eighteenth-Century Hasidic Thought*,

trans. Jonathan Chipman (Princeton, N.J., and Jerusalem: Princeton University Press and Magnes Press, 1993), 10–11.

5. Israel Loebel claimed that "Zemir Aritzim" was written by Elijah himself; see his "Glaubwürdige Nachrichten von einer neuen und zahlreichen Sekte unter den Juden in Polen und Lithauen, Chassidim nennt," *Shulamit* (1807). Simon Dubnow refutes Loebel's claims, arguing convincingly that its editor was the eighteenth-century Brody scribe Areyh Leib ben Mordekhai; see Dubnow, *Toldot ha-Hasidut*, 128. See also Wilensky, *Hasidim u-Mitnagdim*, 1:30–31.

6. On the nature of the rumors circulating about followers of the Baal Shem Tov, see Dubnow, *Toldot ha-Hasidut*, 116; and Israel Klausner, *Vilna be-Tekufat ha-Gaon* (Jerusalem: Reuven Mas, 1942), 22. On Menachem Mendel, see Moshe Hallamish, "The Teachings of Rabbi Menachem Mendel of Vitebsk," in Rapoport-Albert, *Hasidism Reappraised*, 268–287. On the role that Shklov leadership played in starting the fight, see Wilensky, *Hasidim u-Mitnagdim*, 1:29–30; and David Fishman, *Russia's First Modern Jews: The Jews of Shklov* (New York: New York University Press, 1995), 8. Regarding Hasidism's popularity with Jewish youth, see Gershon Hundert, *Jews in Poland-Lithuania in the Eighteenth Century: A Genealogy of Modernity* (Berkeley: University of California Press, 2004), 21–32, 179–181.

7. See Wilensky, *Hasidim u-Mitnagdim*, 1:43 fn.47.

8. On the Mitnagdic version of the meeting, see David Maków's claim that this happened prior to 1772 in ibid., 64 fn.4. On the Hasidic description of events, see Shneur Zalman of Liadi's 1797 letter to his followers in Vilna, also in ibid., 198.

9. See Shneur Zalman of Liadi's letter to his followers in Vilna in ibid., 198.

10. See "Zemir Aritzim" in ibid., 42, 65.

11. Ibid., 64.

12. Ibid., 65.

13. While "Issar's" identity is difficult to decipher, David Kamenetsky tries to identify Hayyim in his article "Le-Havdil bein Hayyim le-Hayyim," *Yeshurun* 22 (2010): 876–900.

14. Wilensky, *Hasidim u-Mitnagdim*, 1:42.

15. Ibid., 65.

16. Ibid., 43, 66.

17. See Klausner, *Vilna be-Tekufat ha-Gaon*, 153.

18. See "Zemir Aritzim," 1:66.

19. See David Maków, *Shever Poshim*, reprinted in Wilensky, *Hasidim u-Mitnagdim*, 2:76.

20. See the 1773 letter sent from Vilna leaders to Brody in ibid., 1:71–74.

21. See ibid., 1:106, and Shmuel Joseph Fuenn, Matisyahu Strashun, and Hillel-Noah Maggid Steinschneider, *Kiryah Ne'emanah: Korot Adat Yisrael be-Ir Vilna* (Vilna: Yitzchak Funk, 1915), 139. On the publication history of *Toldot Ya'akov Yosef*, see Zeev Gries, "The Hasidic Managing Editor," in Rapoport-Albert, *Hasidism Reappraised*, 149–150. On the role played by geographic conditions in the spread of Hasidism, see most recently Adam Teller, "Hasidism and the Challenge of Geography: The Polish Background to the Spread of the Hasidic Movement," *AJS Review* 30, no. 1 (2006): 1–29.

22. See Wilensky, *Hasidim u-Mitnagdim*, 1:107.

23. On how Shneur Zalman and other Hasidic leaders used print to spread their message, see Zeev Gries, *Sefer, Sofer, ve-Sippur be-Reishit ha-Hasidut* (Tel Aviv: 1992), 47–67.

24. On the effect of the excommunication within Vilna, see Klausner, *Vilna be-Tekufat ha-Gaon*, 85.

25. See *Solomon Maimon: An Autobiography*, trans. J. Clark Murray (Urbana: University of Illinois Press, 2001), 175.

26. See Shneur Zalman of Liadi's letter to the Mogeliv Jewish community in Wilensky, *Hasidim u-Mitnagdim*, 1:164.

27. See "Zemir Aritzim," 1:42; and Avigdor ben Hayyim's letter to Tsar Paul I (1799) in ibid., 260. See also Shneur Zalman's letter to his Vilna followers in ibid., 20; and the letter of the Vilna Kahal (1797) in ibid., 182. While historical documentation suggests that there was a book burning of Ya'akov Yosef's *Toldot Ya'akov Yosef* and the anonymously compiled *Tzava'at ha-Rivash* (Zolkiew: 1793), it is unclear when exactly this happened and on how many occasions. On the editing and printing of *Tzava'at ha-Rivash*, see Zeev Gries, "Arikhat *Tzava'at ha-Rivash*," *Kiryat Sefer* 52 (1997): 187–210.

28. See Moshe ben Eliezer's letter to Tzvi of Sieliszcza, in Wilensky, *Hasidim u-Mitnagdim*, 1:333.

29. Samuel J. Yatzkan, *Rabenu Eliyahu mi-Vilna* (Warsaw: 1900), 69.

30. Wilensky, *Hasidim u-Mitnagdim*, 1:135.

31. See the 1781 letter of condemnation issued by Elijah and the Vilna communal leadership in ibid., 108; and Fuenn, Strashun, and Steinschneider, *Kiryah Ne'emanah*, 139.

32. See Wilensky, *Hasidim u-Mitnagdim*, 1:182.

33. It should be noted that the Hasidic scholar Yehoshua Mondshine, in his "Parnasei Vilna ve-ha-Gra ve-Milchamtam be-Hasidut," *Kerem Habad* 4, no. 1 (November–December 1992): 208, argues that these letters were written by the leaders of the *kehilah*. Immanuel Etkes challenges Mondshine's arguments in Etkes, *The Gaon of Vilna: The Man and His Image* (Berkeley: University of California Press, 2002), 130–138.

34. See Wilensky, *Hasidim u-Mitnagdim*, 1:184 fn.6.

35. Gershom Scholem, "Dvekut or Communion with God," in *The Messianic Idea in Judaism* (New York: Schocken Books, 1971), 203–227. On Elijah's theological opposition to Hasidism, see Haim Hillel Ben-Sasson, "Ishiyuto shel ha-Gra ve-Hashpa'ato ha-Historit," *Zion* 31, nos. 1–2 (1966): 39–86; and Etkes, *The Gaon of Vilna*, 91–95.

36. For those who challenge Scholem's ideas on Hasidism and *dvekut* see, most notably, Ada Rapoport-Albert, "God and the Zaddik as the Two Focal Points of Hasidic Worship," *History of Religions* 18, no. 4 (May 1979): 305–307.

37. On the similarities between Mitnagdic and Maskilic perceptions of the Hasidim, see Dynner, *Men of Silk*, 45–46; and Marcin Wodziński, *Haskalah and Hasidism in the Kingdom of Poland* (Oxford: Littman Library, 2005), 9–33. On Maskilic and secular perceptions of Hasidism, see Israel Bartal, "The Imprint of Haskalah Literature on the Historiography of Hasidim," in Rapoport-Albert, *Hasidism Reappraised*, 369–388.

38. On the antinomian aspects of *dvekut*, see Shaul Magid, "Deconstructing the Mystical: The Anti-Mystical Kabbalism in Rabbi Hayyim of Volozhin's *Nefesh Ha-Hayyim*," *Journal of Jewish Thought and Philosophy* 9, no. 1 (1999): 52 fn.93. On the historical precedents for Hasidism see Moshe Idel, *Hasidism: Between Ecstasy and Magic* (Albany: State University of New York Press, 1995), 209–215. On those who have mistakenly downplayed the theological differences between the Hasidim and Mitnagdim, see the list compiled in Nadler, *Faith of the Mithnagdim*, 2–4. On the notion that there was little difference between the early Hasidim and their opponents, see Rapoport-Albert, "God and the Zaddik," 313.

39. Scholem does not address Elijah's work. But his personal library now housed in the National Library in Givat Ram, Jerusalem, contains a number of kabbalistic works written by Elijah in which Scholem made extensive bibliographic notes.

40. Moshe Halbertal, *People of the Book: Canon, Meaning, and Authority* (Cambridge, Mass.: Harvard University Press, 1997), 10.

41. See the argument in *Tractate Menachot* 96b over the obligation to study Torah texts versus what is described as "Greek wisdom."

42. See Halbertal, *People of the Book*, 94–103.

43. On the topic of secular studies in early modern Jewish intellectual history, see David Ruderman, *Jewish Thought and Scientific Discovery in Early Modern Europe* (Detroit: Wayne State University Press, 1995).

44. See Israel M. Ta-Shma, *Minhag Ashkenaz ha-Kadmon: Cheker ve-Iyyun* (Jerusalem: Magnes Press, 1992), 85–88.

45. See Norman Lamm, *Torah Lishmah: Torah for Torah's Sake in the Works of Rabbi Hayyim of Volozhin and His Contemporaries* (New York: Ktav, 1989); and Nadler, *Faith of the Mithnagdim*, 152–163.

46. On Elijah's similarities and uniqueness vis-à-vis other contemporary rabbinic leaders, see Maoz Kahane, "Mi-Prague le-Pressburg: Ktivah Hilkhatit be-Olam Mishtaneh me-ha-Nodah be-Yehudah le-ha-Hatam Sofer, 1730–1839," Ph.D. diss., Hebrew University, 2010, 113–121.

47. On Elijah's radical break with accepted practices (*minhag*), see the sources listed in Yehoshua Mondshine, "Kinat ha-Mitnagdim le-Minhagei Ashkenaz," *Kerem Habad* 4, no. 1 (November–December 1992): 153–157.

48. See Elijah's commentary in Elijah ben Solomon, *Sefer Yetzirah* (Vilna: 1828), chapter 1, section 8. On the issue of covenant (*brit*), see *Sefer Yetzirah*, 1:3 and 6:7. See also Elijah ben Solomon, *Peirush al-Kamah Aggadot* (Königsberg: 1862), 8a. Elijah argues that there are two types of covenant. One covenant is made by Israelites through their "mouth(s)." The other covenant is made by Israel through their flesh, through circumcision. On these two covenants see Elijah's comments to *Tikkunei ha-Zohar*, 51a (*ve-zeh shoresh ha-adam*) and 53c (*brit milah*). Ultimately, Elijah privileges the covenant made by the mouth over that made by the flesh. On God and Torah, see his comments on *Tikkunei ha-Zohar*, 2b, "lishmah."

49. See Elijah's comments to Proverbs 3:6 in *Mishlei im Biur ha-Gra*, ed. Moshe Philip (Petach Tikvah: 1991).

50. See Elijah's comments to Proverbs 8:21 in *Mishlei im Biur ha-Gra*.

51. Scholem, "Dvekut or Communion with God," 208.

52. See Shneur Zalman Liady, *Likkutei Amarim: Tanya* (Brooklyn, N.Y.: Kehot, 1984), 8b.

53. See *Maggid Devarav le-Ya'akov*, ed. Rivka Schatz-Uffenheimer (Jerusalem: Magnes Press, 1990), 259 [161].

54. The attainment of *unio mystica*, Max Weber would remark, leads "religion in practice to strive for enjoyment of salvation in this world rather than to engage in the ascetic struggle for certainty about the future world." See Weber, *The Protestant Ethic and the Spirit of Capitalism*, trans. Talcott Parsons (New York: Courier Dover, 2003), 82.

55. See the 1796 letter of condemnation issued by Elijah and the Vilna leadership, reprinted in Wilensky, *Hasidism u-Mitnagdim*, 1:188.

56. On Sofer's proclivity to invoke divine assistance in his legal rulings, see Jacob Katz, "Towards a Biography of the Hatam Sofer," in his *Divine Law in Human Hands: Case Studies in Halakhic Flexibility* (Jerusalem: Magnes Press, 1998), 422–425; and Maoz Kahane, "Hatam Sofer: Posek be-Eynei Atzmo," *Tarbiz* 76 (2007): 542–544.

57. On Elijah's understanding of *tzimtzum* see Alan Brill, "The Mystical Path of the Vilna Gaon," *Journal of Jewish Thought and Philosophy* 3, no. 1 (1993): 134; and Raphael Shuchat, "Peirush ha-Gra mi-Vilna le-Mishnat Hasidim: Mashal ve-Nimshal be-Kitvei ha-Ari," *Kabbalah* 3 (1998): 273–274. For the historical implications of Elijah's notion of *tzimtzum* vis-à-vis the Hasidim, see Nadler, *Faith of the Mithnagdim*, 11–20.

58. Brill, "The Mystical Path of the Vilna Gaon," 147. For a different opinion, see Nadler, *Faith of the Mithnagdim*, 18–21.

59. See Elijah ben Solomon, *Sifra di-Tzeniuta* (Tel Aviv: 1969), 37b–38b.

60. See for example, Elijah's depiction of "Moses" in *Aderet Eliyahu*, Deuteronomy 22:30.

61. Ya'akov Yosef, Avraham Shimshon, and Avraham Dov, *Toldot Ya'akov Yosef* (Korets: Tzvi Hirsh ben Arye Leib va-Chatano Shmuel ben Yissaschar Ber Segal, 1780), 67a. On the role and influence that Rabbi Ya'akov Yosef's work had on spreading Hasidic doctrines and inciting anger among the Mitnagdim, see Wilensky, *Hasidim u-Mitnagdim*, 1:101.

62. See Yehudah Broda et al., *Sefer Likkutim Yekarim* (Lemberg: Defus Y. Sh. Y. Rapaport, 1792), no. 49.

63. See Shneur Zalman Liady, *Likkutei Amarim: Tanya* (Brooklyn, N.Y.: Kehot, 1984), 154b [309].

64. See Kalonymus Kalman Epstein, *Sefer Maor va-Shemesh* (Tel-Aviv: 1965), 59b–60a.

65. See *Darkhei Yesharim* (Lemberg: 1865). My translation is taken from Schatz-Uffenheimer, *Hasidism as Mysticism*, 314. There, Schatz-Uffenheimer explains how the source itself is a radical interpretation of the Maggid's original words, which she claims can be found in a manuscript of *Torat ha-Maggid* written by R. Shmelke of Nikolsburg (listed under the title Ms Jerusalem-National Library 1467, pt. 3, ch. 2, 12b). Schatz's research demonstrates how Elijah's circle took the most radical statements of the Hasidim and claimed that they represented the group's normative views.

66. See Ben-Sasson, "Ishiyuto shel ha-Gra ve-Hashpa'ato ha-Historit," 24–27, 62–65. More recently, see Nadler, *Faith of the Mithnagdim*, 50–51. On Elijah's notion of prayer, see his *Imrei Noam: Peirush ha-Gra le-Berakhot* (Jerusalem: Mesorah, 1954), comments to Mishnah 5:1; and his *Sefer Sedei Eliyahu Biur ha-Gra ha-Shalem al ha-Shas, Masekhet Ketubot* (Jerusalem: Sh. D. ha-Levi Movshovits, 1991), 61a. On Mitnagdic prayer more generally, see Emmanuel Levinas, "Prayer without Demand," in *The Levinas Reader*, ed. and trans. Sean Hand (Cambridge, Mass.: Blackwell, 1989), 232. It would take only a generation before the Gaon's students would co-opt and redefine the language of *dvekut* for their own Torah-centric worldview. Hayyim of Volozhin redefines the concept of

dvekut by investing in Torah study the heightened spiritual experience that Hasidism associated with prayer. According to Rabbi Hayyim, "for by the very act of study they are connected to [*davuk*] His will and Being" (*Nefesh ha-Hayyim* [Vilna: 1824], 4:10). On the ways in which Rabbi Hayyim further develops and removes the mystical elements of Elijah's theosophy, see Magid, "Deconstructing the Mystical," 29, 35. Rabbi Hayyim, however, was insistent on the centrality of Torah study. "With regard to those who take breaks from Torah study to focus on the fear of God," argued Rabbi Hayyim, "such individuals are guilty of stealing time from the Torah they should be studying" (*Nefesh ha-Hayyim*, 4:9). Compare Rabbi Hayyim's comments with those of scholars like Nachman of Bratslav (1772–1811) in his *Likkutei Moharan* (New York: 1957), 2:25.

67. Elijah ben Solomon, *Mishlei im Biur ha-Gra*, 13:12.

68. See Wilensky, *Hasidim u-Mitnagdim*, 1:38.

69. See Elijah's comments to Proverbs 25:17 in *Mishlei im Biur ha-Gra*.

70. Broda et al., *Sefer Likkutim Yekarim*, 18.

71. See David Maków, *Shever Poshim* 37b–38a, in Wilensky, *Hasidim u-Mitnagdim*, 2:119–120. On Leib Melamed see most recently David Biale, *Eros and the Jews: From Biblical Israel to Contemporary America* (Berkeley: University of California Press, 1997), 271 fn.9.

72. See Nachmanides's commentary to Deuteronomy 11:12, viewable in English in *Nachmanides Commentary on the Torah: Deuteronomy* (New York: Shilo, 1976). For an overview of the way *dvekut* was invoked in pre-Hasidic literature, see *The Religious Thought of the Hasidim*, ed. Norman Lamm (New York: Yeshiva University Press, 1999), 133–136. Likewise, Mordekhai Pachter has detailed the numerous sixteenth- and seventeenth-century kabalistic thinkers who invoked the concept of *dvekut* in their writings. See Pachter, "The Concept of 'Devekut' in the Homiletical Ethical Writings of Sixteenth-century Safed," in *Studies in Medieval Jewish History and Literature*, ed. Isadore Twersky, Harvard Judaic Monographs, no. 2 (Cambridge, Mass.: Harvard University Press, 1984), 193–205. Furthermore, as argued by Ada Rapoport-Albert, from the medieval period onward, there was hardly a time when the idea of *dvekut* was not adopted by Jewish thinkers. Similarly, only a few generations before the Hasidic-Mitnagdic debates, Solomon Luria (1510–1574) proposed an egalitarian conception of God's accessibility to humanity. For Luria, the divine was not restricted to the intellectual elite but was open to all. See Rapoport-Albert's discussion on the differences between Israel Baal Shem Tov's and Luria's understanding of God in her "God and the Zaddik as the Two Focal Points of Hasidic Worship," 312–313. See also Sharon Flatto, "Hasidim and Mitnaggedim: Not a World Apart," *Journal of Jewish Thought and Philosophy* 12, no. 2 (August 2003): 107–112.

73. For example, compare Elijah's notion of prayer to that found in Dov Ber of Międzyrzecz's *Maggid Devarav le-Ya'akov*, 161 [257]. The early Hasidic masters adopted one of two positions regarding the nature of prayer. On the one hand, the Maggid of Mezeritch saw prayer as man losing himself in the infinity of the Divine. The Maggid's model of prayer deemphasized petitionary elements. For the Maggid, the problem with petition is not due to the distance between God and man, but rather the proximity. For the Maggid, one's encounter with the Divine engulfs the individual to the point that he or she no longer has any sense of self and thus cannot petition God for anything. See Dov Ber, *Maggid Devarav le-Ya'akov*, ed. Rivka Schatz-Uffenheimer (Jerusalem: Magnes Press, 1990), 147 [248]. Whereas the Maggid saw humanity smothered by its close proximity to the Divine, those such as Rabbi Ya'akov Yosef saw this connection as an invitation to beseech the Divine. See Louis Jacobs, *Hasidic Prayer* (New York: Schocken Books, 1973), 23.

74. While there are some differences, see the striking similarity between Elijah's metaphor of the sun rising (commentary to Job 7:8) and Rabbi Nachman's metaphor of a child being cleaned by his mother. See Nachman of Bratslav, *Likkutei Etzot ha-Shalem* (Warsaw: 1913), 118–121.

75. Such overlap leads some, such as Allan Nadler, to suggest that a "closer examination of the Mithnagdic sources reveals there was virtually no substantive theological difference between the Hasidim and Mithnagdim in their respective theoretical understandings of the nature of Divine immanence." See Nadler, *Faith of the Mithnagdim*, 16. Yet Elijah certainly vehemently objected to the radicalized Hasidic notion of Divine immanence where "God can be found in any tree or in any stone." Likewise Elijah makes it clear that he objects to the Hasidic understanding of the verse "barukh kevod hashem mimkomo" (Ezekiel 3:12). See Elijah's letters of excommunication in Wilensky, *Hasidim u-Mitnagdim*, 1:188 fns.21, 22, 23.

76. I am not dealing here with the question of the roots of the historical rift, which has been most recently addressed by Dynner, *Men of Silk*. Neither am I concerned with which aspect of Hasidism encouraged its popularity, a topic that has been most recently addressed by Yohanan Petrovsky-Shtern in his "Hasidism, Havurot, and the Jewish Street," *Jewish Social Studies* 10, no. 2 (2004): 20–54. My focus is what was it about the Hasidim that bothered the Mitnagdim *enough* for them to wage such a strong battle against the new group. On those who offer a political and economic reading of the Mitnagdic response, see Mendel Piekarz, *Bi-Yemei Tzmichat ha-Hasidut* (Jerusalem: Mossad Bialik, 1978). For Piekarz's critique of Scholem position, see Mendel Piekarz, "Hasidism as a Socio-Religious Movement," in Rapoport-Albert, *Hasidism Reappraised*, 229–240. More generally see the reasons for the divide suggested by Wilensky, *Hasidim u-Mitnagdim*, 1:29;

Fishman, *Russia's First Modern Jews*, 7–11, 101–104; and Etkes, *The Gaon of Vilna*, 130–138.

77. See Ben-Sasson, "Ishiyuto shel ha-Gra ve-Hashpa'ato ha-Historit," 2–3, 40–41; and the sources noted by Etkes, *The Gaon of Vilna*, 106.

78. See Alain Le Boulluec, *La notion d'heresie dans la literature Grecque* (Paris: Etudes Augustiniennes, 1985), 1, 39–91. Similarly, Michel de Certeau, in his *The Mystic Fable*, trans. Michael B. Smith (Chicago: University of Chicago Press, 1992), argues that charges of heresy are brought about when "the content remained, but underwent a new treatment that, already noticeable in the segmentation brought about by the divisions, would soon be expressed as a political management of differences. The inherited furnishings were redistributed within a new space ordered by a new way of arranging them and using them" (1:20–21). De Certeau's theories are given expression in Jewish and Christian contexts by Virginia Burrus, *The Making of a Heretic: Gender, Authority, and the Pricillianist Controversy* (Berkeley: University of California Press, 1995), 16; and Daniel Boyarin, *Borderlines: The Partition of Judaeo-Christianity* (Philadelphia: University of Pennsylvania Press, 2004), 31–32.

79. For a concise overview on Sabbatianism, see Yehudah Liebes, *Studies in Jewish Myth and Messianism* (Albany: State University of New York Press, 1993), 93–115. For a general overview on Sabbatai Tzvi, see Gershon Scholem, *Sabbatai Sevi: The Mystical Messiah*, trans. R. J. Werblowski (Princeton, N.J.: Princeton University Press, 1973). On the spread and opposition to Sabbatianism, see Elisheva Carlebach, *The Pursuit of Heresy: Rabbi Moses Hagiz and the Sabbatian Controversies* (New York: Columbia University Press, 1990). See also Jacob Barnai, *Shabta'ut: Hebetim Chevratiyim* (Jerusalem: Zalman Shazar Center, 2000); and Rachel Elior, ed., *The Sabbatian Movement and Its Aftermath: Messianism, Sabbatianism and Frankism*, 2 vols. (Jerusalem: 2001).

80. See Jacob Emden, *Hitavkut* (Altona: 1769), 152b.

81. On Rabbi Shimon, see Sid Z. Leiman, "When a Rabbi Is Accused of Heresy: The Stance of the Gaon of Vilna in the Emden-Eibeschuetz Controversy," in Ezra Fleischer, Gerald Blidstein, Carmi Horowitz, and Bernard Septimus, eds., *Me'ah She'arim: Studies in Medieval Jewish Spiritual Life in Memory of Isadore Twersky* (Jerusalem: Magnes Press, 2001), 259 fn.17.

82. See Elijah's letter of approbation to Yonatan Eibeschuetz in *Luchot Edut* (Altona: 1755), 71b. For more on Elijah's letter, see Leiman, "When a Rabbi Is Accused of Heresy," 251–263.

83. See *Darkhei Noam* (Königsberg: 1764), 67a. Elijah's endorsement appears on the first page of the book and is dated 1762.

84. See Elijah's 1797 letter of condemnation in Wilensky, *Hasidim u-Mitnagdim*, 1:188 fns.15, 16. See also Rachel Elior, "Rabbi Nathan Adler of

Frankfurt and the Controversy Surrounding Him," in Karl Erich Grozinger and Joseph Dan, eds., *Mysticism, Magic and Kabbalah in Ashkenazi Judaism: International Symposium Held in Frankfurt a.M., 1991* (Berlin: Walter de Gruyter, 1995), 233–235 fn.35. The passage quoted earlier corroborates Elijah Schochet's initial suspicion that "Gra may have accused the Hasidim of practicing some sort of masturbatory religious rite"; see Schochet, *The Hasidic Movement and the Gaon of Vilna* (Northvale, N.J.: Jason Aronson, 1994), 47. See also Elisheva Carlebach, *The Pursuit of Heresy: Rabbi Moses Hagiz and the Sabbatian Controversies* (New York: Columbia University Press, 1994), 277–278.

85. On the letters KRY equaling YKR, see Dov Ber of Międzyrzecz (speaking in the name of the Baal Shem Tov), *Maggid Devarav le-Ya'akov*, ed. Rivka Schatz-Uffenheimer (Jerusalem: Magnes Press, 1990), 256 [160].

86. See "Zemir Aritzim," 1:65, 39 fn.24.

87. *Solomon Maimon: An Autobiography*, trans. J. Clark Murphy (Urbana: University of Illinois Press, 2001), 174.

88. See *Mishmeret ha-Kodesh* (Zolkiew: 1746) and Gershom Scholem's analysis of the word *dvekut* in "Shtei Eduyot Ha-Rishonot al Chavurot ha-Hasidim ve-ha-Besht," *Tarbiz* 20 (1949): 237.

89. On sexual libertarianism in Sabbatai Tzvi's circle, see Scholem, *Sabbatai Sevi*, 387, 669, 880; David Biale, *Eros and the Jews: From Biblical Israel to Contemporary America* (Berkeley: University of California Press, 1997), 118–120; and Ada Rapoport-Albert, "Al Ma'amad ha-Nashim ba-Shabta'ut," in Elior, *The Sabbatian Movement and Its Aftermath*, 1:143–328.

90. As Gershom Scholem noted, this confusion was common in the middle of the eighteenth century. See Scholem, "Shtei Eduyot Ha-Rishonot al Chavurot ha-Hasidim ve-ha-Besht," 238–240; and more generally Scholem, "Ha-Tnuah ha-Shabta'it be-Polin," in Israel Halpern, ed., *Beit Yisrael be-Polin* (Jerusalem: 1954), 2:36–76. See also Bernard Weinryb, *The Jews of Poland to 1800* (Philadelphia: Jewish Publication Society, 1983), 236–261; Yehudah Leibes, "Ha-Tikkun ha-Klali shel R. Nachman mi-Bratslav ve-Yachaso le-Shabta'ut," *Zion* 44 (1980): 201–245; and more recently, Hundert, *Jews in Lithuania in the Eighteenth-Century: A Genealogy of Modernity* (Berkeley: University of California Press, 2004), 184–185, 204.

91. Elijah did not write this accusation himself. The anonymous editor of "Zemir Aritzim ve-Chorvot Tzurim" records it in his name. Still, neither Elijah nor his children nor followers ever distanced themselves from it. See Wilensky, *Hasidim u-Mitnagdim*, 1:66–67.

92. See ibid., 59.

93. See ibid., 60. It is more than likely that Elijah and the Vilna community were referring to the testimony brought against the Frankists in Satanów.

According to their critics, the Frankists were charged with engaging in a host of deviant sexual rituals. On the Frankists and the charges brought against them, see Majer Bałaban, *Le-Toldot ha-Tnuah ha-Frankit* (Tel Aviv: Devir, 1935); Gershom Scholem, "Jacob Frank and the Frankists," in his *Kabbalah* (New York: Dorset, 1987), 287–310; and Paweł Maciejko, *Jacob Frank and the Frankist Movement*, 1755–1816 (Philadelphia: University of Pennsylvania Press, 2011), 21–40. On Jews who converted to Christianity, see Magdalena Teter, "Jewish Conversions to Catholicism in the Polish-Lithuanian Commonwealth of the Seventeenth and Eighteenth Centuries," *Jewish History* 17, no. 3 (2003): 261–262.

94. Recently Yehudah Liebes, in "Tzidkat ha-Tzadik: Yachas ha-Gaon mi-Vilna ve-Chugo Klapei ha-Shabta'ut," *Kabbalah* 9 (2003): 226–306, has argued that some in Elijah's circle adopted kabbalistic ideas popularly associated with Sabbatianism. Leibes suggests that even Elijah, earlier in life (before his battle with Hasidism), followed a Sabbatian theodicy only to reject it at a later stage (232). While he admits that Elijah never even mentions Tzvi in his kabbalistic writings (287), Leibes maintains that Sabbatian concerns shaped Elijah's kabbalistic worldview. Elijah's identification of Hasidism with Sabbatianism further explains why he would have taken care to clearly distinguish his own ideas from anything remotely associated with a Sabbatian theodicy. On Elijah's theodicy see Chapter 2.

95. See, for example, the Zohar's description of *erev rav* (1.25a–b). There, the Zohar states that "on the day that *erev rav* will be wiped off the face of this earth it will be as though the heavens and earth will have been recreated." For an alternative (and more positive) rendering of *erev rav* in the writings of Hayyim Vital, see Shaul Magid, "The Politics of (Un)Conversion: The 'Mixed Multitude' ('Erev Rav) as Conversos in Rabbi Hayyim Vital's 'Ets Ha-Da'at Tov,'" *Jewish Quarterly Review* 95, no. 4 (2005): 636. In the same way that Magid reads Vital's employment of the term in the context of sixteenth-century Safed, Elijah applies the term to describe the historical challenges of eighteenth-century Vilna. Both Elijah and Vital use the term as a placeholder to describe a problematic element in their respective cultures. Where Vital reads *erev rav* in terms of the problematic status regarding certain peoples' religious origins and connection to the Jewish people, Elijah focuses on the socially disruptive role played by a group of individuals.

96. Elijah uses the imagery of the thorn in the rose to describe *erev rav*. See his commentary to *Tikkunei ha-Zohar*, 27d.

97. Elijah ben Solomon, *Tikkunei ha-Zohar*, 46a, 91a–b.

98. See Elijah's comments to Deuteronomy 1:1 in *Aderet Eliyahu* (Dubrovna: 1804).

99. See Elijah ben Solomon, *Peirush al-Kamah Aggadot* (Königsberg: 1862), 10b.

100. See the third letter of condemnation against the Hasidim in Wilensky, *Hasidim u-Mitnagdim*, 2:189, and Wilensky's interpretation of Elijah's comments (fn.27).

101. See Schochet, *The Hasidic Movement and the Gaon of Vilna*, 31–32.

102. See Elijah's commentary to Proverbs 7:8 in *Mishlei im Biur ha-Gra*.

103. See Ben-Sasson, "Ishiyuto shel ha-Gra ve-Hashpa'ato ha-Historit," 24–27, 62–65.

104. See Elijah's commentary to Proverbs 4:4 in *Mishlei im Biur ha-Gra*.

105. For a version of the whole letter, see "Letter of Elijah (Gaon) of Wilna," in *Hebrew Ethical Wills*, ed. and trans. Israel Abrahams (Philadelphia: Jewish Publication Society, 1926), 311–325.

106. Magid, "Deconstructing the Mystical," 57.

107. See Elijah's commentary to Proverbs 9:12 in *Mishlei im Biur ha-Gra*.

108. Adam Teller, "The Gaon of Vilna and the Communal Rabbinate in Eighteenth-Century Poland and Lithuania," in *The Gaon of Vilnius and the Annals of Jewish Culture: Materials of the International Scientific Conference, Vilnius, September 10–12, 1997*, ed. Izrealis Lempertas (Vilnius: Vilnius University Publishing House, 1998), 149.

109. See for example, Elijah's comments to Proverbs 10:12 in *Mishlei im Biur ha-Gra*.

110. See *Darkhei Noam* (Königsberg: 1764), 32a.

111. See Hundert, *Jews in Poland-Lithuania in the Eighteenth Century*, 16–17.

112. See John Klier, "Polish Shtetls under Russian Rule," *Polin* 17 (2004): 102.

113. See Simon Dubnow, *History of the Jews in Russia and Poland*, trans. Israel Friedlaender (Bergenfield, N.J.: Avotaynu, 2000), 148–155; and Fishman, *Russia's First Modern Jews*, 11.

114. On the partitions of Poland, see Jerzy Lukowski, *The Partitions of Poland, 1772, 1793, 1795* (London: Longman, 1999).

115. See Klausner, *Vilna be-Tekufat ha-Gaon*, 60.

116. As Eli Lederhendler argues, "Together with the Hasidic controversy and with other more localized conflicts over kahal powers (in Minsk, Vitebsk, and elsewhere), the Vilna rabbinate affair demonstrates not only the level of civic demoralization in Jewish politics at the end of the eighteenth century but also the structural inability of a Jewish community shorn of supercommunal restraints to maintain even that precarious balance between internal control and external interference that had been maintained over the previous two centuries." See Lederhendler, *The Road to Modern Jewish Politics: Political Tradition and Political Reconstruction in the Jewish Community in Tsarist Russia* (New York:

Oxford University Press, 1989), 46. On the relationship between the spread of Hasidism and dysfunction of the Jewish governing system, see Adam Teller, "Hasidism and the Challenge of Geography: The Polish Background to the Spread of the Hasidic Movement," *AJS Review* 30, no. 1 (2006): 13–14; and with regard to Elijah's leadership see Teller, "The Gaon of Vilna and the Communal Rabbinate in Eighteenth-Century Poland and Lithuania," 145–146.

117. On Shnuer Zalman's testimony to Russian authorities see Yehoshua Mondshine, *Kerem Habad* 4. no. 1 (November–December 1992): 46–47.

118. See "Zemir Aritzim," 1:44, 46. On Hasidism as a response to the disbanding of the *kehilah* in 1764, see Chone Shmeruk, "Mashmautah ha-Chevratit shel ha-Shechitah ha-Hasidit," in David Assaf, ed., *Tzadik ve-Edah: Hebetim Historiyim ve-Chevratim be-Cheker ha-Hasidut* (Jerusalem: Merkaz Zalman Shazar, 2001), 160–185; and Shmeruk, "Ha-Hasidut be-Askei ha-Chakirut," *Zion* 35 (1970): 182–192. On the fantasy of the Council's ability to eliminate the Sabbatians see Ada Rapoport-Albert, "Hasidism after 1772," in Rapoport-Albert, *Hasidism Reappraised*, 108–109.

119. See Avigdor ben Hayyim's letter to Tsar Paul I reprinted in Wilensky, *Hasidim u-Mitnagdim*, 1:241.

120. On Hasidic leaders assuming communal positions see Rosman, *The Lord's Jews*, 210–212, and Moshe Rosman, "Miedzyboz and Rabbi Israel Baal Shem Tov," in Gershon Hundert, ed., *Essential Papers on Hasidism: Origins to Present* (New York: New York University Press, 1991), 209–226; Fishman, *Russia's First Modern Jews*, 17–18, and Dynner, *Men of Silk*, 1–5.

121. See Elijah's 1797 letter in Wilensky, *Hasidim u-Mitnagdim*, 1:184 fn.6.

122. See Rabbi Avigdor ben Hayyim's letter to Tsar Paul I in Wilensky, *Hasidim u-Mitnagdim*, 1:252.

123. See Shneur Zalman of Liadi's letter to his followers sent in 1799 in Wilensky, *Hasidim u-Mitnagdim*, 1:306.

124. See Etkes, *The Gaon of Vilna*, 75–76.

125. Ibid., 85–86.

126. See Avraham Danzig, *Chokhmat Adam* (1825; New York: Yudaika Press: 1991), ruling 147:24. Avraham's words are supported by a fascinating story recorded by Chaikel Lunski in which Elijah storms out of a meeting with *kehilah* members, whom he thought were no better than "Sodom and Gemorrah." See C. Lunski, *Legendes: Vegn Vilner Goen* (Vilna: 1924), 14–15.

127. See *Darkhei Noam*, 24a–25b. On Elijah and Shmuel ben Eliezer, see Adam Teller, "The Gaon of Vilna and the Communal Rabbinate in Eighteenth-Century Poland and Lithuania," 144–150.

128. Ibid., 50a.

129. On the fiasco involving Abba ben Wolf's son see Chapter 1.

130. See Israel Klausner, *Vilna be-Tekufat ha-Gaon*, 236.

131. Elijah's comments appear in his *"likkutim"* (supplemental commentary) to Yosef Karo, *Shulchan Arukh, Choshen Mishpat* (Königsberg: 1856), 21:1. Elijah composed these supplemental comments later in his life. On the dating of Elijah's commentary see Levin, *Aliyot Eliyahu* (Vilna: 1856), 43–44; as well as the introductory comments made by Meir Ya'akov Gintsburg, Ya'akov Tzvi Mecklenburg, and Meir Leibush in *Shulchan Arukh, Choshen Mishpat;* and David Luria's remarks in "Aliyat Kir" in Levin, *Aliyot Eliyahu*, 120.

132. See Fishman, *Russia's First Modern Jews*, 20.

133. On reports regarding Elijah's death, funeral, and burial customs, see Levin, *Aliyot Eliyahu*, 88–89. It is interesting to note that Levin, writing in the mid-nineteenth century, ignores the fight that ensued between the Hasidim and Elijah's supporters following Elijah's death. According to Levin, "the whole town came out to the field to be present at his burial."

134. See David Maków, *Shever Poshim*, 24a, in Wilensky, *Hasidim u-Mitnagdim*, 2:95.

135. Dubnow's assertion (made in his *Toldot ha-Hasidut*, 254) of Mitnagdim killing Hasidim is based on the claims made in the polemical work of David Maków, *Shever Poshim* (which Dubnow refers to as "Zemir Aritzim"). Earlier charges of "bloodshed" are also recorded in Shneur Zalman of Liadi's letter to the community of Mogilev in Wilensky, *Hasidim u-Mitnagdim*, 1:161–167. For a discussion on Shneur Zalman of Laidi's letter, see Fishman, *Russia's First Modern Jews*, 15–16.

136. To be sure, these laws were already voted and agreed on the day before Elijah passed away. The rulings of the Vilna leadership can be found in Wilensky, *Hasidim u-Mitnagdim*, 1:204–209.

137. Simon Dubnow in *Toldot ha-Hasidut* claims that "the fanatical Mitnagdim were the first group to go speak with the police authorities" (259). Israel Klausner refutes Dubnow in *Vilna be-Tekufat ha-Gaon*, 32. Wilensky, *Hasidim u-Mitnagdim*, vol. 1, brings more documentary support for Klausner's claim that it was the Hasidim in Vilna who in fact originally involved state authorities (214).

138. See Israel Klausner's discussion of the letter sent on April 26, 1798, by the Vilna leadership in *Vilna be-Tekufat ha-Gaon*, 30–31.

139. Ibid., 31–33.

140. The first to document the history of the fight from 1798 to 1800 was Israel Klausner in his *Vilna be-Tekufat ha-Gaon*, 256–262. Mordekhai Wilensky, however, details how the two debates ended up overlapping, passing through the hands of two regional governors of Lithuania (Bulgakow, Frizel) before Mikhail Kutuzov assumed the office. See Wilensky, *Hasidim u-Mitnagdim*, 1:214.

141. Roger Parkinson, *The Fox of the North: The Life of Kutuzov, General of War and Peace* (London: Peter Davies, 1976), 39.

142. In 1800 Derzhavin submitted his report "An Opinion on How to Avert the Scarcity of Food in White Russia through the Curbing of the Jews' Avaricious Occupations, Their Reformation and Other Matters." For a discussion of Derzhavin's report see John Doyle Klier, *Russia Gathers Her Jews: The Origins of 'the Jewish Question' in Russia, 1772–1825* (Dekalb: Northern Illinois University Press, 1986), 95–115; Salo Baron, *The Russian Jew under the Tsar and Soviets* (New York: Schocken Books, 1987), 19–20; and Dubnow, *History of the Jews in Russia and Poland*, 158–161.

143. See Dubnow, *Toldot ha-Hasidut*, 276.

144. A Hebrew translation of Kutuzov's analysis can be found in Wilensky, *Hasidim u-Mitnagdim*, 1:264–270.

145. Kutuzov's report was originally published in the Russian Jewish quarterly *Evreiskaia Starina* (1910): 257–261 and was subsequently translated into Hebrew by Wilensky; see ibid., 1:264–268.

146. Wilensky, *Hasidim u-Mitnagdim*, 1:266.

147. On Isaac's thuggish behavior, see Klausner, *Vilna be-Tefukat ha-Gaon*, 154.

148. Compare Kutuzov's words with the nearly identical ones expressed by Isaac ben Leib, which were recorded in town records, then reprinted and translated in Israel Klausner in *Vilna be-Tefukat ha-Gaon*, 157. On Elijah's *kloiz* see Israel Klausner, *Toldot ha-Kehilah ha-Ivrit be-Vilna* (Vilna: 1938), 78–80. Regarding the financial controversy surrounding Elijah's *kloiz* after his death, see Hillel Noah Steinschneider, *Ir Vilna* (Vilna: 1900), 104–105. On the Hasidic disapproval of the elitist pre-modern *kloiz*, see Dynner, *Men of Silk*, 55–59.

149. On the 1804 reforms see Klier, *Russia Gathers Her Jews*, 117–143; Eli Lederhandler, *The Road to Modern Jewish Politics* (New York: Oxford University Press, 1989), 48–49; M. Stanislawski, *Tsar Nicholas I and the Jews: The Transformation of Jewish Society in Russia, 1825–1855* (Philadelphia: Jewish Publication Society, 1983), 8–9; Baron, *The Russian Jew under the Tsar and Soviets*, 20–21, 348 fn.4.; Dubnow, *History of the Jews in Russia and Poland*, 162–166; and Fuenn, Strashun, and Steinschneider, *Kiryah Ne'emanah*, 28–32.

150. See Russian edict of 1804, translated by Vitaly Charney, para. 53, available at www.jewishgen.org/belarus/1804_laws.htm (last accessed March 14, 2012).

151. See Stanislawski, *Tsar Nicholas I and the Jews*, 8.

152. Throughout the first half of the nineteenth century, numerous local feuds erupted throughout eastern Europe between the Hasidism and their opponents. These fights, however, usually had the state playing the role of arbiter. See Glenn

Dynner, "Hasidic Conquest of Central Poland," *Polin* 17 (2004): 52–81. While the Hasidic-Mitnagdic dispute cooled off following Elijah's death and the edicts of 1804, by the early nineteenth century the new Maskilim would try to enlist the government in their own war against the Hasidim. Whereas the Mitnagdic opposition to Hasidism was based on the Hasidim's relationship to Sabbatianism, early Maskilim such as Isaac Ber Levinsohn argued that the Hasidim stood against the interests of Enlightenment. On the early Maskilic opposition to Hasidism, see Stanislawski, *Tsar Nicholas I and the Jews*, 111–113; and Wodziński, *Haskalah and Hasidism in the Kingdom of Poland*.

153. See Shneur Zalman of Liadi's condemnations of Avraham of Kalisk published in Wilensky, *Hasidim u-Mitnagdim*, 1:39, 65.

Chapter 5. The *Biur* and the Yeshiva

1. This shift did not translate into rabbinic Jews ceasing to employ legal and public policy sanctions as social control mechanisms. But as demonstrated by Elijah's attempt to ban the new Hasidic groups, by the late eighteenth century onward such measures no longer conjured up the same fear.

2. On how Isserles made Karo's code the central legal work of the early modern period see Elchanan Reiner, "Yashan mi-Pnei Chadash: Al Temurot be-Tokhnei Limmud be-Yeshivot Polin be-Meah ha-16 ve-Yeshivat ha-Ramah be-Krakow," in Shmuel Glick, ed., *Remember the Word to Your Servant: Essays and Studies in Memory of Dov Rappel* (Jerusalem: 2007), 189. See also Elchanan Reiner, "Aliyat Kehilah ha-Gedolah," *Gal-Ed* 20 (2006): 25–28.

3. On the phenomenon of code writing throughout Europe and specifically in Jewish circles during the sixteenth century, see Joseph Davis, "The Reception of the *Shulchan Arukh* and the Formation of Ashkenazic Jewish Identity," *AJS Review* 26, no. 2 (November 2002): 252–253.

4. See Charles Taylor, *A Secular Age* (Cambridge, Mass.: Harvard University Press, 2007), 86. Taylor builds on Peter Burke's *Popular Culture in Early Modern Europe* (London: Temple Smith, 1978). There, Burke describes the processes that "reformed popular early modern European culture" from a wild polymorphic culture of "Carnival" to a more sober and ordered culture of "Lent" (207–243). On the transformation of popular early modern Jewish culture, see Elliot Horowitz's study on the purifying and legalizing of the pre-circumcision ceremony parties in "On the Eve of the Circumcision: A Chapter in the History of Jewish Nightlife," *Journal of Social History* 23 (1989): 45–69.

5. Moshe Halbertal, *People of the Book: Canon, Meaning, and Authority* (Cambridge, Mass.: Harvard University Press, 1997), 76.

6. John F. Matthews, *Laying Down the Law: A Study of the Theodosian Code* (New Haven: Yale University Press, 2000), 20.

7. Ibid., p. 30.

8. On the debate over the Mishnah's status (as compilation or code), see the opposing positions of Hanokh Albeck and Jacob Nahum Epstein summarized in Hermann L. Strack and Gunter Stemberger, *Introduction to Talmud and Midrash*, trans. Markus Bokhmuehl (Edinburgh: T&T Clark, 1991), 151–156.

9. On the strong criticisms directed at Isserles specifically, see the citations in Halbertal, *People of the Book*, 80–81. See also Menachem Elon, *Jewish Law: History, Sources, Principles*, trans. Bernard Auerbach and Melvin J. Sykes (Philadelphia: Jewish Publication Society, 1994), 3:1375–1417.

10. See the work by Shlomo ben Yechiel Luria (1510–1573/1574) titled *Yam Shel Shlomo* (1717). On Luria, see Chaim Tchernowitz, *Toldot ha-Poskim* (New York: 1947), 3:74–79. To be sure, Luria's work was more a commentary on the Talmud than a "code." Still, its aim was to present a halakhic ruling on a specific subject matter or issue. See also Mordekhai ben Avraham Jaffe's *Levush ha-Malkhut* (N.p.: 1590–1604). On Jaffe see Lawrence J. Kaplan, "Rationalism and Rabbinic Culture in Sixteenth-Century Eastern Europe: Rabbi Mordecai Jaffe's *Levush Pinat Yikrat*," Ph.D. diss., Harvard University, 1975, 43–79.

11. For example, see a letter sent to Jaffe by rabbis living in Israel claiming that after morning services they would sit and diligently study his work, in Kaplan, "Rationalism and Rabbinic Culture," 64.

12. See the comments made by Nathan (Nata) Hannover in *Yeven Metzulah* (Venice: 1653), 11. For an updated bibliography of scholarship on the reception of Karo's and Isserles's codes in Ashkenaz, see Joseph Davis, "The Reception of the *Shulchan 'Arukh* and the Formation of Ashkenazic Jewish Identity," *AJS Review* 26, no. 2 (November 2002): 251 fn.1, 251–259. Moses A. Shulvas argues in "Ha-Torah ve-Limmudah be-Polin u-ve-Lita," in Israel Halperin, ed., *Pinkas Va'ad Arba Aratzot* (Jerusalem: Mossad Bialik, 1945), 20, that by 1640 the opposition against codification had been almost entirely muted and that most rabbinic scholars living in Ashkenazic lands had focused their intellectual energies on writing commentaries to Karo's work. Until the end of the seventeenth century, Karo's code was not being studied en masse. The handy how-to guide *Emek Berakha* (Krakow: 1597), written by Isserles's student Rabbi Avraham Horowitz (1530–1610), highlights just how few lay people could actually read the codes produced by scholars in the sixteenth century. Commenting on Jaffe's and Falk's codes, Horowitz notes "how all of Israel follows the law of Isserles and Karo" (see the introduction to *Emek Berakha*). Yet only a few lines later Horowitz admits that "I have seen that many people do not have the means of acquiring works such as the *Shulchan Arukh*. Likewise, many do not have the intellect to study such books." It would not be until the mid-seventeenth century that code study would gain a popular following.

13. Cited in Simcha Assaf, *Mekorot le-Toldot ha-Chinukh be-Yisrael*, ed. Shmuel Glick (New York: Jewish Theological Seminary of America, 2002), 2:282. See also *The Libes Briv of Isaac Wetzlar*, ed. and trans. Morris Faierstein (Providence: Scholar Press, 1996), 97.

14. Cited in Assaf, *Mekorot le-Toldot ha-Chinukh be-Yisrael*, 2:335.

15. Mordechai Breuer, *Ohalei Torah: Ha-Yeshivah, Tavnitah, ve-Toldoteha* (Jerusalem: Merkaz Zalman Shazar, 2003), 144–145.

16. For an overview of the various methods of Talmudic study adopted by eastern European Jews in the sixteenth to eighteenth centuries, see Jay M. Harris, "Talmud Study," *YIVO Encyclopedia of Jews in Eastern Europe*, available at www.yivoencyclopedia.org/article.aspx/Talmud_Study (last viewed December 25, 2010).

17. Kenneth R. Stow, "The Burning of the Talmud in 1553 in Light of Sixteenth-Century Catholic Attitudes toward the Talmud," *Bibliothèque d'Humanisme et Renaissance* 34 (1972): 435–459.

18. Daniel Boyarin, *Ha-Iyyun ha-Sefaradi: Le-Farshanut ha-Talmud shel Megorshei Sefarad* (Jerusalem: Mekhon Ben-Tzvi le-Cheker Kehilot Yisrael ba-Mizrach, 1989); Ludwig Blau, "Methods of Teaching the Talmud in the Past and in the Present," *Jewish Quarterly Review* 15, no. 1 (October 1903): 121–134; Haim Z. Dimitrovsky, "Al-Derekh ha-Pilpul," in Saul Lieberman and Arthur Hyman, eds., *Salo Wittmayer Baron Jubilee Volume on the Occasion of His Eightieth Birthday* (Jerusalem: American Academy for Jewish Research, 1975), 111–181. See also Elchanan Reiner, "Temurot be-Yeshivot Polin ve-Ashkenaz be-Meot ha-16–ha-18 ve-ha-Vikuach al ha-Pilpul," in Israel Bartal, Ezra Mendelson, and Chava Turniansky, eds., *Ke-Minhag Ashkenaz ve-Polin: Sefer Yovel le-Chone Shmeruk* (Jerusalem: Merkaz Zalman Shazar, 1993), 9–80.

19. Some have referred to this as an "omnisignificant" interpretive approach. On omnisignificance in the rabbinic tradition, see James L. Kugel, *The Idea of Biblical Poetry: Parallelism and Its History* (New Haven: Yale University Press, 1981), 133–134; and Ya'akov Elman, " 'It Is No Empty Thing': Nahmanides and the Search for Omnisignificance," *Torah u-Madda* 4 (1993): 1–83.

20. *Darkhei Ha-Talmud*, ed. Isaac Sampson Langeh (Jerusalem: 1980), 22–23.

21. On each of these methods and their different but similar styles, see most recently David Katz, "A Case Study in the Formation of a Super-Rabbi: The Early Years of Rabbi Ezekiel Landau, 1713–1754," Ph.D. diss., University of Maryland, 2004, 121–125; On Landau more generally see Sharon Flatto, *The Kabbalistic Culture of Eighteenth-Century Prague: Ezekiel Landau (The Noda bi-Yehudah) and His Contemporaries* (Oxford: Littman Library, 2010); Maoz Kahane, "Mi-Prague le-Pressburg: Ktivah Hilkhatit be-Olam Mishtaneh me-ha

Nodah be-Yehudah le-ha-Hatam Sofer, 1730–1839," Ph.D. diss., Hebrew University, 2010.

22. Boyarin modifies Chaim Dimitrovsky's claim that there was a major difference between the analytic Sefardi method, which focused on investigating the meaning of specific words and the synthetic Ashkenazi method of *pilpul*, which offered a broad overarching explanation for the entire *sugya*. According to Boyarin, the synthetic approach already appears in Sefardic learning culture. See Boyarin, *Ha-Iyyun ha-Sefaradi*, 69 fn.1.

23. See *Darkhei Noam* (Königsberg: 1764), 60b–61a.

24. Ibid., 60a–60b.

25. Aaron F. Kleinberg, "Jewish Education in Central and Eastern Europe from the Sixteenth to the Eighteenth Centuries," in *Entziklopediah Chinukhit*, ed. Martin Buber (Jerusalem: Misrad ha-Chinukh ve-ha-Tarbut, 1964), cols. 398–399. See also M. Shulvas A., "Ha-Torah ve-Limudah be-Polin ve-Lita," in *Pinkas Va'ad Arba Aratzot* (Jerusalem: Mossad Bialik, 1945), 2:22–23.

26. On Judah Loew of Prague, see most recently David Sorotzkin, "Kehillat ha-al Zeman be-Idan ha-Temurot: Kavim le-Hithavutan shel Tefisot ha-Zeman ve-ha-Kolektiv ke-Basis le-Hagdarat Hitpatchut ha-Ortodoksiah ha-Yehudit be-Eropah be-Et ha-Chadashah," Ph.D. diss., Hebrew University, 2007.

27. On Maharal's objections, see Elon, *Jewish Law*, 1379–1383. See also Shlomo Zalman Havlin, "Biur ha-Gra le-*Shulchan Arukh*," *Yeshurun* 5 (1999): 704–705 fn.25.

28. Simha Assaf points out that with the exception of Maharal's emphasis on the study of Mishnah, none of his curriculum changes were adopted in his lifetime. See Assaf, "Introduction," in Shmuel Glick, ed., *Mekorot le-Toldot ha-Chinukh be-Yisrael* (New York: Jewish Theological Seminary of America, 2001), 1:23.

29. Israel Ta-Shma, "Seder Hadpasatam shel Chidushei ha-Rishonim le-Talmud: Perek le-Toldot ha-'Pilpul'," *Kiryat Sefer* 50, no. 2 (1975): 335. See also Elchanan Reiner, "Beyond the Realm of the Haskalah," in David B. Ruderman and Shmuel Feiner, ed., *Jahrbuch Des Simon Dubnow Instituts*, vol. 6 (Leipzig: Vandenhoeck and Ruprecht, 2007), 125–129.

30. Havlin, "Biur ha-Gra le-*Shulchan Arukh*," 707.

31. See Yisrael of Shklov's introduction to *Pe'at ha-Shulchan* (Sefad: 1836).

32. It is possible that Hayyim worried dilettantes might try to emulate his master's bold approach and untraditional positions. See Yehoshua Heshel Levin, *Aliyot Eliyahu* (Vilna: 1856), 32.

33. I hope in the future to write a longer study on the publication of Elijah's writings. On the history of the publication of the *Biur ha-Gra*, see Avraham Halevi Shisha, "Seder Hadpasatam shel Biur ha-Gra al Shulchan Arukh,"

Yeshurun 5 (1999): 678–695. On the inaccuracies and problems surrounding the publication of these works, see Ya'akov Shmuel Spiegel, *Amudim be-Toldot ha-Sefer ha-Ivri: Hagahot u-Megahim* (Ramat Gan: Bar-Ilan University Press, 1996), 384–404.

34. See the introductory comments made by Meir Ya'akov Gintsburg, Ya'akov Tzvi Mecklenburg, and Meir Leibush in *Shulchan Arukh, Choshen Mishpat* (Königsberg: 1856).

35. David Luria chastises the editors of the editions of *Orach Chayyim* and *Yoreh De'ah*, claiming that "the first editions of *Orach Chayyim* and *Yoreh De'ah* were not composed properly by their editors, who organized them in a manner that combined Elijah's notes and glosses together as if Elijah had originally written them that way." See David Luria's remarks in "Aliyat Kir" in Levin, *Aliyot Eliyahu*, 1.

36. See the editors' introduction to Elijah's *Biur al Shulchan Arukh, Orach Chayyim* (Shklov: 1803).

37. On the history, politics, and confusion surrounding the publication of the *Biur*, see Havlin, "Biur ha-Gra le-*Shulchan Arukh*," 699–708. Also see Hayyim Devir, "Biur ha-Gra al ha-*Shulchan Arukh*," *Yeshurun* 5 (1999): 3, Moshe Petrover, "Le-Darkho shel ha-Gra bi-Biuro le-*Shulchan Arukh*," *Yeshurun* 4 (1999): 752–753.

38. On Rashi's commentarial genius see Haym Soloveitchik, "Catastrophe and Halakhic Creativity: Ashkenaz 1096, 1242, 1306, and 1298," *Jewish History* 12, no. 1 (1998): 79–81.

39. See Elijah ben Solomon's commentary to *Chabakkuk* (Prague: 1811), 2:2.

40. See Rabbi Hayyim's introduction to *Biur ha-Gra, Orach Chayyim* (Shklov: 1803).

41. See "Shmayta di-Tagrei Lud," in Boyarin, *Ha-Iyyun ha-Sefaradi*, 89–90. On the history of the manuscript "Shmayta di-Tagrei Lud," see 70–72.

42. On the meaning of "Sevara mi-bachutz" as the text's "implicit" question, see Boyarin's explanation and his disagreement with Dimitrovsky in Boyarin, *Ha-Iyyun ha-Sefaradi*, 52–54.

43. See Menachem Mendel of Shklov's introduction to *Avot* (Shklov: 1804).

44. Elijah amplifies other rabbinic authorities that argued *nanos gigantum humeris insidentes*—the generation of dwarfs stands "on the shoulders of giants"—the claim that later generations have the ability to see beyond their predecessors. This metaphor was first recorded in the twelfth century and attributed to Bernard of Chartres (d. 1124). On how it has been employed in rabbinic literature, see Israel Ta-Shma, "'Halakha ke-Batrai,'" *Shenaton la-Mishpat ha-Ivri* 6–7 (1979–1980): 405–423; Shnayer Z. Leiman, "Dwarfs on the Shoulders of Giants," *Tradition* 27, no. 3 (Spring 1993): 90–94; Abraham Melamed, *Al Kitfei*

Anakim: Toldot ha-Pulmus bein ha-Acharonim le-Rishonim ba-Hagut ha-Yehudit bi-Yemei ha-Beinayim u-ve-Reishit ha-Et ha-Chadashah (Ramat-Gan: Bar Ilan University Press, 2003); and more generally, Robert Merton, *On the Shoulders of Giants: A Shandean Postscript* (Chicago: University of Chicago Press, 1993). See also most recently Allan Nadler, "The Gaon of Vilna and the Rabbinic Doctrine of Historical Decline," in David Assaf and Ada Rapoport-Albert, eds., *Yashan mi-Pnei Chadash: Mechkarim be-Toldot Yehudei Mizrach Eropah u-ve-Tarbutam; Shai le-Immanuel Etkes* (Jerusalem: Merkaz Zalman Shazar, 2009), 2:137–161.

45. See *Biur ha-Gra le-Shulchan Arukh Orach Chayyim* (Shklov: 1803), 498:4. I would like to thank Rabbi Barukh Simon of Yeshiva University via Rabbi Yitzchak Abadi for showing me this important source.

46. Avraham Yeshayahu Karelitz, *Kovetz Iggrot* (Jerusalem: Shmuel Grainiman, 1955), 1:32.

47. It is interesting that Yisrael of Shklov, in his introduction *Orach Chayyim* (Shklov: 1803), claims that Elijah's *Biur* actualized the earlier criticisms of code expressed by scholars like Rabbi Shmuel Eidels (1551–1631). Whereas Eidels's criticisms were ignored, Elijah's *Biur* encouraged the Talmud to be brought back as the primary text of study.

48. See Elijah's comments to Proverbs 10:4 in *Mishlei im Biur ha-Gra*, ed. Moshe Philip (Petach Tikvah: 1991). Elijah's comments may have been adapted from Maharal's brother Rabbi Bezalel's critique of *pilpul* in his "Introduction" to *Vikkuach Mayim Chayyim*, where he employs the metaphor of poverty to describe those who study only codes: "Anyone who seeks instruction only from the books of late authors can be compared to a pauper" (4b–5a).

49. See Moshe Petrover, "Le-Darkho shel ha-Gra bi-Biuro le-Shulchan Arukh," *Yeshurun* 4 (1999): 726–735. Elijah's diachronic critique of code is revealed in his comments on *Yoreh De'ah* (Grodno: 1806), 141:2. There, Elijah points out that Karo contradicts himself (see the difference between Karo's statements in *Yoreh De'ah*, 141:2 and 146:11) regarding the permissibility of using fragments of idols. Elijah suggests that the contradiction is already located in the Talmud (see the contradiction between Shmuel's statements recorded in Avodah Zarah 49b and the position of the anonymous voice of the Talmud on 49b). Elijah glosses both of Karo's contradictory comments without attempting to harmonize them or show their coherence. In his gloss to *Yoreh De'ah* 146:11, Elijah simply points out the two different opinions being juggled, "as it is written on 49b all agree [that fragments of idols are worshipped] and see also the position of Rabbi Yochanan." Elijah then notes that the *Shulchan Arukh* goes against "Shmuel's position on 41b and [Karo's own] position [expressed] in 141:2." Finally, he describes how other medieval commentators, most notably Maimonides and

Rashi, explain the contradiction in the Talmud. Elijah's synchronic critique—which creates space for other commentators and Talmudic texts that have been elided by Karo's code—is revealed in his comments to *Yoreh De'ah* 142:4. There Karo discusses the case of one using sticks from an *ashera* tree (an idolatrous tree from which one is not allowed to receive any kind of benefit) to light a fire for an oven or to use as picks to sew a garment. But in the *Mishnah (Avodah Zara* 49b) referenced by the *Shulchan Arukh*, Rabbi Eliezer agues that if the garment made from an *ashera* pick was mixed together with other garments "one may 'throw' the benefit one would have received from the object away [instead of actually throwing away the garment or pick itself]." Medieval commentators hotly debate the nature of Rabbi Eliezer's cryptic comment. Does Rabbi Eliezer mean to say that once a person tosses a sufficient amount of money into the sea they are permitted to use the pick made from the *ashera* tree? Is Rabbi Eliezer saying that as long as a sufficient amount of money was thrown away the garment can be used even if it was not mixed together with other garments? Or does Rabbi Eliezer suggest only that one need not throw away all the clothing mixed together with this garment made from the idolatrous pick? Elijah never takes a position on the exact nature of Rabbi Eliezer's comments (see *Biur ha-Gra, Yoreah Deah,* 142:7, 8), nor does he harmonize the different interpretations. Rather, he reopens the debate over the passage in question, citing the ignored medieval commentators and dividing them into two camps.

50. For a few of the many examples of where Elijah challenges Rambam's reading of Talmudic sources, see *Yoreh De'ah,* 141:1, 141:3, 141:4, 142:9, 143:1.

51. See Petrover, "Le-Darkho shel ha-Gra bi-Biuro le-*Shulchan Arukh,*" 743–745, and the examples he cites to support his claim.

52. See Israel Klausner, *Vilna be-Tekufat ha-Gaon* (Jerusalem: Reuben Mas, 1942), 17; and Jacob Dienstag, "Ha-im Hitnaged ha-Gra le-Mishnato ha-Filosofit shel ha-Rambam?" *Talpiyot* 4, nos. 1–2 (July 1949): 268 fn.82. See also Immanuel Etkes, "Li-She'elat Mevasrei ha-Haskalah be-Mizrach Eropah," in Etkes, ed., *Ha-Da'at ve-ha-Chayyim: Tnuat ha-Haskalah be-Mizrach Eropah* (Jerusalem: Merkaz Zalman Shazar, 1993), 30. Both Klausner and Dienstag base their interpretation on the passage in the Gaon's writing where he is said to have called philosophy *arurah* (the evil philosophy). See also Shmuel Joseph Fuenn, Matisyahu Strashun, and Hillel-Noah Maggid Steinschneider, *Kiryah Ne'emanah: Korot Adat Yisrael be-Ir Vilna* (Vilna: Yitzchak Funk, 1915), 169, where the authors claim that this phrase was put in by later editors. On the way in which this term was supposedly inserted by later editors, see Alan Brill, "Auxiliary to 'Hokhma': The Writings of the Vilna Gaon and Philosophical Terminology," in Moshe Hallamish, Yosef Rivlin, and Raphael Shuchat, eds., *Ha-Gra u-Veit Midrasho* (Ramat Gan: Bar-Ilan University Press, 2003), 9–11. See also Mejeris

Šubas, "The Gaon's Views on Philosophy and Science," in Izraelis Lempertas, ed., *The Gaon of Vilnius and the Annals of Jewish Culture* (Vilnius: Vilnius University Publishing House, 1998), 65–74.

53. Dienstag, "Ha-Im Hitnaged ha-Gra le-Mishnato ha-Filosofit shel ha-Rambam?" 268 fn.82.

54. See Brill, "Auxiliary to 'Hokhma,'" 12.

55. See Moshe Philip, ed., *Sefer Mishlei im Biur ha-Gra* (Petach Tikvah: 2001), 441; and Eliyahu Stern, "Philosophy and Dissimulation in Elijah of Vilna's Writings and Legacy," *Revue Internationale de Philosophie* (forthcoming). On Elijah reading Aristotle, see his letter to Rabbi Shaul of Amsterdam recorded in Tzvi ha-Levi Horowitz, *Kitvei ha-Geonim* (Warsaw: 1938), 3–10.

56. It is important to note that just because Elijah disagreed with certain aspects of philosophical thought, as seemingly claimed by his later students Menachem Mendel of Shklov in his introduction to Elijah's commentary to *Avot de-Rebbe Natan* (Shklov: 1804), and Yisrael of Shklov in his introduction to *Pe'at ha-Shulchan* (Safed: 1836), this disagreement did not mean that Elijah was against reading philosophy and adopting certain philosophic ideas. Furthermore, a more careful reading of the earlier mentioned students' writings suggests that Elijah was secretly positively inclined to the study of philosophy. On this point see Stern, "Philosophy and Dissimulation in Elijah of Vilna's Writings and Legacy."

57. Moses Maimonides, *The Guide of the Perplexed*, trans. Shlomo Pines (Chicago: Chicago University Press, 1963), 12.

58. On Elijah and his relationship to Maimonides's *Guide*, see Levin, *Aliyot Eliyahu*, 17–18, specifically fn.5 under the heading "Philosophy." Even in *Aliyot Eliyahu*, where Elijah is depicted as standing in opposition to the new Maskilim, Elijah (according to David Luria) is still said to have not only read and cited the *Guide*, but also supported a study group for the *Guide* that met in front of his *kloiz*.

59. See Menashe's recollection of Elijah's criticism of the preacher Jacob Kranz, the Dubno Maggid, in *Alfei Menashe* (Vilna: 1822), "likkutim to siman 129," unpaginated.

60. Michael Shasher, in his *Sambatyon: Essays on Jewish Holidays*, ed. and trans. Edward Levin (Jerusalem: World Zionist Organization, 1987), 62, contends that Elijah's commentary to Jonah follows Maimonides's approach to allegory. Elijah follows Maimonides by rejecting the notion that Jonah was eaten by a real whale and survived inside its stomach for days on end. Instead, he claims that the story is an allegory about the human soul. Unlike Maimonides, however, Elijah's allegory never ignores the specific wording of Jonah. Both neutralize the idea of the existence of irrational forces, but whereas Maimonides ignores the specific

wording of a seemingly irrational text, Elijah feels the need to give sufficient reason for the existence of each word, sentence, and phrase. Maimonides's interpretive behavior makes it impossible to understand how he contextually reads biblical verses and words. With Elijah, the exact opposite is the case. Each word has a reason and contributes to a larger conceptual picture. On those who disagree with Shashar's reading, see Yosef Rivlin, "Biur ha-Gra le-Sefer Yonah," *Kiryat Sefer* 62 (1989): 920–924.

61. For a more in-depth discussion of Elijah's understanding of philosophy and his relationship to Maimonides, see Stern, "Cosmogony, Anthropogony, and Dissimulation in Elijah of Vilna's Philosophy."

62. Jay M. Harris, *How Do We Know This? Midrash and the Fragmentation of Modern Judaism* (Albany: State University of New York Press, 1995), 5–6 alludes to this tendency in modern rabbinic culture.

63. See Maimonides's "Letter to Pinchas Ha-Dayan," cited and translated in Isadore Twersky, *Introduction to the Code of Maimonides (Mishneh Torah)* (New Haven: Yale University Press, 1980), 33. To be sure, as Twersky points out (18 fn.25), one should not make too much of Maimonides's distinction between "commentary" and "compilation." In other contexts, Maimonides seems to use the two words somewhat interchangeably. That said, Maimonides never refers to the *Mishneh Torah* as a commentary (*peirush*).

64. See Maimonides's comments in Hilchot Yesodei ha-Torah, *Mishneh Torah*, 4:13. See also ibid., 65–67.

65. Elijah's son Avraham recounts the following story in his introduction to *Biur ha-Gra:* "In his later years I asked him on a number of occasions why he did not travel to the Holy Land [the land of Israel]. He did not, however, give me an answer. One time I bothered him incessantly, he replied, 'I do not have permission from Heaven.' Likewise, he assured me that he would write a practical legal code on the four sections of halakha. He would write one decisive straightforward answer with strong and powerful proofs. I asked him many times before his death to write such a book and he responded to me 'I do not have permission from Heaven.'" A similar story appears in Judah Leib Maimon, *The History of the Vilna Gaon* (Jerusalem: Mossad ha-Rav Kook, 1954), 93.

66. On the printing of the *Shulchan Arukh* and the Talmud in the eighteenth century see Zeev Gries, *The Book in the Jewish World, 1700–1900* (Oxford: Littman Library, 2007), 35–40.

67. See Davis, "The Reception of the *Shulchan 'Arukh* and the Formation of Ashkenazic Jewish Identity," 273 fn.87.

68. On the method of "glossing" in seventeenth- and eighteenth-century rabbinic writing, see Elchanan Reiner, "The Ashkenazi Elite at the Beginning of the Modern Era: Manuscript versus Printed Book," *Polin* 10 (1977): 85–98.

69. See also Jay Harris, "Rabbinic Literature in Lithuanian after the Death of the Gaon," in Izraeis Lempertas, ed., *The Gaon of Vilnius and the Annals of Jewish Culture: Materials of the International Scientific Conference, Vilnius, September 10–12, 1997* (Vilnius: Vilnius University Publishing House, 1998), 90.

70. See Rabbi Hayyim's introduction to *Biur ha-Gra, Orach Chayyim*.

71. Shaul Stampfer contests Rabbi Hayyim's historical assessment by arguing that Elijah had only minimal intellectual influence in early nineteenth-century Jewish learning culture. His fame, he proffers, was not the result of his intellectual innovations, but a product of the perpetuation of his saintly image. "After the Gaon's death," claims Stampfer, his "memory was not perpetuated by the study of his writings. [Rather], the key to the Gaon's prominence was his personal charisma." Stampfer has written two articles on the subject; see his "On the Creation and Perpetuation of the Image of the Gaon of Vilna," 52–61; and "The Gaon, Yeshivot and the Printing Press: A Complicated Relationship between a Scholar and Society," in Lempertas, *The Gaon of Vilnius*, 142–153. It is incorrect to assert that the underwhelming number of Elijah's texts published in the first half of the nineteenth century reflects a lack of intellectual interest. Rather, according to Gil S. Perl, "the fact that fifty works were published between 1798 and 1808 may be just as significant as the fact that one hundred works of the Gaon were published between 1855 and 1865." See Perl, "Emek ha-Neziv: A Window into the Intellectual Universe of Rabbi Naftali Zvi Yehudah Berlin," Ph.D. diss., Harvard University, 2006, 223, 229, 280. Advancements in printing during the nineteenth century undoubtedly contributed to the increased publication of Elijah's writings starting in the mid-1800s.

72. See Frederick Beiser, *The Fate of Reason: German Philosophy from Kant to Fichte* (Cambridge, Mass.: Harvard University Press, 1987), 177–178.

73. It was not before the publication of Karl Leonhard Reinhold's *Briefe über die Kantische Philosophie* published in 1787 that one sees any sort of critical mass readership of Kant. See ibid., 217–218.

74. See the opening pages of *Shenot Eliyayu* (Lvov: 1799).

75. See Avraham ha-Levi, "Rabbienu ha-Gadol mi-Vilna u-Biur le-Shulchan Aruch," *Yeshurun* 6 (1999): 691. See also Rabbi Avraham Simcha's introduction to Elijah's commentary to *Midrash Ruth Rabbah* reprinted in *Sefer Malkhut Eliyahu* (New York: Makhon ha-Gra, 2000), 124–128.

76. See Yehudah Epstein, *Minchat Yehudah* (Warsaw: 1877). On Yehudah Epstein see Hillel Noah Steinschneider, *Ir Vilna* (Vilna: 1900), 248–249 fn.5. In some later editions of Yehudah's work his critical comments on various rabbinic figures were censored and he offers an apology for his earlier dismissal of certain rabbinic figures. The story is also cited in its original form by Simcha Assaf, *Mekorot le-Toldot ha-Chinukh be-Yisrael*, ed. Shmuel Glick (New York:

Jewish Theological Seminary of America, 2002), 1:622–624. On Yehudah's connection to Elijah's legacy, see midway through Eliyahu Landau's introduction to *Sefer Minchat Eliyahu* (Jerusalem: 1927), unpaginated.

77. Epstein, *Minchat Yehudah* (Warsaw: 1877).

78. On Tevel and his relationship to Rabbi Hayyim of Volozhin, see Levin, *Aliyot Eliyahu*, fn.121.

79. Assaf, *Mekorot le-Toldot ha-Chinukh be-Yisrael*, 1:622–624.

80. Shaul Stampfer, in his essay "On the Creation and Perpetuation of the Image of the Gaon of Vilna," claims that "R. Haim of Volozhin had no dealings with the publication of his venerated teacher's works, nor is there any evidence that he tried to obtain hand written copies of the Gaon's notes to classical text" (57). Yet in the introduction to *Shenot Eliyahu* (Lvov: 1799) we are told by Rabbi Yehudah Leib ben Rabbi Shneur that Rabbi Hayyim of Volozhin was responsible for editing Elijah's commentary to *Mishnah Zeraim*. On this point, see Yeshayahu Winograd, *Otzar Sifrei ha-Gra* (Jerusalem: Kerem Eliyahu, 2003), 37 fn.66.

81. See Dov Eliakh, *Kol ha-Katuv le-Hayyim* (Jerusalem: 1988), 153; see also Dov Eliakh, *Sefer ha-Gaon: Le-Toldot Chayav u-Verur Mishnato shel Morenu ve-Rabenu ha-Gaon Rabenu Eliyahu mi-Vilna* (Jerusalem: Moreshet Yeshivot, 2002), 3:1232–1233.

82. Israel Salanter, *Sefer Tevunah* (Königsberg: August Strobbe, 1861), 3 fn.1.

83. Immanuel Etkes, *The Gaon of Vilna: The Man and His Image* (Berkeley: University of California Press, 2002), 230.

84. On Elijah's indirect role in the founding of the Volozhin yeshiva, see Shaul Stampfer, *Ha-Yeshiva ha-Litait be-Hithavutah* (Jerusalem: Merkaz Zalman Shazar, 1995), 37–38.

85. See Eli Lederhendler, *The Road to Modern Jewish Politics: Political Tradition and Political Reconstruction in the Jewish Community in Tsarist Russia* (New York: Oxford University Press, 1989), 26.

86. See Elchanan Reiner, "Temurot be-Yeshivot Polin ve-Ashkenaz be-meot ha-16–ha-18 ve-ha-Vikuach al ha-Pilpul," in Israel Bartal, Ezra Mendelson, and Chava Turniansky, eds., *Ke-Minhag Ashkenaz ve-Polin: Sefer Yovel le-Chone Shmeruk* (Jerusalem: Merkaz Zalman Shazar, 1993), 33; and Mordechai Breuer, "Appointment and Succession among the Yeshiva Deans," *Jewish History* 13, no. 1 (Spring 1999): 16; and Breuer, *Ohalei Torah* (Jerusalem: Merkaz Zalman Shazar, 2003), 461.

87. Immanuel Etkes, "Mavo," in *Yeshivot Lita: Pirkei Zikhronot*, ed. Immanuel Etkes and Shlomo Tikochinski (Jerusalem: Hebrew University Press, 2004), 14.

88. Breuer, *Ohalei Torah*, 442, 458.

89. Ibid., 459.

90. See Reiner, "Temurot be-Yeshivot Polin ve-Ashkenaz be-Meot ha-16–ha-18 ve-ha-Vikuach al ha-Pilpul," 33; Breuer, "Appointment and Succession among the Yeshiva Deans," 16.

91. Edward Fram, *Ideals Face Reality: Jewish Law and Life in Poland, 1550–1655* (Cincinnati: Hebrew Union College Press, 1997), 45.

92. See Adam Teller, "The Laicization of Early Modern Jewish Society: The Development of the Polish Rabbinate in the Sixteenth Century," in *Schöpferische Momente des europäischen Judentums in der frühen Neuzeit*, ed. Michael Graetz (Heidelberg: Universitätsverlag C. Winter, 2000), 344–349.

93. On seventeenth-century aspirations to create a supra-communal body to adjudicate halakhic matters for all of European Jewry, see Jacob Katz, *Tradition and Crisis: Jewish Society at the End of the Middle Ages*, trans. Bernard Dov Cooperman (New York: New York University Press, 1993), 101–102.

94. See Shmuel Ettinger, "The Council of the Four Lands," in *The Jews in Old Poland, 1000–1795*, ed. Antony Polonsky, Jakub Basista, and Andrzej Link-Lenczowski (London: I.B. Tauris, 1993), 93–109, esp. 101.

95. On Jaffe see Lawrence J. Kaplan, "Rabbi Mordekhai Jaffe and the Evolution of Jewish Culture in the Sixteenth Century," in Bernard Dov Cooperman, ed., *Jewish Thought in the Sixteenth Century* (Cambridge, Mass.: Harvard University Press, 1983), 273. More generally, see Kaplan, "Rationalism and Rabbinic Culture." On Jaffe's scientific interests and rationalism, see David Ruderman, *Jewish Thought and Scientific Discovery in Early Modern Europe* (Detroit: Wayne State University Press, 2001), 87–89.

96. On the *kehilah* and its breakdown, see Jacob Katz, *Tradition and Crisis: Jewish Society at the End of the Middle Ages* (New York: New York University Press, 1973), 65–112. It should be noted that Gershon Hundert has recently challenged Katz's thesis on the extent of the breakdown of the *kehilah*. See Hundert, *Jews in Poland-Lithuania in the Eighteenth Century: A Genealogy of Modernity* (Berkeley: University of California Press, 2004), 99–118.

97. Richard Butterwick, *Poland's Last King and English Culture: Stanislaw August Poniatowski, 1732–1798* (Oxford: Oxford University Press, 1998).

98. On the erosion of the autonomous halakhic system and the emergence of the semi-neutral society in late eighteenth-century Jewish life, see Jacob Katz, *Out of the Ghetto: The Social Background of Jewish Emancipation, 1770–1870* (Syracuse, N.Y.: Syracuse University Press, 1973), 42–56.

99. Moshe Rosman, *The Lord's Jews: Magnate-Jewish Relations in the Polish-Lithuanian Commonwealth* (Cambridge, Mass.: Harvard University Center for Jewish Studies, 1990), 192.

100. See Fuenn, Strashun, and Steinschneider, *Kiryah Ne'emanah*, 150.

101. See Elijah's children's introduction to *Biur ha-Gra al Shulchan Arukh, Orach Chayyim* (Shklov: 1803).

102. On the history of the "Slutzki" home, see ibid., 81.

103. On the history of the *kloiz* as a social and intellectual institution in eastern Europe see Elchanan Reiner, "Hon Ma'amad Chevrati ve-Talmud Torah: Ha-Kloiz be-Chevrah ha-Yehudit be-Mizrach Eropah ba-Meot 17–19," *Zion* 58 (1993): 287–328. As seen from the controversy involving the early eighteenth-century Vilna philanthropist Rabbi Yehudah Lieb Safra (d. 1772), known as "the Yesod" (the "foundation"), who dedicated a new *kloiz* in his own name, establishing new learning institutions in Vilna was a complicated process. Communal leaders did not easily cede power in spiritual or educational matters. On Safra see Fuenn, Strashun, and Steinschneider, *Kiryah Ne'emanah*, 121–123. While Elijah was still alive, his living and study quarters did not have the official status of a "learning institution" (*kloiz*) supported by the community. Instead Elijah's study chamber was granted only the status of a *minyan*, which meant that Elijah was allowed to learn there and prayer services could be held there (but not on the High Holidays or Festivals). Only after Elijah's death, with the official purchase of Elijah's living quarters and study chamber by communal leaders from the descendants of Eliyahu Pesseles (and in agreement with Elijah's children), could Elijah's "study house" be considered a *kloiz* and be dedicated in Elijah's name. See *Kiryah Ne'emanah*, 78–80; and Israel Cohen, *The Jews of Vilna* (Philadelphia: The Jewish Publication Society, 1943), 109–111. On the establishment of Elijah's *kloiz* after his death, see most recently David Kamenetsky, "Sefer 'Ma'aseh Rav,'" *Yeshurun* 21 (2009): 781–791; and Arie Morgenstern, "Bein Banim le-Talmidim: Ha-Ma'avak al Moreshet ve-al ha-Ideologia," *Dat* 53 (2004): 83–92. On the history of the kloizim in Vilna see the reflections of C. Lunski, *Fun Vilner Geto: Geshtaltn un bilder* (Vilna: 1920), 57–68.

104. Contrary to common belief, Elijah did not found or order the founding of the Volozhin yeshiva. Dov Eliakh is the latest biographer of Elijah to claim that Elijah founded or ordered the modern yeshiva at Volozhin; see Eliakh, *Sefer ha-Gaon*, 1:395–414 and *Avi ha-Yeshivot* (Jerusalem: 1991), 95–100. Eliakh's sources are in large measure historically unverifiable, having been recorded by mid- to late nineteenth-century rabbinic figures. Rabbi Hayyim actually addresses his relationship to Elijah in a letter explaining the need for the yeshiva that was written in 1803 and published in 1816. There Hayyim makes clear that "from all of the time he spent with Gra he was only privileged to gain an understanding of Elijah's 'method' (tzurata)." See Fuenn, Strashun, and Steinschneider, *Kiryah Ne'emanah*, 170.

105. See Stampfer, *Ha-Yeshiva ha-Litait be-Hithavutah*, 41.

106. Berlin, *Fun Volozhin biz Yerushalayim* (New York: 1933), 1:13.

107. Stampfer, *Ha-Yeshiva ha-Litait be-Hithavutah*, 41.

108. The injunction to study the same tractate must be understood in the context of printing costs; see Breuer, *Ohalei Torah*, 463.

109. Etkes, "Mavo," 17.

110. See Breuer, *Ohalei Torah*, 394–395; and further, Etkes, *The Gaon of Vilna*, 228–229.

111. On the funding of students and rabbinical positions see Berlin, *Fun Volozhin biz Yerushalayim*, 1:103–111, and on curricula see 1:77–86.

112. See Charles Taylor, *Sources of the Self: The Making of Modern Identity* (Cambridge, Mass.: Harvard University Press, 1989), 462; see also José Casanova, *Public Religions in the Modern World* (Chicago: University of Chicago Press, 1994), 215.

113. On the curriculum of the Volozhin yeshiva and Elijah's influence, see Stampfer, *Ha-Yeshiva ha-Litait be-Hithavutah*, 44. It should be noted that in the same way that code-style learning never eliminated the study of Talmud but only stressed the role of codes, so too did the shift to Talmudic study in the nineteenth century never eliminate halakhic and code-oriented learning. Rather, as Stampfer explains, in the nineteenth century codes were studied but the "emphasis was on the Gemara" (48). On yeshiva culture in the nineteenth century see Abraham Menes, "Patterns of Jewish Scholarship in Eastern Europe," in Louis Finkelstein, ed., *The Jews: Their History, Culture and Religion* (New York: Harper, 1960), 1:376–392.

114. Reiner, "Beyond the Realm of the Haskalah," 129.

115. Even deep into the nineteenth century, Volozhin's head, Naftali Tzvi Yehudah Berlin, was known to have had sympathies for Enlightenment sentiments. See his son's recollections in Berlin, *Fun Volozhin biz Yerushalayim*, 1:83.

116. See *Madreigat ha-Adam* (Paltava: 1918), 17. On Hurwitz and the Mussar movement in modernity see David Fishman, "Musar and Modernity: The Case of Novaredok," *Modern Judaism* 8, no. 1 (1988): 41–64; and Mordekhai Pachter, "Tnu'at ha-Mussar ve-ha-Kabbalah," in David Assaf and Ada Rapoport-Albert, eds., *Yashan mi-Pnei Chadash* (Jerusalem: Merkaz Zalman Shazar, 2009), 1:243–251.

117. On the active public role and respect given to rabbinic figures in nineteenth-century eastern Europe see Michael Stanislawski, *Tsar Nicholas I and the Jews: The Transformation of Jewish Society in Russia, 1825–1855* (Philadelphia: Jewish Publication Society, 1983), 133–137; and Lederhendler, *The Road to Modern Jewish Politics*, 68–83.

118. See the roles played by Rabbi Isaac of Volozhin and Menachem Mendel Schneersohn in the 1843 St. Petersburg Conference. At the conference the rabbis were forced to support the state-sponsored schools for Jewish pupils, which

mandated the study of secular subjects. See Lederhendler, *The Road to Modern Jewish Politics*, 70–72; and Stanislawski, *Tsar Nicholas I and the Jews*, 77–88.

119. Breuer, *Ohalei Torah*, 47.

120. On the spread of Hasidism in the nineteenth century see Mordechai Zalkin, "Between Dvinsk and Vilna: The Spread of Hasidism in Nineteenth-Century Lithuania," in I. Etkes, D. Asaf, I. Bartal, and E. Reiner, eds., *Within Hasidic Circles: Studies in Hasidism in Memory of Mordechai Wilensky* (Jerusalem: Mossad Bialik Hebrew University Press, 1999), 21–50; and Raphael Mahler, *Hasidism and the Jewish Enlightenment: Their Confrontation in Galicia and Poland in the First Half of the Nineteenth Century* (Philadelphia: Jewish Publication Society of America, 1985), 25.

121. See Meir Wunder, "Ha-Yeshiva be-Galitziyah," *Moriah* 3 (1992): 97–98; Allan Nadler, "Ha-Sintezia be-Hasidut Slonim bein Hasidut le-Limmud Torah be-Nusach ha-Mitnagdim," in Immanuel Etkes, ed., *Yeshivot u-Vatei Midrashot* (Jerusalem: Merkaz Zalman Shazar, 2006), 395; and Hayyim Gertner, "Batei Midrash be-Galitsiyah be-Meah ha-19," also in Etkes, *Yeshivot u-Vatei Midrashot*, 174–206.

122. On the development and emergence of the Hasidic Yeshiva in the interwar period, see Shaul Stampfer, "Hasidic Yeshivot in Inter-War Poland," *Polin* 11 (1998): 12.

Chapter 6. The Genius

1. On the role played by race science in nineteenth-century Jewish history, see John Efron, *Defenders of the Race: Jewish Doctors and Race Science in Fin-de-Siècle Europe* (New Haven: Yale University Press, 1994), 47–55 and 71–73; also Raphael Patai and Jennifer Patai, *The Myth of the Jewish Race* (Detroit: Wayne State University Press, 1994), 156–160. Specifically, on the nineteenth-century "scientific" conceptualization of "Jewish Genius" see Sander Gillman, *Smart Jews: The Construction of the Image of Jewish Superior Intelligence* (Lincoln: University of Nebraska Press, 1996), 42–51; and Noah B. Strote, "The German Birth of the 'Psychological Jew' in an Age of Ethnic Pride," *New German Critique* 39, no. 1 (2012): 199–224.

2. The most cited testimonies written by the Gaon's sons, Avraham (1765–1808) and Yehudah Leib (1764–1816), appear as introductions to their father's commentaries *Biur ha-Gra al Shulchan Arukh, Orach Chayyim* (Shklov: 1803), *Aderet Eliyahu* (Dubrovna: 1804), and *Peirush al Kamah Aggadot* (Vilna: 1800). The Gaon's grandson, Ya'akov Moshe of Słonim (1779–1849), also recorded his impressions in his introductions to the following works by Elijah: the Gaon's commentary to *Zohar* (Vilna: 1810), *Sifra di-Tzniuta* (Vilna: 1820), *Biur ha-Gra al Shulchan Arukh, Orach Chayyim,* and the mathematical work *Ayil Meshulash*

(Vilna: 1834). The Gaon's prized student, Hayyim of Volozhin (1749–1821), wrote oft-cited stories about his master as introductions to Elijah's commentaries to *Orach Chayyim* (Shklov: 1803), *Mishnah Zeraim, Shenot Eliyahu* (Lvov: 1799), *Zohar* (Vilna: 1810), and *Sifra di-Tzniuta* (Vilna: 1820). Among the most read testimonies are those written by Menachem Mendel of Shklov (1750–1827) in *Pirkei Avot* (Shklov: 1804); and by Yisrael of Shklov (1770–1839) in *Taklin Chadatin* (Minsk: 1812) and *Pe'at ha-Shulchan* (Safed: 1836). Finally, reflections on the Gaon by his in-law Avraham Danzig (1748–1820) appear in Danzig's popular legal digests *Chayyei Adam* (Vilna: 1819) and *Chokhmat Adam* (Vilna: 1825), as well as in his *Zikhru Torat Moshe* (Vilna: 1827). To be sure, there are numerous other accounts produced by students such as Menashe of Illya (1767–1831), Pinchas of Połock (d. 1822), Dov Ber Treves (d. 1803), and Rabbi Binyamin Rivlin (1728–1810), to name but a few. Likewise, Elijah's son Avraham's posthumously published *Sa'eret Eliyahu* (Warsaw: 1877) offers a meditation on the greatness of his father and the loss incurred by his passing. On the most updated list of Elijah's students and subsequent followers, see Raphael Shuchat, *Olam Nistar be-Memadei ha-Zeman* (Ramat Gan: Bar Ilan University Press, 2008), 74–75.

3. See Levin, *Aliyot Eliyahu*, 12.

4. See ibid., 28.

5. Levin left Volozhin after a protracted battle with Rabbi Naftali Tzvi Yehudah Berlin over the institution's direction and curriculum. The disagreement revolved around whether Volozhin was to be an elitist institution meant purely for study (Berlin) or a more populist institution focused on training communal rabbis (Levin). Both were related to Volozhin's founder, Rabbi Hayyim. Levin's and Berlin's disagreement was finally adjudicated by leading rabbinic European authorities, who handed the keys of the yeshiva to Berlin. On the fight between Berlin and Levin, see Shaul Stampfer, *Ha-Yeshiva ha-Litait be-Hithavutah* (Jerusalem: Merkaz Zalman Shazar, 1995), 74–80. For a firsthand account of the dispute and the brutal war fought between Levin and Berlin, see Shmuel Leib Tzitron, "Milchamta ha-Dinastiyot bi-Yeshivat Volozhin," in *Yeshivot Lita: Pirkei Zikhronot*, ed. Immanuel Etkes and Shlomo Tikotsinski (Jerusalem: Merkaz Zalman Shazar, 2004), 81–93. On Levin and the Haskalah see Immanuel Etkes, "Parashat ha-Haskalah mi-Ta'am ve-ha-Temurah be-Ma'amad Tnuat ha-Haskalah be-Rusiyah," *Zion* 43 (1978): 312–313, republished in Etkes, ed., *Ha-Da'at ve-ha-Chayyim: Tnuat ha-Haskalah ha-Yehudit be-Mizrach Eropah* (Jerusalem: Merkaz Zalman Shazar, 1993), 215–216 (167–216). On a less than flattering firsthand description of Levin, see the reflections of Isaac Kovner, *Sefer ha-Matzref* (1868), ed. Shmuel Fiener (Jerusalem: Mossad Bialik, 1998), 136–149.

6. The politics and relationships among the people involved in the publication of *Aliyot Eliyahu* is worthy of its own study. In short, in 1855 the printer, Nachman ben Tzvi Hirsch of Grodno, persuaded Levin that the time was ripe to produce a full-length study on Elijah. This task, which would involve the gathering of myriad sources, texts, and testimonies, could not be achieved by Levin alone. Nachman thus enlisted the help of, among others, Rabbi David Luria, who only a couple of years earlier had signed the letter that removed Levin from his post in Volozhin (see M. Rabinowitz, "Teudot le-Toldot ha-Yeshiva bi-Volozhin," cited in Stampfer, *Ha-Yeshiva ha-Litait be-Hithavutah*, 79). By the time Luria was informed of the work, Levin had already produced a manuscript and sent it to Nachman to print. Nachman, however, was not yet ready to publish the work. Perhaps it was the controversy surrounding Levin in Volozhin or maybe he wanted more experts involved in this delicate project. Whatever the reason, he decided to send the manuscript to Luria. Letters published at the beginning of *Aliyot Eliyahu* attest that Luria very graciously agreed to offer his assistance. Luria congratulated Levin on the manuscript, offered his support, and detailed which aspects of Elijah's life and learning that he might be able to shed more light on. What most impressed Luria about Levin's undertaking was his urgent need to tell the story about the way that Elijah lived and behaved. "Such a work," Luria remarked, need not "praise (*le-Shvach*) Elijah's memory, but rather should be aimed at awakening the hearts of its readers and bring them to follow the path paved by Gra" (see Levin, *Aliyot Eliyahu*, 8). Luria agreed with Levin that they should not try to "honor the Gaon through praise or glorify him through stories." Levin's endeavor to keep Elijah "next to us" was a response to what he felt was the waning influence exerted by Elijah on eastern European Jewry. Levin believed that "Gra's students had gone out to the streets to spread the teaching of their master and his ways of holiness. Throughout all of Israel these students have become a light in the places they reside." As the days progress, however, Levin feared "that this light might be diminished." It is also important to make mention of the other co-contributor to *Aliyot Eliyahu*, Ya'akov Tzvi Mecklenburg, who played a critical role in the publication and promotion of Elijah's work in western Europe. Mecklenburg promoted Elijah's worldview in western European learning circles to combat certain Maskilic tendencies. He himself published numerous editions of Elijah's notes on various texts. From 1840–1864 more than twenty volumes of Elijah's notes were printed in Königsberg, where Mecklenburg served as chief rabbi. Unlike Luria and Levin who only slightly embellish or add stories (usually only from eyewitnesses), most of Mecklenburg's entries in *Aliyot Eliyahu* seem almost entirely fictional and deal almost exclusively with Elijah's relationship to the Haskalah. On Mecklenburg see Edward Breuer,

"Between Haskalah and Orthodoxy: The Writings of R. Jacob Zvi Meklenburg," *HUCA Annual* 66 (1995): 259–287.

7. See Avraham Mapu's letter to his brother on May 9, 1957, published in *Mikhtivei Avraham Mapu*, ed. Ben-Zion Dinur (Jerusalem: Mossad Bialik, 1970), 21. The fact that Mapu's *Ayit Tzavua* was directed at the very hypocrisy, lies, and obscurantisms he believed to be reflected in *Aliyot Eliyahu's* exaggerations only added insult to injury. Mapu's comments highlight the extent of Elijah's popularity with the public, as well as nineteenth-century Jews' attachment to a rabbinic worldview.

8. *Sefer Ma'aseh Rav* was compiled by the Vilna rabbi Yissaschar ben Tanchum (1769–1846) from the notes of Rabbi Sa'adya ben Natan Nata of Vilna and Menachem Mendel of Shklov. Yissaschar's son, Mordechai, received their notes from the land of Israel. The text was published by Mordechai in Vilna in 1832. In 1833, Yissaschar's other son, Rabbi Eliyahu Peretz, published a second edition in Lwów with corrections to the original manuscript. Correcting and adding to *Sefer Ma'aseh Rav* seems to have been an intellectual pastime of nine-teenth-century rabbinic luminaries. Like *Aliyot Eliyahu*, *Sefer Ma'aseh Rav* details Elijah's behaviors and idiosyncrasies, telling us everything from when the Gra permitted one to pick one's nose (even when reciting the holiest prayers, Shema and the Amidah, 44) to the amount of time one should allot for earning a livelihood (only two hours a day, 72). The book's late publication date resulted from the author's discomfort with his own work. When he asked Rabbi Hayyim of Volozhin if it should be sent to press, Rabbi Hayyim demurred, dismissing the project as something to be undertaken by lesser minds. Even more damning, Rabbi Hayyim cautioned that he could not verify its testimonies. Rabbi Hayyim noted correctly that *Sefer Ma'aseh Rav* was of a different genre from the earlier sketches produced by Elijah's students. It was more popular and thus "of lesser value." See the letter written by Rabbi Hayyim to Rabbi Yissaschar published posthumously in the first edition of *Sefer Ma'aseh Rav* (Vilna: 1832). Before *Sefer Ma'aseh Rav*, Elijah was known to European Jews primarily by his dense and voluminous commentaries. *Sefer Ma'aseh Rav* and *Aliyot Eliyahu* were written in Hebrew with numerous references to details of Jewish law. On the complicated history behind the publication of and constant revisions to *Sefer Ma'aseh Rav*, see the "introduction" to *Sefer Ma'aseh Rav* (Jerusalem: 2008), 7–22. On *Sefer Ma'aseh Rav* and Sa'adya ben Natan Nata, see David Kamenetsky, "Sefer 'Ma'aseh Rav,'" *Yeshurun* 21 (2009): 774–827. It should be noted that *Sefer Ma'aseh Rav* had a very different objective than did *Aliyot Eliyahu*. *Sefer Ma'aseh Rav* focused primarily "on those traits that were applicable to Elijah's observance of law," according to Yissaschar ben Tanchum's anonymous introduc-tion to the first edition of *Sefer Ma'aseh Rav*.

9. The first printing of the Gaon's Haggadah was in 1805, in Grodno. For a complete publication history, see Winograd, *Otzar Sifrei ha-Gra* (Jerusalem: 2003), 97–116.

10. *Alim li-Terufah* was printed just four times from 1800 to 1849 and only in Hebrew. In 1850 it was translated into Yiddish and from that point on it was republished more than twenty-five times, until 1900. The Yiddish translation is further evidence of the interest and popularization of the Gaon's image in the second half of the nineteenth century.

11. Ibid., 56.

12. See the letter sent by Rabbi Tzvi Hirsch Lehren to Solomon Shapira in *Iggerot ha-Pekidim ve-ha-Amarkalim*, ed. Yosef Yoel and Benjamin Rivlin, vols. 1–3 (Jerusalem: 1965), 1:263, 2:182. On Lehren see Richard Cohen, "Representations of the Jewish Body in Modern Times: Forms of Hero Worship," in *Representation in Religion: Studies in Honor of Moshe Barasch*, ed. Moshe Barasch, Jan Assmann, and Albert Baumgarten (Leiden: Brill, 2001), 263.

13. See Zusia Efron, "Portrait of the Gaon of Vilna: Two Centuries of Imagination," in *The Gaon of Vilnius and the Annals of Jewish Culture*, ed. Izraelis Lempertas (Vilnius: Vilnius University Publishing House, 1998), 164–166.

14. See Rachel Schnold, "Elijah's Face: The Portrait of the Vilna Gaon in Folk Art," in Schnold, *Aderet Eliyahu: Ha-Gaon mi-Vilna, Demuto ve-Hashpa'ato* (Tel Aviv: Beit ha-Tefutsot al shem Nahum Goldmann, 1998), 55. On the Gaon's wardrobe, Hayyim of Volozhin claims, "He was known not to walk further than four handbreadths without wearing phylacteries and a prayer shawl all day." See Hayyim of Volozhin, introduction to *Sifra di-Tzniuta* (Vilna: 1820) and *Sefer Ma'aseh Rav* (Jerusalem: 2008), subject heading 60, 63. Elijah may have also been inspired by early medieval German Pietists who, according to Ivan Marcus in his *Piety and Society: The Jewish Pietists of Medieval Germany* (Leiden: E.J. Brill, 1981), "attached ritual fringes . . . to the four corners of an outer garment, thereby making it into a prayer shawl . . . which they wore, not only during the morning prayers but 'all day' " (98).

15. Montefiore had deep ties to the Gaon's students and biographers. A copy of *Aliyot Eliyahu* appears with Levin's personal stamp on its title page in Montefiore's library. The book can be found in Montefiore's library housed at Yarnton Manor, Oxford Center for Hebrew and Jewish Studies, under the call number 60e17. It is also interesting that Levin's personal stamp can be found in the book, suggesting that he may have personally given the book to Montefiore. In 1846 Montefiore prayed and cried before the Gaon's grave during his visit to Vilna. On Montefiore's visit to Elijah's grave, see Abigail Green, *Moses Montefiore: Jewish Liberator, Imperial Hero* (Cambridge, Mass.: Harvard University Press, 2010), chapter 9.

16. See Efron, "Portrait of the Gaon of Vilna," 166.

17. See Laura Engelstein, *Slavophile Empire: Imperial Russia's Illiberal Path* (Ithaca, N.Y.: Cornell University Press, 2009), 102.

18. Shaul Stampfer claims that the spurts in the publication of the Gaon's commentaries came in the wake of the publication of biographies about the Gaon. The first such increase in the publication of Elijah's commentaries, according to Stampfer, was the result of the publication of *Ma'aseh Rav* (1832), and the second spurt was the result of *Aliyot Eliyahu* (1857). Stampfer is correct that between the years of 1832 and 1840 there were 28 books published with Elijah's notes in them (compared to 14 such books published from 1824 to 1832), whereas from 1841 to 1849 there were only 11 books published (not even half the number published from 1832 to 1840). Biographies alone, however, should be used cautiously to gauge Elijah's intellectual influence. If one looks at the broad publication history of the Gaon's writings laid out by Yehoshua Winograd in the introduction to his *Otzar Sifrei ha-Gra* (Jerusalem: 2003), 33–34, there is a steady increase in the publication of Elijah's works throughout the nineteenth century, suggesting that advancements in printing probably are a more significant cause. Stampfer is correct that the biographies greatly contributed to Elijah's *social* popularization. But Elijah's social popularity should be distinguished from his intellectual influence. Those who read Elijah's commentary to *Zohar* were probably not the same people who read *Aliyot Eliyahu*. Likewise, those capable of reading *Aliyot Eliyahu* may not have included those who hung pictures of Elijah in their homes.

19. See Walter Benjamin, "The Work of Art in the Age of Mechanical Reproduction," in *Illuminations*, trans. Harry Zohn, ed. Hannah Arendt (New York: Schocken Books, 1968), 223. For an example of the way Elijah's "*geonut*" hovered over nineteenth-century eastern European Jewish homes, see the recollections of Louis Ginzberg (1873–1953) in Eli Ginzberg, *Louis Ginzberg: Keeper of the Law* (Philadelphia: Jewish Publication Society, 1996), 18.

20. See the observation made by Mendel Silber, *The Gaon of Wilna: A Review of His Life and Influence* (New York: Maccabaean Publishing Company, 1905), 21. Rachel Schnold notes that "up to WWII more than thirty versions of the Vilna Gaon's portrait were in circulation." While she modifies M. Gertz's exaggerated claim that the portrait of the Gaon was "used to adorn nearly every house" in eastern Europe, she nonetheless argues that such a situation "is undoubtedly true of Vilna." See Rachel Schnold, "Elijah's Face: The Portrait of the Vilna Gaon in Folk Art," in Schnold, ed., *Gaon of Vilna: The Man and His Legacy* (Tel Aviv: Beit Hatfutsot, 1998), 51–53.

21. On the use and definition of the honorific "Gaon" in the Middle Ages, see the entry on "Gaon" written by Yehoshua Brand, Simha Assaf, and David

Derovan in *Encyclopedia Judaica*, ed. Michael Berenbaum and Fred Skolnik (Detroit: Macmillan Reference, 2007), 7:380–386. See also Tsvi Groner, "A List of Rav Hai Gaon's Responsa," *Alei Sefer* 13 (1986): 79–80.

22. See Alexander Kohut's comments to the word "gaon" in Nathan ben Yehiel, *Arukh ha-Shalem*, ed. Alexander Kohut (Vienna: 1878), 1:218.

23. Marina Rustow, *Heresy and the Politics of Community: The Jews of the Fatmid Caliphate* (Ithaca, N.Y.: Cornell University Press, 2008), 84.

24. Ibid., 87.

25. See Israel Klausner, *Vilna be-Tekufat ha-Gaon* (Jerusalem: Reuben Mas, 1942), 18 fn.1.

26. For an excellent overview of the way the term was invoked in the medieval period, see Max Weinreich, *History of the Yiddish Language*, ed. Paul Glasser, trans. Shlomo Nobel (New Haven: Yale University Press, 2008), 1:A344–A345.

27. The Jewish medieval usage of the term gaon follows the *doctrine classique* of genius, whereby the public determines and appreciates what it considers intellectual excellence. See Peter Bürger, *The Decline of Modernism*, trans. Nicholas Walker (State College, Pa.: Penn State University Press, 1992), 60–63. On the relationship between rules and genius, see Martin Jay, *Songs of Experience: Modern American and European Variations on a Universal Theme* (Berkeley: University of California Press, 2005), 149–155.

28. See "Seder ha-kabbalah," in *Beit ha-Bechirah al Mesekhet Avot* (Jerusalem: 1964), 53.

29. See David ben Zimra, *Shut ha-Radvaz* (Jerusalem: 1882) vol. 4, responsa 79.

30. See Eliyahu Bachur, *Sefer ha-Tishbi* (Bnei Brak: 1976), 9. According to his son, Avraham, Bachur himself claimed that the number sixty referred to kingship as well as the sixty tractates of the Talmud. See Avraham's introduction to his commentary to *Midrash Aggadat Bereishit* (Vilna: 1802). Eliezer Brodt in an unpublished paper also makes the connection between the Gaon and Bachur with regard to sixty tractates and the term Gaon. See also the comments made by Nachman ben Tzvi (the publisher) in Yehoshua Heschel Levin, *Aliyot Eliyahu* (Vilna: 1856), fn.111. There, Nachman ben Tzvi cites Bachur's work and makes note of the shift that has taken place in the definition of the term "gaon."

31. See *Koreh ha-Dorot* (Berlin: 1842), 5b.

32. See Joseph David Azulay, *Sefer Shem ha-Gedolim ha-Shalem* (Jerusalem: 1992), Kuntres Achron (final appendix), 49. On the publication and formation of *Shem ha-Gedolim* see Yohanan Lederman, "Sur l'influence du Shem ha-Guedolim du rabbin Haim Joseph David Azoulai ('Hida) dans la bio-bibliographie hébraïque, de la fin du XIII siècle au XX siècle," *Bulletin du CRFJ* 2 (1998): 29–30.

33. See the comments made by Yehudah Leib ben Shneur Zalman of Shklov in his introduction to Elijah's work *Shenot Eliyahu* (Lvov: 1799). See also the story recorded by C. Lunski in *Legendes: Eynike vegn Vilner Goen* (Vilna: 1924), 12, about Aryeh Leib ben Asher Gunzberg's visit to Vilna. According to Lunski, Gunzberg crowned Elijah with the title "Gaon" and lowered the chief rabbi to the title of "Gadol."

34. Shuchat, *Olam Nistar be-Memadei ha-Zeman*, 1 notes that throughout Abraham's work *Ma'alot ha-Torah* (1828) he refers to his brother as "Gaon" (12, 37).

35. "Gaon olam" can be translated as either "the genius of the world" or "the eternal genius." On Elijah's claiming that *malkhut* stands for sixty tractates, see his comments on *Tikkunei ha-Zohar im Tikkunim mi-Zohar Chadash im Biur ha-Gra* (Vilna: Rosenkranz, 1867), 44b.

36. Menachem Mendel of Shklov, introduction to Elijah's commentary to *Pirkei Avot* (Shklov: 1804).

37. See the second eulogy of Avraham Danzig for the Gaon first published in 1871 in Vilna and republished in *Mussar Adam* (Jerusalem: Hadrat Yerushalayim, 1992), 108–109 and republished with annotations in *Tehilot Eliyahu* (New York: Machon ha-Gra, 1999), 14–15.

38. For a general overview of the term "genius," see the entries of Edward Lowinsky, Giorgio Tonelli, and Rudolph Wittkower in *Dictionary of the History of Ideas: Studies of Selected Pivotal Ideas*, ed. Philip P. Weiner (New York: Charles Scribner & Sons, 1973), 2:293–296. On the social construction of "genius" see Tia DeNora, *Beethoven and the Construction of Genius* (Berkeley: University of California Press, 1997), 189–191.

39. See the first eulogy of Avraham Danzig for the Gaon published in *Mussar Adam* (Jerusalem: Hadrat Yerushalayim, 1992), 99.

40. Ibid., 109.

41. See Ya'akov Kana'ani, *Otzar ha-Lashon ha-Ivri*, ed. Abraham Shlunsky and David Levin (Tel-Aviv: 1961), 2:294.

42. Peter Brown, *Augustine of Hippo: A Biography* (Berkeley: University of California, 2000), 254; and Brown, "The Rise and Function of the Holy Man in Late Antiquity," *Journal of Roman Studies* 61 (1971): 80–101.

43. Pierre Hadot, in his *What Is Ancient Philosophy?* trans. Michael Chase (Cambridge, Mass.: Harvard University Press, 2002), 69, describes the "philosopher"; and Ivan Marcus, in his *Piety and Society: The Jewish Pietists of Medieval Germany* (Leiden: E. J. Brill, 1981), 71–73, describes the "sage."

44. Peter Burke, *The Fabrication of Louis XIV* (New Haven: Yale University Press, 1992), 11–12.

45. See Zalman Epstein's memoir "Yeshivat Volozhin," 77.

46. See Levin, *Aliyot Eliyahu*, 85.

47. See Shlomo ben Yisrael Moshe's introduction to *Ma'aseh Rav*.

48. On Hasidei Ashkenaz see Marcus, *Piety and Society*, 21–37, 55–75, and specifically, Ivan Marcus, "The Politics and Ethics of Pietism in Judaism: The Hasidim of Medieval Germany," *Journal of Religious Ethics* 8 (1980): 227–258; Eliot Wolfson, "The Mystical Significance of Torah Study in German Pietism," *Jewish Quarterly Review* 84, no. 1 (July 1993): 43–78; Haym Soloveitchik, "Piety, Pietism and German Pietism: 'Sefer Hasidim I' and the Influence of Hasidei Ashkenaz," *Jewish Quarterly Review* 92, nos. 3–4 (January–April 2002): 455–493; and Talia Fishman, "The Penitential System of Hasidei Ashkenaz and the Problem of Cultural Boundaries," *Journal of Jewish Thought and Philosophy* 9 (1999): 1–29. On the reception of pietistic practices in the early modern period, see Edward Fram, "German Pietism and Sixteenth- and Early Seventeenth-Century Polish Rabbinic Culture," *Jewish Quarterly Review* 96, no. 1 (Winter 2006): 50–59.

49. See Isadore Twersky, *Introduction to the Code of Maimonides (Mishneh Torah)* (New Haven: Yale University Press, 1980), 453–457; Raymond Weiss, *Maimonides' Ethics: The Encounter of Philosophic and Religious Morality* (Chicago: University of Chicago Press, 1991), 1–9; and David Shatz, "Maimonides' Moral Theory," in *Cambridge Companion to Maimonides*, ed. Kenneth Seeskin (Cambridge: Cambridge University Press, 2005), 170–171.

50. On the reception of Maimonides in the early modern period, see Allan Nadler, "The 'Rambam Revival' in Early Modern Jewish Thought: Maskilim, Mitnagdim, and Hasidism on Maimonides' *Guide for the Perplexed*," in *Moses Maimonides: Communal Impact, Historic Legacy*, ed. Benny Kraut (New York: Queens College Press, 2005), 36–61.

51. See his commentary to Proverbs 26:7 in *Mishlei im Biur ha-Gra*, ed. Moshe Philip (Petach Tikvah: 1991).

52. See Saba Mahmood's discussion of positive ethics and the post-Kantian conception of virtue ethics in *Politics of Piety: The Islamic Revival and the Feminist Subject* (Princeton, N.J.: Princeton University Press, 2005), 27, 120; and Alasdair MacIntyre, *After Virtue* (Notre Dame, Ind.: University of Notre Dame Press, 1984), 146–164. On those who have written on the role of positive ethics in modern rabbinic thought, see most recently Yehudah Mirsky, "An Intellectual and Spiritual Biography of Rabbi Avraham Yitzhaq Ha-Cohen Kook from 1865 to 1904," Ph.D. diss., Harvard University, 2007, 30–32.

53. See Levin, *Aliyot Eliyahu*, 85.

54. The Gaon, however, is rarely described as possessing a photographic memory like Rabbi Aryeh Leib Gunzburg (1695–1785), who was known "to be able to organize and see a picture of the Talmud in his head." See Micah Yosef Berdichevsky, "Olam ha-Atzilut," reprinted in *Yeshivot Lita*, 133.

55. Moshe Idel, *Hasidism: Between Ecstasy and Magic* (Albany: State University of New York Press, 1995), 172.

56. Avraham ben ha-Gra, *Sa'eret Eliyahu* (Warsaw: 1877), 6b.

57. See Ya'akov Moshe of Słonim's introduction to *Sifra di-Tzniuta* (Vilna: 1820).

58. Levin, *Aliyot Eliyahu*, 57.

59. See Elijah's commentary to Proverbs, 2:3 in *Mishlei im Biur ha-Gra*.

60. See Roland Barthes's reflections on Einstein's genius in Barthes, "The Brain of Einstein," in *Mythologies*, trans. Annette Lavers (New York: Macmillan, 1972), 68–69.

61. The authors of *Aliyot Eliyahu* repeatedly stress that Elijah was not a recipient of divine inspiration. As seen from the letters written between Luria and Levin, *Aliyot Eliyahu*'s purpose was to promote the idea that Elijah's genius was self-generated (8, 22, 24, 25). *Aliyot Eliyahu* is not, as some have argued, a polemic against the Haskalah, nor an attempt to make Elijah into a Hasidic rebbe. To be sure, the first pages of the work (1–2) are directed toward the government and try to depict Elijah in enlightened terms. Likewise, *Aliyot Eliyahu* contains a few stories about Elijah that border on Hasidic tales. In general, however, *Aliyot Eliyahu* tries to demonstrate Elijah's genius and the way it should be distinguished from the traits associated with the Hasidic rebbe. The refrain appearing throughout *Aliyot Eliyahu* is that Gaon "did everything on his own" without any help from heaven or outside guidance (51). For nineteenth-century rabbinic Jews such as David Luria, Yisrael of Shklov, and Yehoshua Heschel Levin, Elijah's life of "actions" stood in marked contrast to that of the Hasidic rebbe celebrated and memorialized in "books of praise" such as *Shivchei ha-Besht* (Kapost: 1814). *Shivchei ha-Besht* contains 250 stories about the prophecy, miracles, and divine encounters of Israel Baal Shem Tov and his circle. The book was not the first of its kind; in many ways it copied earlier models such as Shlomo ben Hayyim's *Shivchei ha-Ari* (Basle: 1629), which describes the miracles and wonders surrounding the life of Rabbi Isaac Luria. *Shivchei ha-Ari* and *Shivchei ha-Besht* highlight the mystical and spiritual greatness of their protagonists. These books disempower their readers by showing the distance between the simple lives they lead versus the awesome and supernatural one lived by the book's hero. The stories in these *Shivchei* (praise) books convey that only one individual in a generation, if even that many, can be given access to the Divine. According to David Luria, *Aliyot Eliyahu* (8), "Books of Praise" deify and mystify their protagonist, encouraging readers to see their own leaders through such a lens. In other words, these works created "Hasidim," those who acquired their spiritual sustenance through the wondrous works and divine encounters of their rebbe. In contrast, *Aliyot Eliyahu* details its protagonist's "will," "actions,"

and "achievements"—the steps needed to become, or at least emulate, Elijah's genius. The distance between the reader and the protagonist is not the vast field that separates the divine and human realms, but rather the surmountable hurdles that stand between being merely human and being learned.

62. On the shift in eighteenth-century discourse from *"having"* to *"being"* a "genius," see Kineret S. Jaffe, "The Concept of Genius: Its Changing Role in Eighteenth-Century French Aesthetics," *Journal of the History of Ideas* 41, no. 4 (1980): 581.

63. Jonathan Bate, *The Genius of Shakespeare* (New York: Oxford University Press, 1998), 160–165. On the differences between "genius" as an outcome of an individual's melancholic horoscope versus a supernatural momentary experience, see Noel L. Bran, *The Debate over Genius in the Italian Renaissance* (Leiden: Brill, 2002), 2–5.

64. On the rise of *maggidim* in the eighteenth century, see Raphael Patai, *The Hebrew Goddess: Jewish Folklore and Anthropology* (Detroit: Wayne State University Press, 1990), 202–221.

65. See Haim-Hillel Ben-Sasson, "Ishiyuto shel ha-Gra ve-Hashpa'ato ha-Historit," *Zion* 31, nos. 1–2 (1966): 44–53; and Immanuel Etkes, *The Gaon of Vilna: The Man and His Image*, trans. Jeffrey Green (Berkeley: University of California Press, 2002), 26–29.

66. See Elijah's commentary to Proverbs 19:32 in *Mishlei im Biur ha-Gra*.

67. See Levin, *Aliyot Eliyahu*, 60.

68. See *Ma'aseh Rav*, subject heading 112.

69. See Levin, *Aliyot Eliyahu*, 48.

70. Elijah's comments can be found in his commentary to Mishnah Shabbat in *Shenot Eliyahu*, 8:1. I wish to thank Prof. Bernard Septimus for bringing this source to my attention. Elijah's comments also appear in the work of Benjamin Rivlin, *Geviei Gavia ha-Kessef* (Warsaw: 1897), 9–10. There Rivlin offers a lengthy discussion on "what he heard on this topic from Gra." Rivlin further develops Elijah's metaphors, arguing that hunger and financial handicaps are prerequisites for a greater appreciation of Torah knowledge and communal leadership.

71. Elijah's writings consistently emphasize that desire and lust are the embodiment of evil. See, for example, Elijah ben Solomon, *Peirush al Kamah Aggadot* (Königsberg: 1862), 11a.

72. On the importance of accounting for one's basic material needs, see ibid., 9b, specifically see his comments on the word "shem."

73. Ralph Waldo Emerson, "Self-Reliance," in Emerson, *Essays: First Series* (Boston: James Munroe and Company, 1841).

74. See the introduction of Yisrael of Shklov to *Pe'at ha-Shulchan* (Safed: 1836). To be sure, this trope of self-sufficiency can also be found among "Holy

Men" of Late Antiquity. On this point see Brown, "The Rise and Function of the Holy Man in Late Antiquity," 91–92.

75. See Levin, *Aliyot Eliyahu*, 29 fn.30.

76. See ibid., 49. Depicting Elijah as stoic and unaffected was a conscious decision on the part of the authors and editors of *Aliyot Eliyahu*. Avraham Simcha Mścisław notes that there were those who considered removing (for reasons unknown to him) one of the stories told about Elijah that depict him as being affected by the death of his mother (9).

77. Heinrich Graetz, *The History of the Jews*, ed. and trans. Bella Löwy (London: David Nutt, Strand, 1892), 5:412–419.

78. See Fuenn, Strashun, and Steinschneider, *Kiryah Ne'emanah*, 146.

79. The emphasis placed on the Gaon's intellectual sovereignty expresses what Harold terms an "anxiety of influence." See Harold Bloom, *The Anxiety of Influence: A Theory of Poetry*, 2d ed. (New York: Oxford University Press, 1997), xix. On "fierce originality" as a definition of genius see Bloom, *Genius: A Mosaic of One Hundred Exemplary Creative Minds* (New York: Warner Books, 2002), 11.

80. See Elijah's commentary to Proverbs 11:18 in *Mishlei im Biur ha-Gra*. Collaborative learning played a critical role in nineteenth-century yeshiva culture. Nonetheless, for all the lively debate and discussion bouncing off the walls inside these Jewish centers of learning, these walls were soundproof, blocking out those with radically different and conflicting opinions. In the early modern period, eastern European rabbinic Jews had been forced to work within the confines of a Jewish corporate structure, their internal differences notwithstanding. Defined by outside governments led by non-Jewish noblemen and princes, Jews had to manage various groups and ideologies. While pre-modern eastern European Jewish life was far from "tolerant," it forced extreme elements of the community to engage and work with one another. The yeshiva, with its strong, defined walls, mirrored Elijah's practice of ignoring and refusing to recognize those who challenged or undermined his ideological predispositions. Though a plethora of different ideological voices could be heard within the yeshiva, the new learning institution severely curtailed the range of acceptable positions and practices tolerated by the lay-led early modern corporate structure.

81. See the comments of Rabbi Zundel of Salant recorded in the most recent edition of *Sefer Ma'aseh Rav*, which was published in 2009 in Jerusalem with additional notes (153).

82. Yisrael of Shklov, *Pe'at ha-Shulchan*.

83. See Levin, *Aliyot Eliyahu*, 80, and Yisrael of Shklov's reflections on Elijah's reading with candles in *Pe'at ha-Shulchan*.

84. Levin, *Aliyot Eliyahu*, 19, 35.

85. Winograd, *Otzar Sifrei ha-Gra*, 308.

86. Menachem Mendel of Shklov invokes this phrase in his introduction to Elijah's commentary to *Pirkei Avot* and by Hayyim of Volozhin in his introduction to *Sifra di-Tzniuta*. It should be noted that seeing only as much as candlelight permits is also a metaphor for ignoring that which exists over an ever expanding horizon of greed, desire, and lust. In his commentary to Proverbs 28:24 (see *Mishlei im Biur ha-Gra*), the Gaon scolds those "who constantly move around from State to State in search of money-making opportunities." Satisfaction always stands beyond the grasp of those looking beyond four hand-breadths. Pursuing money generates worry and insecurity. Individuals, in the Gaon's spatial metaphor, have "expansive desires" and "are never fulfilled by what they possess." Needy individuals are unfulfilled; for there is a "world which is not theirs [that they believe] awaits conquering." Limiting one's horizons and practicing a frugal ethic toward material goods generate appreciation of what stands before one's eyes.

87. See Levin, *Aliyot Eliyahu*, 49–50 fn.24; this was also recorded in Shmuel Maltzan, *Even Shlomo* (Vilna: 1863), 13b–14a.

88. Yissaschar interpreted the Gaon's words as follows: "One ought not rely upon others / Don't wait for tomorrow / and throw yourself into your studies with fervor." Yissaschar's words are taken from a manuscript and are recorded by Eliakh, *Sefer ha-Gaon*, 116.

89. Avraham ben ha-Gra's eulogy for his father, *Sa'eret Eliyahu*, 6a.

90. Ibid.

91. Elijah ben Solomon, commentary to Proverbs 6:26 in *Mishlei im Biur ha-Gra*.

92. See Elijah's comments on "Zivchei Shlamim" and "Shabbat" in his commentary to Proverbs 7:14 in *Mishlei im Biur ha-Gra*.

93. See Benjamin Rivlin, *Geviei Gavia ha-Kessef* (Warsaw: 1897), 58.

94. See Elijah's children's introduction to *Biur ha-Gra al Shulchan Arukh, Orach Chayyim;* and Levin, *Aliyot Eliyahu*, 65. For an interesting example of a contemporary of the Gaon who also sought to control his eating practices, see Arthur Green's description of Nachman of Bratslav's eating practices in *Tormented Master: A Life of Rabbi Nahman of Bratslav* (Tuscaloosa: University of Alabama Press, 1979), 38–39.

95. Chaim Grade, "My Quarrel with Hersh Rasseyner," trans. Milton Himmelfarb, in *A Treasury of Yiddish Stories*, ed. Irving Howe and Eliezer Greenberg (New York: Viking, 1954), 565. Reb Hersh's words are taken word for word from the Gaon's letter to his wife.

96. See Rabbi Hayyim's introduction to *Shenot Eliyahu*.

97. On Alexander the Sleepless see most recently Daniel Caner, *Wandering, Begging Monks: Spiritual Authority and the Promotion of Monasticism in Late Antiquity* (Berkeley: University of California Press, 2002), 126–150.

98. See Elijah's farewell letter to his wife, *Alim li-Terufah*.

99. See the comments made by the late nineteenth-century Vilna rabbi Shlomo ben Yisrael Moshe in *Sefer Ma'aseh Rav* (Vilna: 1888), 10–11.

100. The portrait of Elijah with a clock hanging over his left shoulder appears in numerous nineteenth-century pictures of Elijah. See for example, the pictures compiled in Winograd, *Otzar Sifrei ha-Gra*, 308.

101. See Elijah's sons' introduction to *Biur ha-Gra al Shulchan Arukh Orach Chayyim* (Shklov: 1803). See also Levin, *Aliyot Eliyahu*, 65, 82 fn.97.

102. See Yisrael of Shklov's introduction to *Pe'at ha-Shulchan*.

103. See the comments made by Rabbi Judah he-Hasid and cited by Marcus, *Piety and Society*, 84, 94. On Judah he-Hasid, see also Ephraim Kanarfogel, "Rabbi Judah he-Hasid and the Rabbinic Scholars of Regensburg: Interactions, Influences, and Implications," *Jewish Quarterly Review* 96, no. 1 (2005): 17–37.

104. See Elijah's children's introduction to *Biur ha-Gra al Shulchan Arukh, Orach Chayyim*.

105. Ibid.

106. Ibid.

107. Ibid.

108. On the history and authenticity of Ya'akov Moshe's testimony, see Shuchat, *Olam Nistar be-Memadei ha-Zeman*, 41.

109. See Levin, *Aliyot Eliyahu*, 67–68 fn.51.

110. See *Peirush al Kamah Aggadot*, 5–6.

111. See Elijah's commentary to Proverbs 11:30 in *Mishlei im Biur ha-Gra*. Elijah's privileging of students over children is part of a much larger revaluation of the relationship between the world of knowledge and family life. On the familial and education repercussions of privileging students, teachers, and knowledge (which Elijah classifies under the rubric of the "covenant of the mouth") over children, parents, and family (which Elijah classifies under the rubric of the "covenant of circumcision"), see Elijah's comments to *Tikkunei ha-Zohar*, 47a.

112. Levin, *Aliyot Eliyahu*, 65.

113. Ibid., 67.

114. Solomon Schechter, *Studies in Judaism*, vol. 1, facsimile reproduction of the original ed., Philadelphia, 1896–1924 (Piscataway, N.J.: Gorgias Press, 2003), 92.

115. See William Jackson, "Whether Genius Be Born or Acquired," in Jackson, *The Four Ages* (London: 1798), 186–187.

116. On the popularity of the Gaon's picture and the role it played in nineteenth-century European Jewry, see Cohen, "Representations of the Jewish Body in Modern Times," 235–276, esp. 266. For an analysis of the way Elijah was popularized and depicted in the twentieth century, see most recently David E. Fishman's chapter "Commemoration and Cultural Conflict: The Vilna Gaon's Bicentenary," in his work *The Rise of Modern Yiddish Culture* (Pittsburgh: University of Pittsburg Press, 2005), 114–126.

117. Jonathan Bate, *The Genius of Shakespeare* (New York: Oxford University Press, 1998), 166.

118. On the emergence of the *pushke* (charity box) in nineteenth-century eastern European Jewish households, see Shaul Stampfer, *Families, Rabbis, and Education: Traditional Jewish Society in Nineteenth-Century Eastern Europe* (Oxford: Littman Library, 2010), 102–120.

119. See the list in Mark Zborowski and Elizabeth Herzog, *Life Is with People: The Jewish Little Town of Eastern Europe* (New York: International Press, 1952), 80.

120. The translation is taken from Stanley Nash, "Kotso Shel Yud," *CCAR Journal* (Summer 2006): 177. Gordon in his youth was taught by a disciple of Hayyim of Volozhin. On Gordon's relationship to the intellectual heritage of the Gaon, see Michael Stanislawski, *For Whom Do I Toil? Judah Leib Gordon and the Crisis of Russian Jewry* (New York: Oxford University Press, 1988), 9–11. On the popularization of honorifics in the nineteenth century, see Fuenn, Strashun, and Steinschneider, *Kiryah Ne'emanah*, 99, esp. para. 33.

121. See Fritz Ringer, *The Decline of the German Mandarins* (1969; Hanover, N.H.: Wesleyan University Press by University Press of New England, 1990), 87. On the idea of *Bildung* see Norbert Elias, *The Civilizing Process*, trans. Edmund Jephcott (Malden, Mass.: Blackwell, 2000), 24; and David Sorkin, "The Genesis and Ideology of Emancipation, 1806–1840," *Leo Baeck Institute Yearbook* 32, no. 1 (1987): 19.

122. On idea of the *mensch* and the trait of *edelkayt* in nineteenth-century European Jewish culture, see Daniel Boyarin, *Unheroic Conduct: The Rise of Heterosexuality and the Invention of the Jewish Male* (Berkeley: University of California Press, 1997), 51–73.

123. See Elijah's comments to *Pirkei Avot*, 6:8.

124. On those who objected to the community supporting Gra, see Israel Klausner, *Vilna be-Tekufat ha-Gaon* (Jerusalem: Reuben Mas, 1942), 153, 155.

125. Levin, *Aliyot Eliyahu*, 70.

126. See ibid., 26–27; see also Elijah's sons' introduction to *Biur ha-Gra al Shulchan Arukh Orach Chayyim*.

127. Levin, *Aliyot Eliyahu*, 27.

128. On Nathan Adler see Rachel Elior, "Rabbi Natan Adler of Frankfort and the Controversy Surrounding Him," in *Mysticism, Magic Kabbalah in Ashkenazi Judaism*, ed. Karl-Erich Grözinger and Joseph Dan (Berlin: Walter de Gruyter, 1995), 223–243; and Jacob Katz, "Towards a Biography of the Hatam Sofer," in Katz, *Divine Law in Human Hands: Case Studies in Halakhic Flexibility* (Jerusalem: Magnes Press, 1998), 403–443.

129. See the impressions of the Rabbi Yisrael Gordon, who witnessed the spectacle, recorded in Levin, *Aliyot Eliyahu*, 12–13. On Gordon and his relationship to the Vilna Haskalah, see the impressions of Max Lilienthal in David Philipson, *Max Lilienthal, American Rabbi: Life and Writings* (New York: Bloch, 1915), 268–269. These testimonies refer to events that transpired in the last quarter of Elijah's life. From 1758 on, Elijah lived next door to the main synagogue. On the eastern wall of the Gra's *kloiz* there was a plaque stating that the study house of the Gra was founded during his lifetime, in the year 1758, and was renovated in 1768. In 1768 Eliyahu Pesseles renovated and expanded his dwellings to include a study and a prayer room. On Elijah's living quarters and study, see Israel Klausner, *Toldot ha-Kehilah ha-Ivrit be-Vilna* (Vilna: 1938), 78–80. It is unclear when Elijah would have had reason to leave his dwellings by carriage to go to a study house. In 1780, Elijah raised the funds needed to purchase the "Slutzki" home, located outside the courtyard of the synagogue. Elijah had hoped to turn the Slutzki home into a study house; it is likely that these testimonies refer to Elijah's passage from his living quarters to the Slutzki house. On the Slutzki house, see Chapter 1.

130. Abraham Cahan, *The Education of Abraham Cahan*, trans. Leon Stein, Abraham Conan, and Lynn Davison (Philadelphia: Jewish Publication Society, 1969), 30.

131. See the statement recorded in Cecile E. Kuznitz, "On the Street: Yiddish Culture and the Urban Landscape in Interwar Vilna," in *Yiddish Language and Culture: Then and Now*, ed. Leonard Jay Greenspoon (Omaha, Neb.: Creighton University Press, 1998), 66.

Conclusion

1. See Gershon Hundert's discussion of the Germano-centric reading of modern Jewish history laid out in his book *Jews in Poland-Lithuania in the Eighteenth Century* (Berkeley: University of California Press, 2004), 233–240, and masterfully condensed in Gershon David Hundert, "Re(de)fining Modernity in Jewish History," in Jeremy Cohen and Moshe Rosman eds., *Rethinking European Jewish History* (Oxford: Littman Library, 2009), 133–145.

2. Ibid., 135.

3. See David Ruderman, "Jewish Cultural History in Early Modern Europe: An Agenda for Future Study," in Cohen and Rosman, *Rethinking European Jewish History*, 99.

4. On the influence of the eastern European Haskalah, see most recently Michael Stanislawski, *For Whom Do I Toil? Judah Leib Gordon and the Crisis of Russian Jewry* (Oxford: Oxford University Press, 1988), 18; Immanuel Etkes's "Parashat ha-Haskalah mi-Ta'am ve-ha-Temurah be-Ma'amad Tnuat ha-Haskalah be-Rusiyah," in Etkes, ed., *Ha-da'at ve-ha-Chayyim: Tnuat ha-Haskalah ha-Yehudit be-Mizrach Eropah* (Jerusalem: 1993), 167–216; Mordekhai Zalkin, "Scientific Literature and Cultural Transformation in Nineteenth-Century East European Jewish Society," *Aleph* 5 (2005): 249–271; Marcin Wodziński, *Haskalah and Hasidism in the Kingdom of Poland* (Oxford: Littman Library, 2005); and Wodziński, "Haskalah and Politics Reconsidered: The Case of the Kingdom of Poland, 1815–1860," in David Assaf and Ada Rapoport-Albert, eds., *Yashan mi-Pnei Chadash: Mechkarim be-Toldot Yehudei Mizrach Eropah u-ve-Tarbutam: Shai le-Immanuel Etkes* (Jerusalem: Merkaz Zalman Shazar, 2009), 2:163–197; Shmuel Feiner, "Ha-Mifneh be-Ha'arakhat ha-Hasidut: Eliezer Zweifel ve-ha-Haskalah ha-Metunah be-Rusiyah," in Etkes, *Ha-Da'at ve-ha-Chayyim*, 336–379; and Steven Zipperstein, *The Jews of Odessa: A Cultural History, 1794–1881* (Palo Alto, Calif.: Stanford University Press, 1985).

5. See the recent studies by Yohanan Petrovsky-Shtern, such as "Hasidism, Havurot, and the Jewish Street," *Jewish Social Studies* 10, no. 2 (Winter 2004): 20–54, and "Hasidism and the Challenge of Geography: The Polish Background to the Spread of the Hasidic Movement," *AJS Review* 30 (2006): 1–29; see also Glenn Dynner, *Men of Silk: The Hasidic Conquest of Polish Jewish Society* (New York: Oxford University Press, 2006).

6. See Yohanan Petrovsky-Shtern, *Jews in the Russian Army, 1827–1917: Drafted into Modernity* (Cambridge: Cambridge University Press, 2009); and Olga Litvak, *Conscription and the Search for Modern Russian Jewry* (Bloomington: Indiana University Press, 2006).

7. See Immanuel Etkes, *Rabbi Israel Salanter and the Mussar Movement*, trans. Jonathan Chipman (Philadelphia: Jewish Publication Society, 1993); and

David Fishman, "Musar and Modernity: The Case of Novaredok," *Modern Judaism* 8, no. 1 (1988): 41–64.

8. Gershon Hundert himself admits as much when he writes: "The responses of many Jews in east-central Europe to the Hasidic movement, for example, are an important part of the same [modern] story." See Hundert, "Re(de)fining Modernity in Jewish History," 144.

9. See ibid., 139–140.

10. See Judah Leib Gordon, "Awake My People" (1863) republished and translated by Michael Stanislawski in his *For Whom Do I Toil?* 49–50. See also Stanislawski's important explanation of this term and the differences between what Gordon meant when invoking the phrase and similar but ultimately different statements made by western European Jews (50–53).

11. On the use of governmental force in the fight between Maskilim and Hasidim, see Etkes, "Parashat ha-Haskalah mi-Ta'am ve-ha-Temurah be-Ma'amad Tnuat ha-Haskalah be-Rusiyah," 183–215; Wodziński, "Haskalah and Politics Reconsidered," 163–197; and Eli Lederhendler, *The Road to Modern Jewish Politics: Political Tradition and Political Reconstruction in the Jewish Community in Tsarist Russia* (New York: Oxford University Press, 1989), 84–153. On the use of local governing structures in the spread of Hasidism in the nineteenth century, see Mordekhai Zalkin, "Mekomot Shelo Matza Adayin ha-Hasidut Ken Lah Clal," in Immanuel Etkes, David Assaf, et al., eds., *Be-Ma'aglei Hasidim: Kovetz Mechkarim le-Zikhro shel Professor Mordekhai Wilensky* (Jerusalem: Mossad Bialik, 1999), 21–50.

12. See José Casanova, *Public Religions in the Modern World* (Chicago: University of Chicago Press, 1994), 214–215.

13. See Mordekhai Pachter, "Tnuat ha-Mussar ve-ha-Kabbalah," in Assaf and Rapoport-Albert, *Yashan mi-Pnei Chadash*, 1:223–246.

14. Ada Rapoport-Albert argues that almost from the beginning of the Hasidic movement, leaders were wary of allowing individuals to claim a direct relationship to God. See Ada Rapoport-Albert, "God and the Zaddik as the Two Focal Points of Hasidic Worship," *History of Religions* 18, no. 4 (May 1979): 305–307. This curtailing of the claims to the Divine was ignored by the Mitnagdim, who tried to depict the Hasidism as God-intoxicated. On Hasidic yeshivot see Shaul Stampfer, "Hasidic Yeshivot in Inter-War Poland," *Polin* 11 (1998): 12.

15. See Arie Morgenstern, *Hastening Redemption: Messianism and the Resettlement of the Land of Israel* (Oxford: Oxford University Press, 2006).

16. On the curriculum of the state-sponsored Jewish school in Vilna, see Michael Stanislawski, *Tsar Nicholas I and the Jews: The Transformation of Jewish Society in Russia, 1825–1855* (Philadelphia: Jewish Publication Society, 1983), 100–101.

17. Raphael Shuchat, *Olam Nistar be-Memadei ha-Zeman* (Ramat Gan: Bar Ilan University Press, 2008), 295–315.

18. See Benjamin Harshav's preface in Herman Kruk, *The Last Days of the Jerusalem of Lithuania: Chronicles from the Vilna Ghetto and the Camps, 1939–1944*, ed. Benjamin Harshav, trans. Barbara Harshav (New Haven: Yale University Press, 2002), xxx. On the Gaon's image in the Haskalah, see Shmuel Werses, "Ha-Gaon mi-Vilna bi-Olamah shel Safrut ha-Haskalah," in Werses, *Hakitzah Ami: Sifrut ha-Haskalah be-Idan ha-Modernizatziah* (Jerusalem: Magnes Press, 2000), 25–66. On late twentieth-century French intellectuals' adoption of the Gaon, see Judith Friedlander, *Vilna on the Seine: Jewish Intellectuals in France since 1968* (New Haven: Yale University Press, 2000), 3.

Bibliography

Aarsleff, Hans. *From Locke to Saussure: Essays on the Study of Language and Intellectual History*. Minneapolis: University of Minnesota Press, 1982.

Abraham ben Solomon. *Ma'alot ha-Torah*. Edited by Michael Feinstein and Nissan Waxman. New York: Peninim, 1946.

Abramsky, Chimen. "The Crisis of Authority within European Jewry in the Eighteenth Century." Pp. 13–28 in *Jewish Religious and Intellectual History: Presented to Alexander Altmann on the Occasion of His Seventieth Birthday*, edited by Siegfried Stein and Raphael Loewe. Tuscaloosa: University of Alabama Press, 1979.

Albeck-Gidron, Rachel. *Ha-Meah shel ha-Monadot: Ha-Metafizikah shel Leibniz ve-ha-Moderniyut shel ha-Meah ha-Esrim*. Ramat-Gan: Bar-Ilan University Press, 2007.

Albo, Joseph. *Sefer ha-Ikarim*. Edited and translated by Isaac Husik. 4 vols. Philadelphia: Jewish Publication Society, 1946.

Alter, Robert. *The Art of Biblical Poetry*. New York: Basic Books, 1985.

Altmann, Alexander. *Moses Mendelssohn: A Biographical Study*. Philadelphia: Jewish Publication Society of America, 1973.

Anderson, Benedict. *Imagined Communities: Reflections on the Origin and Spread of Nationalism*. 1983; New York: Verso, 1991.

Arkush, Allan. *Moses Mendelssohn and the Enlightenment*. Albany: State University of New York Press, 1994.

————. "The Questionable Judaism of Moses Mendelssohn." *New German Critique* 77 (Spring–Summer 1999): 29–44.

Arranoff, Deena. "Elijah Levita: A Jewish Hebraist." *Jewish History* 23 (2009): 17–40.

Asad, Talal. *Formations of the Secular: Christianity, Islam, Modernity*. Palo Alto, Calif.: Stanford University Press, 2003.

Assaf, David. *The Regal Way: The Life and Times of Israel of Ruzhin*. Palo Alto, Calif.: Stanford University Press, 2002.

Assaf, Simcha. *Mekorot le-Toldot ha-Chinukh be-Yisrael*. Edited by Shmuel Glick. 3 vols. New York: Jewish Theological Seminary of America, 2002.

Auerbach, Erich. *Mimesis: The Representation of Reality in Western Literature*. Translated by Willard Trask. New York: Doubleday, 1957.

Augustine. *On Christian Doctrine*. Translated by D. W. Robertson. New York: Liberal Arts Press, 1958.

Avivi, Yosef. *Kabbalat ha-Gra*. Jerusalem: Kerem Eliyahu, ha-Makhon le-Hotsa'at Sifrei ha-Gra, 1992.

————. *Kerakh Ktivat Yad ha-Kollel be-Tokho Shlosha Sefarim*. Jerusalem: Asufa Auction House, 2001.

Avraham, Danzig. *Chayyei Adam*. Vilna: 1819.

————. *Chokhmat Adam*. 1825; New York: Yudaika Press: 1991.

————. *Zikhru Torat Moshe*. Vilna: 1827.

Avraham ben Elijah of Vilna (Avraham ben ha-Gra). *Sa'eret Eliyahu*. Warsaw: 1877.

————. *Sefer Rav Pe'alim*. Warsaw: Shuldenberg Halter Vaizenshtadt, 1894.

Azulay, Joseph David. *Sefer Shem ha-Gedolim ha-Shalem*. Jerusalem: 1992.

Baer, Dov. *Maggid Devarav le-Ya'akov*. Jerusalem: Magnes Press, Hebrew University, 1990.

Bałaban, Majer. *Le-Toldot ha-Tnuah ha-Frankit*. Tel Aviv: Devir, 1935.

Barnai, Jacob. *Shabta'ut: Hebetim Chevratiyim*. Jerusalem: Zalman Shazar Center, 2000.

Baron, Salo. *The Russian Jew under the Tsar and Soviets*. New York: Schocken Books, 1987.

Bartal, Israel. *Galut ba-Aretz*. Jerusalem: Ha-Sifriya ha-Tzionit, 1994.

————. "The Image of Germany and German Jewry in East European Jewish Society during the 19th Century." Pp. 3–17 in *Danzig, between East and West*, edited by Isadore Twersky. Cambridge, Mass.: Harvard University Press, 1985.

————. "The Imprint of Haskalah Literature on the Historiography of Hasidim." Pp. 369–388 in *Hasidism Reappraised*, edited by Ada Rapoport-Albert. Oxford: Littman Library of Jewish Civilization, 1996.

———. "On Periodization, Mysticism and Enlightenment: The Case of Moses Hayyim Luzzatto." Pp. 201–214 in *Jahrbuch Des Simon Dubnow Instituts*, vol. 6, edited by David B. Ruderman and Shmuel Feiner. Leipzig: Vandenhoeck and Ruprecht, 2007.

Barthes, Roland. *Mythologies*. Translated by Annette Lavers. New York: Macmillan, 1972.

Barzilay, Isaac. *Manasseh of Ilya: Precursor of Modernity among the Jews of Eastern Europe*. Jerusalem: Magnes Press, Hebrew University, 1999.

Bate, Jonathan. *The Genius of Shakespeare*. New York: Oxford University Press, 1998.

Bates, David William. *Enlightenment Aberrations: Error and Revolution in France*. Ithaca, N.Y.: Cornell University Press, 2002.

Beck, Ulrich. *Risk Society: Towards a New Modernity*. Translated by Mark Ritter. London: Sage, 1992.

Beiser, Frederick. *The Fate of Reason: German Philosophy from Kant to Fichte*. Cambridge, Mass.: Harvard University Press, 1987.

Beit-Arie, Malakhi. "Sefatim Dovivot: Hagahot ve-ha-Shleimut be-Ketivat Yad le-*Siftei Yeshenim*." *Kiryat Sefer* 40 (1965): 124–133.

Benjamin, Walter. *The Correspondence of Walter Benjamin, 1910–1940*. Translated by Manfred R. Jacobson and Evelyn M. Jacobson and edited by Gershom G. Scholem and Theodor W. Adorno. Chicago: University of Chicago Press, 1994.

———. *Illuminations*. Translated by Harry Zohn and edited by Hannah Arendt. New York: Schocken Books, 1968.

Ben-Sasson, Haim Hillel. "Ishiyuto shel ha-Gra ve-Hashpa'ato ha-Historit." *Zion* 31, nos. 1–2 (1966): 39–86.

Berdichevsky, Micah Yosef. "Olam ha-Atzilut." Reprinted as pp. 132–152 in *Yeshivot Lita: Pirkei Zichronot*, edited by Immanuel Etkes and Shlomo Tikotsinski. Jerusalem: Merkaz Zalman Shazar, 2004.

Berlin, Meir. *Fun Volozhin biz Yerushalayim*. 2 vols. New York: 1933.

Berlin, Naftali Tzvi Yehudah. *Ha-Emek Davar*. 6 vols. Jerusalem: 1999.

Bernfeld, Simon. *Dor Tapuchot*. Warsaw: 1897.

Bersohn, Nehama R. "Isaac Satanow, the Man and His Work: A Study in the Berlin Haskalah." Ph.D. diss., Columbia University, 1975.

Biale, David. *Cultures of the Jews: A New History*. New York: Schocken Books, 2002.

———. *Eros and the Jews: From Biblical Israel to Contemporary America*. Berkeley: University of California Press, 1997.

Blau, Ludwig. "Methods of Teaching the Talmud in the Past and in the Present." *Jewish Quarterly Review* 15, no. 1 (October 1903): 121–134.

Blažytė, Danutė. "The Vilnius Magistracy and the Jewish Community in the Eighteenth Century." Pp. 313–320 in *The Gaon of Vilnius and the Annals of Jewish Culture*, edited by Izraelis Lempertas. Vilnius: Vilnius University Publishing House, 1998.

Bloom, Harold. *The Anxiety of Influence: A Theory of Poetry*. New York: Oxford University Press, 1997.

———. *Genius: A Mosaic of One Hundred Exemplary Creative Minds*. New York: Warner Books, 2002.

Blumenberg, Hans. *The Legitimacy of the Modern Age*. Translated by Robert M. Wallace. Cambridge, Mass.: MIT Press, 1983.

Boyarin, Daniel. *Border Lines: The Partition of Judaeo-Christianity*. Philadelphia: University of Pennsylvania Press, 2004.

———. *Ha-Iyyun ha-Sefaradi: Le-Farshanut ha-Talmud shel Megorshei Sefarad*. Jerusalem: Mekhon Ben-Tzvi le-Cheker Kehilot Yisrael ba-Mizrach, 1989.

———. "Internal Opposition in Talmudic Literature: The Case of the Married Monk." *Representations* 36 (Autumn 1991): 87–113.

———. *Intertextuality and the Reading of Midrash*. Bloomington: Indiana University Press, 1990.

———. *Unheroic Conduct: The Rise of Heterosexuality and the Invention of the Jewish Male*. Berkeley: University of California Press, 1997.

Bran, Noel L. *The Debate over Genius in the Italian Renaissance*. Leiden: Brill, 2002.

Brandt, Richard B. *The Philosophy of Schleiermacher: The Development of His Theory of Scientific and Religious Knowledge*. Westport, Conn.: Greenwood Press, 1941.

Breuer, Edward. *The Limits of Enlightenment: Jews, Germans, and the Eighteenth-Century Study of Scripture*. Cambridge, Mass.: Harvard University Press, 1996.

Breuer, Mordechai. "Appointment and Succession among the Yeshiva Deans." *Jewish History* 13, no. 1 (Spring 1999): 11–23.

———. *Modernity within Tradition: The Social History of Orthodox Jewry in Imperial Germany*. Translated by Elizabeth Petuchowski. New York: Columbia University Press, 1992.

———. *Ohalei Torah: Ha-Yeshivah, Tavnitah, ve-Toldoteha*. Jerusalem: Merkaz Zalman Shazar, 2003.

Briedis, Laimondas. *Vilnius: City of Strangers*. Budapest: Central European University Press, 2009.

Brill, Alan. "Auxiliary to 'Hokhma': The Writings of the Vilna Gaon and Philosophical Terminology." Pp. 9–37 in *Ha-Gra u-Veit Midrasho*, edited by

Moshe Hallamish, Yosef Rivlin, and Raphael Shuchat. Ramat Gan, Israel: Bar Ilan University Press, 2003.

———. "The Mystical Path of the Vilna Gaon." *Journal of Jewish Thought and Philosophy* 3, no. 1 (1993): 131–151.

Broda, Yehuda, et al. *Sefer Likkutim Yekarim*. Lemberg: Defus Y. Sh. Y. Rapaport, 1792.

Brown, Peter. *Augustine of Hippo: A Biography*. Berkeley: University of California Press, 2000.

———. "The Rise and Function of the Holy Man in Late Antiquity." *Journal of Roman Studies* 61 (1971): 80–101.

Brown, Stuart. "Some Occult Influences on Leibniz's Monadology." Pp. 1–21 in *Leibniz, Mysticism and Religion*, edited by Allison Coudert, Richard Popkin, and Gordon Weiner. Dordrecht: Kluwer Academic Press, 1998.

Buber, Salomon. *Toldot Eliyahu ha-Tishbi*. Leipzig: C.L. Fritzsche, 1856.

Budzyński, Zdzisław. *Ludność Pogranicza Polsko-Ruskiego w Drugiej Połowie XVII Wieku*. Przemyśl and Rzeszów: 1993.

Bürger, Peter. *The Decline of Modernism*. Translated by Nicholas Walker. State College, Pa.: Penn State University Press, 1992.

Burke, Peter. *The Fabrication of Louis XIV*. New Haven: Yale University Press, 1992.

———. *Popular Culture in Early Modern Europe*. London: Temple Smith, 1978.

Burrus, Virginia. *The Making of a Heretic: Gender, Authority, and the Pricillianist Controversy*. Berkeley: University of California Press, 1995.

Butterwick, Richard. *Poland's Last King and English Culture: Stanislaw August Poniatowski, 1732–1798*. Oxford: Oxford University Press, 1998.

Cahan, Abraham. *The Education of Abraham Cahan*. Translated by Leon Stein, Abraham Conan, and Lynn Davison. Philadelphia: Jewish Publication Society, 1969.

Campanton, Isaac. *Darkhei ha-Talmud*. Edited by Isaac Sampson Langeh. Jerusalem: Yitzchak Shimshon Langeh, 1980.

Caner, Daniel. *Wandering, Begging Monks: Spiritual Authority and the Promotion of Monasticism in Late Antiquity*. Berkeley: University of California Press, 2002.

Carlebach, Elisheva. "Early Modern Ashkenaz in the Writings of Jacob Katz." Pp. 65–83 in *The Pride of Jacob: Essays on Jacob Katz and His Work*, edited by Jay Michael Harris. Cambridge, Mass.: Harvard University Press, 2002.

———. *The Pursuit of Heresy: Rabbi Moses Hagiz and the Sabbatian Controversies*. New York: Columbia University Press, 1990.

Casanova, José. *Public Religions in the Modern World*. Chicago: University of Chicago Press, 1994.

Cassirer, Ernst. *The Philosophy of Symbolic Forms*. Translated by Ralph Mannheim. 3 vols. New Haven: Yale University Press, 1953.

———. *The Philosophy of the Enlightenment*. Princeton, N.J.: Princeton University Press, 1979.

Certeau, Michel de. *The Mystic Fable*. Translated by Michael B. Smith. 2 vols. Chicago: University of Chicago Press, 1992.

Chladenius, Johann. *Einleitung zur richtigen Auslegung vernünftiger Reden und Schriften*. Düsseldorf: Stern-Verlag Janssen, 1969.

Cohen, David. "Mavo." Pp. 16–25 in *Siddur Eizur Eliyahu*, edited by Yehoshua Winograd. Jerusalem: Kerem Eliyahu, 2000.

———. *Sefer Kol Nevuah*. Jerusalem: Mossad ha-Rav Kook, 1970.

Cohen, Gerson D. "The Blessings of Assimilation." Pp. 145–156 in *Jewish History and Jewish Destiny*. New York: Jewish Theological Seminary of America, 1997.

Cohen, Israel. *Vilna*. Philadelphia: Jewish Publication Society, 1943.

Cohen, Paul A. *China Unbound: Evolving Perspectives on the Chinese Past*. New York: Routledge, 2003.

Cohen, Richard. *Jewish Icons: Art and Society in Modern Europe*. Berkeley: University of California Press, 1998.

———. "Representations of the Jewish Body in Modern Times: Forms of Hero Worship." Pp. 237–276 in *Representation in Religion: Studies in Honor of Moshe Barasch*, edited by Moshe Barasch, Jan Assmann, and Albert Baumgarten. Leiden: Brill, 2001.

Conforte, David. *Koreh ha-Dorot*. Berlin: 1842.

Connolly, William E. *Political Theory and Modernity*. Ithaca, N.Y.: Cornell University Press, 1993.

Cook, Daniel. "Leibniz on Creation: A Contribution to His Philosophical Theology." Pp. 449–460 in *Leibniz: What Kind of Rationalist? Logic, Epistemology, and the Unity of Science*, edited by Marcelo Dascal. Tel Aviv: Tel Aviv University Press, 2008.

Copperman, Yehuda L. *Li-Feshuto shel Mikra: Kovets Ma'amarim*. Jerusalem: Hotsa'at Haskel le-Yad Mikhlalah Yerushalayim le-Vanot, 1974.

———. *Pirkei Mavo la-Peirush ha-Ketav ve-ha-Kabbalah al ha-Torah*. Jerusalem: Hotsa'at Haskel le-Yad Mikhlalah Yerushalayim le-Vanot, 1985.

Coudert, Allison. "Introduction." Pp. vii–xxxiii in Anne Conway, *The Principles of the Most Ancient and Modern Philosophy*, edited and translated by Allison Coudert and Taylor Corse. Cambridge: Cambridge University Press, 1996.

———. *Leibniz and the Kabbalah*. Boston: Kluwer Academic, 1995.

Coxe, William. *Travels in Poland, Russia, Sweden and Denmark*. London: J. Nicholas, 1784.

Culbertson, Philip. "Multiplexity in Biblical Exegesis: The Introduction to *Qohelet* by Moses Mendelssohn." *Cincinnati Judaica Review* 2 (Spring 1991): 10–18.

Curtius, Ernst R. *European Literature and the Latin Middle Ages*. Translated by Willard R. Task. Princeton, N.J.: Princeton University Press, 1967.

Dahlstrom, Daniel O. *Moses Mendelssohn: Philosophic Writings*. Cambridge: Cambridge University Press, 1997,

David ben Zimra. *Shut ha-Radvaz*. Jerusalem: 1882.

Davidson, Herbert. "Maimonides' Secret Position on Creation." Pp. 16–40 in *Studies in Medieval Jewish History and Literature*, edited by I. Twersky. Cambridge, Mass.: Harvard University Press, 1979.

Davis, Joseph. "The Reception of the *Shulchan Arukh* and the Formation of Ashkenazic Jewish Identity." *AJS Review* 26, no. 2 (2002): 251–276.

DeNora, Tia. *Beethoven and the Construction of Genius*. Berkeley: University of California Press, 1997.

de' Rossi, Azariah. *The Light of the Eyes*. Translated and with an introduction by Joanna Weinberg. New Haven: Yale University Press, 2001.

Derrida, Jacques. *Of Grammatology*. Translated by Gayatri Spivak. Baltimore: Johns Hopkins University Press, 1997.

———. *Writing and Difference*. Translated by Alan Bass. Chicago: University of Chicago Press, 1978.

Devir, Haim. "Biur ha-Gra al ha-*Shulchan Arukh*." *Yeshurun* 5 (1999): 3–13.

Dienstag, Jacob Israel. "Ha-im Hitnaged ha-Gra le-Mishnato ha-Filosofit shel ha-Rambam?" *Talpiyot* 4, nos. 1–2 (1949): 269–356.

Dimitrovsky, Haim Z. "Al-Derekh ha-Pilpul." Pp. 111–181 in *Salo Wittmayer Baron Jubilee Volume on the Occasion of His Eightieth Birthday*, edited by Saul Lieberman and Arthur Hyman. Jerusalem: American Academy for Jewish Research, 1975.

Dinur, Ben-Zion. *Be-Mifneh ha-Dorot*. Jerusalem: Mossad Bialik, 1955.

Dolgopolski, Sergey. *What Is Talmud? The Art of Disagreement*. New York: Fordham University Press, 2009.

Dotan, Aron. "Prolegomenon." Pp. vii–xlvi in William Wickes, *Two Treatises on the Accentuation of the Old Testament: On Psalms, Proverbs, and Job, on the Twenty-one Prose Books*. New York: Ktav Publishing House, 1970.

Dubnow, Simon. *History of the Jews in Russia and Poland*. Translated by Israel Friedlaender. Bergenfield, N.J.: Avotaynu, 2000.

———. "The Maggid of Miedzyrzecz, His Associates, and the Center in Volhynia." Pp. 67–75 in *Essential Papers on Hasidism: Origins to Present*. New York: New York University Press, 1991.

———. *Toldot ha-Hasidut*. Tel-Aviv: Devir, 1967.

Dynner, Glenn. "Hasidic Conquest of Central Poland." *Polin* 17 (2004): 52–81.

———. *Men of Silk: The Hasidic Conquest of Polish Jewish Society*. New York: Oxford University Press, 2006.

Edel, Yehudah L. *Afikei Yehudah*. Lvov: 1803.

Efron, John M. *Defenders of the Race: Jewish Doctors and Race Science in Fin-de-Siècle Europe*. New Haven: Yale University Press, 1994.

———. *Medicine and the German Jews: A History*. New Haven: Yale University Press, 2001.

Efron, Zusia. "Portrait of the Gaon of Vilna: Two Centuries of Imagination." Pp. 164–168 in *The Gaon of Vilnius and the Annals of Jewish Culture*, edited by Izraelis Lempertas. Vilnius: Vilnius University Publishing House, 1998.

Eibeschuetz, Yonatan. *Luchot Edut*. Altona: 1755.

Elbaum, Jacob. *Lehavin Divrei Chakhamim*. Jerusalem: Mossad Bialik, 2000.

Eliakh, Dov. *Avi ha-Yeshivot*. Jerusalem: Moreshet ha-Yeshivot, 1991.

———. *Kol ha-Katuv le-Hayyim*. Jerusalem: 1988.

———. *Sefer ha-Gaon: Le-Toldot Chayav u-Verur Mishnato shel Morenu ve-Rabenu ha-Gaon Eliyahu mi-Vilna*. 3 vols. Jerusalem: Makhon Moreshet ha-Yeshivot, 2002.

Elias, Norbert. *The Civilizing Process*. Translated by Edmund Jephcott. Malden, Mass.: Blackwell Publishers, 2000.

Elijah ben Solomon. *Aderet Eliyahu*. 1804; Warsaw: 1887; Tel Aviv: Sinai, 1961.

———. *Meskhet Avot*. Shklov: 1804.

———. *Biur ha-Gra al Shulchan Arukh, Choshen Mishpat*. Köningsberg: 1856.

———. *Biur ha-Gra al Shulchan Arukh, Even ha-Ezer*. Grodno: 1819.

———. *Biur ha-Gra al Shulchan Arukh, Orach Chayyim*. Shklov: 1803.

———. *Biur ha-Gra al Shulchan Arukh, Yoreh Deah*. Grodno: 1806.

———. *Biur ha-Gra le-Nevi'im*. Jerusalem: Mossad ha-Rav Kook, 2002.

———. *Biur ve-Hagahot al Kol Sefer Zohar*. Vilna: 1810.

———. *Imrei Noam: Peirush ha-Gra le-Berakhot*. Jerusalem: Mesorah, 1954; Jerusalem: Mossad ha-Rav Kook, 2006.

———. *Kol Eliyahu*. Pietrokov: 1905.

———. "Letter of Elijah (Gaon) of Wilna." In *Hebrew Ethical Wills*, 311–325. Edited and translated by Israel Abrahams. Philadelphia: Jewish Publication Society, 1926.

———. *Megilat Ester im Peirush ha-Gra ha-Shalem*. Jerusalem: Yeshivat Tiferet ha-Talmud, 1989.

———. *Me'il Tzedek*. Berlin: 1856.

———. *Mishlei im Biur ha-Gra*. Shklov: 1798; Petach Tikvah: 1991.

———. *Peirush al Kama Aggadot*. Prague: 1810.

———. *Peirush ha-Gra le-Tehilim.* Prague: 1812.

———. *Sefer Alim li-Terufah.* Minsk: 1836.

———. *Sefer Ayil Meshulash: Al Chokhmat ha-Meshulashim ve-ha-Handasah.* Vilna: 1833.

———. *Sefer Divrei Eliyahu.* Bnei Brak: Mishor, 1999.

———. *Sefer Malkhut Eliyahu.* New York: Makhon ha-Gra, 2000.

———. *Sefer Mishlei im Biur ha-Gra.* Edited by Moshe Philip. Petach Tikvah: 1992.

———. *Sefer Sedeh Eliyahu: Biur ha-Gra ha-Shalem al ha-Shas, Masekhet Ketubot.* Jerusalem: Sh. D. ha-Levi Movshovits, 1991.

———. *Sefer Yahel Or.* Vilna: 1882.

———. *Sefer Yetsirah.* Grodno: 1806.

———. *Shenot Eliyahu.* Lvov: 1799.

———. *Sifra di-Tzeniuta.* Vilna: 1820; Tel Aviv: 1969.

———. *Tikkunei ha-Zohar im Tikkunim mi-Zohar Chadash, im Biur ha-Gra.* Vilna: 1867.

Elior, Rachel. *The Paradoxical Ascent to God: The Kabbalistic Theosophy of Habad Hasidism.* Albany: State University of New York Press, 1993.

———. "Rabbi Nathan Adler of Frankfurt and the Controversy Surrounding Him." Pp. 223–242 in *Mysticism, Magic and Kabbalah in Ashkenazi Judaism: International Symposium Held in Frankfurt a.M. 1991,* edited by Karl Erich Grozinger and Joseph Dan. Berlin: Walter de Gruyter, 1995.

Eliot, T. S. "Tradition and the Individual Talent." Pp. 47–59 in Eliot, *The Sacred Wood: Essays on Poetry and Criticism.* London: Methune, 1920.

Ellenson, David H. *After Emancipation: Jewish Religious Responses to Modernity.* Cincinnati: Hebrew Union College Press, 2004.

———. *Between Tradition and Culture: The Dialectics of Modern Jewish Identity.* Atlanta: Scholars Press, 1994.

———. "A Disputed Precedent: The Prague Organ in Nineteenth-Century Central-European Legal Literature and Polemics." *Leo Baeck Institute Yearbook* 40 (1995): 251–264.

Elman, Ya'akov. "Derekh ha-Gra u-Megamato be-Likkut Midrashei Halakha be-Aderet Eliyahu al Sefer Vayikra." Pp. 63–80 in *Ha-Gra u-Veit Midrasho,* edited by Moshe Hallamish, Joseph Rivlin, and Raphael Shuchat. Ramat Gan, Israel: Bar Ilan University Press, 2003.

———. " 'It Is No Empty Thing': Nahmanides and the Search for Omnisignificance." *Torah u-Madda* 4 (1993): 1–83.

———. "The Rebirth of Omnisignificant Biblical Exegesis in the Nineteenth and Twentieth Centuries." *Jewish Studies: An Internet Journal* 2 (2003): 199–249.

Elon, Menahem. *Jewish Law: History, Sources, Principles*. Translated by Bernard Auerbach and Melvin J. Sykes. 4 vols. Philadelphia: Jewish Publication Society, 1994.

Emden, Jacob. *Hitavkut*. Altona: 1769.

Emerson, Ralph Waldo. "Self-Reliance." In Emerson, *Essays: First Series*. Boston: James Munroe and Company, 1841.

Engelstein, Laura. *Slavophile Empire: Imperial Russia's Illiberal Path*. Ithaca, N.Y.: Cornell University Press, 2009.

Epshtain, Ephraim M. *Sefer Gevurot ha-Ari: Tahalukhot ve-Korot Yemei Chayav*. Vilna: 1870.

Epstein, Barukh ha-Levi. *Torah Temimah*. 5 vols. Jerusalem: Makhon Ha-Torah, 2005.

Epstein, Kalonymus Kalman. *Sefer Maor va-Shemesh*. Tel-Aviv: 1965.

Epstein, Yehudah. *Minchat Yehudah*. Warsaw: 1877.

Etkes, Immanuel. *The Gaon of Vilna: The Man and His Image*. Berkeley: University of California Press, 2002.

———. *Ha-Dat ve-ha-Chayyim: Tnuat ha-Haskalah ha-Yehudit be-Mizrach Eropah*. Jerusalem: Merkaz Zalman Shazar, 1993.

———. "Immanent Factors and External Influences in the Development of the Haskalah Movement in Russia." Pp. 13–32 in *Toward Modernity: The European Jewish Model*, edited by Jacob Katz. New Brunswick, N.J.: Transaction Press, 1987.

———. "Mavo." Pp. 9–56 in *Yeshivot Lita: Pirkei Zikhronot*, edited by Immanuel Etkes and Shlomo Tikochinski. Jerusalem: Merkaz Zalman Shazar, Hebrew University, 2004.

———. "Parashat ha-Haskalah mi-Ta'am ve-ha-Temurah be-Ma'amad Tnuat ha-Haskalah be-Rusiyah." *Zion* 43 (1978): 264–313.

———. *R. Yisrael Salanter ve-Reishita shel Tnuat ha-Mussar*. Jerusalem: Hebrew University Press, 1982.

Ettinger, Shmuel. "The Council of the Four Lands." Pp. 93–109 in *The Jews in Old Poland, 1000–1795*, edited by Antony Polonsky, Jakub Basista, and Andrzej Link-Lenczowski. London: I.B. Tauris and the Oxford Institute for Polish-Jewish Studies, 1993.

———. "Hasidism and the Kahal in Eastern Europe." Pp. 63–75 in *Hasidism Reappraised*, edited by Ada Rapoport-Albert. Oxford: Littman Library of Jewish Civilization, 1996.

Euclid. *Euclid: Explanation of all the Geometric Sciences*. Translated by Barukh Schick. The Hague: Leb Zusmensh, 1780.

Fefer, Nehemiah. *Tehilot Eliyahu*. New York: Makhon ha-Gra, 1999.

Feiner, Shmuel. "Ha-Mifneh be-Ha'arakhat ha-Hasidut: Eliezer Zweifel ve-ha-Haskalah ha-Metunah be-Rusiyah." Pp. 336–379 in Immanuel Etkes, ed., *Ha-Dat ve-ha-Chayyim: Tnuat ha-Haskalah ha-Yehudit be-Mizrach Eropah*. Jerusalem: Merkaz Zalman Shazar, 1993.

———. *Haskalah and History: The Emergence of a Modern Jewish Historical Consciousness*. Oxford: Littman Library of Jewish Civilization, 2002.

———. *The Jewish Enlightenment*. Translated by Chaya Naor. Philadelphia: University of Pennsylvania Press, 2003.

———. *The Origins of Jewish Secularization in Eighteenth-Century Europe*. Translated by Chaya Naor. Philadelphia: University of Pennsylvania Press, 2010.

Feiner, Shmuel, and David J. Sorkin, eds. *New Perspectives on the Haskalah*. Oxford: Littman Library of Jewish Civilization, 2001.

Feldman, Seymour, trans. and ed. *The Wars of the Lord*, by Levi ben Gershom. New York: Jewish Publication Society and Jewish Theological Seminary of America Press, 1999.

Fishman, David E. "Musar and Modernity: The Case of Novaredok." *Modern Judaism* 8, no. 1 (1988): 41–64.

———. "A Polish Rabbi Meets the Berlin Haskalah: The Case of R. Barukh Schick." *AJS Review* 12, no. 1 (1987): 95–121.

———. *The Rise of Modern Yiddish Culture*. Pittsburgh: University of Pittsburg Press, 2005.

———. *Russia's First Modern Jews: The Jews of Shklov*. New York: New York University Press, 1995.

Fishman, Joshua. "The Gaon of Vilne and the Yiddish Language." Pp. 18–26 in *The Gaon of Vilnius and the Annals of Jewish Culture: Materials of the International Scientific Conference, Vilnius, September 10–12, 1997*, edited by Izraelis Lempertas. Vilnius: Vilnius University Publishing House, 1998.

Fishman, Talia. "The Penitential System of Hasidei Ashkenaz and the Problem of Cultural Boundaries." *Journal of Jewish Thought and Philosophy* 9 (1999): 1–29.

Flatto, Sharon. "Hasidim and Mitnaggedim: Not a World Apart." *Journal of Jewish Thought and Philosophy* 12, no. 2 (2003): 99–121.

———. *The Kabbalistic Culture of Eighteenth-Century Prague: Ezekiel Landau (The Noda bi-Yehudah) and His Contemporaries*. Oxford: Littman Library of Jewish Civilization, 2010.

———. "Prague's Rabbinic Culture: The Concealed and Revealed in Ezekiel Landau's Writings." Ph.D. diss., Yale University, 2000.

Foucault, Michel. *The Order of Things: An Archaeology of Human Sciences*. New York: Vintage Books, 1970.

Fox, Menahem Tzvi. "Hagahot ha-Gra le-Midrashei Halakha ke-Yesod le-Tfisat Olamo ha-Ruchani." *Sidra* 15 (1999): 111–117.

Fram, Edward. "German Pietism and Sixteenth- and Early Seventeenth-Century Polish Rabbinic Culture." *Jewish Quarterly Review*, 96, no. 1 (2006): 50–59.

———. *Ideals Face Reality: Jewish Law and Life in Poland, 1550–1655.* Cincinnati: Hebrew Union College Press, 1997.

———. "Perception and Reception of Repentant Apostates in Medieval Ashkenaz and Premodern Poland." *AJS Review* 21, no. 2 (1996): 299–339.

Franks, Paul. *All or Nothing: Systematicity, Transcendental Arguments, and Skepticism in German Idealism.* Cambridge, Mass.: Harvard University Press, 2005.

Freedman, Chaim. *Eliyahu's Branches: The Descendents of the Vilna Gaon and His Family.* Bergenfield, N.J.: Avotaynu, 1997.

Frei, Hans W. *The Eclipse of Biblical Narrative: A Study in Eighteenth- and Nineteenth-Century Hermeneutics.* New Haven: Yale University Press, 1974.

Frick, David. "Jews and Others in Seventeenth-Century Wilno: Life in the Neighborhood." *Jewish Studies Quarterly* 12, no. 1 (2005): 8–42.

Friedlander, Yehudah. "Le-Birur Yachaso shel ha-Gaon mi-Vilna la-Haskalah be-Reishitah: Ha-Gaon ve-N. H. Wesseley." Pp. 197–205 in *Ha-Gra u-Veit Midrasho*, edited by Moshe Hallamish, Joseph Rivlin, and Raphael Shuchat. Ramat Gan: Bar-Ilan University Press, 2003.

Friedman, Menachem. "Life Tradition and Book Tradition in the Development of Ultra-Orthodox Judaism." Pp. 235–255 in *Judaism Viewed from Within and from Without*, edited by Harvey E. Goldberg. Albany: State University of New York Press, 1987.

———. "The Lost "Kiddush" Cup: Changes in Ashkenazic Haredi Culture: A Tradition in Crisis." Pp. 175–186 in *The Uses of Tradition: Jewish Continuity in the Modern Era*, edited by Jack Wertheimer. New York: Jewish Theological Seminary, 1992.

Fuenn, Shmuel Y. *Knesset Yisrael.* Warsaw: 1886.

Fuenn, Shmuel Y., Matisyahu Strashun, and Hillel-Noah Maggid Steinschneider. *Kiryah Ne'emanah: Korot Adat Yisrael be-Ir Vilna.* Vilna: Yitzchak Funk, 1915.

Funkenstein, Amos. *Perceptions of Jewish History.* Berkeley: University of California Press, 1993.

———. *Theology and the Scientific Imagination: From the Late Middle Ages to the Seventeenth Century.* Princeton, N.J.: Princeton University Press, 1986.

Gafni, Chanan. "Hirsch Mendel Pineles and His Work *The Way of Torah*." Master's thesis, Hebrew University, 1999.

Garb, Jonathan. "Ha-Model ha-Politi be-Kabbalah ha-Modernit Iyyun be-Kitvei Ramchal." Pp. 13–45 in *Al Da'at ha-Kahal*, edited by Benjamin Brown,

Menahem Lorberbaum, Avinoam Rosenak, and Yedidyah Stern. Jerusalem: The Zalman Shazar Center and Israel Democracy Institute, forthcoming 2012.

———. "The Modernization of Kabbalah: A Case Study." *Modern Judaism* 30, no. 1 (2010): 1–22.

Garber, Daniel. "Leibniz on Form and Matter." *Early Science and Medicine* 2, no. 3 (1997): 326–352.

Geiger, Abraham. *Urschrift und Übersetzungen der Bibel in ihrer Abhängigkeit von der innern Entwicklung des Judenthums*. Breslau: J. Hanauer, 1857.

Genuzot ha-Gra. Jerusalem: Y.D. Kroizer, 2000.

Gertner, Hayyim. "Batei Midrash be-Galitsiyah be-Meah ha-19." Pp. 163–186 in *Yeshivot u-Vatei Midrashot*, edited by Immanuel Etkes. Jerusalem: Merkaz Zalman Shazar and Merkaz Dinur le-Cheker Toldot Yisrael, Hebrew University, 2006.

Gillman, Sander. *Smart Jews: The Construction of the Image of Jewish Superior Intelligence*. Lincoln: University of Nebraska Press, 1996.

Ginsburg, Christian D. *The Massoreth ha-Massoreth of Elias Levita*. London: Longmans, Green, Reader & Dyer, 1867.

Ginzberg, Eli. *Louis Ginzberg: Keeper of the Law*. Philadelphia: Jewish Publication Society, 1996.

Ginzberg, Louis. "The Gaon, Rabbi Elijah of Wilna." Pp. 125–144 in *Students, Scholars and Saints*, edited by Louis Ginzberg. Philadelphia: The Jewish Publication Society of America, 1928.

Goldberg, Jacob. *Ha-Mumarim be-Mamlekhet Polin-Lita*. Jerusalem: 1985.

Goldstein, Jonathan. "The Origins of the Doctrine of Creation Ex-Nihilo." *Journal of Jewish Studies* 35 (1984): 127–135.

Goodman, Lenn E. "Maimonides and Leibniz." *Journal of Jewish Studies* 31, no. 2 (1980): 214–236.

Gordon, Yehudah Leib. "Kotso Shel Yud." Translated by Stanley Nash. *CCAR Journal* (Summer 2006): 107–108.

Grade, Chaim. "My Quarrel with Hersh Rasseyner," translated by Milton Himmelfarb. Pp. 625–651 in *A Treasury of Yiddish Stories*, edited by Irving Howe and Eliezer Greenberg. New York: Viking Press, 1954.

Green, Abigail. *Moses Montefiore: Jewish Liberator, Imperial Hero*. Cambridge Mass.: Harvard University Press, 2010.

Green, Arthur. *Tormented Master: A Life of Rabbi Nahman of Bratslav*. Tuscaloosa: University of Alabama Press, 1979.

Gries, Zeev. "Arikhat *Tzava'at ha-Rivash*." *Kiryat Sefer* 52 (1997): 187–210.

———. "The Hasidic Managing Editor." Pp. 141–155 in *Hasidism Reappraised*, edited by Ada Rapoport-Albert. Oxford: Littman Library of Jewish Civilization, 1996.

————. *Sefer, Sofer, ve-Sippur be-Reishit ha-Hasidut*. Tel Aviv, 1992.

Gross, David. *The Past in Ruins: Tradition and the Critique of Modernity*. Amherst: University of Massachusetts Press, 1992.

Grossman, Jeffrey. *The Discourse on Yiddish in Germany: From the Enlightenment to the Second Empire*. New York: Camden House, 2000.

Güdemann, Moritz. "Die Gegner Hartwig Wessely's Divrei Shalom ve-Emet." *Monatsschrift für Geschichte und Wissenschaft des Judentums* 19, no. 10 (1870): 478–480.

Gutmann, Tuviah. *Kol Nehei*. Warsaw: 1797.

Hacohen, Aviya. "Be-Ikvei Biur ha-Gra le-Parshat Amah Ivriyah." Pp. 77–91 in *Sefer ha-Yovel le-Rav Mordekhai Breuer: Asufat Ma'amarim be-Maddaei ha-Yahadut*, vol. 1. Jerusalem: Akademon, 1992.

Hadot, Pierre. *What Is Ancient Philosophy?* Translated by Michael Chase. Cambridge, Mass.: Harvard University Press, 2002.

Halbertal, Moshe. *People of the Book: Canon, Meaning, and Authority*. Cambridge, Mass.: Harvard University Press, 1997.

Halivni, David. *Peshat and Derash: Plain and Applied Meaning in Rabbinic Exegesis*. New York: Oxford University Press, 1991.

Hallamish, Moshe. "The Teachings of Rabbi Menahem Mendel of Vitebsk." Pp. 268–287 in *Hasidism Reappraised*, edited by Ada Rapoport-Albert. Oxford: Littman Library of Jewish Civilization, 1996.

Hanau, Shlomo Zalman. *Sha'arei Tefila*. Jessnitz: 1725.

Hands, Alfred W. *An Introduction to the Study of Hebrew Synonyms*. Gloucester: H. Osborne, Printer, 1891.

Hardwick, Lorna, and Christopher Stray. *A Companion to Classical Receptions*. Malden, Mass.: Blackwell, 2008.

Harkavi, Abraham. "Appendix." *Divrei Yemei Yisrael*, vol. 9. Warsaw: 1893.

Harris, Jay. *How Do We Know This? Midrash and the Fragmentation of Modern Judaism*. Albany: State University of New York Press, 1995.

————. "Rabbinic Literature in Lithuania after the Death of the Gaon." Pp. 88–95 in *The Gaon of Vilnius and the Annals of Jewish Culture: Materials of the International Scientific Conference, Vilnius, September 10–12, 1997*, edited by Izraelis Lempertas. Vilnius: Vilnius University Publishing House, 1998.

————. "Talmud Study." *YIVO Encyclopedia of Jews in Eastern Europe*. Available at www.yivoencyclopedia.org/article.aspx/Talmud_Study. Last accessed December 25, 2010.

Harvey, Warren Zev. "A Third Approach to Maimonides' Cosmogony-Prophetology Puzzle." *Harvard Theological Review* 74, no. 3 (1981): 287–301.

Haver, Yitzchak. *Magen ve-Tzinah*. Bnei Brak: 1985.

Havlin, Shlomo Zalman. "Biur ha-Gra le-*Shulchan Arukh*." *Yeshurun* 5 (1999): 696–721.

Hayyim, Volozhiner. *Nefesh ha-Hayyim*. Bnei Brak: I. D. Rubin, 1989.

Heidegger, Martin. *Being and Time*. Translated by J. Macquarrie and E. Robinson. New York: Harper & Row, 1962.

Heine, Heinrich. *Zur Geschichte der Religion und Philosophie in Deutschland*. Frankfurt am Main: Insel Verlag, 1964.

Helmer, Christine. "Transhistorical Unity of the New Testament Canon from Philosophical, Exegetical, and Systematic Perspectives." Pp. 13–50 in *One Scripture or Many? Canon from Biblical, Theological and Philosophical Perspectives*, edited by Christine Helmer and Christoff Landmesser. Oxford: Oxford University Press, 2004.

Hertz, Deborah. *Jewish High Society in Old Regime Berlin*. New Haven: Yale University Press, 2005.

Hess, Jonathan M. *Germans, Jews, and the Claims of Modernity*. New Haven: Yale University Press, 2002.

Heyd, Michael. *"Be Sober and Reasonable": The Critique of Enthusiasm in the Seventeenth and Early Eighteenth Centuries*. Leiden: E.J. Brill, 1995.

Hildesheimer, Meir. "Moses Mendelssohn in Rabbinic Literature." *Proceedings of the American Academy for Jewish Research* 55 (1988): 79–133.

Hobsbawm, Eric J., and Terence O. Ranger. *The Invention of Tradition*. Cambridge: Cambridge University Press, 1992.

Holub, C. Robert. *Reception Theory: A Critical Introduction*. London: Methuen, 1984.

Horowitz, Eliot. "On the Eve of the Circumcision: A Chapter in the History of Jewish Nightlife." *Journal of Social History* 23 (1989): 45–69.

Horowitz, Tzvi ha-Levi. *Kitvei ha-Geonim*. Warsaw: 1938.

Horwitz, Rivka. " 'Kabbalah' in the Writings of Mendelssohn and the Berlin Circle of 'Maskilim.' " *Leo Baeck Institute Yearbook* 45 (2000): 3–24.

Hoy, David Couzens. *The Critical Circle: Literature, History, and Philosophical Hermeneutics*. Berkeley: University of California Press, 1978.

Humboldt, Wilhelm von. *On Language: On the Diversity of Human Language Construction and Its Influence on the Mental Development of the Human Species*. Edited by Michael Losonsky and translated by Peter Heath. New York: Cambridge University Press, 1999.

Hundert, Gershon D. *Jews in Poland-Lithuania in the Eighteenth Century: A Genealogy of Modernity*. Berkeley: University of California Press, 2004.

———. "Re(de)fining Modernity in Jewish History." Pp. 133–145 in *Rethinking European Jewish History*, edited by Jeremy Cohen and Moshe Rosman. Oxford: Littman Library of Jewish Civilization, 2009.

Hurwitz, Yosef Yozel. *Madreigat ha-Adam*. Paltava: 1918.

Hyman, Paula. "Jacob Katz as Historian." Pp. 85–96 in *The Pride of Jacob: Essays on Jacob Katz and His Work*, edited by Jay Harris. Cambridge, Mass.: Harvard University Press, 2002.

Ibn Kaspi, Joseph. *Gevia Kesef: A Study in Medieval Jewish Philosophic Bible Commentary*. Edited by Basil Herring. New York: Ktav Publishing House, 1982.

———. *Sharshot Kesef*. Ms. Rome-Angelica, republished by I. H. Last in "*Sharshot Kesef: The Hebrew Dictionary of Roots*, by Joseph Ibn Kaspi." *Jewish Quarterly Review* 19 (1907): 651–687.

Idel, Moshe. *Hasidism: Between Ecstasy and Magic*. Albany: State University of New York Press, 1995.

———. "Jewish Kabbalah and Platonism in the Middle Ages and Renaissance." Pp. 319–351 in *Neoplatonism and Jewish Thought*, edited by Lenn E. Goodman. Albany: New York State University Press, 1992.

———. *Kabbalah: New Perspectives*. New Haven: Yale University Press, 1988.

———. "Kabbalat R. Menachem Mendel mi-Shklov." Pp. 176–183 in *Ha-Gra u-Veit Midrasho*, edited by Moshe Hallamish, Yosef Rivlin, and Raphael Shuchat. Ramat Gan: Bar-Ilan University Press, 2003.

———. *Language, Torah, and Hermeneutics in Abraham Abulafia*. Translated by Menahem Kallus. Albany: State University of New York Press, 1989.

———. *The Mystical Experience in Abraham Abulafia*. Translated by Jonathan Chipman. Albany: State University of New York Press, 1988.

Iggerot ha-Pekidim ve-ha-Amarkalim. Edited by Yosef Yoel and Benjamin Rivlin, 3 vols. Jerusalem: 1965.

Ishiguro, Hidé. *Leibniz's Philosophy of Logic and Language*. Ithaca, N.Y.: Cornell University Press, 1972.

Israel, Jonathan. *Radical Enlightenment: Philosophy and the Making of Modernity, 1650–1750*. New York: Oxford University Press, 2001.

Jackson, William. "Whether Genius Be Born or Acquired." In Jackson, *The Four Ages*. London: 1798.

Jacobs, Louis. *Hasidic Prayer*. New York: Schocken Books, 1973.

Jaffe, Kineret S. "The Concept of Genius: Its Changing Role in Eighteenth-Century French Aesthetics." *Journal of the History of Ideas* 41, no. 4 (1980): 579–599.

Jay, Martin. *Songs of Experience: Modern American and European Variations on a Universal Theme*. Berkeley: University of California Press, 2005.

Jellinek, Adolf. *Kuntres ha-Klalim*. Vienna: 1878.

Kahane, Maoz. "Mi-Prague le-Pressburg: Ktivah Hilkhatit be-Olam Mishtaneh me-ha Nodah be-Yehudah le-ha-Hatam Sofer, 1730–1839." Ph.D. diss., Hebrew University, 2010.

Kalik, Yehudit. "Patterns of Contact between the Catholic Church and the Jews in the Polish-Lithuanian Commonwealth: The Jewish Debts." In *Studies in the History of the Jews in Poland in Honor of Jacob Goldberg*, edited by Adam Teller. *Scripta Heirosolymitana* 38 (1998): 102–122.

Kamenetsky, David. "Haskamot Gedolei ha-Rabbanim le-Chumashei Rabbi Shlomo Dubno." *Yeshurun* 8 (2001): 718–759.

———. "Lehavdil bein Hayyim le-Hayyim." *Yeshurun* 22 (2010): 876–900.

———. "Peirush Rabbi Avraham ben ha-Gra le-Sefer Bereishit." *Yeshurun* 4 (1998): 322–344.

———. "Sefer 'Ma'aseh Rav.'" *Yeshurun* 21 (2009): 774–827.

Kana'ani, Ya'akov. *Otzar ha-Lashon ha-Ivri*. Edited by Abraham Shlunsky and David Levin. Tel-Aviv: 1961.

Kanarfogel, Ephraim. "Rabbi Judah he-Hasid and the Rabbinic Scholars of Regensburg: Interactions, Influences, and Implications." *Jewish Quarterly Review* 96, no. 1 (2005): 17–37.

Kant, Immanuel. *Immanuel Kant: Correspondence*. Edited and translated by Arnulf Zweig. Cambridge: Cambridge University Press, 1999.

Kaplan, Lawrence J. "Maimonides on the Miraculous Element in Prophecy." *Harvard Theological Review* 70, nos. 3–4 (1977): 233–256.

———. "Rationalism and Rabbinic Culture in Sixteenth-Century Eastern Europe: Rabbi Mordecai Jaffe's *Levush Pinat Yikrat*." Ph.D. diss., Harvard University, 1975.

Karelitz, Avraham Yeshayahu. *Kovetz Iggrot*. 3 vols. Jerusalem: Shmuel Grainiman, 1955.

Kasher, Menachem. *Torah Shleima, Exodus*. Vol. 17. Jerusalem: 1927.

Katz, Ben-Zion. *Rabbanut, Hasidut, Haskalah*. 2 vols. Tel Aviv: Agudat ha-Sofrim ha-Ivrim le-Yad Devir, 1956.

Katz, David. "A Case Study in the Formation of a Super-Rabbi: The Early Years of Rabbi Ezekiel Landau, 1713–1754." Ph.D. diss., University of Maryland, 2004.

Katz, Jacob. "The Concept of Social History and Its Possible Use in Jewish Historical Research." Pp. 292–312 in *Scripta Hierosolymitana*, edited by Roberto Bachi. Vol. 3. Jerusalem: Magnes Press, Hebrew University, 1955.

———. *Divine Law in Human Hands: Case Studies in Halakhic Flexibility*. Jerusalem: Magnes Press, 1998.

———. "Introduction." Pp. 1–12 in *Toward Modernity: The European Jewish Model*, edited by Jacob Katz. New Brunswick, N.J.: Transaction, 1987.

———. *Out of the Ghetto: The Social Background of Jewish Emancipation, 1770–1870*. Syracuse, N.Y.: Syracuse University Press, 1973.

————. "Towards a Biography of the Hatam Sofer." Pp. 223–266 in *Profiles in Diversity: Jews in a Changing Europe, 1750–1870*, edited by Frances Malino and David Sorkin and translated by David Ellenson. Detroit: Wayne State University Press, 1998.

————. *Tradition and Crisis: Jewish Society at the End of the Middle Ages*. Translated by Bernard Dov Cooperman. New York: New York University Press, 1993.

Katzman, Asher. "Zikhronot mi-Kloiz shel ha-Gaon mi-Vilna." *Yeshurun* 6 (1999): 684–691.

Kavolis, Vytautas. "The Devil's Invasion: Cultural Changes in Early Modern Lithuania." *Lituanus* 34, no. 4 (Winter 1989): 123–139.

Keidosiute, Elena. "Missionary Activity of Mariae Vitae Congregation." *PaRDeS: Zeitschrift der Vereinigung für Jüdische Studien* 16 (2010): 57–72.

Kennecke, Andreas. *Isaac Abraham Euchel: Architekt der Haskala*. Göttingen: Wallerstein Verlag, 2007.

Kennedy, James. *Studies in Hebrew Synonyms*. Oxford: Williams and Norgate, 1898.

Kertzer, David. *The Kidnapping of Edgardo Montara*. New York: Alfred Knopf, 1997.

Klausner, Israel. *Ha-Gaon Rabbi Eliyahu mi-Vilna*. Tel Aviv: Ha-Kongres ha-olami, ha-Hanhalah ha-Yisraelit, 1969.

————. *Toldot ha-Kehilah ha-Ivrit be-Vilna*. Vilna: 1938.

————. *Vilna bi-Tekufat ha-Gaon*. Jerusalem: Reuven Mas, 1942.

————. *Vilna, Yerushalayim de-Lita*. Edited by Shmuel Barantchok. Vol. 2. D.N. Western Galilee, Israel: Ghetto Fighter's House, 1983.

Kleinberg, Aaron F. "Jewish Education in Central and Eastern Europe from the Sixteenth to the Eighteenth Centuries." In *Entziklopediah Chinukhit*, edited by Martin Buber. Vol. 4. Jerusalem: Misrad ha-Chinukh ve-ha-Tarbut, 1964.

Klier, John D. "Polish Shtetls under Russian Rule." *Polin* 17 (2004): 97–108.

————. *Russia Gathers Her Jews: The Origins of 'the Jewish Question' in Russia, 1772–1825*. De Kalb: Northern Illinois University Press, 1986.

Koselleck, Reinhart. *Futures Past: On the Semantics of Historical Time*. Translated by Keith Tribe. Cambridge: Mass.: MIT Press, 1985.

Kovner, Isaac. *Sefer ha-Matzref*. Edited by Shmuel Fiener. Jerusalem: Mossad Bialik, 1998.

Krochmal, Nachman. *Moreh Nevukhei ha-Zeman*. Lemberg: M. Volf, 1863.

Kruk, Herman. *The Last Days of the Jerusalem of Lithuania: Chronicles from the Vilna Ghetto and the Camps, 1939–1944*. Edited by Benjamin Harshav and translated by Barbara Harshav. New Haven: Yale University Press, 2002.

Kugel, James L. *The Idea of Biblical Poetry: Parallelism and Its History*. New Haven: Yale University Press, 1981.

Kuznitz, Cecile E. "On the Street: Yiddish Culture and the Urban Landscape in Interwar Vilna." In *Yiddish Language and Culture: Then and Now*, edited by Leonard Jay Greenspoon. Omaha, Neb.: Creighton University Press, 1998.

Lamm, Norman, ed. *The Religious Thought of the Hasidim*. New York: Yeshiva University Press, 1999.

———. *Torah Lishmah: Torah for Torah's Sake in the Works of Rabbi Hayyim of Volozhin and His Contemporaries*. New York: Ktav, 1989.

Landau, Bezalel. *Ha-Gaon ha-Hasid mi-Vilna*. Jerusalem: 1964.

Landau, Eliyahu. *Sefer Minchat Eliyahu*. Jerusalem: 1927.

Le Boulluec, Alain. *La notion d'heresie dans la literature Grecque*. Vol. 1. Paris: Etudes Augustiniennes, 1985.

Lederhendler, Eli. *The Road to Modern Jewish Politics: Political Tradition and Political Reconstruction in the Jewish Community in Tsarist Russia*. New York: Oxford University Press, 1989.

Leibniz, Gottfried W. *The Correspondence between Leibniz and Arnauld*. Edited and expanded by Jonathan Bennet (2010). Available at http://www.earlymoderntexts.com/pdfbits/leiba2.pdf. Last accessed May 1, 2011.

———. "Discourse on Metaphysics (1686)." Pp. 53–93 in *Philosophical Texts*, translated by Richard Francks and R. S. Woolhouse. Oxford: Oxford University Press, 1998.

———. *Monadology: An Edition for Students*. Edited by Nicholas Rescher. Pittsburgh: University of Pittsburgh Press, 1991.

———. *New Essays on Human Understanding*. Edited and translated by Peter Remnant and Jonathan Bennett. Cambridge: Cambridge University Press, 1981.

———. "Observationes ad Rabbi Mosis Maimonidis librum qui inscribitur Doctor Perplexorum." In *La philosophie juive et la cabale*, edited by Alexandre Foucher de Careil. Paris: 1861.

———. "On Nature Itself." Translated by Jonathan Bennett. 2005. Available at www.earlymoderntexts.com/pdf/leibnat.pdf. Last accessed May 1, 2011.

———. *Philosophical Papers and Letters*. Edited and translated by Leroy E. Loemker. 1st ed. Chicago: University of Chicago Press, 1956; 2d ed. Dordrecht: D. Reidel, 1970.

———. *Die Philosophische Schriften von Gottfried Wilhelm Leibniz*. Edited by C. I. Gerhardt. 7 vols., 1875–1890. Reprint, Hildesheim: Olms, 1960.

———. *Textes inédits*. Edited by G. Grua. Paris: 1948.

———. *Theodicy*. Edited by Austin Farrer and translated by E. M. Huggard. New Haven: Yale University Press, 1952.

Leibowitz, Nechamah. *Iyyunim Chadashim be-Sefer Shemot*. Jerusalem: World Jewish Agency, 1969.

Leiman, Shnayer. "Dwarfs on the Shoulders of Giants." *Tradition* 27, no. 3 (Spring 1993): 90–94.

———. "When a Rabbi Is Accused of Heresy: The Stance of the Gaon of Vilna in the Emden-Eibeschuetz Controversy." Pp. 251–263 in *Me'ah She'arim: Studies in Medieval Jewish Spiritual Life in Memory of Isadore Twersky*, edited by Ezra Fleischer, Gerald Blidstein, Carmi Horowitz, and Bernard Septimus. Jerusalem: Magnes Press, Hebrew University, 2001.

———. "Who Is Buried in the Vilna Gaon's Tomb? A Mysterious Tale with Seven Plots." *Jewish Action* 59, no. 2 (1998). Available at http://www.ou.org/publications/ja/5759winter/leiman.htm. Last accessed September 1, 2011.

Leventhal, Robert S. *The Disciplines of Interpretation: Lessing, Herder, Schlegel and Hermeneutics in Germany, 1750–1800*. New York: Walter de Gruyter, 1994.

Levin, Yehoshua Heschel. *Aliyot Eliyahu*. Vilna: 1856.

Levinas, Emmanuel. "Prayer without Demand." Pp. 225–234 in *The Levinas Reader*, edited by Sean Hand. Cambridge, Mass.: Blackwell, 1989.

Levine, Hillel. *The Kronika on Jacob Frank and the Frankist Movement*. Jerusalem: Israel Academy of Sciences and Humanities, 1984.

Levinsohn, Isaac Baer. *Teudah be-Yisrael*. Vilna: 1828.

Levita, Elijah. *Sefer Masoret ha-Masoret*. Venice: 1538.

Lewis, Arthur James. *Zinzendorf the Ecumenical Pioneer: A Study in the Moravian Mission to Christian Mission and Unity*. Philadelphia: Westminster, 1962.

Liady, Shneur Zalman. *Likkutei Amarim: Tanya*. Brooklyn, N.Y.: Kehot, 1984.

Lieberman, Saul. *Tosefet Rishonim*. Jerusalem: Bamberger Vahrman, 1937.

Liebes, Yehuda. "Hatikkun ha-Klali shel R. Nachman mi-Bratslav ve-Yachaso le-Shabta'ut." *Zion* 44 (1980): 201–245.

———. *Studies in Jewish Myth and Messianism*. Albany: State University of New York Press, 1993.

———. "Tzidkat ha-Tzadik: Yachas ha-Gaon mi-Vilna ve-Chugo Klapei ha-Shabta'ut." *Kabbalah* 9 (2003): 226–306.

Liebeschutz, Hans. "Max Weber's Historical Understanding of Judaism." *Leo Baeck Institute Yearbook* 9 (1964): 41–68.

Lifshitz, Yehudah. *Nachal Yehudah*. Kovno: 1920.

Lifshitz, Yisrael. Introduction to *Biur ha-Gra al Shulchan Arukh Choshen Mishpat*. Königsberg: 1856.

Little, David. *Religion, Order, and Law: A Study in Pre-Revolutionary England*. Chicago: University of Chicago Press, 1984.

Litvak, Olga. *Conscription and the Search for Modern Russian Jewry*. Bloomington: Indiana University Press, 2006.

Loewinger, David S., and Bernard D. Weinryb. *Catalogue of the Hebrew Manuscripts in the Library of the Juedisch-Theologisches Seminar in Breslau, a Publication of the Leo Baeck Institute, New York*. Wiesbaden: Harrassowitz, 1965.

Lorentz, Stanislaw. *Jan Krzysztof Glaubitz, Architekt Wileński XVIII wieku*. Warsaw: 1937.

Lowenstein, Steven. *The Berlin Jewish Community: Enlightenment, Family, and Crisis, 1770–1830*. New York: Oxford University Press, 1994.

———. "The Readership of Mendelssohn's Bible Translation." *Hebrew Union College Annual* 53 (1982): 179–213.

Lowth, Robert. *Isaiah: A New Translation, with a Preliminary Dissertation and Notes, Critical, Philological and Explanatory*. Reprint, London: Thomas Tegg, 1835.

———. *Lectures on the Sacred Poetry of the Hebrews*. Hildesheim: Georg Olms Verlag, 1969.

Lukowski, Jerzy. *The Partitions of Poland, 1772, 1793, 1795*. London: Longman, 1999.

Lunski, Chaikel. *Fun Vilner Geto: Geshtaltn un bilder*. Vilna: 1920.

———. *Legendes: Eynike vegn Vilner Goen*. Vilna: 1924.

Luria, David. "Aliyat Kir." In Yehoshua Heschel Levin, *Aliyot Eliyahu*. Vilna: 1856.

Luzzatto, Moses Hayyim. *Da'at Tevunot*. Jerusalem: 1943.

———. *Derekh Tevunot*. Amsterdam: 1742; Jerusalem: Eshkol, 1973.

Maciejko, Paweł. *Jacob Frank and the Frankist Movement, 1755–1816*. Philadelphia: University of Pennsylvania Press, 2011.

MacIntyre, Alasdair. *After Virtue: A Study in Moral Theory*. Notre Dame, Ind.: University of Notre Dame Press, 1981.

Mack, Michael. *German Idealism and the Jews: The Inner Anti-Semitism of Philosophy and German Jewish Responses*. Chicago: University of Chicago Press, 2003.

Magid, Shaul. "Deconstructing the Mystical: The Anti-Mystical Kabbalism in Rabbi Hayyim of Volozhin's *Nefesh Ha-Hayyim*." *Journal of Jewish Thought and Philosophy* 9, no. 1 (1999): 21–67.

———. "The Politics of (Un)Conversion: The 'Mixed Multitude' ('Erev Rav) as Conversos in Rabbi Hayyim Vital's 'Ets Ha-Da'at Tov.'" *Jewish Quarterly Review* 95, no. 4 (2005): 625–666.

Mahler, Raphael. *Hasidism and the Jewish Enlightenment: Their Confrontation in Galicia and Poland in the First Half of the Nineteenth Century*. Philadelphia: The Jewish Publication Society of America, 1985.

Mahmood, Saba. *Politics of Piety: The Islamic Revival and the Feminist Subject*. Princeton, N.J.: Princeton University Press, 2005.

Maimon, Judah Leib. *Sefer ha-Gra*. 2 vols. Jerusalem: Mossad ha-Rav Kook, 1953.

———. *Toldot ha-Gra*. Jerusalem: Mossad ha-Rav Kook, 1954.

Maimon, Solomon. *Solomon Maimon: An Autobiography*. Trans. J. Clark Murray. Urbana: University of Illinois Press, 2001.

Maimonides, Moses. *The Guide of the Perplexed*. Translated by Shlomo Pines. Chicago: Chicago University Press, 1963.

Maltzan, Shmuel. *Barak ha-Shachar*. Vilna: 1863.

———. *Even Shlomo*. Berlin, 1889.

Mannheim, Karl. "Conservative Thought." Pp. 156–161 in *Karl Mannheim*, edited by Kurt Wolf. New York: Oxford University Press, 1971.

Mapu, Abraham. *Mikhtivei Avraham Mapu*. Edited by Ben-Zion Dinur. Jerusalem: Mossad Bialik, 1970.

Marcus, Ivan. "Israeli Medieval Jewish Historiography: From Nationalist Positivism to New Cultural and Social Histories." *Zion* 74 (2009): 109–140.

———. *Piety and Society: The Jewish Pietists of Medieval Germany*. Leiden: E.J. Brill, 1981.

———. "The Politics and Ethics of Pietism in Judaism: The Hasidim of Medieval Germany." *Journal of Religious Ethics* 8 (1980): 227–258.

Margoliot, Yehudah Leib. *Atzei Eden*. Frankfurt am Main: 1802.

Matthews, John F. *Laying Down the Law: A Study of the Theodosian Code*. New Haven: Yale University Press, 2000.

McDonough, Jeffrey K. "Leibniz: Creation *and* Conservation *and* Concurrence." *Leibniz Review* 17 (2007): 31–60.

Mecklenburg, Ya'akov T. *Ha-Ketav ve-ha-Kabbalah*. Leipzig: O.L. Fritzsche, 1839.

Meier, Georg Friedrich. *Versuch einer Allgemeinen Auslegungskunst*. Düsseldorf: Stern-Verlag, 1965.

Meir ben Shmuel. *Rashbam's Commentary on Leviticus and Numbers: An Annotated Translation*. Edited and translated by Martin Lockshin. Providence: Brown Judaic Studies, 2001.

Melamed, Abraham. *Al Kitfei Anakim: Toldot ha-Pulmus bein ha-Achronim le-Rishonim ba-Hagut ha-Yehudit be-Yemei ha-Beinayim u-ve-Reishit ha-Et ha-Chadashah*. Ramat-Gan: Bar Ilan University Press, 2003.

Menahem ben Shlomo. *Beit ha-Bechira al Mesekhet Avot*. Jerusalem: 1964.

Menahem Mendel of Shklov. *Sefer Derekh ha-Kodesh*. Reprint, Jerusalem: Kolel Torat ha-Chakham, 1998.

Menashe ben Yosef. *Alfei Menashe*. Vilna: Ha-Meshutafim ha-Negidim, 1822.

———. *Sefer Binat Mikra*. Grodno: 1817.

Mendelssohn, Moses. *Gesammelte Schriften Jubiläumsausgabe*. Edited by F. Bamberger, A. Altmann, et al. Stuttgart: Frommann, 1971–1975.

———. *Jerusalem; or, On Religious Power and Judaism*. Trans. Allan Arkush. Hanover, N.H.: Brandeis University Press by University Press of New England, 1983.

Mendes-Flohr, Paul R., and Jehuda Reinharz, eds. *The Jew in the Modern World: A Documentary History*. 2d ed. Oxford: Oxford University Press, 1995.

Menes, Abraham. "Patterns of Jewish Scholarship in Eastern Europe." Pp. 376–392 in *The Jews: Their History, Culture and Religion*, vol. 1, edited by Louis Finkelstein. New York: Harper, 1960.

Merton, Robert. *On the Shoulders of Giants: A Shandean Postscript*. Chicago: University of Chicago Press, 1993.

Meyer, Michael A. *Judaism within Modernity: Essays on Jewish Historiography and Religion*. Detroit: Wayne State University Press, 2001.

———. *The Origins of the Modern Jew: Jewish Identity and European Culture in Germany, 1749–1824*. Detroit: Wayne State University Press, 1967.

———. "Tradition and Modernity Reconsidered." Pp. 465–469 in *The Uses of Tradition: Jewish Continuity in the Modern Era*, edited by Jack Wertheimer. New York: Jewish Theological Seminary of America, 1992.

Michaelis, Johann D. *Mosaisches Recht*. Frankfurt am Main: Johann Gottlieb Garbe, 1770.

Mirsky, Yehudah. "An Intellectual and Spiritual Biography of Rabbi Avraham Yitzhaq Ha-Cohen Kook from 1865 to 1904." Ph.D. diss., Harvard University, 2007.

Momigliano, Arnaldo. "A Note on Max Weber's Definition of Judaism as a Pariah Religion." *History and Theory* 29, no. 1 (1980): 313–318.

Mondshine, Yehoshua. "Kinat ha-Mitnagdim le-Minhagei Ashkenaz." *Kerem Habad* 4, no. 1 (November–December 1992): 158–181.

———. "Parnasei Vilna ve-ha-Gra ve-Milchamtam be-Hasidut." *Kerem Habad* 4, no. 1 (1992): 182–221.

Morgenstern, Arie. "An Attempt to Hasten the Redemption." *Jewish Action* 58, no. 1 (Fall 1997): 38–44.

———. "Bein Banim le-Talmidim: Ha-Ma'avak al Moreshet ve-al ha-Ideologia." *Dat* 53 (2004): 83–125.

———. *Meshichiyut ve-Yishuv Eretz Yisrael: Ba-Machatzit ha-Rishonah shel ha-Meah ha-19*. Jerusalem: Yad Yitzchak Ben Tzvi, 1985.

————. *Mysticism and Messianism: From Luzzatto to the Vilna Gaon*. Jerusalem: Meor, 1999.

Moshe of Satanów. *Mishmeret ha-Kodesh*. Zolkiew: 1746.

Mueller-Vollmer, Kurt. *The Hermeneutics Reader: Texts of the German Tradition from the Enlightenment to the Present*. New York: Continuum, 2006.

Mühlau, Ferdinand. "Geschichte hebräischen Synonymik in the Zeitschrift der Deutschen Morgenländschen Gesellschaft." *Band* 17 (1863): 316–335.

Myers, David M. *Resisting History: Historicism and Its Discontents in Jewish Thought*. Princeton, N.J.: Princeton University Press, 2003.

Nachman of Bratslav. *Likkutei Etsot ha-Shalem*. Warsaw: 1913.

————. *Likkutei Moharan*. 2 vols. New York: 1957.

Nadler, Allan. *The Faith of the Mithnagdim: Rabbinic Responses to Hasidic Rapture*. Baltimore: Johns Hopkins University Press, 1997.

————. "The Gaon of Vilna and the Rabbinic Doctrine of Historical Decline." Pp. 137–161 in *Yashan mi-Pnei Chadash: Mechkarim be-Toldot Yehudei Mizrach Eropah u-ve-Tarbutam; Shai le-Immanuel Etkes*, edited by David Assaf and Ada Rapoport-Albert. Vol. 2. Jerusalem: Merkaz Zalman Shazar, 2009.

————. "Ha-Sintezia be-Hasidut Slonim bein Hasidut le-Limmud Torah be-Nusach ha-Mitnagdim." Pp. 395–415 in *Yeshivot u-Vatei Midrashot*, edited by Immanuel Etkes. Jerusalem: Merkaz Zalman Shazar, Hebrew University, 2006.

————. "The 'Rambam Revival' in Early Modern Jewish Thought: Maskilim, Mitnagdim, and Hasidism on Maimonides' *Guide for the Perplexed*." Pp. 36–61 in *Moses Maimonides: Communal Impact, Historic Legacy*, edited by Benny Kraut. New York: Queens College Press, 2005.

Nathan ben Yechiel. *Arukh ha-Shalem*. Edited by Alexander Kohut. Vienna: 1878.

Nathan (Nata) Hannover. *Yeven Metzulah*. Venice: 1653.

Niebuhr, H. Richard. *Schleiermacher on Christ and Religion: A New Introduction*. New York: Scribner, 1964.

Pachter, Mordekhai. "The Concept of 'Devekut' in the Homiletical Ethical Writings of 16th-Century Safed." Pp. 171–230 in *Studies in Medieval Jewish History and Literature*, Harvard Judaic Monographs, vol. 2. Cambridge, Mass.: Harvard University Press, 1984.

————. "Tnu'at ha-Mussar ve-ha-Kabbalah." Pp. 223–251 in *Yashan mi-Pnei Chadash: Mechkarim be-Toldot Yehudei Mizrach Eropah u-ve-Tarbutam; Shai le-Immanuel Etkes*, edited by David Assaf and Ada Rapoport-Albert. Vol. 1. Jerusalem: Merkaz Zalman Shazar, 2009.

Panitz, Michael. "Modernity and Mortality: The Transformation of Central European Jewish Responses to Death, 1750–1850." Ph.D. diss., Jewish Theological Seminary of America, 1989.

Parkinson, Roger. *The Fox of the North: The Life of Kutuzov, General of War and Peace*. London: Peter Davies, 1976.

Patai, Raphael. *The Hebrew Goddess: Jewish Folklore and Anthropology*. Detroit: Wayne State University Press, 1990.

Patai, Raphael, and Jennifer Patai. *The Myth of the Jewish Race*. Detroit: Wayne State University Press, 1994.

Pedersen, Johannes. *Israel: Its Life and Culture*. Translated Aslaug Mikkelsen Møller, A.I. Fausbell, and Johannes Pedersen. London: Oxford University Press, 1926.

Perl, Gil S. "'Emek ha-Neziv': A Window into the Intellectual Universe of Rabbi Naftali Zvi Yehudah Berlin." Ph.D. diss., Harvard University, 2006.

———. "No Two Minds Are Alike: Tolerance and Pluralism in the Work of Netziv." *Torah u-Madda* 12 (2004): 74–98.

Petrover, Moshe. "Le-Darkho shel ha-Gra bi-Biuro le-Shulchan Arukh." *Yeshurun* 4 (1999): 726–735.

Petrovsky-Shtern, Yohanan. "Hasidism, Havurot, and the Jewish Street." *Jewish Social Studies* 10, no. 2 (2004): 20–54.

———. *Jews in the Russian Army, 1827–1917: Drafted into Modernity*. Cambridge: Cambridge University Press, 2009.

Philipson, David. *Max Lilienthal, American Rabbi: Life and Writings*. New York: Bloch Publishing, 1915.

Piekarz, Mendel. *Bi-Yemei Tzmichat ha-Hasidut*. Jerusalem: Mossad Bialik, 1978.

———. "Hasidism as a Socio-Religious Movement." Pp. 225–248 in *Hasidism Reappraised*, edited by Ada Rapoport-Albert. London: Vallentine Mitchell, 1996.

Pinkas Medinat Lita. Edited by Simon Dubnow. Berlin: 1925.

Plungian, Mordekhai. *Sefer Ben Porat*. Vilna: R. Yosef Reuven Bar Menahem Man Romm, 1858.

Politella, Joseph. "Platonism, Aristotelianism and Cabalism in the Philosophy of Leibniz." Ph.D. diss., University of Pennsylvania, 1938.

Rabe, Johann Jacob. *Mischnah oder der Text des Talmuds*. Ansbach: 1760–1763.

Ran, Leyzer, collector and arranger. *Yerushalayim de-Lita: Ilustrirt un Dokumentirt*. 3 vols. New York: Vilna Album Committee, 1974.

Rapoport-Albert, Ada. "Al Ma'amad ha-Nashim ba-Shabta'ut." Pp. 143–328 in R. Elior, ed., *The Sabbatian Movement and Its Aftermath: Messianism, Sabbatianism and Frankism*, vol. 1. Jerusalem: 2001.

————. "God and the Zaddik as the Two Focal Points of Hasidic Worship." *History of Religions* 18, no. 4 (May 1979): 296–325.

————, ed. *Hasidism Reappraised*. Oxford: Littman Library, 1996.

Redding, Paul. *Continental Idealism: Leibniz to Nietzsche*. New York: Routledge, 2009.

Reif, Stefan. "A Defense of David Qimhi." *Hebrew Union College Annual* 44 (1973): 211–226.

Reiner, Elchanan. "Aliyat ha-Kehilah ha-Gedolah." *Gal-Ed* 20 (2006): 13–37.

————. "Beyond the Realm of the Haskalah." Pp. 123–133 in *Jahrbuch Des Simon Dubnow Instituts*, edited by David B. Ruderman and Shmuel Feiner, vol. 6. Leipzig: Vandenhoeck and Ruprecht, 2007.

————. "Hon Ma'amad Chevrati ve-Talmud Torah: Ha-kloiz be-Chevrah ha-Yehudit be-Mizrach Eropah ba-Meot 17–19." *Zion* 58 (1993): 287–328.

————. "Temurot be-Yeshivot Polin ve-Ashkenaz be-Meot ha-16–ha-18 ve-ha-Vikuach al ha-Pilpul." Pp. 9–80 in *Ke-Minhag Ashkenaz ve-Polin: Sefer Yovel le-Chone Shmeruk*, edited by Israel Bartal, Ezra Mendelson, and Chava Turniansky. Jerusalem: Merkaz Zalman Shazar, 1993.

————. "Yashan mi-Pnei Chadash: Al Temurot be-Tocknei Limmud be-Yeshivot Polin be-Meah ha-16 ve-Yeshivat ha-Ramah be-Krakow." Pp. 183–206 in *Remember the Word to Your Servant: Essays and Studies in Memory of Dov Rappel*, edited by Shmuel Glick. Jerusalem: 2007.

Ringer, Fritz. *The Decline of the German Mandarins*. Hanover, N.H.: Wesleyan University Press by University Press of New England, 1990.

Rivlin, Benjamin. *Geviei Gavia ha-Kessef*. Warsaw: 1897.

Rivlin, Yosef. "Biur ha-Gra le-Sefer Yonah." *Kiryat Sefer* 62 (1989): 920–924.

Rosin, David. *Peirush ha-Torah asher Katav Rashbam*. (Cover title: "Peirush ha-Rashbam ha-Shalem al ha-Torah 'Mahadurat Rozin.'") Breslau: S. Shottlender, 1881.

Rosman, Moshe. *The Lord's Jews: Magnate-Jewish Relations in the Polish-Lithuanian Commonwealth*. Cambridge, Mass.: Harvard University Center for Jewish Studies, 1990.

————. "Miedzyboz and Rabbi Israel Baal Shem Tov." Pp. 209–226 in *Essential Papers on Hasidism: Origins to Present*, edited by Gershon Hundert. New York: New York University Press, 1991.

Ross, George MacDonald. "Leibniz and the Origin of Things." Pp. 241–257 in *Leibniz and Adam*, edited by M. Dascal and E. Yakira. Tel Aviv: University Publishing Projects, 1993.

Ruderman, David. *Jewish Thought and Scientific Discovery in Early Modern Europe*. Detroit: Wayne State University Press, 2001.

Rudolph, Lloyd, and Susanne H. Rudolph. *The Modernity of Tradition: Political Development in India*. Chicago: University of Chicago Press, 1967.

Russell, Bertrand. *A Critical Exposition of the Philosophy of Leibniz*. Boston: Longwood Press, 1989.

Rustow, Marina. *Heresy and the Politics of Community: The Jews of the Fatmid Caliphate*. Ithaca, N.Y.: Cornell University Press, 2008.

Salanter, Israel. *Sefer Tevunah*. Köningsberg: August Strobbe, 1861.

Samet, Moshe. *He-Chadash Asur min ha-Torah*. Jerusalem: Merkaz le-Cheker Toldot Yisrael, 2005.

Sandler, Peretz. *Ha-Biur le-Torah shel Moshe Mendelssohn ve-Siato, Hithavuto ve-Hashpa'ato*. Jerusalem: Reuven Mas, 1940.

———. "On the Problem of *PaRDeS* and the Fourfold Method." Pp. 222–237 in *Sefer Urbach*, edited by Arthur Biram. Jerusalem: Kiryat Sefer, 1955.

Satanov, Isaac. *Sefer ha-Shorashim*. Berlin: 1780; Prague: S. Hamburger & J. Bamberger, 1803.

Schacter, Jacob J. "Editor's Introduction." *Torah u-Madda* 2 (1990): 5–6.

———. "Haskalah, Secular Studies, and the Closing of the Yeshiva in Volozhin in 1892." *Torah u-Madda* 2 (1990): 76–133.

———. "Rabbi Jacob Emden: His Life and Major Works." Ph.D. diss., Harvard University, 1988.

Schatz, Andrea. "Incomplete Revolution." *Jewish Quarterly Review* 97, no. 1 (2007): 137–146.

———. " 'Peoples Pure of Speech': The Religious and Secular, and the Jewish Beginnings of Modernity." Pp. 169–187 in *Jahrbuch Des Simon Dubnow Instituts*, vol. 6, edited by David B. Ruderman and Shmuel Feiner. Leipzig: Vandenhoeck and Ruprecht, 2007.

Schatz-Uffenheimer, Rivka. *Hasidism as Mysticism: Quietistic Elements in Eighteenth-Century Hasidic Thought*. Translated by Jonathan Chipman. Princeton, N.J.: Princeton University Press; Jerusalem: Magnes Press, Hebrew University, 1993.

———. "Moshe Hayim Luzzatto's Thought against the Background of Theodicy Literature." Pp. 173–199 in *Justice and Righteousness: Biblical Themes and Their Influence*, edited by Henning Graf Reventlow and Yair Hoffman. Sheffield, Eng.: JSOT Press, 1992.

Schechter, Salomon. *Studies in Judaism*. 2 vols. Piscataway, N.J.: Gorgias Press, 2003.

Schlereth, Thomas. *The Cosmopolitan Ideal in Enlightenment Thought: Its Form and Function in the Ideas of Franklin, Hume, and Voltaire, 1694–1790*. Notre Dame, Ind.: University of Notre Dame Press, 1977.

Schnold, Rachel. *Aderet Eliyahu: Ha-Gaon mi-Vilna, Demuto ve-Hashpa'ato*. Tel Aviv: Beit ha-Tefutsot al shem Nahum Goldmann, 1998.

Schochet, Elijah J. *The Hasidic Movement and the Gaon of Vilna*. Northvale, N.J.: Jason Aronson, 1994.

Scholem, Gershom. "Dvekut or Communion with God." Pp. 203–227 in Scholem, *The Messianic Idea in Judaism*. New York: Schocken Books, 1971.

———. "Ha-Maggid shel R. Yosef Titatzak." *Sefunot* 11, no. 1 (1971–1977): 69–112.

———. *Kabbalah*. New York: 1987.

———. "Martin Buber's Interpretation of Hasidism." Pp. 227–250 in Scholem, *The Messianic Idea in Judaism*. New York: Schocken Books, 1971.

———. *Sabbatai Sevi: The Mystical Messiah*. Trans. R. J. Werblowski. Princeton, N.J.: Princeton University Press, 1973.

———. "Shtei Eduyot Ha-Rishonot al Chavurot ha-Hasidim ve-ha-Besht." *Tarbiz* 20 (1949): 228–240.

Schreiber, Aaron M. "Hashkafato Shel ha-Gra: Al Chashivut ha-Haskalah ha-Kelalit ve-al ha-Kesher le-Yemot ha-Mashiach." *Bekhol Derakhekha Daehu* 9 (Summer 1999): 5–28.

———. "The Hatam Sofer's Nuanced Attitude towards Secular Learning, Maskilim, and Reformers." *Torah u-Madda* 11 (2003): 123–173.

Schwarzschild, Steven, and Henry Schwarzschild. "Two Lives in the Jewish Frühaufklärung: Raphael Levi Hannover and Moses Abraham Wolff." *Leo Baeck Institute Yearbook* 29 (1984): 229–276.

Scuchard, Marcia Keith. "Leibniz, Benzelius and the Kabbalistic Roots of Swedish Illuminism." Pp. 84–106 in *Leibniz, Mysticism and Religion*, edited by Allison P. Coudert, Richard H. Popkin, and Gordon M. Weiner. Boston: Kluwer Academic, 1998.

Seeskin, Kenneth. *Maimonides on the Origins of the World*. New York: Cambridge University Press, 2007.

Shapiro, Marc. *Between the Yeshiva World and Modern Orthodoxy: The Life and Works of Rabbi Jehiel Jacob Weinberg*. Oxford: Littman Library of Jewish Civilization, 1999.

Shapiro, Yisrael. "Askolot Chalukot be-She'elat Torah u-Madda'im be-Veit Midrasho shel ha-Gra." *Bekhol Derakhekha Daehu* 13 (2003): 5–53.

Shashar, Michael. *Sambatyon: Essays on Jewish Holidays*. Jerusalem: World Zionist Organization, 1987.

Shatz, David. "Maimonides' Moral Theory." Pp. 167–193 in *Cambridge Companion to Maimonides*, edited by Kenneth Seeskin. Cambridge: Cambridge University Press, 2005.

Shatzky, Jacob. "Kulture-Geschichte fun der Haskole bei Yidden in Lita." Pp. 691–758 in *Lita*, edited by Mark Wishnitzer, vol. 1. New York: Futuro Press, 1951.

Sheehan, Jonathan. *The Enlightenment Bible: Translation, Scholarship, Culture.* Princeton, N.J.: Princeton University Press, 2005.

Shils, Edward. *Tradition.* Chicago: University of Chicago Press, 1981.

Shisha, Avraham H. "Seder Hadpasatam shel Biur ha-Gra al Shulchan Arukh." *Yeshurun* 5 (1999): 678–696.

Shmeruk, Chone. "Ha-Hasidut be-Askei Ha-Chakirut." *Zion* 35 (1970): 182–192.

———. "Mashmautah ha-Chevratit shel ha-Shechitah ha-Hasidit." Pp. 160–185 in *Tsadik ve-Edah: Hebetim Historiyim ve-Chevratim be-Cheker ha-Hasidut,* edited by David Assaf. Jerusalem: Merkaz Zalman Shazar, 2001.

Shmuel ben Eliezer. *Darkhei Noam.* Köningsberg: 1764.

Shuchat, Raphael. "The Debate over Secular Studies among the Disciples of the Vilna Gaon." *Torah u-Madda* 8 (1999): 283–294.

———. "Ha-Gra mi-Vilna ve-Limmud ha-Chokhmot ha-Klaliot." *Bekhol Derakhekha Daehu* 2 (1996): 89–106.

———. *Olam Nistar be-Memadei ha-Zeman.* Ramat Gan: Bar-Ilan University Press, 2008.

———. "Peirush ha-Gra mi-Vilna le-Mishnat Hasidim: Mashal ve-Nimshal be-Kitvei ha-Ari." *Kabbalah* 3 (1998): 265–302.

Shulvas, Moses A. *From East to West: The Westward Migration of Jews from Eastern Europe during the Seventeenth and Eighteenth Centuries.* Detroit: Wayne State University Press, 1971.

———. "Ha-Torah ve-Limmudah be-Polin ve-Lita." P. 2 in *Pinkas Va'ad Arba Aratzot: Acta congressus generalis Judaeorum regni Poloniae (1580–1764) quae supersunt omnia cum deperditorum fragmentis et testimonies.* Jerusalem: Mossad Bialik, 1945.

Silber, Michael K. "The Emergence of Ultra-Orthodoxy: The Invention of a Tradition." Pp. 23–84 in *The Uses of Tradition: Jewish Continuity in the Modern Era,* edited by Jack Wertheimer. New York: Jewish Theological Seminary of America, 1992.

———. "A Hungarian Rhapsody in Blue: Jacob Katz's Tardy Surrender to Hagar's Allure." Pp. 141–161 in *The Pride of Jacob: Essays on Jacob Katz and his Work,* edited by Jay Harris. Cambridge, Mass.: Harvard University Press, 2002.

Silberstein, Laurence J. *The Postzionism Debates: Power and Knowledge in Israeli Culture.* New York: Routledge Press, 1999.

Simon, Uriel. "Le-Darko ha-Parshanit shel Ibn Ezra al-pi Shloshet Biurav le-Pasuk Echad." *Sefer ha-Shanah shel Universitat Bar Ilan* 3 (1965): 92–138.

Sinkoff, Nancy. *Out of the Shtetl: Making Jews Modern in the Polish Borderlands*. Providence: Brown Judaic Studies, 2004.

Sklare, Marshall. *Conservative Judaism: An American Religious Movement*. Lanham, Md.: University Press of America, 1985.

Socher, Abe. *The Radical Enlightenment of Solomon Maimon: Judaism, Heresy, and Philosophy*. Stanford: Stanford University Press, 2006.

Soloveitchik, Haym. "Catastrophe and Halakhic Creativity: Ashkenaz 1096, 1242, 1306, and 1298." *Jewish History* 12, no. 1 (1998): 71–85.

———. *Derekh ha-Limmud*, 1989. Recording available at http://www.yutorah. org/. Last accessed May 2006.

———. "Halakhah, Hermeneutics, and Martyrdom in Medieval Ashkenaz (Part I of II)." *Jewish Quarterly Review* 94, no. 1 (Winter 2003): 77–109.

———. "Halakhah, Hermeneutics, and Martyrdom in Medieval Ashkenaz (Part II of II)." *Jewish Quarterly Review* 94, no. 2 (Spring 2004): 278–299.

———. "Piety, Pietism and German Pietism: 'Sefer Hasidim I' and the Influence of Hasidei Ashkenaz." *Jewish Quarterly Review* 92, nos. 3–4 (2002): 455–493.

———. "Rupture and Reconstruction: The Transformation of Contemporary Orthodoxy." *Tradition* 28, no. 4 (1994): 64–130.

Sorkin, David J. *The Berlin Haskalah and German Religious Thought: Orphans of Knowledge*. London: Vallentine Mitchell, 2000.

———. "The Early Haskalah." Pp. 9–26 in *New Perspectives on the Haskalah*, edited by Shmuel Feiner and David J. Sorkin. Oxford: Littman Library of Jewish Civilization, 2001.

———. "The Genesis and Ideology of Emancipation, 1806–1840." *Leo Baeck Institute Yearbook* 32, no. 1 (1987): 11–40.

———. *Moses Mendelssohn and the Religious Enlightenment*. Berkeley: University of California Press, 1996.

———. *The Religious Enlightenment: Protestants, Jews, and Catholics from London to Vienna*. Princeton, N.J.: Princeton University Press, 2008.

Sorotzkin, David. "Kehillat ha-al Zeman be-Idan ha-Temurot: Kavim le-Hithavutan shel Tefisot ha-Zeman ve-ha-Kolektiv ke-Basis le-Hagdarat Hitpatchut ha-Ortodoksiah ha-Yehudit be-Eropah be-Et ha-Chadashah." Ph.D. diss., Hebrew University, 2007.

Spalding, Moses Paul. "Toward a Modern Torah: Moses Mendelssohn's Use of a Banned Bible." *Modern Judaism* 19, no. 1 (1999): 67–82.

Spiegel, Ya'aḳov. *Amudim be-Toldot ha-Sefer ha-Ivri: Hagahot u-Megihim*. 2 vols. Ramat Gan: Bar-Ilan University Press, 1996.

Stampfer, Shaul. *Families, Rabbis and Education: Traditional Society in Nineteenth-Century Eastern Europe*. Oxford: Littman Library of Jewish Civilization, 2010.

BIBLIOGRAPHY

———. "Hasidic Yeshivot in Inter-War Poland." *Polin* 11 (1998): 3–24.

———. *Ha-Yeshivah ha-Litait be-Hithavutah.* Jerusalem: Merkaz Zalman Shazar, 1995.

———. "Heder Study, Knowledge of Torah and the Maintenance of Social Stratification in Traditional East European Jewish Society." *Studies in Jewish Education* 3 (1988): 271–289.

———. "On the Creation and the Perpetuation of the Image of the Gaon of Vilna." Pp. 39–69 in *Ha-Gra u-Veit Midrasho*, edited by Moshe Hallamish, Yosef Rivlin, and Raphael Shuchat. Ramat Gan: Bar Ilan University Press, 2003.

———. "The 1764 Census of Lithuanian Jewry and What It Can Teach Us." Pp. 91–121 in *Papers in Jewish Demography, 1993*. Jerusalem: 1997.

Stanislawski, Michael. *For Whom Do I Toil? Judah Leib Gordon and the Crisis of Russian Jewry*. New York: Oxford University Press, 1988.

———. "Towards an Analysis of the *Bi'ur* as Exegesis." Pp. 137–147 in *Neti'vot le-David: Jubilee Volume for David Weiss Halivni*, edited by Ya'akov Elman et al. Jerusalem: Ohrot Press, 2004.

———. *Tsar Nicholas I and the Jews: The Transformation of Jewish Society in Russia, 1825–1855*. Philadelphia: Jewish Publication Society, 1983.

Steinschneider, Hillel Noah Maggid. *Ir Vilna*. Edited by M. Zalkin. Vilna: 1900; Jerusalem: Magnes Press, Hebrew University, 2002.

Stern, Eliyahu. "Cosmogony, Anthropogony, and Dissimulation in Elijah of Vilna's Philosophy." *Revue Internationale de Philosophie* (forthcoming).

———. "Modern Rabbinic Historiography and the Legacy of Elijah of Vilna: A Review Essay." *Modern Judaism* 24, no. 1 (February 2004): 79–90.

Stewart, Matthew. *The Courtier and the Heretic: Leibniz, Spinoza, and the Fate of God in the Modern World*. New York: Norton, 2006.

Stoeffler, F. Ernst. *German Pietism during the Eighteenth Century*. Leiden: E.J. Brill, 1973.

Stone, Daniel. *The Polish-Lithuanian State: 1386–1795*. Saint Louis: Washington University Press, 2001.

Stow, Kenneth R. "The Burning of the Talmud in 1553 in Light of Sixteenth-Century Catholic Attitudes toward the Talmud." *Bibliothèque d'Humanisme et Renaissance* 34 (1972): 435–459.

Strack, Hermann L., and Gunter Stemberger. *Introduction to Talmud and Midrash*. Translated by Markus Bokhmuehl. Edinburgh: T&T Clark, 1991.

Strote, Noah B. "The German Birth of the 'Psychological Jew' in an Age of Ethnic Pride." *New German Critique* 39, no. 1 (2012): 199–224.

Stroumsa, Gedaliahu G. "Form(s) of God: Some Notes on Metatron and Christ." *Harvard Theological Review* 76, no. 3 (July 1983): 269–288.

Šubas, Mejeris. "The Gaon's Views on Philosophy and Science." Pp. 65–74 in *The Gaon of Vilnius and the Annals of Jewish Culture*, edited by Izraelis Lempertas. Vilnius: Vilnius University Press, 1998.

Szondi, Peter. *Introduction to Literary Hermeneutics*. Translated by Martha Woodmansee. Cambridge: Cambridge University Press, 1995.

Tabori, Yosef. "Siddur ha-Gra." Pp. 11–25 in *Ha-Gra u-Veit Midrasho*, edited by Moshe Hallamish, Yosef Rivlin, and Raphael Shuchat. Ramat Gan: Bar-Ilan University Press, 2003.

Talmage, Frank. *Apples of Gold in Settings of Silver: Studies in Medieval Jewish Exegesis and Polemics*. Edited by Barry Dov Walfish. Toronto: Pontifical Institute of Medieval Studies, 1999.

Tamulynas, Alfonsas. "Demographic and Social Professional Structure of the Jewish Community of Vilnius." Pp. 331–335 in *The Gaon of Vilnius and the Annals of Jewish Culture*, edited by Izrealis Lempertas. Vilnius: Vilnius University Publishing House, 1998.

Ta-Shma, Israel. " 'Halakha ke-Batrai.' " *Shenaton la-Mishpat ha-Ivri* 6–7 (1979–1980): 405–423.

———. *Minhag Ashkenaz ha-Kadmon: Cheker ve-Iyyun*. Jerusalem: Magnes Press, Hebrew University, 1992.

———. "Seder Hadpasatam shel Chidushei ha-Rishonim le-Talmud: Perek le-Toldot ha-'Pilpul.' " *Kiryat Sefer* 50, no. 2 (1975): 325–336.

———. "The Vilna Gaon and the Author of 'Sha'agat Aryeh,' the 'Pnei Yehoshua' and the Book 'Tziyon le-Nefesh Chaya': On the History of New Currents in Rabbinic Literature on the Eve of the Enlightenment." *Sidra* 15 (1999): 181–191.

Taylor, Charles. *Sources of the Self: The Making of Modern Identity*. Cambridge: Harvard University Press, 1989.

Tchernowitz, Chaim. *Toldot ha-Poskim*. 3 vols. New York: 1947.

Tchorsh, Katriel Fishel. "Sirtutim le-Demuto shel ha-Gra." *Talpiyot* 4 (1949): 155–166.

Teller, Adam. "The Gaon of Vilna and the Communal Rabbinate in Eighteenth-Century Poland and Lithuania." In *The Gaon of Vilnius and the Annals of Jewish Culture: Materials of the International Scientific Conference, Vilnius, September 10–12, 1997*. Edited by Izrealis Lempertas, 142–153. Vilnius: Vilnius University Publishing House, 1998.

———. "Hasidism and the Challenge of Geography: The Polish Background to the Spread of the Hasidic Movement." *AJS Review* 30, no. 1 (2006): 1–29.

———. *Koach ve-Hashpa'ah: Ha-Yehudim be-Achuzot Beit Radzhivil be-Lita be-Meah ha-18*. Jerusalem: Merkaz Zalman Shazar, 2005.

————. "The Laicization of Early Modern Jewish Society: The Development of the Polish Rabbinate in the Sixteenth Century." Pp. 33–349 in *Schöpferische Momente des europäischen Judentums in der frühen Neuzeit*, edited by Michael Graetz. Heidelberg: Universitätsverlag C. Winter, 2000.

Teter, Magdalena. "Jewish Conversions to Catholicism in the Polish-Lithuanian Commonwealth of the Seventeenth and Eighteenth Centuries." *Jewish History* 17, no. 3 (2003): 257–283.

Thompson, P. Martyn. "Reception Theory and the Interpretation of Historical Meaning." *History and Theory* 32 (1993): 248–272.

Tipps, Dean C. "Modernization Theory and the Comparative Study of Societies: A Critical Perspective." *Comparative Studies in Society and History* 15, no. 2 (1973): 199–226.

Tirosh-Samuelson, Hava. "Philosophy and Kabbalah: 1200–1600." Pp. 218–258 in *The Cambridge Companion to Medieval Jewish Philosophy*, edited by Daniel H. Frank and Oliver Leaman. Cambridge: Cambridge University Press, 2003.

Tishby, Isaiah. *Messianic Mysticism: Moses Hayyim Luzzatto and the Padua School*. Translated by Morris Hoffman. Oxford: The Littman Library of Jewish Civilization, 2008.

Twersky, Isadore. *Introduction to the Code of Maimonides (Mishneh Torah)*. New Haven: Yale University Press, 1980.

————, trans. and ed. *Maimonides Reader*. New York: Behrman House, 1972.

Tzimrion, Tzemach. *Moshe Mendelssohn ve-ha-Ideologia shel ha-Haskalah*. Tel Aviv: Tel Aviv University Press, 1984.

Tzitron, Shmuel Leib. "Milchamta ha-Dinastiyot bi-Yeshivat Volozhin." Pp. 81–93 in *Yeshivot Lita: Pirkei Zichronot*, edited by Immanuel Etkes and Shlomo Tikotsinski. Jerusalem: Merkaz Zalman Shazar, 2004.

Tzvi Hirsh ben Shmuel Zanvil Segal. *Margolit ha-Torah*. Fritzk: 1788.

Venclova, Tomas. "Vilnius/Wilno/Vilna: The Myth of Division and the Myth of Connection." Pp. 11–28 in *History of the Literary Cultures of East-Central Europe: Junctures and Disjunctures in the Nineteenth and Twentieth Centuries*, edited by Marcel Cornis-Pope and John Neubauer, vol. 2. Philadelphia: John Benjamins Publishing, 2004.

Walzer, Michael. *The Revolution of the Saints: A Study in the Origins of Radical Politics*. Cambridge, Mass.: Harvard University Press, 1965.

Waters, Malcolm, ed. *Modernity: Critical Concepts*. New York: Routledge, 1999.

Waxman, Chaim I. "From Institutional Decay to Primary Day: American Orthodox Jewry since World War II." *American Jewish Historical Society* 91, nos. 3–4 (2003): 405–421.

Weber, Max. *General Economic History*. Translated by Frank H. Knight. New Brunswick, N.J.: Transaction Publishers, 1981.

————. *The Protestant Ethic and the Spirit of Capitalism*. Translated by Talcott Parsons. New York: Courier Dover, 2003.

————. *The Theory of Social and Economic Organization*. Edited by Talcott Parsons. New York: Free Press, 1964.

Weiner, Philip P. *Dictionary of the History of Ideas: Studies of Selected Pivotal Ideas*. New York: Scribner, 1973.

Weinreich, Max. *History of the Yiddish Language*. Edited by Paul Glasser and translated by Shlomo Nobel. New Haven: Yale University Press, 2008.

Weiss, Raymond. *Maimonides' Ethics: The Encounter of Philosophic and Religious Morality*. Chicago: University of Chicago, 1991.

Welch, Claude. *In This Name: The Doctrine of the Trinity in Contemporary Theology*. New York: Scribner, 1952.

————. *Protestant Thought in the Nineteenth Century*, vol. 1. 2 vols. New Haven: Yale University Press, 1972.

————. *Protestant Thought in the Nineteenth Century*, vol. 2. 2 vols. Eugene, Ore.: Wipf and Stock, 1985.

Wellbery, David. *Lessing's Laocoon: Semiotics and Aesthetics in the Age of Reason*. Cambridge: Cambridge University Press, 1984.

Werblowski, Zwi. *Joseph Karo: Lawyer and Mystic*. Philadelphia: Jewish Publication Society, 1977.

Werses, Shmuel. *Hakitzah Ami: Sifrut ha-Haskalah be-Idan ha-Modernizatziah*. Jerusalem: Magnes Press, 2000.

Wertheimer, Jack. "The Orthodox Moment." *Commentary* 107, no. 2 (February 1999): 18–24.

Westerhoff, Jan. "Poeta Calculans: Harsdöorffer, Leibniz, and the *Mathesis Universalis*." *Journal of the History of Ideas* 60, no. 3 (1999): 449–467.

Wetzler, Isaac. *The Libes Briv of Isaac Wetzlar*. Edited and translated by Morris Faierstein. Providence: Scholars Press, 1996.

White, Hayden. *Figural Realism: Studies in the Mimeses Effect*. Baltimore: Johns Hopkins University Press, 1999.

————. *Metahistory: The Historical Imagination in Nineteenth-Century Europe*. Baltimore: Johns Hopkins University Press, 1973.

Wiernik, Peter. "Der Vilner Goen." Pp. 213–249 in *Lebens-beshraybungen fun ale Goenim un Gdoylim fun Yidishen Folk*, edited by Philip Krantz, vol. 3. New York: International Publishing, 1910.

Wiesen, Israel. *Geonei ve-Gedolei Yisrael*. Kettwig: 1881.

Wilensky, Mordekhai. "Hasidic and Mitnagdic Polemics in the Jewish Communities of Eastern Europe: The Hostile Phase." Pp. 89–113 in *Tolerance and Movements of Religious Dissent in Eastern Europe*, edited by Bela K. Kiraly. New York: Columbia University Press, 1975.

———. *Hasidim u-Mitnagdim: Le-Toldot ha-Pulmus she-Beinehem ba-Shanim, 5532–5565.* 2 vols. Jerusalem: Mossad Bialik, 1990.

Williams, Richard R. *Schleiermacher the Theologian: The Construction of the Doctrine of God.* Philadelphia: Fortress Press, 1978.

Wilson, Catherine. *Leibniz's Metaphysics: A Historical and Comparative Study.* Manchester, Eng.: Manchester University Press, 1989.

Winograd, Yeshayahu. *Otzar Sifrei ha-Gra.* Jerusalem: Kerem Eliyahu, 2003.

Wishnitzer, Mark. "Die Geschichte fun Yiddin in *Lita.*" Pp. 43–88 in *Lita.* New York: Futuro Press, 1951.

Wodziński, Marcin. *Haskalah and Hasidism in the Kingdom of Poland.* Oxford: Littman Library of Jewish Civilization, 2005.

———. "Haskalah and Politics Reconsidered: The Case of the Kingdom of Poland, 1815–1860." Pp. 163–197 in *Yashan mi-Pnei Chadash: Mechkarim be-Toldot Yehudei Mizrach Eropah ve-Tarbutam,* edited by David Assaf and Ada Rapoport-Albert, vol. 2. Jerusalem: Merkaz Zalman Shazar, 2009.

Wolf, Friedrich August. *Prolegomena to Homer, 1795.* Translated with introduction and notes by Anthony Grafton, Glenn W. Most, and James E.G. Zetzel. Princeton, N.J.: Princeton University Press, 1985.

Wolff, Christian. *Logic; or, Rational Thoughts on the Powers of the Human Understanding, with Their Use and Application in the Knowledge and Search of Truth.* Translated by Baron Wolfius. Vol. 77 of Wolff, *Gesammelte Werke, Materialien und Dokumente.* Hildesheim: Olms, 2003.

Wolfson, Elliot R. "From Sealed Book to Open Text: Time, Memory, and Narrativity in Kabbalistic Hermeneutics." Pp. 145–178 in *Interpreting Judaism in a Postmodern Age,* edited by Steven Kepnes. New York: New York University Press, 1996.

———. *Language, Eros, Being: Kabbalistic Hermeneutics and Poetic Imagination.* New York: Fordham University Press, 2005.

———. "The Mystical Significance of Torah Study in German Pietism." *Jewish Quarterly Review* 84, no. 1 (July 1993): 43–78.

Woolhouse, Roger S. "Gottfried Wilhelm Leibniz." Pp. 260–279 in *A Companion to Early Modern Philosophy,* edited by Steven M. Nadler. Malden, Mass.: Blackwell, 2002.

Wunder, Meir. "Ha-Yeshivah be-Galitsiyah." *Moriah* 3 (1992): 95–100.

Wuthnow, Robert. *Meaning and Moral Order: Explorations in Cultural Analysis.* Berkeley: University of California Press, 1987.

Yaffe, Avraham. "He'arot be-Sharshei ha-Gra." *Moriah* 11 (1998): 31–48.

Yatzkan, Samuel J. *Rabenu Eliyahu mi-Vilna.* Warsaw: 1900.

Yechezkel Feivel. *Toldot ha-Adam.* Dyhernfurth: 1801.

Yehuda, Zvi. "Hazon Ish on Textual Criticism and Halakha." *Tradition* 18, no. 2 (1980): 172–180.

Yerushalmi, Yosef H. *Zachor: Jewish History and Jewish Memory.* Seattle: University of Washington Press, 1989.

Yisrael (ben Shmuel) of Shklov. *Pe'at ha-Shulchan.* Safed: 1836.

———. *Taklin Chadatin.* Minsk: 1812.

Yissaschar ben Tanchum. *Ma'aseh Rav.* Vilna: 1832; Jerusalem: Machon M.A., 2009.

Yla, Stasys. *Šiluva žemaičių istorijoje.* Vol. 1. Boston: Krikščionis gyvenime, 1970.

Yosef, Ya'akov. *Toldot Ya'akov Yosef.* Korets: 1780.

Yosef ben Ya'akov. *Rosh Yosef.* Kitin: 1717.

Zalkin, Mordechai. "Between Dvinsk and Vilna: The Spread of Hasidism in Nineteenth-Century Lithuania." Pp. 21–50 in *Within Hasidic Circles: Studies in Hasidism in Memory of Mordechai Wilensky,* edited by I. Etkes, D. Asaf, I. Bartal, and E. Reiner. Jerusalem: Mossad Bialik Hebrew University, 1999.

———. "Scientific Literature and Cultural Transformation in Nineteenth-Century East European Jewish Society." *Aleph* 5 (2005): 249–271.

Zborowski, Mark, and Elizabeth Herzog. *Life Is with People: The Jewish Little Town of Eastern Europe.* New York: International Press, 1952.

Zinberg, Israel. *A History of Jewish Literature,* vols. 10–12. Translated by Bernard Martin. Tel Aviv: 1959; Cincinnati: Hebrew Union College Press, 1974.

———. "Hosafot 1." In Zinberg, *Toldot Sifrut Yisrael,* vol. 5. 6 vols. Tel Aviv: Y. Shreberk, 1959.

Zipperstein, Steven. *Imagining Russian Jewry: Memory, History, and Identity.* Seattle: University of Washington Press, 1999.

———. *The Jews of Odessa: A Cultural History, 1794–1881.* Palo Alto, Calif.: Stanford University Press, 1985.

Zobel, Menachem. "Bibliography." *Kiryat Sefer* 28, no. 2 (1941): 126–132.

Index

Solomon); Yehuda Leib (son of Elijah ben Solomon)

Chladenius, Johann Martin, 40, 49

chokhmah, 47, 51, 61, 95, 197n19, 198n20, 198n24

Christianity, 17, 18, 22–23, 31–32, 65–66, 71, 78, 81, 102, 184n35, 222n83, 222n91, 234n93

citation style of the Gaon, 9, 20, 38, 100, 126, 179n30

civil authorities' involvement in Jewish affairs, 16–18, 31–33, 71, 106–108, 110–113, 237n137, 237n140, 238n152, 270n11

codes of law: acceptance by Ashkenazic Jewry, 117–118, 240n12; *Mishneh Torah* (Maimonides), 117, 130; Talmud study, 116–118, 120, 132–135, 252n113. See also *Biur al Shulchan Arukh; Shulchan Arukh* (Karo)

Coudert, Allison, 43

Council of the Four Lands, 105, 106, 136, 137, 142

Council of the Yeshivot, 142

covenant, 93, 228n48

Coxe, William, 22

creation of the world: ex nihilo, 45–47; form-based world in, 47–48; God's imposition of form on matter, 47–48; harmonization of oral and written law, 54; human ability to create, 48; human manipulation of nature, 48–49; mathematics, 40–44, 196–197n19, 199n32; on a neo-Platonic notion of creation, 45; *sefar/sippur/sefer*, 41, 42, 196n19, 197n19, 198n24; world-book trope, 40–41, 49–50, 198n22, 218n56. *See also* evil

Critique of Pure Reason (Kant), 132

custom, 23, 24, 77, 92, 93, 109, 120, 127, 155

Danzig, Avraham, 23, 107, 149, 160, 254n2

Darkhei ha-Gemara (Campanton), 60, 118, 204n83

Darkhei Noam (Shmuel ben Eliezer), 100, 108, 119

David ben Zimra (Radvaz), 148

death of Elijah ben Solomon: eulogies, 34, 35, 36, 149; Hasidic movement's reactions to, 34, 35, 109–113, 237n135, 237n137, 238n152; iconography after, 1, 145–146, 149, 157, 159, 162, 257n14, 258n20, 267n116; legacy, 34–36, 150–151, 248n71; Mitnagdim's reactions to, 34, 35, 109–113, 237n135, 237n137, 238n152; posthumous tributes, 144, 145, 152, 153, 161, 253n2, 255n6, 258n18, 262n61

de Certeau, Michel, 232n78

Derekh Tevunot (Luzzatto), 53, 56, 205n91

Derrida, Jacques, 58

Derzhavin, Gabriel Romanovich, 111, 238n142

Descartes, René, 47, 201n56

desire/materiality, 154–155, 157–159, 164, 265n86

Dienstag, Jacob, 128–129

disciples of the Gaon: beadles, 28, 33, 189n98; the Gaon's relationship with, 19–21, 24, 28, 29–30, 160–161, 189n97, 190n112, 266n111; on his genius, 29, 151–153, 262n61; on his isolation, 156–157; on his pietistic behavior, 29, 151–152, 158–160, 159; his privileging students over

220n77. *See also* Maskilim; Mendelssohn, Moses; Wessely, Naftali Herz

Epstein, Kalonymus Kalman, 96

Epstein, Yehudah, 133, 134, 151, 248n76

Epstein, Zalman, 150–151, 239n4

Eretz Yisrael, 25, 145, 169–170

erev rav (mixed multitude), 102–103, 104, 105, 234n95

eroticism, 97, 100–101, 233n84, 234n93

error (concept), 38, 39–41, 50–51, 54, 56–57, 196n14

Etkes, Immanuel, 107, 134, 226n33

Euclid, 26, 43, 169

evil: darkness as, 195n13; error (concept), 38, 39–41, 50–51, 54, 56–57, 196n14; God and the creation of, 38, 39, 47; harmony of the world, 39, 40, 49, 54, 56–57, 60–61; humanity and the production of, 40, 49, 57, 58; mathematics used to identify, 40–41; textual emendation and the eradication of, 54–55

excommunications, 85, 87, 88, 89, 100, 106, 109, 220

exegetical method of the Gaon: citation style in, 9, 20, 38, 100, 126, 179n30; concision in, 55, 125; divine versus human knowledge, 59–60; divinity of biblical literature, 57–58; harmonization of oral and written law, 54–57, 207n99; human error addressed in, 55, 57–58, 59–60, 61, 208n103; influences on, 7, 9–10, 179n30, 194n6; Iyyun School, 60–61, 204n83, 205n91; Mendelssohn's methods compared with, 75–76, 220–221n77; rabbinic hermeneutic principles 220n77; rabbinic tradition challenged by, 75–76, 121–123,

220–221n77; radical nature of, 55–56, 205n93, 209n109; *sefar/ sippur/sefer* in, 41, 42, 196n19, 197n19, 198n24; *sensus literalis*, 67, 73–76, 79, 81, 128, 220n77; speech, 41–42, 196n19; synonymy, 57–58, 60, 73; world-book trope in, 40–41, 49–50, 198n22, 218n56

Falk, Joshua, 117, 137

Fatel, Michael ben (Fatel house), 18, 21

Feiner, Shmuel, 6

Finkelstein, Louis, 209n107

Fox, Menachem Tzvi, 203n74, 207n97

Fram, Edward, 136

Frank, Jacob, 100, 184n35

Frankist movement, 100, 101–102, 113, 184n35

Franks, Paul, 193n1

Frei, Hans, 72

Friedländer, David, 26, 69, 70

Fuenn, Samuel Joseph, 137–138, 155

Galton, Francis, 143–144

gaon (use of term), 146–151, 155, 162–163, 164, 259n27, 259n30, 260n35

Gaon of Vilna. *See* Elijah ben Solomon

Geiger, Abraham, 55–56

genius: formation of, 80–82; of Mendelssohn, 80–82; *mensch* as opposite of, 164; as self-generated, 20, 152–155, 262n61; sixty tractates as determining *geonut*, 148, 259n30, 260n35

genius of the Gaon: asceticism, 154–155, 157–161, 164, 265n86; erudition, 19–20, 27–28, 29–30, 131, 195n10; knowledge of Talmud, 28, 57–58, 60, 113–135, 156–160; in the popular

Hayyim of Sereje, 15

Hayyim of Vilna, 86, 87

Hayyim of Volozhin: on biographies of Elijah ben Solomon, 256n8; co-option of Hasidic concepts by, 230n66; on Elijah's approach to learning, 27, 56, 133, 134; on Elijah's genius, 153, 154, 254n2; Elijah's works edited by, 134, 206n94, 249n80; on significance of the *Biur*, 131–132, 248n71; Volozhin Yeshiva founded by, 28, 138, 141, 251n104

Hebrew language, 77, 78, 222n83, 222n91

Heidegger, Martin, 50–51

Herder, Johann Gottfried von, 66

heresy, 98, 232n78

hermeneutics, the Gaon's, 67, 72–81, 128, 218n59, 219n70, 220n71, 220n77; importance of introductions to, 51–53; readers and, 50–51; subject-predicate propositions, 52–53, 56; theory of authorship, 49–50, 51, 59–60, 202n70

Hertz, Elkan, 67

Hirsch ben Abba Wolf kidnapping case, 31–33, 71, 108

Hirsch ben Yosef, 110

Horowitz, Avraham, 137, 240n12

Hundert, Gershon, 22, 140, 166–167

Hurwitz, Yosef Yoizel, 141

Ibn Kaspi, Joseph, 92

idealism, 38–39, 45, 46, 61, 63–64, 193n1

Isaac ben Leib, 31, 112

Isaac of Volozhin, 141, 252n118

Isaac the Blind, 45

Israel ben Eliezer (the Baal Shem), 83–84, 95, 100

Issar (denouncer of Elijah ben Solomon), 86, 87

Isserles, Moshe, 17, 116

Iyyun School, 60–61, 204n83, 205n91

Jablonski, Daniel Ernst, 222n91

Jackson, William, 161–162

Jacob, Joseph, 144

Jacob ben Wolff Kranz (Dubner Maggid), 30

Jaffe, Mordekhai, 117, 137

Jerusalem (Mendelssohn), 67

Judah the Hasid, 159

kabbalah: the Gaon on, 19–20, 27–28, 38, 95, 169, 197–198n19; in Leibniz's philosophy, 43; Luzzatto's messianic, 194n6; mathematics, 43, 44; *mathesis universalis*, 42, 43–44; Sabbatianism, 100; *Sefer Yetzirah*, Elijah ben Solomon's commentary to, 41, 42, 43, 196n19; *sefirot*, 47, 51, 61, 95, 197n19, 198n20, 198n24

Kagan, Yisrael Meir, 206n94

Kana'ani, Ya'akov, 150

Kant, Immanuel, 132

Karelitz, Avraham Yeshaya, 126

Karlin Hasidim, 86, 111, 113

Karo, Joseph. See *Shulchan Arukh* (Karo)

Katz, Jacob, 3, 4, 7, 136–137, 224n2

kehilah: code-based learning supported by, 11, 115, 137, 140; decline of, 11, 135, 137, 140, 167–168; Elijah ben Solomon's relations with, 30–31, 107–108, 112; founding of the modern yeshiva, 135, 137–138, 140; as governing body, 135–137; Hasidic movement and, 107, 115, 168; Hirsch ben Abba Wolf kidnapping case,

194n6; subject-predicate
propositions, 53
Luzzatto, Simcha, 136

Ma'aseh Rav, 77–78, 145, 256n8
Mack, Michael, 82
Maggid of Międzyrzecz, 94, 98, 100
Magid, Shaul, 234n95
Maimon, Solomon, 88, 100–101
Maimonides: citation style of, 9,
    179n30; on creation of the world,
    45–46, 200n47; Elijah ben Solomon
    on, 127–128, 129–130, 246n60;
    essentialism of, 130; on ethical
    behavior, 151; on evil, 195n13; on
    parables, 129; Torah text study, 92;
    use of Aristotelian terms, 129; works
    of, 44–45, 117, 129, 130, 179n30,
    196n13, 246n58
Maków, David, 97, 102
Malebranche, Nicolas de, 47
Malick, Terrance, 48
Manishes, Isaac (Sar Shalom), 87, 89
Mannheim, Karl, 6, 7
Mapah (Isserles), 17, 116
Mapu, Abraham, 144–145, 256n7
Marcus, Ivan, 159, 174n5, 257n15,
    261n48
Mariavite missionaries, 18, 22, 184n35
Maskilim: Elijah ben Solomon's
    relations with, 26, 27, 69, 75–76, 83,
    220–221n77; David Friedländer, 26,
    69, 70; Shlomo Zalman Hanau, 77,
    221n83; Isaac Ber Levinsohn, 169,
    239n152; Menashe of Illya, 27, 129;
    rabbinic Judaism defended by,
    66–68, 79, 81, 213n27, 223n93; Isaac
    Satanov, 79; Kalman Shulman, 70;
    on study of rabbinic texts, 139–140;
    in Vilna, 26, 68–69, 168; Naftali

Herz Wessely, 26, 69, 73–74. *See also*
    Mendelssohn, Moses
masorah, 77–79, 222n85, 222n91
Masoret ha-Masoret (Levita), 77, 78
Massalski, Ignacy, Bishop, 22–23, 24,
    71, 107
mathematics, 40–44, 58, 196–197n19,
    199n32
mathesis universalis, 42, 43–44
Mathews, John, 116
ha-Me'asef (Maskilic periodical), 69
Mechotievitz, Yitzchak ben Yosef, 30
Mecklenburg, Ya'akov Tzvi, 144, 255n6
Meier, Georg Friedrich, 42, 49
Mekhilta, 20, 53, 54
Melamed, Leib, 97
Menachem ben Shlomo (Meiri), 147
Menachem Mendel of Shklov, 28, 29,
    44, 121, 122, 126, 148–149, 192n33,
    198n19, 245n56
Menachem of Vitebsk, 26, 85–86
Menashe of Illya, 27, 129
Mendel, of Przemyśl, 96
Mendelssohn, Moses: on authorship of
    text, 202n70; biblical exegesis of,
    79–81, 223n100; *Biur* of, 67–70, 78,
    214n34, 218n56; Christian anti-
    rabbinic bias in Germany, 66, 81;
    Ecclesiastes commentary, 67; Elijah
    ben Solomon compared with, 63–64;
    exegetical method of, 72–73;
    German translations of works, 67,
    68, 69; interaction with Protestant
    community, 65–66; on Levita's
    work, 78; rabbinic Judaism
    defended by, 66–68, 75–76, 79, 81,
    213n27, 220n77, 223n93; on rabbinic
    tradition and interpretive practices,
    65–66, 73, 75–76, 220–221n77; on
    Rashbam's exegesis, 79, 80

Shmuel ben Avigdor, 22–23, 24, 25, 30, 31, 69, 106, 187n15

Shmuel ben Eliezer, 100, 105, 108, 119

Shmuel ben Meir (Rashbam), 77, 78–79, 222n91

Shneur Zalman of Liadi, 26, 86, 88, 94, 96, 107, 112

Shraga Feivush of Dubrowna, 27, 63–64

Shuchat, Raphael, 175n13, 177n25, 194n6, 201n49, 229n57, 253n2, 270n17

Shulchan Arukh (Karo): acceptance of by Ashkenazic Jewry, 117–118, 240n12; influence of, 117–118, 126, 131; ·on Maimonides's legal opinions, 127–131; *Mapah* (Isserles) as gloss on, 115–116; prohibition against Jews going to civil courts in, 108–109; rearrangement of established commentaries in Elijah ben Solomon's *Biur*, 121–123; Talmud study and texts, 116–118, 120, 123, 125–127, 132–135, 252n113. See also *Biur al Shulchan Arukh*

Shulman, Kalman, 70

Sifra, 20, 53, 54, 55, 208n103

Sifra di-Tzniuta, Elijah ben Solomon's commentary to, 47–48, 153, 197n19, 218n56

Silber, Michael K., 4, 5, 7

Slutzki house, 21–22, 24, 27, 35, 137–138, 268n129

Sofer, Moses, 4–5, 7, 156

Solomon Zalman (father of Elijah ben Solomon), 14–15, 21

Soloveitchik, Haym, 131, 179n32, 243n38, 261n48

Soloveitchik, Hayyim, 139

Soloveitchik, J. B., 128

Sorkin, David, 6

Spector, Isaac Elchanan, 141

Spektor, Joel, 87

Spener, Philip Jakob, 7

Spiegel, Shmuel, 2065n93

Spiegel, Ya'akov, 57

Stampfer, Shaul, 138, 180n34, 182n10, 191n119, 192n136, 248n71, 249n80, 252n113, 254n5, 258n18

study houses, 15, 21–22, 24, 25, 27, 35, 120, 137–138, 251n103

subject-predicate propositions, 52–53, 56

Sulzer, Johann Georg, 65

synonymy, 57–58, 60, 73, 206n94

Talmud and Talmud study: Iyyun School, 60–61, 204n83, 205n91; mastery of, as indication of *geonut*, 148, 260n35; and *Midrash Halakha*, 53–57, 205n93, 206n94, 207n97, 208n103; *pilpul*, 118–119, 120, 125, 133; recitation of texts, 151–152; and status of code-based learning, 116–118, 120, 132–135, 252n113

Tam, Jacob Meir, 92

Taylor, Charles, 140

Tekhunot ha-Shamayim (Raphael Levi of Hannover), 37–38

Teller, Adam, 105, 136, 194n141, 217n52, 235n108, 235n116, 250n92

theodicy, 38–40, 47, 49, 194n6, 234n94

Tikkunei ha-Zohar, Elijah ben Solomon's commentary to, 19, 20, 197n19, 207–208n101, 228n48

Timaeus (Plato), 45

Tishbi, Eliyahu. *See* Levita, Eliyahu (Bachur)

Tishby, Isaiah, 194n6

Ya'akov Yosef of Połonne, 87–88, 96–97, 100

Yatzken, Shmuel Ya'akov, 89

Yehudah ha-Nassi, 117, 126

Yehuda Leib (son of Elijah ben Solomon), 33, 35, 160, 194n4

yeshiva/yeshivot: centrality of, 140–142; decline of the *kehilah*, 135, 137–138, 139; degrees of student knowledge in, 162–163; founding of, 108, 141; genius identified with, 150–151, 162–163; goals of, 138, 139; insularity of, 264n80; *milchamta shel Torah* (war of Torah), 139; practical halakha, 139; privatization of religious life, 141; selectivity of, 11; students in, 162; Talmud study in, 11; teaching method of Elijah ben Solomon, 133–134

Yeven Metzulah (Nathan of Hannover), 119

Yisrael of Shklov, 56, 121, 126, 152, 157, 159, 209n109, 212n5, 262n61

Yissaschar ben Tanchum, 145, 256n8

Yissaschar Ber (Elijah ben Solomon's brother), 44

Yitzchak, Levi, 89

Yoreh De'ah, 121, 244n49

Yosef Zundel of Salant, 156, 222n85

Zalman Ber (grandson of Elijah ben Solomon), 160–161

"Zemir Aritzim ve-Chorvot Tzurim," 85–86

Zerachia ha-Levy, 120

Zinzendorf, Nikolaus von, 7

Zohar, 19, 20, 44, 80, 197n19, 234n95

Zuckermandel, M. S., 205n93